GLOBAL LATIN/O AMERICAS

Frederick Luis Aldama and Lourdes Torres, Series Editors

LA VERDAD

An International Dialogue on
Hip Hop Latinidades

EDITED BY

Melissa Castillo-Garsow and Jason Nichols

The Ohio State University Press • *Columbus*

Library of Congress Cataloging-in-Publication Data
Names: Castillo-Garsow, Melissa, 1984– editor. | Nichols, Jason, 1978– editor.
Title: La verdad : an international dialogue on hip hop Latinidades / edited by Melissa
    Castillo-Garsow and Jason Nichols.
Other titles: Global Latin/o Americas.
Description: Columbus : The Ohio State University Press, [2016] | Series: Global Latin/o
    Americas | Includes bibliographical references and index.
Identifiers: LCCN 2016021659 | ISBN 9780814213155 (cloth ; alk. paper) | ISBN 0814213154
    (cloth ; alk. paper)
Subjects: LSCH: Rap (Music)—Social aspects—United States. | Rap (Music)—Social
    aspects—Latin America. | Rap (Music)—United States—History and criticism. |
    Rap (Music)—Latin America—History and criticism. | Hip-hop—United States—
    Influence. | Hip-hop—Latin America—Influence.
Classification: LCC ML3918.R37 V47 2016 | DDC 782.421649089/68—dc23
LC record available at https://lccn.loc.gov/2016021659

Cover design by Janna Thompson-Chordas
Text design by Juliet Williams
Type set in Adobe Minion Pro and Bitstream Vera

9 8 7 6 5 4 3 2 1

contents

A Little Hip Hop History from the Bronx and Beyond

H ip Hop was born multicultural. Its earliest Bronx jams were spaces where DJs, nurtured in the sound system culture of the Anglophone Caribbean, as well as the musical wizardry found in Manhattan clubs catering to the new Black middle class, inspired dancers whose moves fused mambo dancing, capoeira, the movements of James Brown, and what they drew from Bruce Lee movies. It was Afro-diasporic cultural space par excellence, where language didn't matter and people from the Spanish-speaking portion of the African diaspora played a central role. However, four or five years later, when rapping or MCing became a distinguishing feature of Hip Hop, allowing the music to be easily recorded and marketed, Hip Hop became powerfully identified with the groups who had the most developed traditions of English-language vernacular improvisation, African Americans and West Indians. The poetic genius that quickly emerged, from the ground up to accompany the beats, transformed Hip Hop, at least in the public eye, into a pre-eminently African American discourse, a voice of a newly disfranchised section of the Black U.S. population left behind by deindustrialization, austerity, and a rejection of the redistributionist policies of the 60s. Those whose primary language was not English remained important in Hip Hop spaces, but their contributions were eclipsed as charismatic English-language rappers defined Hip Hop's public profile globally as well as in the United States. Even today, terms drawn from African American vernacular discourse are part of how rappers in a score of different language traditions define their authenticity.

In the short run, the African-Americanization of what was once a diasporic musical and social space appeared to leave out, or at least marginalize, non-English speakers attracted to the music. They were relegated to the three other elements, DJing, B-boying, and Graffitti, leaving the most prestigious and commercially viable Hip Hop performance skills to those fluent in African American vernacular English, which included a small number of artists from Spanish-language or French-language families who grew up around African Americans. However, this pattern of language exclusion not only proved to be temporary, it ended up strengthening the ultimate dissemination of Hip Hop culture through the diaspora by foregrounding a Blackness which many non-Anglophone, none U.S.-based national cultures tended to submerge in a fiction of "mestizaje" in which racial mixture was applauded and Blackness denigrated or rendered invisible. All through the Western Hemisphere, irrespective of the language traditions, Black and indigenous people found their cultural traditions and identities under siege even while they were proclaimed to be part of the mixing of peoples that defined entire nations. So when Hip Hop finally did come to them, through the medium of records, and tapes and films and music videos, its unabashed BLACKNESS gave it a revolutionary edge even when the language tradition that it embodied was not their own.

This revolutionary volume displays the consequences of that insurgency among the non-English-speaking peoples of the Americas, peoples whose primary languages are Spanish, Portuguese, French, indigenous, or creolized versions of all three that incorporated African language survivals. The authors have amassed an extraordinary record of how peoples under duress in every corner of the hemisphere have made Hip Hop culture their own, and have reinvented the art forms associated with it in the process. In doing so, they have challenged head-on language chauvinism, gender chauvinism, and the ways even revolutionary and insurgent cultures can become exclusionary. The essays in this book are filled with a celebration of the creativity of the invisible, of the prophetic power of the marginalized, and the irrepressible energy that Hip Hop unleashes. Because Blackness, as Marcus Garvey reminded us, was everywhere denigrated, music that foregrounds Blackness in the most explicit form, that indeed uses it as a mark of authenticity, ends up validating all cultures despised and denied and gives hope to all peoples. So tune in and see how from L.A. to Queens to Port-au-Prince to São Paulo to Nicaragua to Oakland and sometimes back and forth between those places, Hip Hop has been reinvented as a culture for all, irrespective of language, who have been marginalized and rendered invisible by those with wealth and power. The spirit of grass roots democracy pulsates through these essays, reminding us that the most beautiful flowers are those which come up through cracks in the sidewalk.

Mark D. Naison
Professor of African American Studies and History
Fordham University
Co-Founder, Badass Teachers Association

acknowledgments

Jason Nichols

As I sat to write this, the words of Hector Lavoe echoed in my head, "hoy te dedico, mis mejores pregones." I would like to thank my partner Melissa, who took this project from an idea in my head to the book you are now reading. My collaborators and friends Mazi Mutafa and Jared Ball helped nurture my career with their valuable advice. The African American Studies Department at the University of Maryland made this work possible with the mentorship and guidance they have offered me through this process. My hippie guru and Managing Editor, Kristina Byrne, has been an encouraging presence and has filled me with joy and optimism for my future. I would also like to thank the mother of my children, Michelle Gomez. If not for her tireless work with our kids, I would not have had the time or the freedom to engage in this scholarship. I would like to thank all of our contributors, Kristen Elias Rowley, and The Ohio State University Press, for the special attention they have paid to our project.

Melissa Castillo-Garsow

This book has been an unexpected journey filled with many unexpected collaborators. In many ways it began in Brazil in 2005, when I was studying abroad as an undergraduate and found my face in the midst of not just a growing Hip Hop scene that was not in English but with the realities of Latin America's often unacknowledged African diaspora. From there I discovered Mexican Hip Hop in my very own playground, New York City, and I was hooked forever. So, first and foremost, I am forever indebted to the artists who live, breathe, and share Hip Hop, in all its forms, not for money or fame but out of pure love for the culture and their diverse communities. In particular, I am thankful for the friendship of groups like Hispanos Causando Pániko, crews like Buendia BK, grafiterros Sarck and Pisket, as well as others from the Har'd Life Arts Collective, and MCs Versos, Audry Funk, Rhappy, and Bocafloja, who have always been so generous with their work. Their creativity, like the groundbreaking research of the authors presented in this volume, is what kept me going when putting together and then completing this volume seemed like an impossible task. On that note, I would like to thank my collaborator, Jason, for seeing my potential as a junior scholar and empowering me to run with my often nontraditional ideas about the volume. In our conversations, disagreements and finally compromise, I learned so much about how I want to approach, study, and teach Latinidades. I am also always indebted to my mentor Mark Naison, who was the first to really introduce me to the power and potential of Hip Hop studies, first when I was his teaching assistant at Fordham University, and now, as he continues to advise me on various publications. And last but always first in mi corazón, I dedicate this to mi máma— I would be nothing without your unwavering support and belief in me.

PART I

UNDEFINING HIP HOP LATINIDADES

chapter 1

Hip Hop Latinidades

More Than Just Rapping in Spanish

Melissa Castillo-Garsow and Jason Nichols

Jason's Rap

I welcomed the audience as they quietly prepared to hear new academic perspectives on Hip Hop at the 2013 Words Beats & Life Teach-In entitled "Remixing the Art of Social Change." The beauty of the event was that Hip Hop was a location in which scholars and practitioners from many different disciplines met to dialogue about a topic that most of them felt personally invested in. It was a living testament to the cliché that Hip Hop brings together people from all different linguistic, racial, and cultural—and in this particular case, academic—backgrounds. The truth is, Hip Hop still struggles to gain respect and legitimacy among the old guard and gatekeepers of the academy. Some still fail to see that Hip Hop is often an early warning sign of social unrest, an expression of angst and economic or political dissatisfaction, and a site for community building and sustainability.

I feel I was born into Hip Hop culture. Some of my earliest sonic memories involve hearing Melly Mel's famous "It's like a jungle sometimes / it makes me wonder how I keep from going under." Just as Nas once said he was a "fiend for hip-hop / it got me stuck like a crack pipe," I got more and more hooked as I grew. My older sister spent her teenage years moving back and forth between our suburban Maryland home and the dank basement apartment in our grandmother's brownstone in East Harlem. She would play me vinyl records, then tapes, then CDs of the music she collected. She told me stories of sneaking into the Roxy and watching b-boys battle. I would visit her in New York and see all of her friends who wore Zulu beads. The more I saw, the more I craved. Like a junkie whose addiction progressed from recreational use to dependence, I evolved from spectator to participant. I can remember trying to recruit kids in my quiet neighborhood to become a b-boy crew. We had no rivals and, ultimately, very little talent. I tried my hand at graffiti, but I wasn't good at it, and the lack of public transportation or walls on our tree-lined cul-de-sacs didn't make it very conducive to that particular visual art medium. More than anything, though, I loved music. I fell in love with the idea of being an MC. I wrote rhymes in my notebook during slow classes and study hall periods in school. One day, on the back of the school bus, I shared a rhyme with a couple of kids. "Yo, that was pretty dope," responded one listener. That was all I needed. I went on to later become a big part of the Washington, DC, scene. I eventually put out albums on labels like Universal and EMI and was even featured in the "Hip Hop bible" of the era, *The Source*.

Still, despite this background, it was after witnessing and preparing questions for the presenters, that one woman's presentation rang in my head, and prodded me to rethink what I knew. She wrote a paper about a Mexican rap group from New York City. I started to reflect on my notions of Chicano and Latino rap growing up. I am a self-taught Spanish speaker who loves salsa music and tostones. I knew Puerto Rican kids who loved and performed Hip Hop like I did. I recognized their Latinidad, but never viewed us as separate. When I heard Fat Joe, it felt like the Hip Hop I knew, or, as Raquel Z. Rivera (2003) would say, that it was from Hip Hop's core. However, when I heard Kid Frost as a young teenager, it felt different.

That was my first exposure to West Coast Chicano rap. The lyrics made it clear that I was not even a part of his intended audience, because the refrain stated, "This is for La Raza." As I reflected on these differences, I knew I had to find this woman, whose name, Melissa Castillo-Garsow, was hard to forget. I wanted to edit a book that explored this Hip Hop and Latinidad, and that hopefully further clarified the distinction (if one exists) between Latino Hip Hop and Hip Hop performed by Latinos. Is all Spanish-language Hip Hop therefore Latino Hip Hop? Is Hip Hop performed by people of Latin American descent necessarily Latino Hip Hop?

Soon after, I met with Melissa and invited her to embark on this project with me. She only stipulated that she wanted to broaden the project beyond the U.S. borders. I excitedly agreed. Melissa had experience that I hadn't yet had. She lived overseas and is not only a fluent Spanish speaker but can also read, write, and speak Portuguese. In our early discussions about framing she also was adamant about including Brazil. Brazil is the largest country in the region and yet Brazilians are often not considered Latinos. From those conversations we agreed that this project could not be bounded by simple Spanish/English considerations, which frequently and uncritically bounded considerations of Latinidad. My only reservation was why we would stop there. Why not include Haiti, a nation bordered by an unmistakably Latino nation? The history of Haiti and the Dominican Republic are intertwined, and there are close to a million ethnic Haitians living in the DR, working and switching between Spanish and Creole. Though Haitian Creole is primarily a francophone-derived language, French is still a Romance language much like Spanish and Portuguese.

In the end, we both agreed that the primary reason for excluding Haiti was racial bias. Latino cultural studies must explore more than an English/Spanish binary; they must look into the hundreds of Indigenous languages that are still spoken in pockets of Central and South America. Through Melissa's contacts and language skills we sought out submissions from scholars and artists in every country of Latin America, including those where Spanish or even Portuguese was not the primary language, including Anglophone West Caribbean countries which are never talked about in studies of Latin America and yet share the same waters as Puerto Rico, Cuba, and the Dominican Republic. Meanwhile, I worked to find articles about U.S. Latinos that did not replicate the artificial East Coast Puerto Rican / West Coast Chicano Rap divide that Melissa's work originally opened my eyes to. In doing so, we hope to open the door for further research, while kicking in the door of the dominant yet limited English/Spanish binary in Latin American Studies.

Melissa's Rap

I came to Hip Hop from quite a different perspective than Jason. Growing up Mexican American in upstate New York, Hip Hop was not part of my culture. And while the sounds of 1990s gangsta rap followed by the commercial rap of the 2000s played in the background, it was not a music that I identified with or sought out. When I moved to New York City in 2003 to study journalism at New York University, I was assaulted by a very different sound or music than the traditional Mexican music I grew up with, the mainly white rock that was popular in my small college town, or the Hip Hop I saw on MTV.

The "Latin Alternative" music scene had arrived in New York. I began listening to artists like Manu Chao, Café Tacvba, Calle 13, The Beatnuts, Ana Tijoux, La Ley, Los Amigo Invisibles, Control Machete, and many others. Although they reflected diverse countries, cultures, and backgrounds, what drew me to them was the way they lyrically, sonically, and stylistically represented hybrid cultures and linguistic traditions with an urban feel. They didn't define themselves and didn't feel the need to. Freelancing as a music journalist, before I could often legally gain entrance into these venues, I was able to meet, talk to, and most importantly listen to a diverse set of Latin American and Latino artists.

In particular, Yerba Buena was one of the first groups to really speak to me. Against the backdrop of a highly masculinized and sexualized Reggaeton music that was popular among college Latinos, but that often made me uncomfortable, Yerba Buena was decidedly different. Blending some of my favorite Latin music styles—cumbia, salsa, rumba—with music from the African diaspora and performed by a band of musicians from all over the world, they showed me a different side to Hip Hop. And I liked it. From there I worked backward, listening to and seeking out both Latin American acts that incorporated Hip Hop and rap en español, but still largely preferring international acts to those grown closer to home.

In 2005 I studied in Belo Horizonte, Brazil for six months. I went to study Portuguese and was again surprised by what I found. A Hip Hop movement was in full swing, and it was racially conscious, unapologetically political, and incredibly infectious. Largely ignored by the mainstream music industry, nevertheless, thousands of youth gathered in soccer arenas to listen to artists like Racionais MC, Rappin' Hood, Marcelo D2, and Sabotage who rapped about racial inequality, prison systems, and life in favelas. When I came back to the United States, I noticed how articles about Brazilian Hip Hop kept referencing the country as a home for conscious rap, a scene very reminiscent of the genre's U.S. origins.

Nevertheless, while these experiences piqued my interest in U.S. Hip Hop's history and older music, I never considered Hip Hop mine until I heard "La Verdad," by the Mexican New York Hip Hop group Hispanos Causando Pániko (HCP) in 2010. It was that same year that legendary Mexican American Los Angeles Hip Hop artist Sick Jacken was visiting with members of New York based group HCP when he heard a beat he couldn't resist. That very day Jacken would record a verse for HCP's new song, "La Verdad." A classic Hip Hop tale of survival and street life, "La Verdad" is significant because it represents both the history and the future of Latino Hip Hop in the United States. A member of Psycho Realm and frequent collaborator of Cypress Hill, Sick Jacken has been an important member of the West Coast Hip Hop scene since the early '90s. Hispanos Causando Paniko, composed of Mexican immigrants to New York City who rap entirely in Spanish and market themselves mainly to Latin America, represent the new and international landscape for Latino Hip Hop.

Blending lyrics about the Mexican community in Queens, immigration issues, and daily struggles in the city with a clean, classic New York sound, the music spoke to me in a different way. The backdrop of the now destroyed 5 Pointz and live Mexican migrants painting graffiti localized the Hip Hop expression into something I could both sonically and lyrically relate to. At a time when the Mexican community in New York, though substantial, was largely invisible—even to me—HCP's music represents a statement, a presence, I desperately needed. They demonstrated that there are different ways to be a Mexican rapper, or to be Mexican and love Hip Hop other than Chicano Rap. It proved that there were more ways to be Latino in New York than caribeño. It showed that Latino Hip Hop was a lot bigger and more complicated than we thought. As I saw academics and artists alike express surprise at HCP's swagger and background, I realized that we were at a new frontier for Hip Hop. Latinos (mostly Puerto Ricans) are among Hip Hop's pioneers, but not only has Hip Hop spread throughout Latin America, creating new sounds and genres, but changes to the U.S. Latino makeup as well as a long-standing presence of Hip Hop in those home countries is also changing what is being produced here.

La Verdad

This is *La Verdad*; "The Truth." Over the past forty years, Hip Hop has grown into a multilingual, multiethnic, intergenerational, global yet localized and regional collection of cultural expressions. Descendants of Latin American immigrants in the United States were instrumental in the foundations of Hip Hop's four elements on both the East and West coasts, adapting some of the cultural traditions of their ancestors' homelands to a different environment and time. On the East Coast, those early stages of development took place primarily within the Puerto Rican and African American communities of the South Bronx, while on the West Coast, artists like Mellow Man Ace and Kid Frost opened doors by infusing Spanish into their lyrics.

Clearly, from the earliest days, Hip Hop has been not just about music, but about community and exchange, in which Latinos have been extremely instrumental and influential. However, for the past several decades that cultural exchange has expanded by traveling to Latin America and back as visual artists, music producers, MCs, vocalists, and dancers from Latin America create localized art combining their surrounding culture with influences from north of the U.S. border. Hip Hop in Latin America has grown to the point where Latin American artists are now major influences for some U.S. Latino and non-Latino artists, traveling around the world and performing in large non-English-language showcases. One excellent example of this is Mexican poet, rap artist, scholar, cultural ambassador, and founder of the Quilomboarte Collective, Bocafloja, who authored an important piece for this volume. One of the most revered icons in Spanish-speaking Hip Hop communities, Bocafloja travels widely and collaborates with numerous U.S. Latino artists, encouraging and spreading his redefined version of Hip Hop's four elements, "Decolonize, self-manage, transgress, emancipate" (130).

Still, there is another truth—that Hip Hop still struggles to gain the respect and legitimacy among the old guard and gatekeepers of the academy. *La Verdad* is that existing literature on Hip Hop often downplays Latinos and generally omits Latin America. Instead, the current trend in Hip Hop studies is to examine, historicize, and contextualize localized Hip Hop scenes in the United States. Recent books such as Maco Faniel's *Hip-Hop in Houston: The Origin and the Legacy* (2013), Matt Miller's *Bounce: Rap Music and Local Identity in New Orleans* (2012), and Schmelling, Sanneh, and Welch's *Atlanta: Hip-Hop and the South* (2010) demonstrate this trend. In a U.S. Latino/a context Juan Flores, Raquel Z. Rivera, and Pancho McFarland have produced work on New York Puerto Ricans and West Coast Chicano Rap. While Rivera's *New York Ricans from the Hip Hop Zone* (2003) addresses the New York City Puerto Rican contribution to the development of Hip Hop and McFarland's *Chicano Rap: Gender and Violence in the Postindustrial Barrio* (2008) gave an important history of Mexican American MCs, both books were written purely from a U.S. context and within a bounded East Coast / West Coast divide. *La Verdad* represents the next step, as we bring together pieces written about non-Anglo localized scenes in international communities. It will serve both as an introduction to questions of Latinidad and Latino Hip Hop and as a resource for those who want to do more research.

At this point, those who are interested in Latin American and Latino Hip Hop have very limited options. Several readers have been published that attempted to show the broad scope of Hip Hop culture traditions and history. Murray Forman, author of *The 'Hood Comes First: Race, Space, and Place in Rap and Hip-Hop* (2002), and Mark Anthony Neal, who authored *Soul Babies: Black Popular Culture and the Post-Soul Aesthetic* (2001), joined forces to edit *That's the Joint: The Hip-Hop Studies Reader* (2004). The reader was a virtual who's who of scholars, public intellectuals, and practitioners. However, there was very little that focused specifically on Hip Hop outside of U.S. borders, and only two pieces covered U.S. Latinos. Likewise, Jeff Chang's seminal work, *Can't Stop Won't Stop: A History of the Hip-Hop Generation* (2005), tells a story of Hip Hop's beginnings and trajectory, but solely in a U.S. context. Though the book covers three decades of the culture, stories about how Hip Hop spread or developed or about where it is headed in other nations are not found in the book. Even *Global Linguistic Flows: Hip-Hop Cultures, Youth Identities, and the Politics of Language* (2009), edited by Alim, Ibrahim, and Pennycook, which dealt with international Hip Hop expression, incorporates only one article about Latin America and focuses mainly on language.

La Verdad: An International Dialogue on Hip Hop Latinidades addresses this glaring hole in Hip Hop scholarship. Only three books within U.S. academia currently address Hip Hop in South America: *Afro-Colombian Hip-Hop: Globalization, Transcultural Music, and Ethnic Identities* (2012), by Christopher Dennis, and two books about Brazil by Derek Pardue (2008, 2011). Although there has been a significant interest in Cuban Hip Hop from both academics[1] and the Hip Hop community more generally, this attention has not been applied to other countries. This represents very little work for the more than 500 million people in Latin America, and the United States' largest minority (53 million).[2] For this reason, as much as possible we invited and aimed to include scholars from outside the United States whose expertise "on the ground" could provide new perspectives. In this way, we also mean to make a step toward ending U.S. academic cultural imperialism, especially on the subject of Hip Hop, Latin America, and Latinos, welcoming a number of the contributors from beyond U.S. borders. This dialogue is what *La Verdad* is all about. As the Hispanos Causando Pániko song describes, "La Verdad" is about respect—across crews, coasts, cultures, and countries. Likewise, this reader is not just about Hip Hop but about the possibilities of Hip Hop to open a dialogue for scholars and practitioners all across Latin America and the United States.

La Verdad breaks new ground in Hip Hop studies by introducing the world to the vast diversity of Latin American Hip Hop histories and expressions. We further a short legacy of writers who highlight Hip Hop's global impact beyond the United States and Europe as well as those who have focused on Hip Hop's past and current Latino character. *La Verdad* endeavors to broaden the definition of what Hip Hop America "is" and where it plays. Hay un dicho

---

1. See books by Tanya Saunders (2015), Marc D. Perry (2015), Geoffrey Baker (2011), and Sujatha Fernandes (2006).

2. There are also two books on Reggaeton: Raquel Rivera, Wayne Marshall, and Deborah Pacini Hernandez's 2009 *Reggaeton,* and Petra Rivera-Rideau's 2015 *Remixing Reggaeton.*

(there is a saying) that home is where the heart is. Our reader will prove that Hip Hop's heart is where the homies are, and there are plenty of homies, male and female, who are rhyming in ciphers on the corners of La Paz, b-boying in the alleys of Quito, and spray-painting murals on the walls of Santiago de Chile.

Undefining Hip Hop Latinidades

Perhaps that is why we begin this book not by defining Latinidad or Latino Hip Hop, but by undefining it. What we learned in our initial conversations (and at times heated debates) was that for every Latino "theme" (immigration, discrimination, lack of opportunities) or "style" (Spanish, English, sampling from salsa or Tejano music) there were numerous artists who were both Latino or Latin American and doing something completely different. These weren't outliers, but real diversity that could not be contained in a single category. Likewise, the more we spread our search geographically and unhinged it linguistically, the more enthusiasm we found among those groups who found themselves marginalized by hispanophone definitions of Latinidad. The pieces in this volume represent Hip Hop production in Spanish, English, Spanglish, Portuguese, French, Creole, Aymara with influences from various African languages and from the following countries: U.S./Puerto Rico, Colombia, Brazil, Mexico, Nicaragua, Costa Rica, Bolivia, Cuba, Haiti, Trinidad, Jamaica, Martinique, and Guadalupe. The submissions demonstrated active Hip Hop cultures in numerous other countries including Peru, Ecuador, Venezuela, Dominican Republic, Guatemala, and Chile as well as rapping in other Indigenous languages besides just Aymara.

This book takes a theoretical leap in the understanding of Latinidad. The brilliant activist journalist Juan Gonzalez acknowledges in his book *Harvest of Empire* that there is debate about what constitutes Latinidad. However, he concedes that it can be used interchangeably with Hispanic and hispanicity. Hispanic is a term created by the U.S. government and emphasizes Spanish language and ultimately the European colonial oppressor of a majority of the region, Spain. Latino is not a term without problems, but it stresses Latin America as the ancestral homeland of the inhabitants and the hybridity of its cultural expressions.

Due to the complexity of these issues, we complete this introductory section with two perspectives on Latinidad and Hip Hop other than ours. In "Borderland Hip Hop Rhetoric: Identity and Counterhegemony," Robert Tinajero explores U.S.-based Latino/a Hip Hop, which he defines as "Hip Hop produced by those of Latino/a/Hispanic origins and/or those that self-identify, either fully or partially, with that ethnolinguistic group. Linguistically, this may include Hip Hop that is written, spoken, or performed entirely in English, Spanish, or a mixture of the two languages. Culturally, the Hip Hop artist(s) will usually have strong ties to the Latino/a community not only in terms of language but also in rhetorical references to specific experiences, food, dress, Latino/a popular culture, and so forth" (18). While this reader takes a more expansive view of Latinidad, Tinajero's definition allows him to analyze the power of everyday rhetorics by rethinking the field of rhetorical studies and its "terrain" to include English-, Spanish-, and Spanglish-language Hip Hop by Latinos and its counterhegemonic and multi-conscious properties. Getting close up and lyrical, Tinajero analyzes what rappers like South Park Mexican and Cypress Hill say in their lyrics but, more important, rhetorically how they are saying it.

While Tinajero takes on the field of rhetoric, Pancho McFarland and Jared A. Ball round out the section with a critique of the term Latino itself as one which erases Indigeneity and Africanity from our understanding of this diverse group of people and as the latest iteration of the centuries-long attempt to erase Indigenous people from the planet. For McFarland and Ball, "Re-Indignization and re-Africanization begin as attempts from among the colonized to remember and reappropriate precolonial self-concepts and self-definitions and as processes are seen as necessary precursors to protracted political struggle . . . We group them because within the Latin American identity are both Indigenous and African people, culture and histories" (45). Nevertheless, in Hip Hop they find ways in which Latinos are similarly rejecting these terms. While Mexican Americans / Chicanos have developed an Indigenous or Mexica form of Hip Hop, a Panamanian-descended MC whose reclamation in eponym of the African maroon Bayano provides un otro cuadro (another tableau) through which to examine efforts at re-Indigenization (50).

Thus, rather than attempt to determine what constitutes Latino Hip Hop and what is just Hip Hop done by Latinos, we wanted to expose our audience to scholarship from Latin America, as well as about Latin America, and allow the readers to determine whether categorization is possible or even useful. At its core Hip Hop is rebellious and defies convention. Our categories for class, gender, race, and ethnicity, however arbitrary at times, simplify the world. As the articles in this reader demonstrate, Hip Hop can have simultaneous and multiple meanings, affiliations and interpretations that are too complicated to be confined within the limits of categorization. In essence, the key to understanding what Latino Hip Hop is lies in self-definition. If you identify as a practitioner or fan of "Latino Hip Hop" then that name fits you.

Latin American Hip Hop is too broad a term and not one used or identified by those in Latin America and the Caribbean. For this reason, this book discusses Hip Hop *Latinidades* rather than "Latino Hip Hop."

Contents

In order to encourage dialogue about Latinidad and Hip Hop across borders, we decided against imposing our own in structuring the book. Rather than organize the book by region, geography, or language, we organized it thematically. Nonetheless, these themes are not meant to be separations but suggestions for further conversations. Most of these articles could have fit into one or more of the other sections, and a whole other set of themes could also be brainstormed. We encourage readers to do just that.

Just as Pancho McFarland and Jared Ball critiqued the term "Latino" due to its erasure of Indigenous and African aspects of the culture, in many cases Hip Hop in Latin America has been attached to an ethos of social justice—Afro-descendants and Indigenous peoples have used the form to call for racial and social equality. This is what the second section, "Whose Black Music?: Afro-Latinidades and African Legacies in Latin American and Latino Hip Hop," aims in part to address. The section opens with Petra Rivera-Rideau's exploration of Los Rakas, a Panamanian rap duo from the Bay Area. While their music and self-fashionings re-center Panama as an important site of Hip Hop performance, Los Rakas also promote pride in their Afro-Latino identity that contests the devaluation of Blackness in Panama and the relative invisibility of Afro-Latino communities in the Bay Area. Similarly, just as Los Rakas's music demands a more inclusive understanding of Latinidad, Jason Nichols troubles standard views of Reggaeton to explore how it is a reflection of a uniquely Black Puerto Rican spiritual identity. While Nichols highlights Puerto Rico's significant positioning as in between Latin America and the United States and the complications that presents to Afro–Puerto Rican identities, Christopher Dennis takes us to the vibrant but much overlooked Hip Hop of Afro-Colombia. Focusing on the renowned Hip Hop group ChocQuibTown, Dennis demonstrates how these Afro-Colombian artists recuperate, re-elaborate, and preserve cultural memories that emerge from their day-to-day lives within their communities.

Together, these essays complicate prevalent critiques of the global appropriation of Black youth culture of the United States, underscoring the usefulness of such appropriations in establishing visibility and mobilization of similarly marginalized peoples often of Afro-Latino or Afro-Latin American descent. The final essay, "Now Let's Shake to This: Viral Power and Flow from Harlem to São Paulo," by Honey Crawford, offers a vocabulary of motion and viral exchange in negotiating the cultural currency between scattered and displaced African legacies across the Americas, tapping into a potential for viral Hip Hop performance to *shake* established compartmentalization and nationalist identity constructs that divide Black communities of the Americas. In the end, Hip Hop becomes the possibility for a balanced cultural interplay between the two largest Black populations of the Western Hemisphere, a conversation which informs and broadens the sociopolitical perspectives of both communities.

In his opening to the third section, "Chicano? Mexican?: On the Borderlands of Mexican and Mexican American Hip Hop," Mexican rapper, poet, and activist Bocafloja immediately destabilizes ideas about Mexicans and Hip Hop by grappling with Mexico's largely invisible African history. According to Bocafloja, "Historically, in Mexico, racial stratification has been concealed within a false discourse of harmonious miscegenation, with the aim of destroying any possibility of questioning race within the fabric of an apparently homogenous society" (127). For this reason his Hip Hop collective is named "Quilomboarte," to recognize the Quilombos, which during the colonial period on the American continent were established by fugitive Black slaves (also known as maroons and cimarrones), Indigenous peoples and others who rejected colonialism's domination, who preferred to live as free people in communal form. To follow up Bocafloja's deft dismantling of Mexicanidad, Melissa Castillo-Garsow similarly unlinks Mexican Hip Hop in the United States from Chicano Rap. In "'Yo soy Hip Hop': Transnationalism and Authenticity in Mexican New York," she explores the implications of a growing New York scene with strong transnational ties to Mexico City. The last two articles take us to both the familiar and the widely unfamiliar limits of Mexican Hip Hop. While Lisset Anahí Jiménez Estudillo explores new youth identities of the borderlands forged from participation in graffiti and rap, Daniel Zarazua tells the unlikely story of the spread of Chicano rap to Taipei, Taiwan, demonstrating that the way Hip Hop travels around the world and gains currency is not always what we assume.

Part IV, "Somos Mujeres, Somos Hip Hop," addresses what most research about Hip Hope fails to examine, female participation. For many of the authors of Hip Hop, this is due to the reality that even more than mainstream Hip Hop, in Latin America and Latino communities Hip Hop is heavily dominated by men, so much so that women are even greatly outnumbered as an audience. Nevertheless, important female MCs, DJs, producers, and graffiti artists do exist in these communities, which this section highlights.

In "Chicana Hip Hop: Expanding Knowledge in the L.A. Barrio," Diana Carolina Peláez Rodríguez presents powerful ethnographic work on women of Mexican origin who have decided to actively participate in Hip Hop and the struggles they face from their families, neighborhoods, and male rappers. In the end, she finds that the cultural nationalism of the Chicana rappers endowed with this alternative female identity displaces the normative logics of traditional gender relations and shapes their Chicano Hip Hop. Next, in a provocative turn, Jessica Pabón presents an interview with members of the all-female graffiti-writing crew from Nicaragua and Costa Rica, "Ladies Destroying Crew," giving a unique view of a rare group of young women. Last, Sandra Abd'Allah-Álvarez Ramírez discusses the possibilities and limitations of Cuban Conscious Hip Hop through the work of two female groups, Krudas Cubensi and Supercrónica Obsesión. While Krudas Cubensi has created a Hip Hop focused on the treatment of social issues related to sexual diversity, feminism, and sisterhood, Supercrónica Obsesión has chosen to emphasize a discourse of racial and national identity.

In many ways, the final section, "Rap Consciente: Hip Hop's Role in Activism," is hinted at throughout the book and is prominent in many of the previous articles. It is also the section which spans the most geographical and linguistic spaces, none of which include Spanish speakers. María Angela Riveros Pinto's "Ethnicity, Race, Nation, and the Male Voice in Alteño Hip Hop in Bolivia" presents the development of Hip Hop in Bolivia, specifically its growth in the city of El Alto from 2004 to 2008, among Aymara Indigenous youth. Not only was this growth directly after the 2003 "Gas War" during which many Aymara alteños lost their lives, but also their demands for social and political justice demonstrate the possibilities that Hip Hop poses for Indigenous young people as a form of expression and activism. Moving from Aymara to Creole, Stéphanie Melyon-Reinette examines the way second-generation Haitian youth remade a Haitian identity stigmatized as diseased and impoverished through an affiliation with Hip Hop culture. She identifies a new Haitian Heritage Hip Hop movement that is both a transnational and a hybrid expression of the Haitian pride, identity, and determination against racism. Moving to the Anglophone Caribbean, Steven Gadet takes us on a tour of Guadeloupe, Trinidad, Martinique, and Jamaica to discuss the intercultural potential of Hip Hop and its capacity to increase the awareness of young Caribbean people about the notion of citizenship in the region as a whole. Finally, Sarah Soanirina Ohmer's "Brazilian Hip Hop as Social Healing and Activism: AfroReggae and Grupo Cultural AfroReggae" presents Afro-Reggae, a group of multigenre / Hip Hop artists from Rio de Janeiro, and their

Hip Hop as part of a long history of Africana resistance through music in Latin America.

La Verdad connects the Black Atlantic and the African Diasporic cultural landscapes to Latin America, where Blackness has at times been marginalized, denied, or forgotten. It also poses questions about indigeneity, demonstrating how African-influenced soundscapes and dance moves influence Indigenous and Mestizo communities in Latin America. *La Verdad* demonstrates that Latin American Hip Hop is more than just rap en español; it is a multilingual expression performed in Creole, Portuguese, Aymara, and numerous other tongues. And finally, *La Verdad* further explores the role of gender for Latinas and latinoamericanas, asking how female Hip Hop Latinidades are articulated. But this is still not all that encompasses Hip Hop Latinidades. This is just the cusp, the beginning of a conversation. We hope you join in.

Bibliography

Alim, H. Samy, Awad Ibrahim, and Alastair Pennycook, eds. 2009. *Global Linguistic Flows: Hip-Hop Cultures, Youth Identities, and the Politics of Language*. New York: Routledge.

Baker, Geoffrey. 2011. *Buena Vista in the Club: Rap, Reggaetón, and Revolution in Havana*. Durham, NC: Duke University Press.

Chang, Jeff. 2005. *Can't Stop, Won't Stop: A History of the Hip-Hop Generation*. New York: Picador.

Dennis, Christopher. 2012. *Afro-Colombian Hip-Hop: Globalization, Transcultural Music, and Ethnic Identities*. Lanham, MD: Lexington Books.

Faniel, Maco. 2012. *Hip-Hop in Houston: The Origin and the Legacy*. Charleston, SC: History Press.

Fernandes, Sujatha. 2006. *Cuba Represent! Cuban Arts, State Power, and the Making of New Revolutionary Cultures*. Durham, NC: Duke University Press.

Flores, Juan. 2000. *From Bomba to Hip Hop: Puerto Rican Culture and Latino Identity*. New York: Columbia University Press.

Forman, Murray. 2002. *The 'Hood Comes First: Race, Space, and Place in Rap and Hip-Hop*. Music/Culture Series. Middletown, CT: Wesleyan University Press.

Forman, Murray, and Mark Anthony Neal, eds. 2004. *That's the Joint: The Hip-Hop Studies Reader*. New York: Routledge. 105–17.

George, Nelson. 1998. *Hip Hop America*. New York: Penguin.

Gonzalez, Juan. 2000. *Harvest of Empire: A History of Latinos in America*. New York: Viking.

McFarland, Pancho. 2008. *Chicano Rap: Gender and Violence in the Postindustrial Barrio*. Austin: University of Texas Press.

———. 2013. *The Chican@ Hip Hop Nation: Politics of a New Millennial Mestizaje*. East Lansing: Michigan State University Press.

Miller, Matt. 2012. *Bounce: Rap Music and Local Identity in New Orleans*. Amherst: University of Massachusetts Press.

Neal, Mark Anthony. 2001. *Soul Babies: Black Popular Culture and the Post-Soul Aesthetic*. New York: Routledge.

Pardue, Derek. 2008. *Ideologies of Marginality in Brazilian Hip Hop*. New York: Palgrave Macmillan.

———. 2011. *Brazilian Hip Hoppers Speak from the Margins: We's on Tape*. New York: Palgrave Macmillan.

Perry, Marc D. 2015. *Negro Soy Yo: Hip Hop and Raced Citizenship in Neoliberal Cuba*. Durham, NC: Duke University Press.

Rivera, Raquel Z. 2003. *New York Ricans from the Hip Hop Zone*. New York: Palgrave Macmillan.

Rivera, Raquel Z., Wayne Marshall, and Deborah Pacini Hernandez, eds. 2009. *Reggaeton*. Durham, NC: Duke University Press.

Rivera-Rideau, Petra R. 2015. *Remixing Reggaeton: The Cultural Politics of Race in Puerto Rico*. Durham, NC: Duke University Press.

Saunders, Tanya. 2015. *Cuban Underground Hip Hop: Black Thoughts, Black Revolution, Black Modernity*. Austin: University of Texas Press.

Schmelling, Michael, Kelefa Sanneh, and Will Welch. 2010. *Atlanta: Hip Hop and the South*. San Francisco: Chronicle Books, 2010.

chapter 2

Borderland Hip Hop Rhetoric

Identity and Counterhegemony

Robert Tinajero

The discursive practices of Latino/as have been studied and written about by many scholars from a variety of angles and disciplines. This scholarship continues to grow in importance considering the fact that this population is now the largest minority group in the United States and arguably the most influential in political and social matters. Scholars of Rhetoric and Composition have produced a plethora of important works connected to the Latino/a population but have yet to approach Latino/a rhetoric through the lens of Hip Hop discourse/culture. Latino/a Hip Hop is only one piece of the landscape of Latino/a rhetorical studies but it is an important, and thus far underrepresented, area of study.

This essay foregrounds Hip Hop rhetoric in analyzing the identity-showing and identity-shaping discourse of the present-day Latino/a community while emphasizing linguistic practices, culture, and identity. While no single rhetorical analysis ever functions as a full representation of any community, or as an exact representation of all individuals in a specific population, critically analyzing the Latino/a community through the lens of Hip Hop provides important and unique insight and functions as a critically useful tool to approach Latino/a studies. The discourse of this community is identity-showing in that it displays the lived realities of many in the Latino/a community—many of whom live on and in literal and metaphorical borders. The discourse is identity-shaping in that the rhetoric (lyrical, textual, visual) can also shape the lives and worldviews of those who strongly connect with Latino/a Hip Hop rhetoric. As discourse is a showing/telling phenomenon, it is also an epistemic one, and this is no different in the case of the Latino/a community.

More specifically, this essay focuses on issues of identity. Identity among the Latino/a population functions many times in a state of double-consciousness but, as viewed through the community's Hip Hop discourse, more readily functions in a state of multi-consciousness. This is manifested in the placement of Latino/as in cultural, linguistic, physical, and psychological borderlands (Anzaldúa 1999) and their possession of a "contradictory consciousness" (Villanueva 2004). Furthermore, the discourse of many Latino/a Hip Hoppers is counterhegemonic in critical ways: it can function, as much Hip Hop discourse does, in opposition to social "norms" and sensibilities with regard to linguistic practices, identity, and culture, and it is espoused through nontraditional mediums of rhetorical studies such as lyrics, music videos, graffiti, tagging, and "vehicular rhetoric." The multi-consciousness of this community, expressed in linguistic practices and culture, will be addressed first, followed by an analysis of how this multi-consciousness serves as a counterhegemonic force.

Ultimately, the Hip Hop discourse of the Latino/a community is directly connected to the complex identity of this ethnic group and is a powerful tool in displaying some of its central characteristics while also serving as a shaping-tool of the group's identity. Latino/a Hip Hop illustrates the power of everyday rhetorics to affect identity and society. Reaching out toward these untraditional places expands and enriches the rhetorical landscape and teaches us about a historically marginalized population that is growing in numbers and influence.

Defining Latino/a Hip Hop

Although any genre or subgenre of music is nearly impossible to strictly define, it is important to have a working definition of "Latino/a Hip Hop" for the purposes of this essay. Latino/a Hip Hop is Hip Hop produced by those of Latino/a/Hispanic origins and/or by those who self-identify, either fully or partially, with that ethnolinguistic group. Linguistically, this may include Hip Hop that is written, spoken, or performed entirely in English, Spanish, or a mixture of the two languages. Culturally, the Hip Hop artist(s) will usually have strong ties to the Latino/a community in terms of not only language but also in rhetorical references to specific experiences, food, dress, Latino/a popular culture, and so forth.

It is also important to note the presence of nationalistic and geographical differences among Latino/as, which is, of course, not a homogenous group but a diverse group of individuals with some strong, and some loose, connections that bring them together under the umbrella of "Latino/a." Latino/as may have ancestry from Mexico, Puerto Rico, El Salvador, Colombia, and so forth and will also have regionalized experiences depending on where they were raised and live(d). Because of these complexities it is difficult to pinpoint any one "Latino/a" experience, but a major element of this essay is to highlight and analyze some of the rhetorical and ideological underpinnings of the Latino/a Hip Hop community which in turn reveal important characteristics of the Latino/a community at large.

Theoretical Foundations

The theoretical framework of this essay begins with the call of Jacqueline Jones Royster (2003) to critically analyze and re-analyze the field of rhetorical studies and rethink its "terrain." She asks that scholars of rhetoric shift rhetorical subjects, shift the circle of practice, shift where they stand, and shift the theoretical frame (150–62).[1] The work of re-landscaping the terrain of rhetorical studies is important in that it diversifies the field, expands the number of voices and experiences heard and analyzed, adds to the fabric of world discourse, adds legitimacy to lost/forgotten/ignored rhetorics and the populations that produce(d) them, and creates new lenses through which to study the power of discourse in displaying and creating the identity of communities. The study of Latino/a Hip Hop accomplishes these tasks. The very use of Hip Hop lyrics throughout this essay represents a shift from the subjects of traditional rhetorical studies, and the multiplicity of nontraditional mediums incorporated by Latino/a Hip Hop are touched on at the end of the essay.

Beyond the general sense that the study of Hip Hop rhetoric, in this case Latino/a Hip Hop rhetoric, adds to the terrain of rhetorical studies, this essay uses theory that focuses on multi-conscious identity and cultural counterhegemony—with the latter frequently expressed in terms of Homi Bhabha's (2002) notion of "menace." The identity of many Latino/as can be

---

1. These sentiments are echoed by many others in the field, including Michael Leff (2003) and Patricia Bizzell (2003), among others (Charland 2003, Glenn qtd. in Portnoy 2003, Berlin 1994, Jarratt 1991).

described as influenced by two dominant cultures—that of the United States and that of their mother country (and even a third that already is a mixture of U.S. and Latin American cultures). Interestingly, the discourse of Latino/a Hip Hop rhetoric reveals two other cultural layers of influence for those Latino/as strongly connected to the Hip Hop ethos: those of African American culture and Hip Hop culture. These four layers create an organic multi-consciousness among those Latino/as who produce and are highly influenced by Latino/a Hip Hop rhetoric.[2]

A state of multi-consciousness is created as Latino/as become aware of and deal with—linguistically, psychologically, and physically—the influence of a multitude of social forces. The notion of multi-consciousness is rooted in the idea of "double-consciousness" introduced by W. E. B. Du Bois (2007) in his influential work *The Souls of Black Folk*. What he explains about African Americans of his time resonates with Latino/as today:[3]

> [They are] born with a veil, and gifted with a second sight in this American world—a world which yields [them] no true self-consciousness, but only lets [them] see [themselves] through the revelation of the other world. It is a peculiar sensation, this double-consciousness. . . . (896)

This resonates with Latino/as of the new millennium because the consciousness of many Latino/as is split in a multitude of ways as well. This sense of multi-consciousness is thematic in Latino/a discourse and Latino/a Hip Hop rhetoric and has been expressed by Latino/a Hip Hoppers just as it has been expressed through more traditional mediums by scholars like Victor Villanueva, Richard Rodriguez, and Gloria Anzaldúa. Some of these Latino/a Hip Hop texts, and their connection to multi-consciousness in language and culture, are discussed at length in the next section.

Cultural and critical race theory also offer valuable perspectives on Latino/a Hip Hop culture. The work of Homi Bhabha (2002) can be used to complicate and politicize the multi-consciousness of Latino/as. While, on one level, the layered existence of Latino/as can be said to be a common sociological occurrence in most people (i.e., all people exist in different roles in their lives—child, parent, employee, friend, etc.), the multi-consciousness of

---

2. A more expansive analysis could consider other characteristics such as sexuality and region (both the regional home within the United States and the region of the Latino/a's mother country).

3. Not surprisingly, as can be seen in Hip Hop rhetoric in general, the struggles and social concerns of Latino/as and African Americans have historically paralleled each other in important ways.

Latino/as was born out of powerful historical circumstances that have, in many instances, devalued at least a portion of their identity. This diminution of the value of Latino/a existence, experience, and culture in traditionally powerful circles, which has encompassed language, cultural norms, dress, food, and so forth, is part of the history of Latino/as and surfaces in Latino/a Hip Hop. Not only are Latino/as metaphorically colonized, considering their subordinate status in American society, but many of their ancestors were literally colonized when the United States took over parts of Mexico. These historic and present-day realities are connected to the identity of Latino/as, especially many who strongly identify with Latino/a Hip Hop, in that it articulates and creates a sense of struggle and counterhegemony among that population.

These struggles and multi-consciousness lead to discourse, and an identity bound up with this discourse, that is indicative of Bhabha's notions of camouflaging, mimicry, and mockery—but especially "menace," which serves as an aggressive counterhegemonic force against the dominant culture of the United States. Bhabha writes of subaltern groups within a colonialist state who exist "camouflaged" within a society where they are not the dominant group and voice. Within this state the subalterns, in this case Latino/as, are formed and reformed into a "recognizable Other" who, in their difference, are "almost the same [as the dominant group], but not quite" (Bhabha 2002, 114). In this "camouflaged" state, Latino/as often mimic and mock dominant White culture and can also be seen as a social menace to White middle- and upper-class norms and sensibilities. This menacing is at the heart of their counterdominant linguistic practices and culture—both of which have been marginalized by White middle- and upper-class sensibilities.

Furthermore, the unbalanced split between dominant culture and Latino/a culture is a playing out of neocolonialism in that the dominant culture possesses indirect control over the nondominant group. Invaluable to this discussion, as Stuart Hall (2002) reminds us, is the fact that this control is not simply economic—thus we cannot only explain racial or ethnic social divisions through the discussion of economic structures and processes. Hall understands and highlights the complex nature of the situation and uses the term "articulation" to describe the joining up of complex social, historical, ideological, and economic forces in analyzing social strata and racial and ethnic interaction (39). As applied to the Latino/a milieu, articulation highlights the multitude of ways in which Latino/as feel their culture is dominated, which then leads to discourse that expresses counterdominant sentiments that, at once, are born out of Latino/a experience and shape Latino/a identity. Simply put, social, historical, economic, and ideological realities have shaped the multi-conscious Latino/a identity, which in turn produces a discursive output that incorporates, directly and indirectly, a counterhegemonic message. This message, viewed here through the lens of Hip Hop, then becomes a part of Latino/a identity *and* a shaping-tool of that identity, especially for those Latino/as who strongly connect with Latino/a Hip Hop.

Ultimately, the multi-conscious and "othered" identity of Latino/as—which is both dominated by *and* incorporated with dominant culture—serves as a menacing and counterhegemonic force to dominant culture and ideals. Rhetorically, Latino/a Hip Hop works within the realm of this force. As Antonio Gramsci expresses, hegemony is "always constituted by a combination of coercion and consent" (qtd. in Omi and Winant 2002, 130) and much Latino/a Hip Hop, whether knowingly or not, is "coerced" by record labels, social norms, the English language, the sensibilities of dominant culture, and so forth. But, centrally, Latino/a Hip Hop also contests this cultural hegemony with its lyrical, textual, and visual rhetoric. It can serve as "political opposition . . . [with its] insistence on identifying itself and speaking for itself" (Omi and Winant 2002, 132) and with its expression of an *othered* experience—an experience deeply connected with social, cultural, linguistic, and ideological multi-consciousness and struggle. The following section highlights ways in which Latino/a identity is bound up in multi-consciousness, expressed rhetorically through Hip Hop discourse, while the final section delves more deeply into ways this identity grapples with and against the dominant culture.

Multi-Consciousness: Language, Culture, and Identity

> How you know where I'm at / when you haven't been where I've been /
> Understand where I'm coming from?
>
> —Cypress Hill

The discourse of Latino/a Hip Hop highlights integral pieces of the Latino/a experience, and it also creates a rhetorical atmosphere in which many Latino/as who strongly identify with Hip Hop, usually from an early age, are influenced to think and act (verbally and physically) in specific ways—ways "othered" by dominant culture.[4] These experiences and influences come to light in issues of language and culture as Latino/a Hip Hop exists within a multiplicity of linguistic and cultural borders.

---

4. Once again, I find it important to stress that no one section/type of discourse, in this case Latino/a Hip Hop, can fully describe the identity of an entire people; nor does it describe perfectly any one individual of that community.

As John Francis Burke (2002) states in *Mestizo Democracy,* "being open to dialogue with the 'other' that is different from us" is important, and the "use [and analysis] of multiple languages increase[s] the breadth and depth of the understanding [and knowledge] that ensues" (207). In this case, the knowledge that ensues is a deeper understanding of the complex linguistic makeup of Latino/a Hip Hop discourse and how this discourse articulates and influences important pieces of the Latino/a identity.

Linguistically, Latino/a Hip Hop functions at the crossroads of a number of languages/dialects: English, Spanish, Spanglish, African American Vernacular English (AAVE), and Hip Hop. Many have discussed Latino/a linguistics only in relation to the Spanish-English dichotomy, but when looking through the lens of Latino/a Hip Hop discourse, AAVE and Hip Hop linguistic practices must also be considered. These linguistic influences create a layered and complex ethnolinguistic rhetorical situation and are representative of the code-switching ethos of *mestizaje* (Burke 2002). This presentation—and a discussion of its connection to cultural hegemony in the final section—also represents a move toward what Ulla Connor (2004) terms "intercultural rhetoric research," where there is a focus on studying language through "social context and ideology" (295–96). This section focuses on displaying the multilayered linguistic practices of Latino/a Hip Hop rhetoricians, providing lyrics from two representative examples: Cypress Hill and Kid Frost.

Many scholars in the field of rhetoric and writing studies have discussed the importance of studying and valuing ethnolinguistic practices (Gilyard 1991, Elbow 2000, Schroeder, Fox, and Bizzell 2002). Jonathan Kozol in *Savage Inequalities: Children in America's Schools* (1991) discusses the marginalization of Latino/a students and how "language ideologies" have negatively affected Latino/as in general. These negative effects illustrate the effects that devaluing multi-ethnolinguistic practices have on Latino/as in general and create an atmosphere ripe for Latino/a backlash. They also show that valuing layered and ethnolinguistic practices is often not the norm for a dominant culture that applies its linguistic normative gaze to, among others, Latino/a discourse. It is a gaze that often devalues nontraditional and nonstandard English. Thus, the linguistic practices of Latino/a Hip Hoppers constitute not only a multilayered discourse but a discourse that represents opposition to monolinguistic (English) and monocultural (simplified Americanness) leanings. These leanings have been present in the United States from the Americanization movement against Native Americans to contemporary English-only movements and are addressed more fully in the following section on counterhegemony.

The quotation that begins this section is by Cypress Hill, a Latino rap group that utilizes linguistically complex lyrics and that understands that the

Latino/a experience is many times misunderstood—and diminished—in dominant culture. "How you know where I'm at / when you haven't been where I've been" is a defensive statement that emphasizes the fact that others—non-Latino/as, especially those of the middle/upper class—cannot understand the situation of Latino/as. Part of this "situation" involves the common use of a number of languages/dialects and is indicative of how Gloria Anzaldúa (1999) describes her "language of the Borderlands"—it is a space at the juncture of cultures where "languages cross-pollinate and are revitalized" (preface).

The first, and most obvious, is the space that much Latino/a Hip Hop occupies between English and Spanish. This may come in the form of intermixing English and Spanish words within a single phrase/sentence as in "*el* closet" or using Spanglish words/phrases like "troca"[5] which take the English "closet" and "truck" and Spanish-ize them. This linguistic interplay is a common, everyday practice for many Latino/as living on the border or in areas where border-existence has moved into nonborder regions (e.g., Houston, Chicago, Los Angeles, New York). Latino/as who use this mixture of Spanish and English are often criticized by non-Latino/as (and even Latino/as) who look down on this practice of linguistic mixing. The call of "just speak one language" attests to the fact that many, especially those who serve to gain the most from speaking only English, are bothered and/or threatened by the intermixing of languages.[6]

Whether they purposefully employ this linguistic mixing or, more often, are simply speaking a language/dialect they were raised in, the Spanish-English-Spanglish interplay functions as a form of dissent and protest that pushes up against dominant culture and "standard" English. As Cypress Hill states, "they clownin' [ragging/disrespecting] on me 'cause of my language / I have to tell them . . . it's called Spanglish." These Latino rappers understand that their linguistic practices are disrespected and diminished by dominant culture because they do not fit neatly into a linguistic category. And because linguistic practices are linked to one's identity, many Latino/a Hip Hoppers, and Latino/as in general, feel that their identity—their very being—is commonly disrespected by dominant culture.

To add to this dynamic, African American Vernacular English (AAVE) and words, phrases, and imagery that are directly connected to Hip Hop discourse are also a major piece of the linguistic collage that is Latino/a/Borderland Hip Hop. Because African American experience and discourse is the central template from which Hip Hop was created, Hip Hop rhetoric is already

---

5. *El* closet is "the closet," while a proper Spanish word for "truck" is *camion*.

6. The irony here, of course, is that Standard English itself is already an intermixed language.

infused with African American culture. The following example, also from rap group Cypress Hill, illustrates the linguistic interplay of Spanish, English, AAVE, and Hip Hop. These are lines from their song "Latin Lingo":

> But wait, they're clownin' on me 'cause of my language
> I have to tell 'em straight up, it's called Spanglish
> Now who's on the pinga, tha gringo
> Tryin' to get paid, from the funky bilingual . . .
>
> Cuando entro, when I come in, suckers fronted
> Me mira another bilingual from villa
> Vengo con un ejemplo, check the tiempo
>
> Hey homes, pass the cerveza
> Before I have to go and push up on your esa
>
> Where you live, si tu puedes
> Nowadays you ain't shit without your cuetes
> Something like it's gangbang, vatos quieren BANG BANG!
>
> Salte de mi cara, sal de mi camino
> Make way, for the funky bilingual

The back-and-forth of Spanish and English is obvious in the very first line as one of the rappers calls himself the "funky *bilingue.*[7]" This mixture of Spanish and English words is common among Latino/a rappers and among many in the Latino community. Words that are Spanglish slang, and that depend on the country or region the Spanish speaker comes from, are present as well: "pinga," "esa," and "cuetes"[8] are used to mean "penis," "girlfriend," and "guns," respectively. Also, terminology/imagery that is common in Hip Hop discourse is displayed: "homie" is commonly used to mean "friend/comrade"; "el deporte" refers to "the game," which is how many in Hip Hop refer to life in general or to the rap industry or to one's work/hustle to make a living; "*veterano*" is used to refer to a veteran of "the game" and is synonymous with the OG (original gangsta) of African American rap; "check the *tiempo*" is a common Hip Hop phrase—in this case mixing Spanish and English—meaning that one

---

7. *Bilingue* is the Spanish word for "bilingual."

8. These terms are used by Latino/as of various origins and are common among Cubans (*pinga*) and Mexican Americans (*esa* and *cuetes*).

should check/analyze the status of one's place/situation. The general reference to defending one's space/identity (*salte de mi cara, sal de mi camino*; get out of my face, get out of my way) and defending it violently if need be (nowadays you ain't shit without your *cuetes*[9]) are also commonplace in Hip Hop rhetoric.

Beyond that, the complexity of the language issue is caught up in the social structure. The counterhegemonic message—"that gringo / tryin' to get paid, from the funky bilingual"—brings to light the opinion among many in the Latino/a community that some/many White individuals will exploit Latino/a culture and language in order to profit financially. Cypress Hill seems aware that their ability to incorporate Spanish, English, and AAVE in the context of Hip Hop and to connect with Latino/a and African American audiences could be exploited by White-led record labels who may look at the linguistically complex lyrics of Latino/a rappers not as an important rhetorical production but as a means to gain larger profits. It is a matter of linguistic exploitation and appropriation that, as Georgina Born and David Hesmondhalgh (2000) remind us in *Western Music and Its Others,* are necessarily bound up in culture, power, ethnicity, and class (3). So while Cypress Hill believes that society needs to "make way" for Latino/a rappers, the group seems aware, at least at some level, of some of the political, social, and economic implications—a complex web of implications directly connected to Hall's (2002) discussion of "articulation" and cultural hegemony. These implications are connected to the fact that the Latino/a identity—linguistically and otherwise—can function as a form of social protest against the dominant culture. At times it is a purposeful/intentional menacing of dominant culture and other times the organic existence of Latino/a culture is labeled as nonnormal, illegitimate, or menacing by the dominant culture.

Lyrics from the song "La Raza" by Kid Frost, a pioneer of Latino rap, provide another short example of linguistic layering by a Hip Hop rhetorician. In his song, which translates as "the race" but which more closely means "the people" or "the people of the race,"[10] he raps:

What's da matter? Are you afraid, you gonna get hurt?
I'm with my homeboys, my camaradas

Yo soy chingon, ese
Like Al Capone, ese

---

9. *Cuete* is a Spanish slang word, sometimes spelled *quete,* that is used to refer to a gun/pistol; it can also be used to refer to "firecracker" or to "getting "drunk/plastered."

10. The term *la raza* was coined by Mexican writer Jose Vasconcelos in his 1925 book *La Raza Cósmica* (The Cosmic Race).

Once again, the intermixing of English and Spanish words is present, as is the use of Spanish slang like "chingon" (awesome/great/tough), "ese" (used by some Latino/as, many times of Mexican descent, and many times as a slang/street term, to mean "that one," "that guy," or "that guy who is my friend or homeboy"), and even "camaradas" (comrades/friends), which is common in "street" and Latino/a Hip Hop dialect. Even the reference to Al Capone is linked here, in the lyrics of a Latino rapper, to both American culture *and* Hip Hop culture. Al Capone was an American gangster of the 1920s and 1930s, and the image of the "gangster" or "gangsta" is highly prevalent in Hip Hop culture. As an important side note, the 1983 film *Scarface* ("scarface" was a nickname for Al Capone), based on a gangster figure, is extremely popular in Hip Hop culture and in Hip Hop textual and visual rhetoric. Thus, the reference to Al Capone is a discursively implicit way for Kid Frost, who is already rapping in Spanish and English in a Black-dominated medium, to connect to a Hip Hop audience that readily identifies with gangsta and "tough-guy" imagery—imagery that connects with the prominent strand of machismo and self-reliance among Latinos who have strong connections to Latino Hip Hop.

References to a gangster lifestyle—like that of Al Capone—add another layer to the complex rhetorical output of Latino/a Hip Hop discourse—connecting it to popular Hip Hop discursive practices—and show how dynamic this rhetoric is. Latino/a Hip Hop discourse often rhetorically connects itself to the overall Hip Hop ethos of struggle and violence by using words such as "gangsta" and "soldier"—or referencing specific gangsters or soldierlike activities. This not only articulates a self-identity bound up in struggle but directly connects Latino/a Hip Hop to the culture and wordplay of Hip Hop in general. The use of "gangsta" also re-emphasizes the anti-establishment and menacing nature of the discourse—after all, gangsters are characterized as social outsiders proud of their rule-breaking.

Those studying linguistics, sociology, literature, composition, rhetoric, and so forth can find in Latino/a Hip Hop rhetoric, and in Hip Hop rhetoric in general, complex linguistic practices and a deep well of knowledge and experiences. They will find that the multi-mixed discourse of Latino/a Hip Hop is a central piece of the "code-switching ethos of *mestizaje*" (Burke 2002, 209)—a common thread among these "mixed" people—and that this multi-ethnolinguistic discourse represents a challenge to dominant culture and contains a counternormative message. The ability of many Latino/a Hip Hoppers to code-switch between English, Spanish, Spanglish, AAVE, and Hip Hop is a discursively rich and powerful tool embraced by many in the Latino/a community and highlights their identities as multi-conscious *mestizos*.

The examples above, from Cypress Hill and Kid Frost, are but two short instances of this complex interplay, but many other artists are available as examples. A few of these are South Park Mexican, Down A. K. A. Kilo, Lil Rob, Chingo Bling, Big Pun, Fat Joe, A Lighter Shade of Brown, Mellow Man Ace, and Latin Alliance.[11] In all instances there is linguistic and cultural weaving and, in most cases, an emphasis on the "otherness" of the Latino/a experience.

Ultimately, the dynamic and multilinguistic/multidialectical discourse of Latino/a Hip Hop, while diversifying the landscape of rhetorical studies, forces scholars to focus on issues of language, dialect, and identity, and highlights the complexity of Latino/a rhetoric in general. As Khadar Bashir-Ali (2006) argues in "Language Learning and the Definition of One's Social, Cultural, and Racial Identity," linguistic practices help individuals form an allegiance to a group (628)—in this case the allegiance is to the Latino/a population and, more specifically, to the Latino/a population that embraces the Hip Hop ethos. Their discourse reveals and creates identity while complicating our understanding of the practices of a particular section of the Latino/a community whose discourse is often marginalized and labeled as dumbed-down and simplistic. It highlights the fact that Latino/a rhetoric, in general, is linguistically rich and that this richness is actually in opposition to dominant ideals that emphasize standard Americanness and the use of standard English as a leveling tool for those interested in maintaining the linguistic status quo.

Latinas and Borderlands Hip Hop Rhetoric

A final border at which many Latino/as exist/struggle involves gender bias and gender (in)equality. While important strides have been made for women in general, and for Latinas specifically, there is still a strong male-centered ethos present in Latino culture and especially in Latino/a Hip Hop. No Latina Hip Hop artists appear in this essay because there are so few women actively rapping, and none who have, or have been allowed to have, a large impact on the overall Latino/a Hip Hop scene. It is also not surprising that a search through Latinrapper.com produces very little information about Latina rappers but quite a bit on "sexy and hot Latina pictures" and "Latin eye candy."[12]

---

11. There are certainly hundreds of Latino/a artists to choose from, but I chose some of the more influential and commercially popular artists in this short list. Also, Reggaeton and other subgenres of Latino rap were not included in my analysis. See a list of Latino/a rappers at www.brownpride.com.

12. See http://www.latinrapper.com/eyecandy.html.

This lack of Latina Hip Hop discourse is somewhat surprising considering the popularity of rap music among Latino/as in general and the fact that there have been quite a few successful female rappers from the African American community. This lack is representative of a culture that has its struggle with issues of gender equality.

Many traditional values in Latino/a culture are also conservative values when it comes to the role of Latinas. While Latinas are meant to be respected, especially mothers and grandmothers, there is also the sense that Latinas are meant to be silent supporters and caregivers—while the males are viewed by many in the culture as the physical and verbal leaders. Interestingly, in "Racial and Ethnic Variations in Gender-Related Attitudes," sociologist Emily W. Kane finds contradictory results when studying the attitudes of Hispanic Americans toward gender roles. Some propose and defend more traditional and subservient roles for Latinas, while others work against these views. This is not surprising given the complex mix of respect, disrespect, veneration, and gender-role conservatism in Latino/a culture. It is also not surprising that Jezzy P, a female rapper from the slums of Mexico City, expresses often that she is "furious about sexism in macho Mexico" (Grillo 2006). Instead, Jezzy P's anger reflects the realty of the machismo of Latin American countries which trickles into Latino/a culture and then is expressed vividly in its Hip Hop.

As such, in Latino Hip Hop, there is simultaneously a respect-giving and respect-taking with regard to Latinas. On one hand there is, in Latino Hip Hop, the deep respect for and defense of mothers, daughters, grandmothers, and at times wives and girlfriends. This is expressed by South Park Mexican when he raps "My only daughter she's daddy's girl / And for her I'll buy the whole Astro world" and by Lil Rob when he writes "call the *ruca* [girlfriend] on the phone . . . / let her know she looks beautiful to me . . . / . . . she is such a sight to me / the kind of woman that would put up a fight for me." While the woman/girl is willing to fight, it is in the context of fighting for "him"—it is still the male at the center of that action. There is also a strong defense of female family members by males who at once often see these females as women deserving of respect (mainly by other males) but also women who are socially and physically weak and need "their man" to defend them. On the other hand, there is the more common objectification of women in much Latino Hip Hop. As Imani Perry (2008) reminds us, most rappers "exist within . . . a colonized space, particularly in regard to race and gender . . . [which is] full of traditional gender messages" (145). These messages are vivid in Latino Hip Hop, where references to "bitches," "hos," and "*putas*" are common along with visual images of scantily clad Latinas in music videos and on websites.

Thus, though Latino Hip Hoppers at times project female respect/defense/ veneration, it is the female objectifying and misogyny that often wins out. This rhetoric displays and affects the fact that many Latinas, especially those strongly connected to Hip Hop culture and "the streets," are at the crossroads between physical, psychological, and social advancement and the competing rhetoric and images of male dominance and traditional views in regard to gender roles—views perpetuated by both United States culture and the culture of their national roots. This final point is emphasized by Jessica Enoch (2004), though she does not directly discuss Hip Hop, in *"Para la Mujer*: Defining a Chicana Feminist Rhetoric at the Turn of the Century,"* where she highlights the fact that Latinas (she discusses Mexican women here) battle a long history of male-centered views in texts from Anglo writers like "Stephen Crane, Carleton Beals, and Ruth Allen" *and* in Mexican texts where "women's gender roles were clearly defined" (23). This places Latino/as in a web of borders characterized by gender, race, nationality, sexuality, and cultural tradition. More specifically, it highlights the pervasiveness of misogynistic rhetoric among Latin males and the presence of many Latin females who become subservient to male dominance—both of which challenge the dominant discourse of female equality and advancement.

Critically, these complex gender roles can have long-reaching effects on the Latino/a community. They can affect Latina self-esteem, education, career goals (or lack thereof), economics, health,[13] and general social standing. This very "real world" connection between Latino/a Hip Hop discourse and what is happening with many Latino/as points to the importance of studying this discourse and, as it closely pertains to the following section, to the menacing threat that Latino/a Hip Hop poses to dominant culture. After all, dominant culture in the United States champions women's rights and does not want to be reminded of past (and present) gender inequality and injustice. It also fears a popular discourse that espouses misogyny, traditional gender roles, and which may be a rhetorical force in the production of fatherless minority children.

Ultimately, multi-consciousness is an umbrella term that incorporates the many languages, cultures, ideologies, and identities that many Latino/as embody and traverse daily and which are vividly expressed in Latino/a Hip Hop. From the incorporation of Black, White, and Brown culture, to the process of self-labeling, to social and mental struggles of economics and gender roles, Latino/as are physically and ideologically *mestizos* whose

---

13. See *Gender Roles, Power Strategies, and Precautionary Sexual Self-Efficacy: Implications for Black and Latina Women's HIV/AIDS Protective Behaviors,* by Lisa Bowleg, Faye Z. Belgrave, and Carol E. Reisen.

multilayered existence can, implicitly and explicitly, serve as a counterhegemonic force to the dominant culture. This force contains deep and complex connections to historical, cultural, racial, political, and ideological realities of the American social fabric.

Counterhegemony: Expanding the Complex Connections

While the previous section touched on ways that a multi-conscious Latino/a identity runs counter to some dominant social norms and sensibilities, this section delves more deeply into the ways that the linguistic and cultural *mestizaje* of Latino/as, as expressed in Latino/a Hip Hop, challenges, agitates, and disrupts dominant culture. Important to this discussion is the fact that the marginalization of Latino/as in the United States has created a space from which Latino/as have carved out an identity that pulls marginality from the shackles of a rhetorically neutered existence toward a "space for alternative cultural production and alternative epistemologies" (hooks 1994, 171). That is, Latino/a rhetoric, of which Latino/a Hip Hop rhetoric is an important strand, functions not simply as a dominated discourse but as a discourse that points to complex social realities—it helps us see and understand the world, and connections between cultures, through a different lens. More specifically, the alternative discourse of Latino/a Hip Hop rhetoric, in espousing an alternative epistemology, contains the quality of social "menace."

The Latino/a Hip Hopper is a cultural *mestizo*, equipped with a multi-ethnolinguistic tongue, whose culturally and psychologically bordered existence disrupts dominant social ideals. These ideals include strong sentiments toward preserving "the security of a monolingual English public discourse" (Burke 2002, 206) and traditionally White American culture. This border existence highlights much of what Gloria Anzaldúa (1999) wrote of in her seminal *Borderlands / La Frontera: The New Mestiza*. She writes that "to survive the Borderlands / you must . . . / be a crossroads" (217). Anzaldúa acknowledges the interplay between a borderland/multi-conscious existence and survival—survival that happens at the intersection of many social crossroads. That is, existence is not only *within* crossroads but *acts as* a crossroads—a crossroads where "you are the battleground / you are at home, a stranger" (216). This sense of difference, otherness, borderness is many times tinged with angst and anger in the discourse of Latino/a Hip Hop. This discourse suggests that many Latino/as, while being extremely proud of the cultural differences that distinguish them from White American and Black American culture, are highly cognizant of their marginalization from White American, middle-, and upper-class sensibilities—of their subaltern status. As a consequence, the Latino/a Hip Hopper has no trouble understanding—and in fact preaching—the notion of a cultural "battleground" where cultural soldiers and gangsters fight for equality and supremacy.

This multi-conscious Latino/a nature proves antihegemonic and menacing to dominant modes of being, while a more aggressive and direct message of resistance acknowledges and perpetuates a battleground of sorts where the Latino/a Hip Hopper can be presented as not simply a challenger to simplified cultural and racial division but a menacing "gangsta." This type of menace is articulated by Homi Bhabha (2002), who asserts that menace is produced by a "double vision which in disclosing the ambivalence of colonial discourse also disrupts its authority" and by discourse that "articulates those disturbances of cultural, racial, and historical difference that menace the narcissistic demand of colonial authority" (117). Although Bhabha refers to a different group of subalterns in a different place, his theory applies equally well to Latino/as in the United States. In the case of Latino/a hip rhetoric, a mirror is held up to the dominance and neocolonialism of White authority and a challenge presented to the cultural, racial, and ideological history of that dominance. Furthermore, Latino/a Hip Hop, in its multilinguistic and multi-conscious ways, provides a "displacing gaze" where the traditional "observer" (White middle- and upper-class individuals) becomes the "observed" (117). Latino/a Hip Hop, whether aware or unaware of this, reverses the critical gaze of dominant culture by espousing a multilayered existence and in directly revealing and attacking dominance.

Linguistically, the nature of Latino/a Hip Hop serves in opposition to sentiments toward a simplified monolinguistic English public discourse— a sentiment cloaked many times in nationalistic and culturally and politically conservative ideals and most poignantly represented by "English-only" and "official English" movements. While these movements do not look to rid the United States of all other languages per se, they function under an ideological umbrella that seeks the simplification of cultural practices in the United States and the preserving of the social superiority of the English language. While supporters of English-only and official English hold that "reaffirming the preeminence of English means reaffirming a unifying force in American life" (Crawford 1992, 2), they fail to understand the divisiveness that such ideologies and policies breed. At best, such ideologies perpetuate a history of diminishing the linguistic, rhetorical, and cultural output of minority groups; at worst, they "serve[ ] to justify racist and nativist biases under the cover of American patriotism" (ibid., 3).

The ethnolinguistic patterns of Latino/a Hip Hoppers, who regularly use Spanish, English, Spanglish, AAVE, and Hip Hop discourse, also challenge the notion that the discourse these individuals are producing is immature and simplistic—two characteristics viewed as opposite to that of expertise in using one language (i.e., English). Not only are these patterns antihegemonic in that they challenge the push of English dominance, but they also produce multilinguals who, as seen in a psychology study on bilinguals, "enjoy some cognitive advantages over monolinguals in areas such as cognitive flexibility, metalinguistic awareness, concept formation, and creativity" (Padilla et al. 1991). The view that Latino/a Hip Hoppers are more cognitively advanced than White monolinguistic non–Hip Hoppers challenges deeply rooted racial and social stereotypes. Thus as a matter of being/nature, the linguistic patterns of Latino/a Hip Hoppers both reflect and shape multilingual/multidialectical individuals who pose a threat to English monolinguistic hegemony.

Through more direct rhetoric, Latino/a Hip Hoppers move into the realm of social "gangsta"—providing a more aggressive form of menace in that this discourse differs from and threatens the conservative ideal of a monolingual America. When Cypress Hill rap "now who's on the pinga, tha gringo / tryin' to get paid, from the funky bilingual," they are expressing deeply held sentiments of angst, resistance, even hatred, toward the "gringo" who they feel is exploiting their culture and talent. There is also the rap/rock group Molotov, who state in their song "Frijolero"[14] "*no me diges* beaner / *te sacaré un susto* / *por racista y culero* / *no me llames* frijolero / *pinche gringo puñetero.*" The angry and crude lyrics translate to "don't call me a beaner / I'll give you a scare / for being a racist and an asshole / don't call me a beaner / fucking White jerk." This aggressive rhetoric moves Latino/a Hip Hop discourse into the realm of aggressive menace and the Latino/a Hip Hopper into the realm of the cultural "gangsta."

This move is not surprising considering that the genre of Hip Hop was born from "bleak conditions" and, from its early existence, has produced "lyrical elegies" about the "tortuous twists of urban fate" (Dyson 2008, 174)—something that continues in Latino/a Hip Hop. These elegies "force us to confront the demands of racial representation" and can "force our nation to confront crucial social problems" (181) and in doing so serve as a powerful menace to dominant culture. Latino/a Hip Hoppers that deliver these angry elegies envy, and in fact embody, "the lowdown hustlers [and gangsters] . . . who are not slaves to white power" (185) of whom bell hooks writes

---

14. Frijolero is slang for "beaner," a derogatory term used to refer to Latino/as in reference to their skin color and the fact that beans are a popular Latin American food.

in "Gangsta Culture" (2008). The words of Cypress Hill and Molotov express the violent opposition toward dominant White culture and power which is present not only in Latino/a Hip Hop, but also, to varying degrees, in Latino/a culture in general.

Furthermore, Tim Strode and Tim Wood (2008) point out in "Growing Up Gangsta: Gangsta Rap and the Politics of Identity" that White condemnation of gangsta rap and a gangsta message many times demonstrates an ignorance of what is happening in low-income Black and Latino/a Communities (156–57). For many middle- and upper-class Whites, it is almost impossible to understand that a community that lives in the same country can have such a different social experience—a multi-conscious experience connected to economic and ideological struggle. They are in some respects "almost the same but not quite" (Bhabha 2002, 118). The dominant group focuses on the "sameness" between Latino/as and themselves—the push for sameness coming at times through direct means like the English-only movement and at other times through cultural hegemony—while not fully understanding the presence of struggle or valuing a multicultural and multi-ethnolinguistic existence (the "not quite") so expressed in Latino/a Hip Hop.

Certainly, Latino/as have agency in the formation and evolution of their own group identity, but the forces of history and dominant culture impose themselves during this process. It is the "articulation" (Hall 2002) of a number of forces—social, economic, ideological—which form the imposition by dominant forces and provoke the violent backlash found in Latino/a Hip Hop. While all groups and cultures are influenced by other cultures, including the influence Latino/a culture has on the United States, it must be noted that the dynamics are different when this influence involves the diminution of one culture. In a number of ways, Latino/a culture has come under attack for decades in the United States—in recent history there has been openly racist thinking and policies in the early and mid-1900s, to attacks on bilingual education which include the English-only movement, to a vast amount of stereotypical images in popular media, to a plethora of group actions against Latino/as which have included a "find the illegal immigrant" event.[15] In more extreme cases there is race-based violence against Latino/as which includes "the birth of at least 144 'nativist extremist' groups . . . that do not merely target immigration policies they do not agree with, but instead confront or harass individual immigrants" (Lovato 2007). Illustrating the extent of anti-Latino/a sentiment are FBI reports which state that in 2006 "Hispanics comprised 62.8% of

---

15. The College Republicans group at New York University held a "Find the Illegal Immigrant" event on February 2, 2007.

victims of crimes motivated by a bias toward the victims' ethnicity or national origin" (MALDEF) and that hate crimes targeting Latinos increased 40 percent from 2003 to 2007 ("Hate Crimes" 2008).

It is no wonder that many Latino/a Hip Hoppers support an aggressive opposition to dominant culture and that, as also seen in the example of rapper Chingo Bling, this menacing comes alive in their discursive output. In 2007 the Houston, Texas–based rapper rented out billboard space to promote the release of his new album. The billboard read, in large text, "They Can't Deport Us All" and caused controversy. Many conservative pundits attacked the billboard, including Michelle Malkin, who wrote on her blog that it was "obnoxious" and "defiant." It was also reported that Chingo Bling received several death threats after the billboard went up.[16] While the merits of the billboard could be debated at length, there is no doubt that Chingo Bling was acting, and perceived, as a cultural "gangsta" who was aggressively attacking dominant culture. Chingo Bling also highlights the fact that there is strong solidarity between Latino/a Hip Hoppers and Latin immigrants—legal and illegal—in the push against White cultural hegemony. Part of that push also includes Chingo Bling's music video for the song "Like This 'N' Like That," which includes images of Latino/a immigrants running from the border patrol and the repetitive image of people wearing "They Can't Deport Us All" T-shirts.

Thus, from lyrics to billboards to music videos, Latino/a Hip Hop rhetoric functions like the narratives of people of color that Villanueva (2004) commends: it is a narrative that "validates . . . resonates . . . and awakens" (15). The anti-hegemonic message of this genre resonates with millions of Latino/as; it awakens and expresses an anti-dominant ethos. It is an expression of historical struggle and a rhetorical perpetuation of an ethos of struggle and menace.

This struggle/anti-dominant ethos can also be seen in the Latino/a Hip Hoppers' psychological dichotomy between a pursuit of wealth and an interest in remaining connected to modest means. As in much Hip Hop, and society in general, Latino/a Hip Hoppers stress the accumulation of wealth and the things they can buy with that wealth—not surprising considering the "ethic of consumption that pervades our culture" (Dyson 2008, 175). Yet, Latino/a Hip Hoppers make it clear that they are, or once were, connected to social and economic hardship. When South Park Mexican raps that he got sent home because "my head had lice" and that he had to learn how to "keep the rats out [of] the cereal box," he is not only telling his life story but explicitly expressing the fact that he has to deal with economic hardship. So while

---

16. MTV Online, "Artist Profile: Chingo Bling," August 17, 2009, http://www.mtvmusic.com/bling_chingo/.

South Park Mexican and many Latino/a rappers consistently rap about their real or imagined wealth, they make sure to stress their struggle as well.

What pushes this dichotomy into the realm of the aggressive gangsta is when Latino/a rappers begin espousing violence or illegal actions as a way—or *the* way—to accumulate wealth. While many Latino/a Hip Hoppers choose to gain wealth by legal and nonviolent means, the rhetoric of the genre more often stresses aggressive and illegal actions. Michael Eric Dyson (2008) writes, "Gangsta rappers . . . don't merely respond to the values and visions of the marketplace; they shape them as well" (175) and "respond to economic exploitation" with, at times, "vulgar rhetorical traditions" (174). The Latino/a Hip Hop social gangsta does this as well by stressing the accumulation of wealth through the *violent* shaping of the marketplace via illegitimate acts like robbery and/or drug dealing. In the eyes of many Latino/a Hip Hoppers, the accumulation of wealth through any means necessary (hustlin' or playin' the game) is legitimate—especially among a population that deals with economic struggle on a daily basis. Thus, Latino/a Hip Hoppers mimic capitalistic ideals but add the element of violence and "street capitalism" which menaces the dominant "legitimate marketplace."

Finally, this aggressive anti-hegemony is espoused through a number of media, which in themselves challenge the hegemony of the traditional rhetorical landscape. Latino/a Hip Hoppers use lyrics, music videos, traditional websites, social video sites (e.g., YouTube), social networking sites (e.g., Facebook, Twitter), murals, graffiti, tagging, body art, and even their vehicles to broadcast their message. Thus, this multi-conscious and anti-dominant discourse reaches the eyes and ears of millions of people in multiple ways. Importantly, in "Encountering Visions of Aztlan: Arguments for Ethnic Pride, Community Activism and Cultural Revitalization in Chicano Murals," author Margaret R. LaWare points out that "reasoning takes various forms" and that "in order for a minority community to argue that its culture has distinct properties that set it apart from dominant culture, it needs to show those distinctions within cultural artifacts" (1998, 40). These cultural artifacts are often attacked and criminalized by dominant culture—music lyrics and videos demonized, murals and graffiti labeled simply the work of criminals, and loud and colorful vehicles mocked as not conforming to "normal" standards. A debate over the aesthetics of these media is not the focus here, but instead the realization that the anti-dominant message is espoused through multiple avenues and that these media themselves pose a threat to dominant sensibilities.

These sensibilities include the thinking that only certain forms of expression are valid and important. This thinking even creeps into the discipline of rhetorical studies and what is labeled as *the* rhetorical tradition. Patricia Bizzell

(2003), co-author of the influential *The Rhetorical Tradition*, has acknowledged that traditional texts—such as rhetorical manuals, published texts, and political discourse—still dominate the field into the early twenty-first century (110). This is why Jacqueline Jones Royster (2003) argues that "new" rhetorics are valuable in the re-envisioning . . . of what constitutes knowledge" (161). This is echoed by Bizzell (2003) herself, who states, "we must hear from rhetoricians who have struggled with culturally complex venues in which they were marginalized" (112). Latino/a Hip Hoppers are representatives of a new, complex, marginalized rhetoric that is espoused through nontraditional mediums. And because it carries an aggressive anti-hegemonic message through nontraditional means, it is a part of the cultural gangsta-ness that pervades the Latino/a Hip Hop ethos.

Conclusion

Latino/a Hip Hop's identity-showing and identity-shaping rhetoric expresses a multi-conscious and bordered ethos which contains an anti-dominant message and worldview that challenges those who would push for a more unified cultural and national identity—more specifically, a unified identity which places greater value in the linguistic, cultural, historical, and ideological practices of White middle- and upper-class Americans. In more antagonistic instances, the Latino/a Hip Hop ethos works in aggressive opposition toward dominant culture and highlights the presence of the cultural gangsta. These menacing instances include messages which are anti-White, that venerate violence and illegal activity in the accumulation of wealth, that defend illegal immigration, and that use self-labeling to diminish American-ness/White-ness.

Importantly, Latino/a Hip Hop rhetoric also points to the ethos of the greater Latino/a community. Many Latino/as rely on personal experience and the memory of past racial injustice to help shape an identity that is tinged with subtle *and* aggressive anti-hegemony. The Latino/a Hip Hopper affects this formation of a collective—though complex—Latino/a identity. As a "narrative of people of color," Latino/a Hip Hop "jogs our memories as a collective in a scattered world and within an ideology that praises individualism" while asserting "the interconnectedness among identity, memory, and the personal" (Villanueva 2004, 16). This "jogging of memory" occurs for both the Latino/a and the dominant culture and is a reminder of a past and present that is complicated with competing cultural, linguistic, social, economic, and ideological realities.

Latino/a Hip Hop rhetoric is a validation of that memory and of the bordered and layered existence experienced by many Latino/as. It is a rhetoric that shows and complicates "racial and ethnic power dynamics of . . . cultural relations" (Born and Hesmondhalgh 2000, 6) as well as complex connections to linguistic and cultural identity. These complex connections work within Latino/as and produce—in the Latino/a Hip Hopper—a discourse that challenges dominant cultural hegemony. In this rich discourse we find the playing out of Bhabha's notions of "camouflaging, mimicry, and menace," of Stuart Hall's "articulation," and of Anzaldúa's and Villanueva's fight for the validation of multicultural identity. All of these are directly or indirectly connected to the many borders navigated by Latino/as who are strongly connected to Hip Hop culture and, to various extents, Latino/as in general. These borders create a culture of *mestizaje* which is vividly displayed by the Latino/a Hip Hopper and which is worth deep analysis because, ultimately, we must work at increasing our capacity to "acknowledge and combine multiple identities"—work that can help us understand a "shrinking world in which each of us is increasingly 'crossing borders'" (Burke 2002, 245). Latino/a Hip Hop rhetoric can be an important part of this work.

Bibliography

"Anti-Latino Hate Crimes Rise for Fourth Year in a Row." 2008. *Southern Poverty Law Center: Intelligence Report,* Winter. SPLC Online. https://www.splcenter.org/hatewatch/2008/10/29/anti-latino-hate-crimes-rise-fourth-year-row.

Anzaldúa, Gloria. 1999. *Borderlands/Frontera: The New Mestiza.* San Francisco: Aunt Lute Books.

Bashir-Ali, Khadar. 2006. "Language Learning and the Definition of One's Social, Cultural, and Racial Identity." *TESOL Quarterly* 40(3): 628–39.

Berlin, James. 1994. "Revisionary Histories of Rhetoric: Politics, Power, and Plurality." In *Writing Histories of Rhetoric,* edited by Victor Vitanza. Carbondale: Southern Illinois Press. 112–27.

Bhabha, Homi. 2002. "Of Mimicry and Man: The Ambivalence of Colonial Discourse." In *Race Critical Theories,* edited by Philomena Essed and David Theo Goldberg. Malden, MA: Blackwell. 117–18.

Bizzell, Particia. 2003. "Editing the Rhetorical Tradition." *Philosophy and Rhetoric* 36(2): 109–18.

Born, Georgina, and David Hesmondhalgh. 2000. *Western Music and Its Others: Difference, Representation, and Appropriation in Music.* Berkeley: University of California Press.

Burke, John Francis. 2002. *Mestizo Democracy.* College Station: Texas A&M University Press.

Charland, Maurice. 2003. "The Constitution of Rhetoric's Tradition." *Philosophy and Rhetoric* 36(2): 119–34.

Connor, Ulla. 2004. "Intercultural Rhetoric Research: Beyond Texts." *Journal of English for Academic Purposes* 3:291–304.

Crawford, John. 1992. *Language Loyalties: A Source Book on the Official English Controversy.* Chicago: University of Chicago Press.

Du Bois, W. E. B. 2007. "From *The Souls of Black Folks.*" In *The Norton Anthology of American Literature,* 7th ed., vol. C, edited by Jeanne Campbell Reesman and Arnold Krupat. New York: Norton. 894–910.

Dyson, Michael Eric. 2008. "Gangsta Rap and American Culture." In Strode and Wood, 172–81.

Elbow, Peter. 2000. *Everyone Can Write: Essays Toward a Hopeful Theory of Writing and Teaching Writing.* New York: Oxford University Press. 323–50.

Enoch, Jessica. 2004. "*Para La Mujer*: Defining a Chicana Feminist Rhetoric at the Turn of the Century." *College English* 67 (September): 20–37.

Gilyard, Keith. 1991. *Voices of the Self: A Study of Language Competence.* Detroit: Wayne State University Press.

Grillo, Ioan. 2006. "Rapping Out Their Fury." *The Press Enterprise,* October 16. http://www.pe.com/entertainment/stories/PE_Fea_Ent_D_music.mexicanrap.79d45f.html.

Hall, Stuart. 2002. "Race, Articulation, and Societies Structured by Dominance." In *Race Critical Theories,* edited by Philomena Essed and David Theo Goldberg. Malden, MA: Blackwell. 38–49.

hooks, bell. 1994. *Teaching to Transgress: Education as the Practice of Freedom.* New York: Routledge, 1994.

———. 2008. "Gangsta Culture." In Strode and Wood, 185–90.

Jarratt, Susan. 1991. *Rereading the Sophists: Classical Rhetoric Refigured.* Carbondale: Southern Illinois Press.

Kane, Emily W. 2000. "Racial and Ethnic Variations in Gender-Related Attitudes." *Annual Review of Sociology* 26:419–39.

Kozol, Jonathan. 1991. *Savage Inequalities: Children in America's Schools.* New York: Crown.

LaWare, Margaret R. 1998. "Encountering Visions of Aztlan: Arguments for Ethnic Pride, Community Activism and Cultural Revitalization in Chicano Murals." *Argumentation and Advocacy* 34(3): 140–53.

Leff, Michael. 2003. "Tradition and Agency in Humanistic Rhetoric." *Philosophy and Rhetoric* 36(2): 135–47.

Lovato, Roberto. 2007. "Violence Against Immigrants Builds." *New America Media,* May 9. http://news.newamericamedia.org/news/view_article.html?article_id=cb1ac6666cf80f87fd61e4cec5421342.

MALDEF. 2009. "FBI Report Documents Hate Crimes Against Latinos at Record Level." *Delaware Hispanic Online,* July 15. http://www.delawarehispanic.com/Hate%20Crimes%20Latinos.pdf.

Malkin, Michelle. 2007. "Open-Borders Rapper: 'They Can't Deport Us All.'" *Michelle Malkin Online,* August 14. http://michellemalkin.com/2007/08/14/open-borders-rapper-they-cant-deport-us-all/?print=1.

Omi, Michael, and Howard Winant. 2002. "Racial Formation." In *Race Critical Theories,* edited by Philomena Essed and David Theo Goldberg. Malden, MA: Blackwell. 123–45.

Padilla, Amado M., Kathryn J. Lindholm, Andrew Chen, Richard Durán, Kenji Hakuta, Wallace Lambert, and G. Richard Tucker. 1991. "The English-Only Movement: Myths, Reality, and Implications for Society." *American Psychologist* 46(2): 120–30.

Perry, Imani. 2008. "The Venus Hip Hop and the Pink Ghetto: Negotiating Spaces for Women." In Strode and Wood, 134–45.

Pew Hispanic Center. 2009. "Statistical Portrait of Hispanics in the United States, 2007." *Pew Hispanic Center Online,* September 16. http://pewhispanic.org/files/factsheets/hispanics2007/Table-34.pdf.

Portnoy, Alisse Theodore. 2003. "Defining, Using, and Challenging the Rhetorical Tradition." *Philosophy and Rhetoric* 36(2): 103–8.

Rodriguez, Richard. 1982. *Hunger of Memory: The Education of Richard Rodriguez.* New York: David Godine.

Royster, Jacqueline Jones. 2003. "Disciplinary Landscaping, or Contemporary Challenges in the History of Rhetoric." *Philosophy and Rhetoric* 36(2): 148–67.

Schroeder, Christopher, Helen Fox, and Patricia Bizzell, eds. 2002. *Alt Dis: Alternative Discourse and the Academy.* Portsmouth, NH: Boyton/Cook–Heinemann.

Strode, Tim and Tim Wood. 2008. "Growing Up Gangsta: Gangsta Rap and the Politics of Identity." In Strode and Wood, 156–59.

Strode, Tim, and Tim Wood, eds. 2008. *The Hip Hop Reader.* New York: Pearson/Longman.

Villanueva, Victor. 2004. "*Memoria* Is a Friend of Ours." *College English* 67 (September): 9–19.

chapter 3

¡Ya basta con Latino!

The Re-Indigenization and Re-Africanization of Hip Hop

Pancho McFarland and Jared A. Ball

Who Cares about Hip Hop Latino?

Our intent here is to briefly consider the relationship between Hip Hop, identity, and power relations and to critique the ways in which "Latino" functions as a colonial identity as well as how those in (including the study of) Hip Hop consider, apply, and contradict that imposed identity. In so doing, we accept identity formation as essential to the determination of behavior and place within any given society and that identities imposed on Indigenous/African-descended communities are tuned to function as extensions of Western/European Empire. In North America "Residential" (Indigenous) and "Industrial" (African) schools were established to assimilate the colonized to their new appropriate postcolonial/enslavement identities (Churchill 2004). Prior to that the same goal was incorporated, after military conquest, via education and religious instruction by the French, British, Portuguese, Germans, and Spanish states and churches in the establishment of new "symbolic representations" (Wynter 1995) meant to reorder a more suitable consciousness throughout the continent of Africa and in the so-called West Indies, Caribbean, and Americas.

41

Today, similarly, media conglomerates represent an increasingly powerful institution for the organization and distribution of preferable identities for today's colonial subjects (those held internally as well as externally). The imposed identities for these subjects, people, the targeted, define them as material and immaterial commodities to be managed and exploited along more traditional colonial principles, and dominantly placed conceptions of identity, such as "Latino, Black, Indian, etc.," are intended to impact targets directly, materially in terms of lived experienced and access to resources, but also indirectly as established norms against which all other conceptual forms are judged (Ball 2011b). For our purposes, concepts of re-Indigenization and re-Africanization are synonymous in their anticolonial character and as terms are to be used interchangeably to also support our views on Pan-African and Indigenous identities that both predate and transcend Western/imperial geopolitical borders/boundaries.

Our interests regarding identities are their function in support (or denial) of revolutionary change/advance, anticolonial movements. There has been an ever-present struggle over the identities of those forced into or subsumed within the settler colonial development of the Americas. These are the struggles reflected in the fight against European imperialism led by the eighteenth-century pre-Bolivian/Peruvian Bartolina Sisa and Micaela Bastidas Puyucahua in South America, or the struggle over African identities in North America (Alexander 2012), or, for another example, the Garveyite calls of those such as Carlos Cooks for the abandonment of "Negro" in favor of "Black" or "African" (Rivera 2010, 216). More recently, there is Hip Hop activist Rosa Clemente (2001), who has made similar calls to reject limitations of imposed identities, referring to herself as "Black" and as an "Afro-Latina," or now as "Latinx," which challenges gender norms that accompany "colonialism" (Scharrón-del Río and Aja 2015), saying further that "being Puerto Rican is not a racial identity, but rather a cultural and national one. Being black is my racial identity" (Clemente 2001). There are references to pre-Colombian identities in the lyrics of the self-described "Afro-Antillian / Puerto Rican / Boricua sister" MC Lah Tere, in whose lyrics she clarifies further, "Yo soy Taino!" (2010). Or there are the calls of the #NotYourMascot to have Indigenous identities respected and the Mexica Movement whose adherents similarly refuse labels of "Hispanic, Latino, Raza, Mestizo, Illegals, Immigrants, Latin Americans, Indians . . ." as "racist . . . eurocentric" to be rejected as features of attempts at "artificial border divisions" (Mexica Movement 2015). These expressions of pan-Indigeneity and pan-Africanism demonstrate a lineage we seek to extend and highlight in Hip Hop. In fact, we are inspired by (and want to further inspire in others) precolonial, anticolonial thought that encourages recognition of the concept of "Latin@" as one in need of revolutionary transcendence.

Colonial identities such as "Black," "Latino," and "Indian" are themselves extensions of larger processes and mythologies. Attendant to the construction of these identities are the national myths to which they are attached. These identities become ideological moorings that fasten the consciousness to the mythology of linear advance from precolonial, pre-civilization to post-colonial, civilized, post-racial. These state/national myths have simultaneous parallels in Hip Hop. According to its myth of origin, Hip Hop emerged and assisted the post–Civil Rights generations to newer heights and levels of inclusion with accompanying financial and political success. From the plantation and the palenque to the Bronx and the White House, Hip Hop helped make the necessary cultural shifts required for societal change (Nielsen and Gosa 2015). Perhaps Hip Hop did usher in change, revision, but an improvement that is only relative to the horrific standards established in the process of enslavement, colonization, displacement, and other forms of violence. The realities of food and job shortages, mass incarceration, police violence, immigration rights struggles, and calls for increased Afro-Latino rights, freedoms, and independence throughout Latin America all demonstrate the fallacy of the Obama-era "Yes We Can," itself an ironic heist of Caesar Chavez's "Si Se Puede" (Ball and Johnson 2013).

Thus, we want to explore the possibility of "disturbing" liberal political interpretations of Hip Hop that see it as a way of achieving a non-racist society and to challenge also dominant conceptions of race and identity exemplified by the term "Latin@." By examining Indigenous-focused Hip Hop practiced by people of Latin American descent (here we use the European geographic term that for some Indigenous people is known as Abya Yala) in the United States, we argue for an emancipatory Indigenous politics of Hip Hop and for the exploration of new autonomous understandings of ourselves based on our ancestors' place-based cultures and which reject European-derived definitions of us; essentially, we argue for a re-Indigenization of Hip Hop and illustrate what some in "the Hip Hop nation" are already doing.

Re-Indigenization/Re-Africanization

As said above, our intent is to collapse the meanings of re-Indigenization and re-Africanization so as to accept their common anticolonial and Pan-Africanist traits. In short, we mean by these terms attempts at having Hip Hop serve as a method of reconstituting self-images outside of those established by imperialism, colonization, enslavement, and genocide (Ani 1994, Ball 2011b). And while we also recognize the parallel with historical efforts at or references to cultural nationalism, we prefer this notion of re-Indigenization for its particular encouragement of a revolutionary nationalist or supranationalist framework that differs importantly from other nationalisms.

We recognize the arguments and shortcomings of a nationalist approach including the possibility that, as Huey Newton once challenged concepts of nation and decolonization, there are at this point no precolonial nations to decolonize (Rodriguez 2006). But, we insist, following, for example, native scholars such as Alfred (2009) and Deloria and Lytle (1984), that Indigenous nationhood should not be seen and critiqued based on European notions of the state, sovereignty, and nation. Nor should indigeneity be defined by "race" or "ethnicity." In most previous attempts to redefine people of color and the colonized, cultural nationalist discourse has failed to decenter Europe and European tradition. Decolonization using European frameworks of sovereignty is inadequate because such efforts begin from a conception of governance that is incompatible with Indigenous understandings and practices of power. European colonial power is power over; individual power to make others do as you wish. Power for Indigenous people "is the force needed by all to achieve peace and harmony" (Alfred 2009, 73). Indigenous power results from careful and respectful attention to and interaction with "all our relations" including our other-than-human relations. Indigenous nationhood contrasts sharply with the European nation-state, since within traditional Indigenous social organization "there is no absolute authority, no coercive enforcement of decisions, no hierarchy, and no separate ruling entity" (Alfred 2009, 80).

Other nationalisms and critiques of them are based on European settler understandings and practices of power and nation. Indigeneity can assist us in redefining nationalism using traditional Indigenous knowledges. Moreover, our goal here is a modest one. We simply mean to recognize where Hip Hop performs the necessary but insufficient decolonizing task of mercilessly critiquing colonially imposed frames of reference and interpretation. Whereas the colonial process very much includes incorporation of dissent, we want to draw attention to the points at which that mission is incomplete. Significantly, the colonial endeavor has not been able to account for the resiliency of Indigenous identity as illustrated by many in Hip Hop who continuously redefine themselves individually and collectively.

Identity is political. Identity as self/collective-concept determines behavior and is essential for the establishment and maintenance of any level of grouping. From family to nation to state, there can be no proper function without establishing identity and self or collective concept. If not checked, identities can threaten established order rather than play their preferable societal role of managing behavior. From the start, states are "locating" us in order to prepare each for her/his role, to assure that we "replicate the social order and its hierarchizations, usually without the necessary imposition of directly brutal state force" (Sandoval 2000, 164). States are themselves social constructs developed specifically around maintaining identities for the purpose of easing governance, exchange, control (Ball 2011a). Identities are assigned to explain function and place. These are the lingering remnants of never solved conditions of empire that still require and generate various responses. To counter the theft and reorganization of land, people, and space, the "spatial entitlement" (Johnson 2013) or "colonial spatializing" (Navarro 2014) that accompanies imperial expansion, re-Indigenized Indigenous, Latin@, and African American communities still must engage in physical and psychic struggles over land and (temporal) space which allows for diverse yet collective (cultural) resistance to White supremacy and capital (Zibechi 2012). In fact, Jenell Navarro (2014, 106) in her work on Native Hip Hop speaks perfectly to the very radical and material nature of re-Indigenizing identity. She argues that Indigenous identity must be understood "spatially" as opposed to merely "temporally" because it always represents a "radical ethical" relationship to land.

Re-Indigenization and Re-Africanization begin as attempts from among the colonized to remember and reappropriate precolonial self-concepts and self-definitions and as processes are seen as necessary precursors to protracted political struggle (Alfred 2005; Muntaqim 2010). We group them because within the Latin American identity are both Indigenous and African people, culture and histories. Beyond that, Hip Hop is itself of Pan-African origin, emerging amid the African / Latin American diasporas as they responded to an imperial-imposed coalescence in New York City (Ball 2011b). For African-descended people to re-Africanize is for them to re-Indigenize. Each is at minimum a positive reference to memories of lost or stolen histories for the purpose of advancing future collective identities that circumvent those used to maintain inequality. It is an attempt to create a new consciousness among a particular population which encourages various forms of future behavior. Importantly, we recognize also that symbolic forms of decolonization such as renaming and claims to an identity such as Indigenous without a focus on what this means materially can be a reactionary force that becomes one more "white mask" that a privileged few can use to curry favor with colonial elites. Thus, it is necessary, as we do, to define indigeneity through both a place-based epistemology, ontology, and ethic AND decolonial, pro-life activity (Alfred 2009).

Re-Indigenization and the Politics of Gender and Nationalism

Numerous important critiques of "nationalist" politics have been leveled from various political perspectives: many Marxists, anarchists, and postcolonial theorists point out the numerous restrictions upon human freedom and well-being under nationalist regimes or see nationalism as a step or part of a process of advancing toward some other, more laudable goal (Communism or some form of a classless society). Marxists and anarchists see nationalism as creating division and creating a false consciousness among colonized populations. Following Fanon (1963), postcolonial theorists see the limitations, Fanon's "pitfalls," inherent in nationalist struggles that rarely interrogate all forms of oppression, especially, as Fanon points out, economic inequality.

Importantly, nationalist movements often lack deep analyses of and action on issues of women and gender. Anne McClintock's classic postcolonial study of race, gender, and sexuality, *Imperial Leather* (1995), illustrates how racist settler-colonial nationalism uses heteropatriarchal images, ideas, and symbols to further colonial desires and reinvent themselves. In the case of South Africa, Afrikaners created the legend of the Great Trek to justify their position in South African society. Female racial purity and chastity represented the purity and righteousness of the settler cause. Importantly, for our discussion of the re-Indigenization/re-Africanization of Hip Hop, the response of native South Africans to Afrikaner nationalism and White supremacy was to create a patriarchal mythology and organizational structures of their own. To combat settler-colonialism organizations such as the male, well-educated petit bourgeois, the African National Congress (ANC) used gendered nationalism. ANC documents and its organizational structure reveal that they resisted women's interventions, limited their roles within the nationalist struggle, and did not take "women's issues" seriously. South African women pushed back on this patriarchal response by founding their own organizations and presenting South African women as capable, intelligent, warriors for South African nationalism. They reimagined motherhood as revolutionary motherhood and insisted on a voice in the creation of a new South Africa.

Current Indigenous struggles illustrate a similar dynamic as "official" Indigenous organizations and male leaders have, in their efforts to gain concessions and incremental sovereignty from the state, acquiesced to settler-colonial views of women and gender. For example, since the 1960s in Canada, Indigenous political activity has been a game of winning legal battles in Canadian courts to the exclusion of traditional ways of governing and organizing Indigenous economies. Traditional economies and governance delineate gender roles that are equally respected and egalitarian. Often, indigenous communities are matrilineal, with women determining how familial and community resources are distributed and consumed. This elite Indigenous strategy has seen men rise to the fore of Indigenous political engagement with the state. As happened in South Africa and in Hip Hop, native women forced open the masculinist politics of Indigenous nationalism and infused Indigenous struggles with a revolutionary nationalist politics sensitive to gender and sexuality (Coulthard 2014).

Our insistence on a re-Indigenization/re-Africanization of Hip Hop remains wary of nationalist cultural expression that paints nationalism in narrow masculine strokes and does not pay attention to the subtleties (and not-so-subtleties) and complexities of domination in all its forms. Often, male MCs who have been socialized and masculinized in White supremacist settler culture see gender in the colonizer's terms (McFarland 2013). However, women MCs continually challenge masculinist interpretations of nationalism and indigeneity and forge an understanding of women as leaders, warriors, and mothers. They read Indigenous history as one of egalitarian gender relations and emphasize the matriarchal nature of much Indigenous tradition. A re-Indigenization/re-Africanization process in and through Hip Hop would be critical of patriarchal colonial practices, culture, and structures creeping into an almost entirely male mode of expression and organization. This would include interrogation of "tradition" that might enforce unequal gender relations and a recognition of "the fluidity of our traditions, not the rigidity of colonialism" (Leanne Simpson in Coulthard 2014, 156), so that those current practices that allow for domination and/or inequality will be excised from our practices, including especially our cultural expression.

"An American Success Story": Hip Hop Paves the Way for a Postracial "America"

Attendant on imposed identities (gender, racial, national, etc.) and spatial relations are the accompanying dominant narratives/explanations (justifications) that also demand further intervention. We also mean to join existing voices seeking to intervene in the prevailing and imposed narrative, the antithesis to our own, that Hip Hop largely represents the overall success or overcoming of oppression by formerly aggrieved communities (Thomas 2010). While ours is the perspective of those seeking out Hip Hop as a vehicle to decolonize, to re-Indigenize, to re-Africanize, there is obviously the prevailing and fully mobilized (weaponized) perspective that Hip Hop has been progressively assisting the integration into and transformation of an advancing society. As evidenced in exchanges with and critiques of leading "Hip Hop scholars" Tricia Rose (Thomas 2010), Bakari Kitwana (Ball 2012), and Jeff Chang (Ball 2013), there are important and still unresolved interpretations of Hip Hop's role in identity formation and societal transformation.

Today, for example, the dominant narrative tells of Hip Hop's generally positive role in advancing the United States to improved levels of inclusiveness and equality. Whether intentional or unconscious, this narrative stands in opposition to those which do not consider shifts in empire to be advances and who still look to engage Hip Hop (and other methods of interpretation and expression) to more radically critique the absence of change or to promote a variety of more radical interpretations of self, community, and society. These include interpretations based in Indigenous worldviews and practices as opposed to understandings of Hip Hop using a liberal European diversity perspective. While there has been and remains a long tradition of intellectual work that in various ways discusses where Hip Hop has encouraged varying forms of decolonization (Ball 2011, McFarland 2013), there remains an equally tireless attempt to fight for an assimilationist inclusion into the "national store."

For example, there is the most recent and heavily supported mainstream literary and documentary film promotion of Dan Charnas's *The Big Payback* (2011), in which the author claims Hip Hop to be "an American success story." Extending the already powerful national mythology, Charnas claims the commercial mainstreaming of Hip Hop to have a positive impact on further integrating the country while advancing the capitalist dreams of a few of its participants. His is the Hip Hop microcosm of a national narrative of Black/Brown linear and increasing success from plantations, outer colonies, and slums to multiracial business success, Brown Supreme Court judges, and Black presidents. Charnas offers literary support to the claim (out of disappointment with diminished returns) of Sean "Puffy" Combs's recent comments that "We got Obama into office for the give back. Where are the things in our community that have gotten drastically better?" (Kyles 2015). Or there is Steve Stoute's *Tanning of America* (2014), which similarly argues that Hip Hop prepared the country for new colorful leadership. An even more recent update of that argument is Jeff Chang's (2014) latest, *Who We Be*, which also attempts to place Hip Hop in a context of art that has positively advanced the country.

Each of these represents the dominant perspective that puts severe limitations on arguments coming from the very same communities that produce all the various elements of Hip Hop in ways that critique these national mythologies.

In other words, our intent is to critique ideas that shifts in the application of power are themselves revolutionary rather than merely aesthetic. In fact, beyond even the more easily identifiable unchanging material inequalities are the ways in which Hip Hop can often continue to reify the immaterial yet equally unequal facets of life such as identity or ideology. To the extent that Hip Hop has been unable to fully stem the tides of reactionary identification with imposed colonial borders, states (American, Mexican, Panamanian, Nigerian), or identities (Nigger, Black, Latino), it has not been transcendent. There remain too many material/immaterial markers that signify an absence of change, ranging from increased inequality and violent repression of people of color in the imperial "homeland" (the United States) to Afro-Latino forced removal and attempts among the Indigenous to preserve and adapt traditional cultures even as hundreds of languages (for example) around the world face extinction annually (Bolivian/Tupac).

Against "Latino," for Nican Tlaca and the Afro-Indigenous[1]

"Latino" is the latest iteration of the centuries-long attempt to erase Indigenous people, histories, and worldviews. Since the European invasion of the Americas, beginning with Columbus's failed attempt to find a sea route to Asia, Indigenous people of Abya Yala have been assaulted by European violence and cultural erasure. Honest students of history recognize that colonialism requires both physical terror and violence through military slaughter and/or the threat thereof, and ideological dominance (Leanne Simpson in Coulthard 2014). This "poly-dimensional" method includes the imposition of "Latin@" identity as European/Eurocentric ideological dominance over Nican Tlaca (Indigenous people of Abya Yala, Anahuac, Turtle Island, the Americas) and people of the African diaspora in Abya Yala.

The practice of colonizers naming their subjects is as old as the colonial impulse. Today's person of Mexican descent in the United States is often called "Latino." During the twentieth century, the dominant notion of such persons saw them as mestizos (or as mixed Indigenous-Spanish) and attempted to

---

1. This line is adapted from the Zapatista rallying cry, "Against Neoliberalism, For Humanity."

eradicate indigeneity except as a source of nostalgia. This group of people has also been called "Hispanic." Like "Latino," the nomenclature emphasizes European heritage and makes indigeneity invisible. Importantly, the African in the cultural mix has rarely been included (Hernández Cuevas 2004).

Arguing for Latino as a positive unifying identity, some point out that it solidifies a voting bloc and thus increases political power for these marginalized groups. Others suggest that Latinos/as constitute a potentially economically powerful consumer group. Certainly, marketers, advertisers, and public relations specialists see how a new unified Latina/o identity can benefit the bottom lines of corporations that cater to this manufactured "demographic." Importantly, Ball (2008) calls for a more thorough investigation and critique of the "myth of buying power"; popularized notions that poverty results from the irresponsible spending habits of the poor. The creation of "hurban" (Hispanic urban) radio reflects how in a capitalist society colonized and formerly enslaved people become a market segment (McFarland 2013). Consumer power is not the same as the power of self-determination or autonomy. Moreover, the power to consume more and become part of the capitalist system is precisely the goal of assimilative efforts on the part of colonial states. "Hip Hop" as rendered in the global communications media continues this integration and assimilation of Indigenous Americans and Africans in the diaspora.

In addition, "Latino" originates not with the various peoples of Abya Yala but with the colonial masters. The self-determinative nature of adopting precolonial or anticolonial names is a tendency that struggles against its opposing force of the colonial. Tupac Shakur, for example, took his name as a precolonial honorific to Tupac Amaru and to the idea of anti-imperial struggle. This stands in opposition to the tradition expressed by 50 Cent as a tribute to the gangster himself or by Rick Ross as tribute to an equally popular former drug dealer. Indigenous and African rebels throughout history have renamed themselves as a resistant act and as means of re-Indigenizing themselves. The Indigenous, people of the African diaspora in Abya Yala, and other politicized members of Hip Hop take names that signal their indigeneity and/or Africanness. Xicano (an Indigenous spelling of the more common "Chicano") Indigenous MCs include Tolteka, Olmeca, and Kiawitl. Eyedeal Bayano exemplifies a resistant Afro-Latino renaming.

Bayano and the Maroon Narrative

In our interview with Eyedeal Bayano (Ball 2014), much of what concerns us here is evident. Eyedeal, a Panamanian-descended MC in Maryland, makes conscious attempts to re-Indigenize through his adopted name and by acknowledging the limitations of an imposed Western culture in addressing still-extant concerns facing the world's majority people reclassified as "minorities" in White societies. Pointing to many of the obvious material indicators of institutional inequality (poverty, mass incarceration, police violence, etc.), Eyedeal turns inward to the cultural histories of his ancestral home. Like tracing his own personal decolonizing process, Eyedeal first returns to Panama and then, as if recognizing the colonial nature of his parents' country, moves further beyond, to a precolonial (at least pre-"Panamanian") radicalism. Bayano, the sixteenth-century enslaved African whose name was similarly imposed by the Spanish from whom he fled and against whom he fought, represents for Eyedeal a still necessary concept of maroonage or, as he said in explaining his choice of "Bayano," of "using my music to create new paths and going back and bringing others with me." "Bayano was a king," he continued, "so I am saying I am the 'ideal' King" to lead others "fighting this fight." And all who do "fight this fight are Bayanos."

As has been described, Hip Hop can be a site for a "transnational network and alliance of Indigenous mobilization" which can and does carry decolonial concepts back and forth, crossing borders of the "nation-state" and "Indigenous nationality" (Hornberger and Swineheart 2012, 503). They also cross the intangible boundaries of time. The late Tupac Shakur was consciously given a name representative of traditions of re-Indigenizing or anticolonial struggle exemplified by Tupac Amaru and Tupac Katari and still now carries those concepts back to their place of origin through his music, image, and symbol. Eyedeal Bayano, for his part, is seeking to carry similar concepts out of his ancestral homeland into the seat of empire and back again. Further, Eyedeal enacts an anticolonial critique of popular conceptions of "Latino," and "Black" performing what has for centuries been attempts of the enslaved and colonized to redefine the terms of their experience, identity, and prescriptive solutions. As he says,

> Latinos and Africans have more similarities than anyone can imagine, same people, transplanted in different parts of the world, with similar music, customs and struggle regardless of final destination. From Latin America, Colon (a province in) Panama, looking like Accra, Ghana, African customs and struggles persist, separated artificially primarily by name alone.

This Pan-African expression by Eyedeal reflects traditions of "mutually meaningful Black-Brown anti-racism struggles and radical creative affiliations" (Johnson 2013) and is indicative or representative of efforts toward re-Indigenization, part of a long tradition of transcending back to identities, groupings, or civilizations that predate the Western imperial period. It is an expression not institutionally supported. There is no commercial process or industry behind the production of this knowledge. This "cultural memory" of sorts is not necessarily "taught" but is passed on through varying subnarratives including oral traditions such as Hip Hop. Tupac Amaru spoke to Tupac Shakur, who now speaks back to the descendants here and there of both communities, expressing similar ideas even across linguistic and geographic barriers/boundaries (Hornberger and Swineheart 2012).

We think this is what Eyedeal means in his nebulous reference to the continuing African/Black/Latino "fight we're still fighting." That struggle is itself ambiguous, time and place shifting, renaming and constant. And yet it is known, felt, engaged and reacted to, even if "only" in a name.

Postindustrial Maiz Narratives: Creation and Resistance

Okichike ka centeotzintli (made from sacred maiz) is a dicho (saying) that sums up the attitudes toward nature, especially corn, held by the Indigenous corn-based civilization that spans much of Abya Yala, or the Western Hemisphere. It marks maiz as the origins of Nican Tlaca. Various Indigenous peoples throughout Abya Yala have creation stories that point to the centrality of teosinte (maiz or corn). People of the Mesoamerican Diaspora / Mexican Americans / Xican@s can trace maiz narratives from ancient stories like "Quetzalcoatl and the Ants" to codices to murals of the Great Mexican mural movement to art, music, and dance in the Chicano Movement to the Zapatista revolution to today's revolt against genetically modified corn in Mexico (Rodriguez 2014).

Maiz narratives have served as stories of origin and resistance stemming from an ecological land-based ethic exemplified by the principles of in lak ech and Panche Be. Rodriguez (2014) explains that in his courses in lak ech (you are my other me) he "teaches students to see themselves in each other. Thus, it would be difficult to truly hate others because to do so would be to hate oneself" (76). In lak ech results from Nican Tlaca's thousands of years of studying what we call nature. Nican Tlacan philosophy and science are informed by naturally occurring biotic communities. Peña (2005) points out how the value of in lak ech extends to our nonhuman relatives. Our Indigenous ancestors observed that the various species in these biotic communities depended on one another for survival. They recognized our interdependence. Harm to one resulted in harm to all in the community. Mayan social organization, political structures, and agricultural-based subsistence economies develop from the fact of interspecies interdependence. Similarly, Panche Be (to seek the root of the truth) contributes to a Nican Tlacan ethical path and scientific methodology. The methodology of knowledge seeking in Mesoamerica results from the deep study of nature (the root of the truth) in "pursuit of peace, dignity, and justice" (Rodriguez, 176).

The perspective and lyrics of Xicano MCs and groups such as Kinto Sol, Los Nativos, Rainflowa (pka Kiawitl, pka Lady Binx), Tolteka, Aztlan Underground, Olmeca, and El Vuh are part of the Nican Tlaca maiz narrative tradition. Xicano rap is the latest iteration of the ancient tradition of in xochitl, in cuicatl (flor y canto, poetry). Like the centuries of maiz narratives examined by Rodriguez (2014, 9), Xicano Hip Hop "decenter(s) colonization by restoring the centrality of maiz and of Indigenous history, language, culture, and cosmovision to this continent, including voice" (9). Through Xicano Hip Hop narratives, colonized urban youth radically redefine themselves as people of Nican Tlacan descent. Against a European colonial narrative of "war and conquest," Xicano Hip Hop storytellers define ourselves "by our living maiz culture, which includes stories, memory, and daily sustenance" (Rodriguez 2014, 178).

The Xicana MC Cihuatl Ce exemplifies Hip Hop's postindustrial maiz narrative. Her song "Infinite" describes Nican Tlaca as a people of nature. Like centuries of maiz narratives, Cihuatl Ce states that we come from Mother Earth. In a typical line from the song, she states that Nican Tlaca come from "the smoke made signals / fire clouds of embers from out of our Earth Mother's breath / I float from the brown curves of her breasts." Throughout her songs she defends and redefines Xican@s as place-based people stripped of Indigenous knowledge and identity.

Reclaiming ourselves as Nican Tlaca is that part of the decolonial impulse focused on more than 500 years of ideological attack on things Indigenous, including and especially corn (Pilcher 1998). European colonial narratives defined Nican Tlaca as savage, ignorant, and devilish. Indigenous dignity suffered many blows from colonial ideological domination. This explains the Mayan Zapatista focus on building "dignity" as a revolutionary strategy. In addition, many other Xicano Hip Hop narratives respond to the physically violent side of the colonial dynamic. Cihuatl Ce describes women, especially mothers, as warriors in her songs "We Run This" and "Da People Speak." The Xicana MC and danzante Rainflowa takes a similar stand with her lyrics. In her verse on the El Vuh song "Triumph," Lady Binx (Rainflowa's previous name) calls for revolutionary violence rapping in which "revolution comes in stones and forms of violence/on these oppressors."

Xicano Hip Hop reveals Indigenous identity and resistance to colonialism not only in song lyrics but also in rhythms, style, instrumentation, and dance (b-boying and danza Azteca). In a phone interview Zero explained that Indigenous drumming formed the foundation of the music he produces for the Xicano Hip Hop group El Vuh (The Book). Zero's choice of name illustrates the continuity of the maiz-based Nican Tlaca civilization. Rodriguez (2014) explains that maiz seed "allowed them to discover the concept of zero" (4). Further, Nican Tlaca did not conceive of "zero" as absence. Zero was the seed that germinates into "a radically new culture on this continent . . . It is why the Maya mark the beginning of their calendar with a zero that is represented by a seed." Mesoamerican origin stories show that maiz was the "civilizational impulse" and that we are "okichike ka centeotzintli" (made from sacred maiz). The ancient ideas that we are sons and daughters of Mother Earth, Tonantzin, continue to be expressed in Hip Hop through sentiments like Kinto Sol's "somos hijos de maiz" (we are sons of corn). Along with Indigenous drumming and the use of Indigenous naming to reconnect us to our indigeneity (re-Indigenize ourselves), Xicano Hip Hop uses ancient and new instruments to create un sonido índigena (an Indigenous sound).[2]

Emancipatory Indigenous Hip Hop Politics

The planet is facing climate chaos, hunger, violence, repression, miseducation, and public health crises. In addition, people of color, the Indigenous, and the colonized suffer racism, cultural attack, disrespect, and dishonor. How can Hip Hop help solve these problems? Can it be the cultural wing of a revolutionary movement? Can Hip Hop lead youth to a revolutionary Indigenous/African consciousness and to traditional ecological knowledge (TEK) and African heritage knowledge (AHK) with a contemporary urban twist?

Indigenous politics are necessary for the survival of the planet, as argues Daniel Wildcat. These politics reject forms of governance and social organization based in European cultural values (Alfred 2009, 26). Instead of the enforced colonial system of governance in the form of tribal councils and chairmen, for example, Indigenous social organization begins with the values of "harmony, autonomy and respect." Alfred (2009, 29) explains that "pre-contact indigenous societies developed regimes of conscience and justice that

---

2. See the chapter "Sonido Índigena" in McFarland (2013) for a detailed description of Indigenous sounds, imagery, style, and narrative in Xicano Hip Hop, especially the group Los Nativos.

promoted the harmonious co-existence of humans and nature for centuries." This would include the coexistence of different human groups and respect for difference exemplified in the Lakota saying "mitakuye oyasin" (all my relations).

From this philosophical foundation come a number of principles of Indigenous politics. Alfred (2009) describes six principles of Indigenous governance: lack of coercive authority and collective decision-making; active participation of all; balance of many layers of power; decentralization; situational and place-based; respect for diversity (51). These principles lead to a "profoundly egalitarian" society with little distance between "leaders" and others. In fact, in one version of a new autonomous Indigenous political organization, the Zapatistas use a Mayan tradition of "mandar obediciendo" (lead by obeying) to describe leadership. Leaders obey their communities and fulfill their wishes.

Additionally, Indigenous politics is organized around land and space. This is what it means to be place-based. Indigenous knowledge, including TEK and AHK, is rooted in relationships and in a recognition of interdependence between humans and their immediate ecology. European colonialism forcefully took the Indigenous lands of Abya Yala from Nican Tlaca. Indigenous social organization, culture, spirituality, and identity stem from our interdependence with the land that we no longer control. In addition, Nican Tlaca suffered forced assimilation through Catholicism and other religions and "Americanization"-type programs. These things can, of course, be said of Indigenous African society and the African diaspora in Abya Yala. The result is an ongoing but not fully successful genocide. Indigenous people find it hard to remain Indigenous under these conditions. This de-Indigenization results for many of us, including many in Hip Hop, in a cultural politics of re-Indigenization.

Since land and space are key to Indigenous identity, an urban Indigenous politics requires a decolonial reterritorialization of urban spaces.[3] This approach to emancipatory political action is ongoing in social movements in Latin America. The principles of the reterritorialization strategy of many rural and increasingly urban marginalized communities mirror those described by Alfred as characteristic of Indigenous politics discussed above. Zibechi (2012) summarizes these principles as "territorial rootedness" (essentially, place-centered), autonomy, cultural revalorization, development of organic intellectuals, revalorization and recognition of women's roles, attention to

---

3. For a detailed discussion of reterritorialization in Hip Hop, see Murray Forman's work (2004). Forman uses the concept of "alternative geographies" to discuss what we are describing as "reterritorialization."

human–nature relations, especially as concerns work and production, and self-affirming forms of action (14–18).

A re-Indigenized, emancipatory Hip Hop politics necessarily redefines and reterritorializes urban space. Some of this is seen in the use of city walls as common, collective property for art in the form of "graffiti" as well as practices such as cruisin' and stuntin' on streets and sidewalks. While these symbols of the reterritorialization and redefinition of our urban spaces and subjectivities are necessary aspects of a revolutionary indigeneity that will solve our planet's most pressing problems, they are not sufficient for bringing about the required societal reorganization.

A revolutionary Indigenous Hip Hop is more than style and symbol; more than claims to a radical subjectivity. Revolutionary Indigenous Hip Hop can be traced to its African roots. Etymologically, "hip" has origins in the West African Wolof language. Xippi was an important concept in Wolof epistemology. Roughly translated as "to see with one's eyes open," it emphasizes that to know requires being open to and aware of one's environment and one's place in it (Walker 2001). KRS-One adds to our spatial understanding of Hip Hop and its relation to an African indigeneity, defining Hip Hop in his song "Hip Hop Lives" (2007):

> Hip means to know. It's a form of intelligence.
> To be hip is to be update and relevant.
> Hop is a form of movement.
> You can't just observe a hop you got to hop up and do it.
> Hip and hop is more than music.
> Hip is the knowledge. Hop is the movement.
> Hip and hop is intelligent movement or relevant movement.

Emancipatory Indigenous Hip Hop politics requires action or "intelligent bread labor." Gandhi emphasized this strategy of decolonial emancipation as productive labor done consciously with the aim of empowerment and self-determination for colonized Indians. Hip Hop as a continuation of Indigenous African culture in diaspora is by definition conscious labor focused on the betterment of people of the African diaspora. The colonization of Hip Hop and the hijacking of the genre by the entertainment industry attempts to hide this revolutionary fact of Hip Hop by promoting music that they call Hip Hop filled with the genocidal imagery of murders and physical harm done to Black men, drug use, including and especially alcohol, and other community health problems. Fraternal violence (autogenocide, but not really caused by us) becomes normalized along with consumerism as Black male culture. Moreover, the enormous talent and intelligence in Black communities is diverted by the colonial process played out via the music industry from a potentially culturally revolutionary art to that of being a largely imperial functionary. Thus, like in all colonial situations, the resources of the colonized confront them as weapons of their destruction; resources, wealth, and cultural expression produced by the colony becomes, as Fanon (1964) also said, the "inertia" which "testifies against" the colonized.

This proposal for an Indigenous emancipatory Hip Hop politics follows the "indigenous pathways of action and freedom" examined by Alfred (2005). The development of warriors who protect Indigenous lifeways is among the principles that Alfred (2005) proposes for Nican Tlaca (or Onkwehonwe in Alfred's Kanienkeha or Mohawk language) decolonial political action (45). Warrior action requires a re-Indigenizing process recognizing that the loss of knowledge and assimilation have weakened native peoples. Onkwehonwe warriors model indigeneity through "liv[ing] life as an act of indigeneity, mov[ing] across life's landscapes in an indigenous way." Being Nican Tlaca or Onkwehonwe requires acting Indigenous. Non-Indigenous (settler) definitions of indigeneity are based on biological or racial markers, that is, blood quantum levels, that reduce indigeneity to the amount of "Indian blood" one has. Nican Tlaca / Onkwehonwe define indigeneity as living by Indigenous principles in an Indigenous manner as summarized earlier in this essay. Indigeneity "must go beyond reflective practices to an actual political and social engagement with the world based on consensus arrived at through broad conversation among people who are part of that culture" (Alfred 2005, 140). Thus, emancipatory Indigenous Hip Hop politics as proposed here and informed by Indigenous resurgence such as that of the Indigenous Nationhood Movement, Idle No More, and the Zapatistas is an inclusive politics that invites into our nation any who follow an Indigenous pathway exemplified by reciprocity, coexistence with "all our relations" (human and other-than-human beings), a striving for balance/harmony, and deep connection to land and Indigenous land-based traditions.

Bibliography

Alexander, Leslie. 2012. *African or American? Black Identity and Political Activism in New York City, 1784–1861.* Champaign: University of Illinois Press.

Alfred, Taiaiake. *Peace, Power, Righteousness: An Indigenous Manifesto.* 2009. Oxford: Oxford University Press.

———. *Wasase: Indigenous Pathways of Action and Freedom.* 2005. Toronto: University of Toronto Press.

Ani, Marimba. 1994. *Yurugu: An African-Centered Critique of European Cultural Thought and Behavior*. Trenton, NJ: Africa World Press.

Ball, Jared A. 2008. "The Myth of Black Buying Power." *imixwhatilike.org*, March 12. https://imixwhatilike.org/home/mythofblackbuyingpower/.

———. 2011a. "I Mix What I Like! In Defense and Appreciation of the Rap Music Mixtape as 'Dissident' and 'National' Communication." *International Journal of Communication* 5: 278–97.

———. 2011b. *I Mix What I like! A Mixtape Manifesto*. Baltimore: AK Press.

———. 2012. "What Is 'Hip-Hop Activism'? A Conversation with Bakari Kitwana." *imixwhatilike.org*, October 12. https://imixwhatilike.org/2012/10/12/what-is-hip-hop-activism-w-bakari-kitwana/.

———. 2013. "Hip-Hop's Worldviews: Conversations with Jeff Chang and Dr. Dawn Elissa-Fischer." *imixwhatilike.org*, July 1. http://imixwhatilike.org/2013/07/01/060713/.

———. 2014. "In Search of Bayano: An Eyedeal Interview." *imixwhatilike.org*, November 29. http://imixwhatilike.org/2014/11/29/eyedealbayano/.

Ball, Jared A., and Theresa G. Johnson. 2013. "Black and Brown Struggle and Spatial Entitlement." *imixwhatilike.org*, September 9. http://imixwhatilike.org/2013/09/09/gayetheresajohnson/.

Chang, Jeff. 2014. *Who We Be: The Colorization of America*. New York: St. Martin's.

Charnas, Dan. 2011. *The Big Payback: The History of the Business of Hip Hop*. New York: Penguin.

Churchill, Ward. 2004. *Kill the Indian and Save the Man: The Genocidal Impact of American Indian Residential Schools*. San Francisco: City Lights.

Clemente, Rosa. 2001. "Who Is Black?" http://rosaclemente.net/who-is-black/.

Coulthard, Glenn. 2014. *Red Skins, White Masks: Rejecting the Colonial Politics of Recognition*. University of Minnesota Press.

Deloria, Vine Jr., and Clifford M. Lytle. 1984. *The Nations Within: The Past and Future of American Indian Sovereignty*. Austin: University of Texas Press.

Fanon, Frantz. 1963. *The Wretched of the Earth*. New York: Grove.

———. 1964. *Toward the African Revolution*. New York: Grove.

Hernández Cuevas, Marco Polo. 2004. *African Mexicans and the Discourse on Modern Nation*. Lanham, MD: University Press of America.

Hornberger, Nancy, and Karl Swineheart. 2012. "Bilingual Intercultural Education and Andean Hip Hop: Transnational Sites for Indigenous Language and Identity." *Language in Society* 41: 499–525.

Johnson, Gaye T. 2013. "Black and Brown Struggle and Spatial Entitlement." *imixwhatilike.org*, September 9. https://imixwhatilike.org/2013/09/09/gayetheresajohnson/.

McClintock, Anne. 1995. *Imperial Leather: Race, Gender, and Sexuality in the Colonial Contest*. New York: Routledge.

McFarland, Pancho. 2013. *The Chican@ Hip Hop Nation: Politics of a New Millennial Mestizaje*. East Lansing: Michigan State University Press.

Kyles, Yohance. 2015. "Puff Daddy: We Got Barack Obama Elected, Why Hasn't Our Community Gotten Drastically Better?" *AllHipHop.com*, November 6. http://allhiphop.com/2015/11/06/puff-daddy-we-got-barack-obama-elected-why-hasnt-our-community-gotten-better-video/.

Mexica Movement. 2015. http://www.mexica-movement.org/.

Muntaqim, Jalil. 2010. *We Are Our Own Liberators: Selected Prison Writings*. Portland, OR: Arissa Media Group.

Navarro, Jenell. 2014. "Solarize-ing Native Hip-Hop: Native Feminist Land Ethics and Cultural Resistance." *Decolonization: Indigeneity, Education and Society* 3(1): 101–18.

Nielsen, Eric, and Travis Gosa. 2015. "Obama and Hip-Hop: A Break Up Song." *Washington Post,* September 25. https://www.washingtonpost.com/opinions/obama-and-hip hop-a-breakup -song/2015/09/25/47e3787c-6241-11e5-8e9e-dce8a2a2a679_story.html.

Peña, D. G. 2005. *Mexican Americans and the Environment: Tierra y Vida.* Tucson: University of Arizona Press.

Pilcher, J. M. 1998. *Que vivan los tamales! Food and the Making of Mexican Identity.* Albuquerque: University of New Mexico.

Rivera, Pedro. 2010. "Carlos Cooks: Dominican Garveyite in Harlem." In *The Afro-Latin@ Reader: History and Culture in the United States,* edited by Miriam Jiménez Román and Juan Flores. Durham, NC: Duke University Press. 215–19.

Rodriguez, Besenia. 2006. "Long Live Third World Unity! Long Live Internationalism: Huey P. Newton's Revolutionary Intercommunalism." *Souls: A Critical Journal of Black Politics, Culture, and Society* 8(3): 119–41.

Rodriguez, R. C. 2014. *Our Sacred Maiz Is Our Mother: Indigeneity and Belonging in the Americas.* Tucson: University of Arizona Press.

Sandoval, Chela. 2000. *Methodology of the Oppressed.* Minneapolis: University of Minnesota.

Spivey, Donald. 1978. *Schooling for the New Slavery: Black Industrial Education, 1868–1915.* Westport, CT: Greenwood.

Stoute, Steve. 2014. *The Tanning of America: One Nation Under Hip-Hop* [documentary], VH1. http://www.vh1.com/shows/the_tanning_of_america/.

Tere, Lah. 2010. "Crush." On Rebel Diaz, *Otra Guerrillera Mixtape Vol. 1.* https://rebeldiaz .bandcamp.com/album/otra-guerrillera-mixtape-vol-1.

Thomas, G. 2010. "Hip-Hop vs. The Bourgeois West . . . and 'Hip-Hop Studies'?" *imixwhatilike .org,* June 14. http://imixwhatilike.org/2010/06/14/thomasvrose/.

Walker, Sheila. 2001. "Everyday Africa in New Jersey: Wonderings and Wanderings in the African Diaspora." In *African Roots/American Cultures: Africa in the Creation of the Americas,* edited by Sheila Walker. Lanham, MD: Rowman and Littlefield. 45–80.

Wildcat, Daniel. 2009. *Red Alert: Saving the Planet with Indigenous Knowledge.* Golden, CO: Fulcrum.

Wynter, Sylvia. 2005. "1492: A New World View." In *Race, Discourse, and the Origin of the Americas: A New World View,* edited by Vera Lawrence Hyatt and Rex Nettleford. Washington, DC: Smithsonian Institute Press. 5–57.

Zibechi, Raúl. 2012. *Territories in Resistance: A Cartography of Latin American Social Movements.* Chico, CA: AK Press.

PART II

WHOSE BLACK MUSIC?

Afro-Latinidades and African Legacies in
Latin American and Latino Hip Hop

chapter 4

From Panama to the Bay

Los Rakas's Expressions of Afrolatinidad

Petra R. Rivera-Rideau

On April 15, 2014, Los Rakas dropped *El Negrito Dun Dun & Ricardo,* their first album backed by a major record label, Universal Music Latino. The album has two distinct parts: "El Negrito Dun Dun," by Raka Dun (Abdull Domínguez), which features more dancehall-inflected beats to document topics such as immigration, and "Ricardo," by Raka Rich (Ricardo Bethancourt), a combination of house and R&B-style tunes with a more romantic vibe. It followed several independently released singles and LPs, including the tremendously popular "Abrázame," featuring Bay Area artist Faviola, that was remixed by Brooklyn-based DJ Uproot Andy. Los Rakas began distributing their mixtapes in 2006, and obtained a substantial local following within the San Francisco Bay Area. Since receiving a "Discovery Artist" prize at the Latin Alternative Music Conference in 2010, Los Rakas have developed a more international profile, performing at major music festivals and with a wide range of popular artists including Ozomatli, Cypress Hill, Ana Tijoux, and others. Their first, independently released album, *Chancletas y Camisetas Bordadas,* reached number one on the iTunes Reggaeton / Hip Hop charts in 2011. Thus, prior to the release of *El Negrito Dun Dun & Ricardo,* Los Rakas had already received recognition for their fusions of Caribbean music, especially

Panamanian *reggae en español* (also called *plena*), and Hip Hop from the Bay Area in California. Their musical style reflects their experiences growing up in Panama and Oakland. Drawing from their experiences in both places as well as their love of diverse musical styles and genres, Los Rakas produced their unique, self-described "Panabay" (that is, Panama and Bay Area) sound.

Critics have lauded the duo's one-of-a-kind Panabay sound. But beyond its musical qualities, Panabay also reflects important, but often overlooked, aspects of Latino participation in Hip Hop. Generally, scholarship about Latino Hip Hop tends to focus on Puerto Rican contributions to the genre, as in Raquel Z. Rivera's seminal book *New York Ricans from the Hip Hop Zone*, or the Chicano rap of artists like Kid Frost (McFarland 2006, Wang 2010). Moreover, studies of Latino Hip Hop scenes typically emphasize New York City or Los Angeles as the primary spaces where Latinos have played a part in developing Hip Hop. However, Los Rakas have made critical contributions to Oakland's local Hip Hop scene, and Oakland itself figures prominently in Los Rakas's music and self-fashioning. In addition, Los Rakas "rep" their connections to Panama, an understudied location in stories about Latin Hip Hop and reggaetón.[1] Consequently, Los Rakas's promotion of Panabay music and identity fills a critical gap in common narratives about Latino participation in Hip Hop.

Of particular significance is Los Rakas's articulation of a unique afrolatinidad, or Afro-Latino identity. Scholarship about Latinos in California often overlooks the experiences of Afro-Latinos, despite the historical presence of Afro-Latinos there that stretches back to at least the 1700s (Forbes 2010). Contemporary accounts of Afro-Latino experiences in California relate that Blackness is often considered property of African Americans while Latinidad is linked primarily to Mexican or Chicano *mestizo* identities assumed to emerge from race mixture of Spanish and Indigenous populations (Hoy 2010, Jackson 2010). In this context, afrolatinidad is sometimes made virtually invisible, or, at other times, flattened into very limited and problematic tropes. In the rest of this chapter, I examine Los Rakas's unabashed embrace of afrolatinidad. Importantly, this afrolatinidad is translocal, expanding very localized symbols and aesthetics from both Panama and Oakland to create a broader critique of anti-Black racism across the Americas. Los Rakas's music makes an important intervention in not only larger histories of Latino participation in Hip Hop but also our understandings of Afro-Latino identities in the United States.

---

1. This is particularly curious given Panama's critical role in the development of contemporary Reggaeton that, despite debates about origins, is indebted to *reggae en español* by artists such as Renato and El General (see Marshall 2010, Nwankwo 2009, Twickel 2009a, 2009b).

Afrolatinidad in *"Mestizo"* Latin America and California

The category *Latino* encompasses a varied set of experiences and identities, including diverse groups of national origin, language use, religion, citizenship status, and, of course, race. Despite this racial diversity, many scholars have pointed out that the terms *Hispanic* and *Latino* denote a mixed-race pheno-type that often privileges a "whitened" look (Dávila 2008). Theorists such as Miriam Jiménez Román (2005) posit that the whitening of Latino identity in the United States carries over from the hegemonic discourse of *mestizaje* found throughout much of Latin America. Although individual countries pro-mote specific definitions of their respective national identities, many have also embraced race mixture as their foundations.[2] *Mestizaje* allows Latin American elites to align their national identities with the ideals of European modernity while also insisting upon a distinct identity for the region as a whole, in part by promoting the idea that race mixture would integrate the "best" qualities of individual racial groups to create a superior, "cosmic" race (Vasconselos 1997). Notwithstanding the celebratory rhetoric of race mixture and racial harmony, *mestizaje* generally upholds Whiteness. This is most evident in the assump-tions that race mixture would allegedly lead to the whitening of the popula-tion; that is, Indigeneity and Blackness were assumed to eventually phase out of the Latin American population. *Mestizaje* also idealizes European cultural practices and standards while contributions by Indigenous or African popu-lations are deemed inconsequential, or, even in those instances where these cultures are celebrated, considered to exist in a primitive, premodern era. *Mes-tizaje* thus attempts to present Latin America as a modern, whitened region while contradictorily purporting to embrace its non-White populations.[3]

Like other places in Latin America, Panama also presents a national iden-tity rooted in race mixture, called a *"crisol de razas"* (Priestley and Barrow 2009). Panama's race mixture incorporates (albeit problematically) Black communities descended from enslaved Africans in the country, referred to as *"afrocoloniales"* (Craft 2008, 128; Priestley and Barrow 2009, 51). How-ever, Panamanian understandings of Blackness are also constructed vis-à-vis

---

2. For critical analyses of this process, see Andrews 2004, Jiménez Román 2005, Rahier 2003, Wade 1997.

3. *Mestizaje* does not manifest itself the same way in all Latin American countries. For example, in Mexico, discourses of *mestizaje* have primarily incorporated Spanish and Indig-enous ancestry, excluding the presence of Afro-Mexicans (Jones 2013, Sue 2013). In contrast, countries with substantial populations of African descent, such as Puerto Rico, have incorpo-rated Blackness into their definitions of racially mixed national identities, albeit in problematic ways (Godreau 2015).

another significant Black population in the country: West Indian migrants and their descendants. West Indians arrived in Panama as laborers on banana plantations, the Panama railroad, and, especially, the Panama Canal (Craft 2008, Putnam 2010). In fact, once construction on the Panama Canal finished in 1914, West Indians composed almost half the population in the Canal Zone (Craft 2008, 130). Dominant depictions of these communities, referred to as "*afroantillanos*," presented them as "perpetual foreigners" who could not assimilate into the rest of Panama, and thus were subject to multiple laws restricting their citizenship status (Priestley and Barrow 2009, 51; Putnam 2010). While *afrocoloniales* and *afroantillanos* are often imagined as distinct (and, at times, have been pitted against each other), they also have come together to contest colonialism and racism in the country (Craft 2008). Furthermore, both groups are subject to a general devaluation of Blackness in Panama (Modestin 2010, 418).

Los Rakas openly discuss anti-Black racism in Panama. As Raka Dun describes,

> In Panama, I never learned anything about being Afro-Latino, you know, because the family doesn't teach you that and they don't talk about that . . . A lot of Black people in Latin America, they don't feel proud. They know they're Black, but they don't make the connection, like that's African . . . as soon as they find out they have a grandpa who was a Spaniard or something, they talk like "Oh! My *abuelo* was from Spain, man!" And you're like, "Ok, but you're Black as hell!"[4]

Here, not only does Raka Dun relate the general disparagement of Blackness in Panama, but he also links it to other sites in Latin America, thus demonstrating the ways that Panamanian understandings of race reflect common attitudes found throughout the region.

Los Rakas's embrace of afrolatinidad is also important in relation to dominant constructions of Latino identity in the United States, where, generally, Latinos are assumed to be racially mixed and to occupy an intermediary space between the Black and White poles of the U.S. racial binary. Moreover, acknowledgments that Latinos frequently select "some other race" on the U.S. Census are often "taken as proof that [Latinos] are at the crux of transforming the meaning of race itself" (Dávila 2008, 2). However, like *mestizaje* in Latin America more generally, this celebration of the racially mixed Latino

---

4. All quotes from Los Rakas are from a Skype interview with the author conducted on April 3, 2014. A partial transcript of this interview is in Rivera-Rideau, "Panabay Pride."

subject ultimately results in a whitened image of Latinidad (Jiménez Román 2005). It is important to point out that institutions as well as many Latino communities embrace this idea of the racially mixed Latino. For example, the term *Hispanic* surfaced among government agencies in the 1970s to refer to diverse groups of Latin American descent in the United States in order to facilitate the process of taking statistics related to racial and ethnic identities (Oboler 1995). Other industries, such as what Arlene Dávila (2001) calls the "Hispanic marketing" industry, have identified characteristics associated with Latinos in order to market products directly to a large Latino consumer base. Similarly, Spanish-language media such as the television station Univision began to define their audience as more "Latino" rather than Mexican-oriented in order to expand their reach (Mora 2014). As G. Cristina Mora (2014) argues, government agencies, media, private industries, and advocacy groups all adopted the term such that, by the 1980s, "Hispanic" essentially became a distinct category subject to unique processes of racialization. Accordingly, a particular phenotype that Arlene Dávila (2001) terms the "Mediterranean" look, including tan skin and dark hair, became recognized as the typical "Latin look" (111–12). These industries and institutions have played a critical role in defining Latinidad in the United States as racially mixed and distanced from Blackness.

In addition, some U.S. Latino communities also ascribe to a whitened, *mestizo* Latinidad. Many Afro-Latino authors relate experiences with discrimination they encounter from other Latinos, ranging from job discrimination to social isolation to the frequent disparaging of their hair, dark skin, or African features as "ugly" (Jiménez Román and Flores 2010). Such stories belie the fact that racial discrimination within many U.S. Latino communities contributes to the general perception that authentic Latinidad is marked by a whitened, *mestizo* look. As Miriam Jiménez Román (2005) describes, "The normative 'Latino' leaves no room for the unabashedly Black, Indian, Asian, or any of the other racialized peoples who comprise the Americas" (75). In fact, several scholars point out that this whitening of Latinidad has produced very limited representations of Afro-Latino identities or, at worst, made Afro-Latinos virtually invisible in the United States (Hernández 2003, Hoy 2010).

The visibility of Afro-Latino populations in the United States varies somewhat by geographic region. Some scholars point out that Afro-Latinos are often identified as African Americans in places such as the Southwest or New Orleans, Louisiana, where the majority of Latinos are presumed to be Indigenous or *mestizo* (in other words, non-Black) Mexicans or Central Americans.[5]

---

5. See Dowling and Newby (2010) and England (2009–10). I would like to reiterate that there are, in fact, Afro-descendant communities throughout Mexico and Central America.

Similar dynamics can be found in California, where a *mestizo* Chicano identity has dominated definitions of Latinidad (Hoy 2010, Jackson 2010). In her
interviews with Afro-Latino residents in Los Angeles, California, Anulkah
Thomas (2012) found that her respondents who had lived in East Coast cities
such as New York perceived a greater recognition of Afro-Latino identities
there than on the West Coast. Thomas attributes this to the larger presence
of Spanish Caribbean Latinos such as Puerto Ricans and Dominicans on the
East Coast who are assumed to have more African ancestry than "the predominantly Mexican and Central American mestizo and indigenous populations in the West, particularly in California" (211).[6] Vielka Cecilia Hoy (2010)
explains that, as a woman of Afro-Nicaraguan and Afro-Panamanian descent,
she "negotiat[ed] among invisibilities" while growing up in the San Francisco
Bay Area due to pervasive ignorance about Blackness in Central America,
and because in the Bay Area, "Latinidad is Mexicentric" (416). Consequently,
the presumed invisibility of Afro-Latinos in the United States may be more
acute in places like California that presumably harbor more rigid distinctions
between Blackness and Latinidad in the popular imagination.

Although raised partially in Panama, Los Rakas call Oakland, California,
their home. In contrast to many authors' accounts of the invisibility of afrolatinidad in California, Los Rakas credit their experiences in Oakland with
instilling pride in their Afro-Latino identities. Indeed, they claim that their
perceptions of their Afro-Latino identities would be different if they lived in
other cities such as New York or Miami that have large Afro-Latino populations. Raka Rich states that in Latin America "we've learned to praise the
conquistadors" rather than Blackness; however, he sees the same issue in cities
like Miami that have "statues" and monuments to white(ned) Latin Americans. Similarly, Raka Dun says that "a lot of Latinos, even in New York, still
don't feel proud of being African. It's the same mentality as Latin America."

On the other hand, Los Rakas consider Oakland to be a place that celebrates its rich history as a site of African American political organizing and
artistic production that, in turn, influences their understandings of afrolatinidad. As Raka Dun recounts, "We were blessed to come to Oakland . . .

The point here is that within the United States (and, often, in these regions of Latin America),
Blackness is understood to be fundamentally distinct from Mexican or Central American identities, notwithstanding the presence of Afro-Mexicans and Afro-Central Americans. For more
information about Blackness in Central America, see Gudmundson and Wolfe (2010); for more
on Afro-Mexico, see Jones (2013) and Sue (2013).

    6. Such assumptions follow Arlene Dávila's (2001) observations that Spanish Caribbean
people tend to represent dark-skinned Latinos in Latino-oriented television and advertising
(202). Similarly, Juan Flores (2009) contends that Spanish Caribbean Latinos' perceived ties to
Blackness often distinguish them from a broader panethnic Latino identity (64–66).

in Oakland, they teach you about the Black Panthers and about Malcolm X and all of that, you know. So being in Oakland, I was like, wow. OK. We were queens and kings in Africa and all of that." Importantly, this perspective does not impose U.S. ideas about Blackness onto afrolatinidad. Rather, Los Rakas incorporate the lessons about Black pride that they learned from the histories of African Americans in Oakland into their unique articulations of afrolatinidad. In this instance, the social, cultural, and historical celebrations of Blackness in Oakland were much more important for Los Rakas's understandings of afrolatinidad than the relatively small Afro-Latino population in the area.

Despite drawing diasporic connections with Oakland's African American community, Los Rakas's repertoire embraces and celebrates a distinct afrolatinidad. For example, their recent song "Africana" on *El Negrito Dun Dun & Ricardo* praises the beauty of Afro-Latinas and the importance of honoring one's African heritage. On the same album, "Sueño Americano" and "Chica de mi Corazón" describe the challenges of immigration, including living in the United States as an undocumented immigrant and the plight of children back in Panama whose parents immigrate to the United States without them. A 2013 song, "Hablemos del Amor," featuring Raka Stylo, addresses police brutality and inner-city violence, and pays tribute to Oscar Grant and Trayvon Martin, among others. Such songs both celebrate afrolatinidad and explicitly address racism, disenfranchisement, poverty, incarceration, and additional issues that affect Afro-Latinos and other racialized populations in the United States and in Latin America. In so doing, Los Rakas call attention to Afro-Latino communities rendered invisible by dominant representations of a *mestizo* California and Latin America. Beyond their lyrics, however, Los Rakas's unique Panabay sound and self-fashioning also foreground translocal afrolatinidad.

Raka Pride and the Panabay Sound

While some scholars emphasize the relative invisibility of U.S. Afro-Latinos, popular music remains one site where Afro-Latinos' contributions are readily acknowledged. Many scholars have described the contributions of Afro-Latinos to genres such as jazz, salsa, boogaloo, and Hip Hop (Flores 2000, 2009; García 2006; Rivera 2003; Moreno 2004). Interestingly, these discussions tend to focus on Cuban or Puerto Rican musicians, primarily in New York City. Cultural theorist Juan Flores (2009) argues that for Spanish Caribbean Latinos, living in the United States has constituted a "lesson in blackness," referring to the forms of racialization they encounter that emphasize Blackness and provide opportunities to forge connections with other African diasporic populations (47). These new understandings of Blackness become "cultural remittances" that return to the Spanish Caribbean, introducing new modes of being that often jar with hegemonic depictions of national identities in the region (Flores 2009). Flores (2009) identifies Hip Hop as one particularly important space where these processes manifest. Indeed, scholars have noted that participation in Hip Hop has enabled some Latinos, especially Spanish Caribbean groups from the East Coast, to claim membership in the larger African diaspora, thus dismissing the separations between Blackness and Latinidad that dominate the U.S. racial paradigm (Flores 2000, Rivera 2003). On the other hand, scholars studying Hip Hop and other forms of musical collaboration between African Americans and Latinos (namely, Chicanos) in California argue that music has served as a space for them to come together in resistance to systemic racism, contradicting common portrayals of these groups as always at odds with each other (Johnson 2013, McFarland 2006, Wang 2010). The analyses of both California and East Coast Hip Hop stress that Hip Hop can be a space where Latinidad and Blackness intersect, from fostering collaborations between Latinos and African Americans to expressing distinct Afro-Latino identities.

Similar to the Spanish Caribbean communities that Juan Flores studies, the experience of moving between Panama and the United States marks Los Rakas's expressions of afrolatinidad, evident in their Panabay sound and aesthetic. "Panabay is Panama and the Bay Area mixed together. Two countries blended together, a hybrid of what the United States is now," explained Raka Rich when I asked him to describe the Panabay sound. Listening to Los Rakas, one can hear the fusion of dancehall-inflected vocal styles, Panamanian slang, and bass-heavy hyphy beats. Beyond its innovative sounds, Panabay also brings together distinct understandings of Blackness and African diasporic belonging from two places normally neglected in discussions of Latino participation in Hip Hop, and, in the process, articulates a unique afrolatinidad.

Los Rakas's experiences growing up in Panama introduced them to a variety of Caribbean and U.S. musical genres. As Raka Dun explains, "In Panama, they play all kinds of music . . . It'd be rock and roll from the United States, Haitian music, Jamaican music, salsa, merengue, bachata, vallenato, you know. All of that influenced us." Indeed, the influx of West Indians and Americans to Panama as a result of the Panama Canal's construction and U.S. occupation cultivated a diverse musical landscape that included African diasporic musical practices from throughout the Americas. For example, *reggae en español*[7]

---

7. Many descendants of West Indians in Panama have been credited with creating *reggae en español*, one of the precursors of contemporary Reggaeton. *Reggae en español* is characterized

artist Renato recalled listening to R&B music from African American musicians such as the O'Jays, Marvin Gaye, and Whitney Houston alongside Jamaican artists like Bob Marley and Yellow Man, and Haitian groups like Tabou Combo (Nwankwo 2009, 91–92). Similarly, another *reggae en español* artist, El General, described the arrival of calypsonians from Trinidad to perform for West Indian audiences in Panama (Twickel 2009a, 107).[8] As these stories make clear, the movement of various communities into and out of the Panama Canal Zone and surrounding areas had a profound impact on the popular music scene there. Musical practices from throughout the African diaspora in the Americas flourished in Panama, creating the conditions for innovative musical fusions such as *reggae en español* to emerge. One can hear these connections in Los Rakas's music, which often incorporates beats, vocal stylings, and references to *reggae en español*.

Los Rakas integrate musical influences from Panama with aesthetics from Oakland's hyphy scene. Hyphy refers to a style of Hip Hop associated primarily with Oakland, but also other places in the East Bay such as Vallejo. In contrast to the multicultural and presumably more "conscious" San Francisco Hip Hop scene, hyphy music is considered to have a more "apolitical" stance and incorporates a range of cultural practices understood to proliferate in the urban, impoverished, and predominantly African American areas of Oakland (Harrison 2009, 145–56).[9] In addition to its unique musical characteristics, which include heavy bass and funk aesthetics, hyphy involves specific forms of self-fashioning such as wearing "stunna shades" (oversized sunglasses), gold teeth, or dreadlock hairstyles (Ciccariello-Maher and St. Andrews 2010, 282). It also embraces a unique car culture that includes "sideshows," a type of "spontaneous street party where one might 'ghostride the whip' (get out while driving), 'gas brake dip,' or even 'scrape' (spin donuts in the middle of the

by dancehall-style Spanish vocals performed over popular Jamaican riddims. For more information, see Marshall 2009; Nwankwo 2009; Twickel 2009a, 2009b.

8. Carla Guerrón-Montero (2006) notes that calypso was so popular in Panama that Panamanian calypsonians such as Lord Cobra and Lord Panama performed throughout the country, and even in the United States (646).

9. In general, the Bay Area Hip Hop scene is usually described to include two strands, of which hyphy is one. The other is an "underground" scene marked by politicized lyrics, multiracial participants, and an aversion to commercialization. In fact, Anthony Kwame Harrison (2009) argues that participants in this underground scene, which is spatially located in San Francisco rather than Oakland, often make considerable efforts to differentiate themselves from the hyphy movement (205). Nevertheless, he notes that the scenes share certain characteristics, especially their independent avenues of distribution described as the "Bay Area hustle." Likewise, George Ciccariello-Maher and Jeff St. Andrews (2010) argue that, despite the assumption that underground is "political" and hyphy is not, this distinction is not as stark as many would believe.

street)" (ibid., 272). Finally, the hyphy movement has strong associations with the drug ecstasy, in part because the rapper credited with making hyphy, Mac Dre, preferred the drug (Ciccariello-Maher and St. Andrews 2010). George Ciccariello-Maher and Jeff St. Andrews (2010) note that many of the cultural elements associated with hyphy music have been criminalized within Oakland; for example, police frequently target sideshows. At the same time, they contend that "celebrating old cars (scrapers) when that's all you've got, donning your grandma's old sunglasses (stunna shades), and finding a recreational drug worth celebrating (ecstasy) amidst the crack (and malt liquor) epidemic: these are all eminently political gestures" within the context of "postindustrial" Oakland (ibid., 282).

Los Rakas adopt many aesthetics from the hyphy movement in their self-presentations. For example, printed on many of Los Rakas's products, such as T-shirts, hats, and a limited-edition Puma sneaker,[10] is the Raka logo that relies heavily on signifiers of the hyphy movement. The figure wears a trucker hat with his long hair (possibly dreadlocks) visible underneath. He also adorns stunna shades such that one cannot see his eyes, and in his wide smile reveals a gold tooth. Los Rakas themselves incorporate emblems of Oakland and the Bay Area into their style, often wearing T-shirts, jerseys, or hats with local sports teams' logos. In some instances, they fuse together their logo with local symbols; for example, they sometimes wear a black shirt with the words "Raka Raider" that features their logo within the classic Oakland Raiders' gray shield. Los Rakas's logo and fashion thus integrate emblems specific to Oakland that affiliate them with the local hyphy scene.

At the same time, Los Rakas's aesthetic represents a translocal afrolatinidad that links Oakland and Panama together through a shared "ghetto imaginary." Rivke Jaffe argues that ghetto imaginaries contain "ethno-racial and spatial connotations, referring to a condition of urban immobility that is both cause and consequence of social difference" (Jaffe 2012, 675). In particular, she notes that various forms of Black popular culture, including Hip Hop, dancehall, and Reggaeton, have become symbolic of this ghetto imaginary (Jaffe 2012). As a result, despite the assumption of immobility that accompanies the isolation and segregation associated with physical ghettos, the ghetto imaginary holds the potential to unite these populations across geographic borders given their shared experiences of marginality (Jaffe 2012). While Jaffe is careful to note that the ghetto imaginary does not resonate exclusively with Black populations, thinking of Los Rakas's self-fashioning in relation to ghetto

---

10. Los Rakas designed the sneaker as part of the Modelo Especial Blank Canvas Project in 2012.

imaginaries foregrounds how they express links across African diasporic communities in Oakland and urban Panama through acknowledging their comparable experiences of marginalization and disenfranchisement as a result of anti-Black racism. Indeed, this is evident in the rationale behind the group's name. Los Rakas take their name from the word *rakataka,* a derogatory term from Panama that describes someone from the "ghetto." Raka Dun explains that they selected the name to "inspire the people from the ghetto and show the world that everything from the ghetto is not negative, not bad." Black communities in Oakland and urban Panama are subject to similar stereotypes and inequalities shaped by systemic anti-Black racism. In this context, Los Rakas's resignification of the term *raka* into one of "ghetto pride" counters the discrimination faced by urban, working-class African diasporic subjects in Panama, Oakland, and elsewhere, subsequently producing a Panabay ghetto imaginary that celebrates Blackness and, especially, afrolatinidad.

Still, perhaps the best example of Panabay aesthetics is Los Rakas's music. Besides the aforementioned songs that explicitly address social issues facing Afro-Latinos, many of Los Rakas's seemingly apolitical songs emphasize *raka* pride and a translocal afrolatinidad through their Panabay musical fusions. For instance, Los Rakas's 2010 song "Soy Raka," included on their album *Chancletas y Camisetas Bordadas,* exemplifies the Panabay sound. The duo raps in Spanish peppered with Panamanian slang over a hyphy beat. The lyrics boast about being *raka.* At first listen, the song appears to glorify violence connected to the stereotypes of urban ghettos; for example, Raka Dun raps about having his "Glock" ready, and the chorus includes the lyric "*tengo mi pistola y dientes de oro*" [I have my pistol and my gold teeth]. However, ultimately, the song expresses pride in being *raka.* Throughout the song, Los Rakas claim that "*los yeyos*"—a Panamanian term that refers to people from the upper class, essentially the opposite of *raka*—want to be like *rakas,* who are better because *rakas* have "*to' el estilo / to' el talento / to' el flow*" [all the style / all the talent / all the flow]. "Soy Raka" reflects the sort of braggadocio found in much rap music. At the same time, its questioning of the valorization of *yeyos* over *rakas* makes it a call for *raka* pride that challenges racial and class hierarchies.

The music video for "Soy Raka" illustrates the spatial, class, and racial dynamics of the Panabay aesthetic and *raka* identity. The video features Los Rakas walking through various parts of East Oakland, especially the predominantly Latino neighborhood Fruitvale. In the first scene, Los Rakas stand on a street corner with a group of children. Some children are identifiably Black (although we do not know whether they are Latino or not), and some have the *mestizo* phenotype of dominant representations of Mexicans and Central Americans. Some of the *mestizo* children wear clothing associated with folkloric Mexican dance. These children identify the *raka* community as made up of both Black and Latino subjects united through a shared experience in the segregated neighborhood of East Oakland.

The children and Los Rakas gather around a black car, where a group of male dancers from the Oakland-based group Turf Feinz emerge and begin to turf dance. *Turf* stands for "Taking Up Room on the Floor." Associated with East Oakland and the hyphy movement, turf dancing incorporates moves from Hip Hop (e.g., popping), ballet, "bonebreakin'" (contortionist-style movement of the limbs), and "tuttin'" (hand movements) that dancers combine in improvised routines. Turf dancing serves as a form of localized protest that counters the prevalence of violence in Oakland neighborhoods. Turf Feinz gained recognition from a YouTube video of them dancing on the corner of 90th Avenue and McArthur Avenue in Oakland to commemorate the death of one of their crew members by a drunk driver. The "RIP Rich D Dancing in the Rain" video[11] went viral and brought media attention to the dance form, including the MTV reality show *World of Jenks,* which followed crew member Darrell Armstead, known as "D-Real," around Oakland as he coped with the death of his brother to gun violence (Drummond 2013). Since its beginnings as an improvisational street dance, turf dancing has become more formalized, with organized dance battles popping up throughout the city that bring youth together with the hopes of distancing them from gang activity and violence (Payton 2011, Zamora 2007). The Turf Feinz make appearances throughout "Soy Raka," performing in front of the children in the beginning of the video and on the street as Los Rakas wander through Fruitvale. While the video's images of street signs and neighborhood landmarks locate Los Rakas in Oakland, the spontaneous performances by the Turf Feinz throughout the video also situate them within the city's larger Hip Hop scene.

In most of the video for "Soy Raka," common experiences of Black and Latino youth in Oakland link Blackness and Latinidad, reflecting the long histories of collaboration between these groups. Consequently, the video may appear to reproduce dominant distinctions between Blackness and Latinidad; however, it also references a specific Afro-Latino identity tied to Oakland. In the middle of the video, we see Los Rakas enter a clothing store in Fruitvale. The song "Soy Raka" fades out, replaced by the store's music, a Mexican banda song. The store sells products such as cowboy boots, hats, collared shirts with vests, and other clothing styles associated with Mexican popular music, particularly Banda and Ranchera. The duo approaches a rack with several jackets.

---

11. Yakfilms, *TURF FEINZ RIP RichD.* The video can be seen here: http://www.youtube.com/watch?v=JQRRnAhmB58.

Raka Rich tries on a jean jacket emblazoned with a Panamanian flag with the words *"Prohibido Olvidar"* [Never Forget] on the back. Raka Dun gestures and nods in approval, and Los Rakas leave the store. As soon as they enter the street, "Soy Raka" begins again.

The sounds and images associated with the store, as well as its location in Fruitvale, make it emblematic of the *mestizo* Mexican identity commonly associated with Latino communities in California. The discovery of the Panamanian jacket in the store thus inserts an Afro-Panamanian identity within the space of a *mestizo* Latinidad. Los Rakas's facial expressions and Raka Dun's gesture of approval express pride in this afrolatinidad. The words *"Prohibido Olvidar"* on the jacket can be read as a critical reminder of the importance of Afro-Latino identities, especially in places like California where afrolatinidad has been rendered virtually invisible. At the same time, the Panamanian flag also signifies afrolatinidad's translocal dimensions. As mentioned earlier, in contrast to the relative invisibility of afrolatinidad within the Mexican and Chicano spaces of California, Blackness has been integrated into Panamanian identity, albeit in very limited and stereotypical tropes that demonstrate a profound commitment to whitening. In this context, one could read the *"Prohibido Olvidar"* above the Panamanian flag on Raka Rich's jacket as a celebration of afrolatinidad in Panamanian communities, and other sites in Latin America, as well. Though perhaps a fleeting moment in the video, this scene highlights afrolatinidad defined by the Panabay sound and identity that directly contests the marginalization of Blackness within both Latin American and Latino communities.

Throughout the video, the resignifying of Fruitvale from a *mestizo* space to an Afro-Latino one amplifies this call for recognition of afrolatinidad. In the aforementioned scene, Los Rakas never pay for the jacket. Rather, they stride through the store, find the jacket, Raka Rich puts it on, and they walk out. Through claiming ownership of the jacket in this way, Los Rakas also claim ownership of the space of Fruitvale, and Latinidad more generally, which is symbolized by the Mexican store. This defiant reclamation of space occurs elsewhere in the video, too. For example, earlier we see Los Rakas enter a different store to find some trucker hats. We never witness them at the cash register, leaving open the possibility that they may have paid for the hats, but we do see them confidently step out of the store with their new hats that they wear in the rest of the video. Afterwards, they attempt to purchase some CDs from a vendor on the side of the road who refuses their money, a gesture that might be read as a recognition of Los Rakas as members of the Fruitvale community. Likewise, since reclaiming and resignifying space is central to turf dancing, the integration of the Turf Feinz in the video might also be understood as the making of an African diasporic space that brings together African Americans and Afro-Latinos in contrast to the presumably non-Black, *mestizo* Fruitvale. Ultimately, the reclaiming of space through both the Turf Feinz's dance and Los Rakas's wanderings through the neighborhood inserts Blackness into the *mestizo* space of Fruitvale, and thus asserts a sense of belonging for afrolatinidad in the *mestizo* spaces of California more generally.

"Soy Raka" is just one song in Los Rakas's extensive repertoire that exemplifies both *raka* pride and the Panabay sound. The song's combination of Spanish lyrics, hyphy beats, and Panamanian references not only represents a unique fusion within Oakland's Hip Hop scene but also counters the virtual invisibility of Afro-Latino identities within California. Moreover, its message of "*raka* pride" creates transnational links that bring together the ghetto imaginaries of Oakland and urban sites in Panama in ways that privilege Blackness and African diasporic connections. In the final analysis, this move reflects Los Rakas's larger aim to "rep" their Panamanian roots, their Oakland communities, and their pride in afrolatinidad.

Conclusion

Album reviews of *El Negrito Dun Dun & Ricardo* declared that Los Rakas were poised to take over the Latin urban music scene with their unique Panabay sound. Their musical fusions of Caribbean and Latin American genres popular in Panama and elsewhere with the particular aesthetics of Oakland's hyphy movement are indeed innovative within Hip Hop, reggaetón, and other Latin music scenes. But it is also important to note that the Panabay sound is more than a gimmick. Embedded within its bass-heavy beats and dancehall-inflected vocals is a larger call for pride and recognition in Afro-Latino identity.

A critical analysis of Los Rakas's work has broader implications for our understandings of afrolatinidad in the United States. For example, their music illustrates the importance of considering the transnational dynamics of afrolatinidad. In addition to Los Rakas's incorporation of Panamanian aesthetics into their music, their experiences living between Panama and Oakland have profoundly influenced their commitment to representing and celebrating Afro-Latino identity. Los Rakas are also intrinsically connected to the local. Besides their musical and stylistic ties to hyphy music, Los Rakas make visible an Afro-Latino subjectivity that is normally rendered invisible. Their expressions of afrolatinidad intervene in the space of an allegedly *mestizo* California, and simultaneously expose the marginalization of Blackness in Panama and

Latin America more generally. Ultimately, Los Rakas's music demands a more inclusive understanding of Latinidad—one that equally recognizes afrolatinidad and that openly celebrates *raka* pride.

Bibliography

Andrews, George Reid. 2004. *Afro-Latin America, 1800–2000.* New York: Oxford University Press.

Ciccariello-Maher, George, and Jeff St. Andrews. 2010. "Between Macks and Panthers: Hip Hop in Oakland and San Francisco." In *Hip Hop in America: A Regional Guide,* vol. 1, *East Coast and West Coast,* edited by Mickey Hess. Santa Barbara, CA: Greenwood. 257–86.

Craft, Renée Alexander. 2008. "'Una Raza, Dos Etnias': The Politics of Be(com)ing/Performing 'Afropanameño.'" *Latin American and Caribbean Ethnic Studies* 3(2): 123–49.

Dávila, Arlene M. 2001. *Latinos, Inc.: The Marketing and Making of a People.* Berkeley: University of California Press, 2001.

———. 2008. *Latino Spin: Public Image and the Whitewashing of Race.* New York: New York University Press.

Dowling, Julie A., and C. Alison Newby. 2010. "So Far from Miami: Afro-Cuban Encounters with Mexicans and the US Southwest." *Latino Studies* 8(2): 176–94.

Drummond, Tammerlin. 2013. "From Oakland to MTV, D-Real Releases Anger through Turf Dancing." *Contra Costa Times,* March 2. http://www.contracostatimes.com/ci_22701599/drummond-from-oakland-mtv-d-real-releases-anger (accessed June 16, 2014).

England, Sarah. 2009–10. "Afro-Hondurans in the Chocolate City: Garifuna, Katrina, and the Advantages of Racial Invisibility in the Nuevo New Orleans." *The Journal of Latino/Latin American Studies* 3(4): 31–55.

Flores, Juan. 2000. *From Bomba to Hip-Hop: Puerto Rican Culture and Latino Identity.* New York: Columbia University Press.

———. 2009. *The Diaspora Strikes Back: Caribeño Tales of Learning and Turning.* New York: Routledge.

Forbes, Jack D. 2010. "Black Pioneers: The Spanish-Speaking Afro-Americans of the Southwest." In Jiménez Román and Flores, 27–37.

García, David F. 2006. *Arsenio Rodríguez and the Transnational Flows of Latin Popular Music.* Philadelphia: Temple University Press.

Godreau, Isar P. 2015. *Scripts of Blackness: Race, Cultural Nationalism, and U.S. Colonialism in Puerto Rico.* Champaign: University of Illinois Press.

Gudmundson, Lowell, and Justin Wolfe, eds. 2010. *Blacks and Blackness in Central America: Between Race and Place.* Durham, NC: Duke University Press.

Guerrón-Montero, Carla María. 2006. "Can't Beat Me Own Drum in Me Own Native Land: Calypso Music and Tourism in the Panamanian Atlantic Coast." *Anthropological Quarterly* 79(4): 633–63.

Harrison, Anthony Kwame. 2009. "Multiracial Youth Scenes and the Dynamics of Race: New Approaches to Racialization within the Bay Area Hip Hop Underground." In *Twenty-First Century Color Lines: Multiracial Change in Contemporary America,* edited by Andrew Grant-Thomas and Gary Orfield. Philadelphia: Temple University Press. 201–19.

———. 2009. *Hip Hop Underground: The Integrity and Ethics of Racial Identification.* Philadelphia: Temple University Press.

Hernández, Tanya Katerí. 2003. "'Too Black to Be Latino/a': Blackness and Blacks as Foreigners in Latino Studies." *Latino Studies* 1: 152–59.

Hoy, Vielka Cecilia. 2010. "Negotiating among Invisibilities: Tales of Afro-Latinidades in the United States." In Jiménez Román and Flores, 426–30.

Jackson, María Rosario. 2010. "Profile of an Afro-Latina: Black, Mexican, Both." In Jiménez Román and Flores, 434–38.

Jaffe, Rivke. 2012. "Talkin' 'bout the Ghetto: Popular Culture and Urban Imaginaries of Immobility." *International Journal of Urban and Regional Research* 36(4): 674–88.

Jiménez Román, Miriam. 2005. "Looking at That Middle Ground: Racial Mixing as a Panacea?" *Wadabagei: Journal of the Caribbean and Its Diaspora* 8(1): 65–79.

Jiménez Román, Miriam, and Juan Flores, eds. 2010. *The Afro-Latin@ Reader: History and Culture in the United States.* Durham, NC: Duke University Press.

Johnson, Gaye Theresa. 2013. *Spaces of Conflict, Sounds of Solidarity: Music, Race, and Spatial Entitlement in Los Angeles.* Berkeley: University of California Press.

Jones, Jennifer A. 2013. "'Mexicans will take the jobs that even Blacks won't do': An Analysis of Blackness, Regionalism, and Invisibility in Contemporary Mexico." *Ethnic and Racial Studies* 36(10): 1561–81.

Marshall, Wayne. 2009. "From Música Negra to Reggaeton Latino: The Cultural Politics of Nation, Migration, and Commercialization." In Rivera, Marshall, and Hernández, 19–76.

McFarland, Pancho. 2006. "Chicano Rap Roots: Afro-Mexico and Black-Brown Cultural Exchange." *Callaloo* 29(3): 939–55.

Modestin, Yvette. 2010. "An Afro-Latina's Quest for Inclusion." In Jiménez Román and Flores, 417–21.

Mora, G. Cristina. 2014. "Cross-Field Effects and Ethnic Classification: The Institutionalization of Hispanic Pan-Ethnicity, 1965–1990." *American Sociological Review* 79(2): 183–210.

Moreno, Jairo. 2004. "Bauzá-Gillespie-Latin/Jazz: Difference, Modernity, and the Black Caribbean." *South Atlantic Quarterly* 103(1): 81–99.

Nwankwo, Ifeoma C. K. 2009. "The Panamanian Origins of Reggae en Español: Seeing History through 'Los Ojos Café' of Renato." In Rivera, Marshall, and Hernández, 89–98.

Oboler, Suzanne. 1995. *Ethnic Labels, Latino Lives: Identity and the Politics of (Re)Presentation in the United States.* Minneapolis: University of Minnesota Press.

Payton, Brenda. 2011. "Turf Dancing Lets Oakland Teens 'Tut' Their Stuff." *SF Gate,* May 8. http://www.sfgate.com/opinion/article/Turf-dancing-lets-Oakland-teens-tut-their-stuff-2372210.php#photo-1900025 (accessed June 16, 2014).

Priestley, George, and Angela Barrow. 2009. "The Black Movement in Panama: A Historical and Political Interpretation, 1994–2004." In *New Social Movements in the African Diaspora: Challenging Global Apartheid,* edited by Leith Mullings. New York: Palgrave Macmillan. 49–78.

Putnam, Lara. 2010. "Eventually Alien: The Multigenerational Saga of the British West Indians in Central America, 1870–1940." In *Blacks and Blackness in Central America: Between Race and Place,* edited by Lowell Gudmundson and Justin Wolfe. Durham, NC: Duke University Press. 278–306.

Rahier, Jean Muteba. 2003. "Mestizaje, Mulataje, Mestçagem in Latin American Ideologies of National Identities." *The Journal of Latin American Anthropology* 8(1): 40–51.

Rivera, Raquel Z. 2003. *New York Ricans from the Hip Hop Zone.* New York: Palgrave Macmillan.

Rivera, Raquel Z., Wayne Marshall, and Deborah Pacini Hernández, eds. *Reggaeton.* Durham, NC: Duke University Press, 2009.

Rivera-Rideau, Petra R. "Panabay Pride: A Conversation with Los Rakas." In *Afro-Latinos in Movement: Critical Approaches to Blackness and Transnationalism in the Americas,* edited by Petra R. Rivera-Rideau, Jennifer A. Jones, and Tianna S. Paschel. New York: Palgrave Macmillan, 2016.

Sue, Christina A. 2013. *Land of the Cosmic Race: Race Mixture, Racism, and Blackness in Mexico.* New York: Oxford University Press.

Thomas, Anulkah. 2012. "Black Face, Latin Looks: Racial-Ethnic Identity among Afro-Latinos in the Los Angeles Region." In *Latino Los Angeles: Transformations, Communities, and Activism*, edited by Enrique C. Ochoa and Gilda L. Ochoa. Tucson: University of Arizona Press. 197–224.

Twickel, Christoph. 2009a. "Muévelo (Move It!): From Panama to New York and Back Again, the Story of El General." In Rivera, Marshall, and Hernández, 99–108.

———. 2009b. "Reggae in Panama: Bien Tough." In Rivera, Marshall, and Hernández, 81–88.

Vasconselos, José. (1925) 1997. *The Cosmic Race / La Raza Cósmica*. Translated by Didier T. Jaén. Baltimore: Johns Hopkins University Press.

Wade, Peter. 1997. *Race and Ethnicity in Latin America*. London: Pluto, 1997.

Wang, Oliver. 2010. "The Journey of 'Viva Tirado': A Musical Conversation within Afro-Chicano Los Angeles." *Journal of Popular Music Studies* 22(4): 348–66.

Yakfilms. 2009, October 27. *TURF FEINZ RIP RichD Dancing in the Rain Oakland Street | YAK FILMS*, video, 3:56. https://www.youtube.com/watch?v=JQRRnAhmB58 (accessed June 13, 2014).

Zamora, Jim Herron. 2007. "Architeckz Look to Build Outlet for Oakland Youth—Dance Troupe Channels Emotions through 'Turf Dancing,' a Younger Sibling of 1980s Break Dancing." *SF Gate,* March 10. http://www.sfgate.com/bayarea/article/Architeckz-look-to-build-outlet-for-Oakland-youth-2610783.php (accessed June 16, 2014).

chapter 5

Bandoleros

The Black Spiritual Identities of Tego Calderon and Don Omar

Jason Nichols

P uerto Rico's cultural exports to the United States, Latin America, and
other parts of the world rival those of any other nation. Puerto Rico
brought the world Bomba and Plena, and its natives and expatriates were
instrumental to the development of salsa, Hip Hop, and Reggaeton. The latter
two musical/cultural genres have produced some of the world's most recognizable stars. Puerto Rico, an island with a population roughly half the size of
New York City's, has been more successful in establishing an indelible cultural
imprint on the United States, particularly in terms of music and dance, than
any other location outside the mainland. The reason for this can perhaps be
traced to the fact that Puerto Ricans are U.S. citizens and, in the 1950s, staged
"the largest flight of Latin Americans to the United States that the hemisphere
had ever seen" (Gonzalez 2011, xxiii). However, the richness of Puerto Rican
history can be seen, heard, and experienced in the cultural expression of its
natives and expatriates. Despite there being constantly subjugated, colonized,
and exploited, first by Spain and later by the United States, one of the characteristics of the Puerto Rican people that has aided in their survival is that they
are a spiritual people. This spirituality has found its way into their music and
art. This chapter examines religious imagery in rap and Reggaeton videos of

Don Omar and Tego Calderon, and discusses how it reflects a uniquely Black Puerto Rican spiritual identity.

Any story about Puerto Rican music invariably begins with the story of the Puerto Rican people. Though this research focuses on a Black Puerto Rican identity, I contend that a Black Puerto Rican identity still acknowledges the hybridity of the cultural traditions and spirituality of all inhabitants of the island. Though the Ciboney and the Ignery proceeded them, the most recognized indigenous inhabitants of the Island of Puerto Rico were the Taino Arawak, a peaceful group who called the island "Borinquen," a name meaning "Land of Great Lords" (Galvan 2009).

The Taino were said to be excellent farmers and sailors. Evidence suggests that the Taino were no strangers to arts and music, as archeologists have found maracas and drums they created and hand carved out of wood (Galvan 2009). Christopher Columbus landed on the island in 1493. He originally named it San Juan Bautista and claimed it for the Spanish, a reign that would last until the Spanish-American War in 1898 (ibid.). The Spaniards enslaved the thirty to forty thousand that were on the island almost immediately. Galvan describes the Taino as "a sedentary group" prior to the arrival of the Spanish. They died rapidly from "exhaustion, rebellion, overwork, and disease," causing the Spaniards to turn to African slaves to cultivate their newly formed sugar plantations (ibid.).

The Africans, Europeans, and Indigenous forefathers and mothers each contributed to the development of a distinct culture and cultural expressions in Puerto Rico, even through their religious practices. Though little is known about Taino religious beliefs and practices, we do know that they were polytheists, with major and minor gods (Galvan 2009). Remnants of the Taino belief system still exist. For example, some Puerto Rican women still mention Atabei, the "earth mother and goddess of water, and hence of life and fertility," when they pray for a healthy and successful childbirth (ibid., 30).

The African heritage in Puerto Rico is perhaps more visible than the indigenous cultures in elements of the island's "music, food, art, and religious traditions" (Galvan 2009). The Roman Catholic Spaniards who ruled the island for over 400 years forced their African captives to convert to Christianity. However, the Africans secretly paid to homage to Yoruba orishas (gods).

Reggaeton

The roots of Reggaeton are Black, transnational, and spiritual. Though Reggaeton is closely associated with Puerto Rico, where its industry flourished, its roots are in Panama. It was initially Spanish-language Reggae (*reggae en español*). Panama was a major destination for Jamaican immigrant workers since the turn of the century. The Jamaicans, along with other Black English-speaking Caribbean groups, were used as laborers in the construction of the Panama Canal. Many stayed in Panama and transformed into a hybrid culture. The construction of the canal brought 150,000 Caribbean Blacks to Panama. The Afro-Panamanians of Jamaican descent maintained close ties with their country of origin. Reggae had become the soundtrack to the island by the 1960s, and the genre's brightest star, Robert Nesta Marley, also known as "Bob," used it as platform to spread the tenets of his adopted religion, Rastafarianism, globally. The Rastafarians also have an admiration for Africa and Blackness, which is tied to their spirituality.

The earliest recording of Spanish-language Reggae dates back to the 1970s. The Black Consciousness movement in Panama was in full swing, and musicians were innovating by mixing diasporic music genres such as Calypso, Soca, and Kompa with Latin styles such as Cumbia. Eventually, R&B, salsa, Funk, and Rap music from the United States filtered into the country, which led to the creation of a latinized Reggae (Samponaro 2009). However, the rest of the Caribbean and Latin America still looked backed to Jamaica for inspiration.

In the 1980s Jamaica underwent a political regime change. The idealistic democratic socialism of Michael Manley and the People's National Party had failed to produce the social change many poor Jamaicans sought, despite implementing many positive reforms in government. Jamaicans had seen the roots Reggae of Marley and others become a global phenomenon, and many felt that it was no longer a possession and expression of Jamaican identity. Artists began to perform music with less political and spiritual content, and more as a cathartic release in the island's dance halls. Yellowman became the first dancehall reggae "deejay" to rise to international fame after being signed to Columbia Records in 1981. Latin Reggae, or *reggae en espanol*, experienced a split much like the one in Jamaica, with many artists taking on more of the characteristics of dancehall. Edgardo Franco, also known as El General, an Afro-Panamanian, was Spanish-language dancehall's first bona fide star, providing the genre with its first hit record, "Tu Pum Pum."

Dancehall had garnered popularity in Puerto Rico by the early 1990s. It is argued by some that Jamaican artist Shabba Ranks is actually the direct forefather of modern Reggaeton. In 1990 he released a song called "Dem Bow," in which the "riddim" is said to be the foundation for modern Reggaeton instrumental music (Marshall 2010). Puerto Ricans began to master the genre of Reggaeton with a slew of successful acts. This fact is more than a coincidence. Puerto Rico's positioning between Latin America and the United States, its stark Afro-diasporic identity, and its citizens' freedom to enter and live in both the U.S. mainland and the island gave birth to more modern incarnations of Reggaeton. Reggaeton evolved to incorporate elements of U.S. Hip Hop, a culture that Puerto Ricans played a large role in creating. Raquel Z. Rivera (2003) writes:

> Hip Hop is a fluid cultural space, a zone whose boundaries are an internal and external matter of debate. A profoundly diverse, translocal, multiethnic and multiracial cultural phenomenon, Hip Hop expressions also can present themselves as exclusionary, for aesthetic, regional, gender, sexual-orientation, national, ethnic, racial, class or myriad other reasons. The dynamic tensions within Hip Hop and its constant drawing and crossing of borders are better addressed by the somewhat ambiguous concept of a "Hip Hop zone" than by frequently adopted but more limiting (and, in my opinion, questionable) terms like "Hip Hop community" and "Hip Hop nation." (15)

Some would consider Reggaeton to fall within the Hip Hop zone. Vico C is often thought to be Puerto Rico's pioneering MC. He was among the first to link reggae and dancehall rhythms with Hip Hop–style rhymes (Ilich, n.d.). At the very least, Rivera (2003) suggests that Reggaeton could be a "subzone," filled with connections and "overlap" with more standard, English-based rap music. This idea is substantiated by the fact that Reggaeton is unique because it puts the Blackness and Latinidad of Puerto Rican culture on full display. Part of the reason why Puerto Ricans have been the group to grow Reggaeton is because of their high level of transiency. Many Puerto Ricans spend time stateside and have English-dominant family members who are tied to the Hip Hop culture. Hip Hop is an unmistakably Black art form, at least in relation to its inception. To say that Hip Hop is "Black and Latino," as many have stated, is to overstate the involvement of non-Caribbean Latinos and to understate the Diasporic Black identity of Puerto Ricans. Rivera (2003, 19) states that "neighborhood, borough, city, coast, gender, and sexual and class identity take precedence" over ethnic identity in Hip Hop's core audience of African Americans and Puerto Ricans. Some Puerto Ricans do not stress their ethno-nationality, with the understanding that doing so could compromise "common territory shared with African Americans" (ibid.).

This desire for common ground with African Americans is what separates Puerto Rican Hip Hoppers on the East Coast from Chicano Hip Hop on the West. When Kid Frost said "this is for La Raza," he was clearly making a distinction beyond mere celebration of his culture. The song was a driving force in the creation of a new and exclusive subgenre of rap music. In the book

Cholo Style: Homies, Homegirls, and La Raza, Berrios (2011) stated the following mantra about Chicano rap:

> The white boys and black boys have some kind of relationship, and they want kids to either listen to the fucking freaking white boys or the fucking freaking black boys. I say fuck both of them and let's stop being their CDs. Right now I'm traveling, going to the barrios' frontlines to recruit Chicano rappers and see what we can do to expose our kind of music to Aztlan and the rest of the world! (xiii)

Berrios goes on to explain that Puerto Rican pop star Jennifer Lopez is "not one of us" (xiii), particularly because of her association with Blacks. Despite the book addressing issues such as incarceration, gentrification, police brutality, and intracultural violence—all topics that are common in Black rap music—Chicano rap shares little terrain with Black people. Puerto Rican culture marginalizes Blackness also, but doesn't deny its presence. The culture, music, and sometimes the phenotypes of the people make that extremely difficult. As an Afro-Latin territory, the cultural production that emerges from Puerto Rico and its descendants should not be separated from other forms of cultural expression that emerge from the African Diaspora. Brennan (2008) states that "Afro-Latin and African American music belong in the same discussion." He explains further that "it is not the case, in other words (as many argue) that U.S. black musical forms like Jazz, R&B, ragtime, and rap are part of a different musical family than their Latin American and Caribbean counterparts" (1).

Still, Reggaeton in the United States is the possession of Latinos. Artists of many different national origins have adopted the style. It is primarily performed by people for whom Spanish is a first language. However, on the island it is an example of the hybridization that makes Puerto Ricans unique. Reggaeton styles including fashion and hair were more than likely influenced by U.S. Hip Hop culture and the often close proximity to African Americans in major cities like New York and Philadelphia. For example, in the earlier days of Reggaeton, it was not uncommon to find artists and fans donning cornrows, a tradition African hairstyle also popular among African Americans, regardless of skin color or hair texture. It is hard to deny the African diasporic identity of Reggaeton when one see the styles and listens to the syncopated drum-based rhythms and call-and-response refrains. According to Portia Maultsby (2015), "Call-response is ubiquitous in early and contemporary accounts of African musical performance" (12). In addition, "in both early and contemporary forms of Black music expressions, performers also extend the length of notes at climatic points and they manipulate pitch" (ibid., 14).

What exists often in the shadows of much of Puerto Rican secular music is spirituality, particularly that which is linked to the West African theology that came with the African slaves. Many Puerto Ricans still believe in or practice elements of the Yoruba religions in the form of Santeria, but it is done quietly and many will deny it. According to Vidal-Ortiz (2006), Santeria means "the way of the saints." Meanwhile, Tim Brennan (2008), author of *Secular Devotion,* argues that popular music in the Americas is popular in part because it is so heavily influenced by neo-African religious practices.

In Reggaeton, themes of sex, sexual attraction, and sexual conquest take center stage. It is a musical genre practiced by youth all over the island and is not limited to those who identify as Black or even as being of mixed race. Part of ethno-racial or cultural identity, certainly among many Sub-Saharan African descendants, is religiosity and spirituality. Secular music pioneered by African descendants in the Diaspora has historically found its roots in religious music and institutions, perhaps because the separation between the secular and spiritual is a White supremacist social construction. According to Anthony B. Pinn (2009), embedded in the aesthetics of the African Diaspora is something religious. Further, the idea that spirituality must be devoid of sexuality is also a Eurocentric concept. Rather than religion celebrating fertility and the sacred bonds that can be established through sexual relationships, Eurocentric Christianity tends to focus on virginity and celibacy as symbols of sacrifice, asceticism, and piety. Vidal-Ortiz (2006) states that Santeros "educate each other about general sexuality issues and sexual orientation through their communal participation in this religious belief system" (xx).

Reggaeton is born of the Pan-African, Pan-Caribbean, and African Diasporic spiritual continuum, though it does not overtly show religious themes often. This concept is one I have termed "obscured spiritual foundationalism," and one that explains the evolution of many African-based secular musical styles. For example, the blues seemed to be the antithesis of the African American religious tradition that was housed in the Black church. However, many early blues artists invoked God in their lyrics, even when singing about queer sex (Brown Douglass 2012). This shows that the roots of this musical genre were intertwined with religion, though that part of its foundation is obscured by Bessie Smith's raunchy sex tales. Brennan (2008) observes, "Music is devotion in African religion. Its value system is rooted in relaxation, sexual release, collective oral expression and satire" (n.p.).

The examples do not end there. Paravisini-Gebert (2009) links Haitian art to the practice of Vodou. She argues that in this Caribbean country there is a close relationship between "ritual practice, faith and art." Puerto Rican Reggaeton includes evolved versions of the ritual practice through art, but excludes the faith. Reggaeton, much like Brennan (2008) argues for its diasporic artistic relative, Hip Hop, "fill(s) a void in African secular devotion" (n.p.).

Reggaeton reflects the Puerto Rican hybridization and appreciation for all of the elements that make the Boricua people. While Lil Wayne and other United Statesian artists constantly proclaim their desire and preference for fair-skinned women, Hector y Tito featuring Don Omar sang "Baila Morena," an ode to the sensuality and sexiness of dark-complexioned women. It is no surprise that Don Omar would take part in a song that celebrates the beauty (though fetishizing) of Blackness.

Two of Reggaeton's biggest stars have overtly chosen identity that is Black. Don Omar and Tego Calderon not only appeared side by side in *The Fast and Furious* film series, they are the most visible contemporary emissaries of Black Puerto Rican identity. William Omar Landron Rivera, better known by his stage name, Don Omar, grew up in the crime-ridden, impoverished caserio of Villa Palmeras. He refers to himself as el negro, affirming a Black Puerto Rican identity. He boasts a sexualized black masculinity, reflected in the following passage:

> Don Omar does indeed position himself as a black man above all else via sexualized lyrics such as "el potro de chocolate (the chocolate stud)," "el negro te Consuela (el negro will console you)," and "mas negro que la noche (blacker than the night)." In an intimate dialogue with a female voice, when he asks "Ma' due tu quiere (What do you want)?" she responds, "el negrito me de fuerte (I want el negro to give it to me hard)." (Rudolph 2011, n.p.)

Jennifer Domino Rudolph (2008) states that "Don Omar, and the social class connotations ascribed to him in particular, and Reggaeton in general, hold an Afro-centric mirror to the faces of blanquitos who are forced to acknowledge aspects of Puerto Rico's mixed cultural heritage that they do not necessarily (want to) identify with" (46). Don Omar also refers to "palidos," or White people, in his music, and he understands his role as an entertainer in a White supremacist society. Though he is a champion of Pan-Latino identity, especially through his song "Reggaeton Latino," it does not seem to conflict with his understanding of Blackness. Don Omar uses sexual imagery and interweaves it seamlessly with his spiritual lyrics, which is part of the African diasporic tradition of what Brennan (2008) calls "rituals of secular pleasure" in a "world of religious extremes" (n.p.). In songs like "Angelito Vuela" and "Pobre Diabla," he uses religious and spiritual imagery to discuss topics of love, lust, and pain, which illustrate the African tradition of not drawing barriers between spirituality, the spiritual world, and the material one. His songs that speak of "diablos," "angelitos," and "sleeping under the wings of the dead" for a moment unobscured the spiritual foundation of his music and Reggaeton.

According to Enelbasero.com (2009), Tego Calderon "se siente atraido al culto santero" (felt attracted to Santeria) since his early childhood (n.p.). Despite the protest of his parents, he felt called to the religion and its spiritual traditions. He described his reason for being in the religion as a blood inheritance: "Es por mi decendencia Africana" (it's a result of my African heritage). Calderon moved to Miami in 1988, and it was there that he encountered the pro-Black rap of Public Enemy and others (Garsd 2013). Coupled with the Black pride he was taught by his parents and the anti-Black racism he experienced stateside, the music resonated. He exploded on the Reggaeton scene with his large afro hairstyle and his influences from the Afro-Puerto Rican bomba of his native Loiza. However, his musical influences were not Reggaeton. They were artists such as Ismael Rivera, who did not shy away from the topic of racism or intracultural manifestations in the form of skin-tone prejudices. Rivera approached race issues in Puerto Rico through the use of humor, not unlike countless African American comedians, singers, or even visual artists. Ismael Rivera also was outspoken about Black Pride, which can be heard in his classic recording "Las Caras Lindas (de mi gente negra)." Rivera's spirituality was also unequivocally Black. He traveled for many years to the Church of San Felipe in Portobelo, Panama, where he and several thousand others come to worship a shrine of a Black Jesus Christ. The statue is known as El Nazareno. Rivera dedicated a song to the statue, also called "El Nazareno," in which the lyrics holler out "que viva el triste negro de Portobello."

Tego displays a knowledge of social/racial issues rarely heard in Reggaeton or Latin music in general. He rejects the multicultural democracy myth of Latinidad in his music and his interviews. In 2013 Calderon spoke to NPR, stating that the aforementioned myth allowed for the marginalization of Blacks and that he didn't know "which is worse": this covert discrimination, or overt racism.[1]

---

1. In his ode to his hometown, aptly entitled "Loiza," Tego raps the following:

me quiere hacer pensar
que soy parte de una trilogia racial
donde to' el mundo es igual, sin trato especial
se perdonar
eres tu quien no sabe disculpar
so, como justifica tanto mal
es que tu historia es vergonzosa
entre otra cosas
cambiaste las cadenas por esposas

Conclusion

Both Don Omar and Tego Calderon personify the spiritual Blackness of reggaeton and ultimately of the Puerto Rican culture. Though neither talks about Black spirituality specifically, there is an undercurrent of racial identity and religion in their lyrics. In their hit duo song, "Bandoleros," the two thank God for where they are today. In addition, Tego refers to William Landron as "nigga," which racializes the latter as Black. They are examples that spawn from the continuum of Black consciousness and identity, which does not create borders between art and life, or spirituality, sex, and music. Ismael Rivera is part of this continuum and an influence on modern reggaetoneros like Tego during a time when Blackness is often denied or whitewashed by a rhetoric of racial hybridity that marginalizes Blackness. One need only delve deeper into contemporary cultural expressions like Reggaeton to see where mother Africa has left an indelible, spiritual mark through an obscured spiritual foundationalism.

Bibliography

Berrios, Reynaldo. 2011. *Cholo Style: Homies, Homegirls, and La Raza*. Los Angeles: Feral.

Brennan, Tim. 2008. "Rorotoko." *Rorotoko*, December 5. http://rorotoko.com/interview/20081205 _brennan_timothy_secular_devotion_afro-latin_music_imperial_jazz/.

Brown Douglass, Kelly. 2012. "The Black Church, the Blues, and Black Bodies" *Feminism and Religion*. September 27. https://feminismandreligion.com/2012/09/27/the-black-church-the -blues-and-black-bodies-by kelly-brown-douglass/.

enelbrasero.com. 2009, June 23. http://www.enelbrasero.com/2009/06/23/tego-calderon-dice-si -soy-santero/.

Galvan, Javier. 2009. *Culture and Customs of Puerto Rico*. Westport, CT: Greenwood.

Garsd, Jasmine. 2013. "Black, Puerto Rican, and Proud: Guest DJ Tego Calderon." *NPR*, May 23. http://www.npr.org/blogs/altlatino/2013/05/20/185511016/black-puerto-rican-and-proud -guest-dj-tego-calder-n.

Gonzalez, Juan. 2011. *Harvest of Empire: A History of Latinos in America*. New York: Penguin.

Ilich, Tijana. n.d. "Reggaeton—From Puerto Rico to the World." *About.com*. http://latinmusic .about.com/od/genres/p/PRO019BASIC.htm.

Landron, William. 2004. *Pobre Diabla*.

Landron, William, and Tego Calderon. 2005. *Los Bandoleros*.

Marshall, Wayne. 2010, June 27. "*The Rise of Reggaeton*." *Norient.com*, http://norient.com/en /stories/reggaeton/.

Maultsby, Portia. 2015. "The Translated African Cultural and Musical Past." In *African American Music: An Introduction*, by Mellonee V. Burnim and Portia K. Maultsby. New York: Routledge. 3–22.

Paravisini-Gebert, Lizabeth. 2009. "Sacred Forms: Ritual, Representation, and the Body in Haitian Painting." In *Black Religion and Aesthetics: Religious Thought and Life in Africa and the African Diaspora*, edited by Anthony B. Pinn. New York: Palgrave Macmillan. 91–112.

Pinn, Anthony B. 2009. "Introduction: The Black Labrinth, Aesthetics, and Black Religion." In *Black Religion and Aesthetics: Religious Thought and Life in Africa and the African Diaspora,* edited by Anthony B. Pinn. New York: Palgrave Macmillan. 1–18.

Rivera, Ismael. 1974. *Las Caras Linda.* Comps. Ismael Rivera and Tite Curet Alonso.

Rivera, Raquel Z. 2003. *New York Ricans from the Hip Hop Zone.* New York: Palgrave Macmillan.

Rudolph, Jennifer Domino. 2008. *"Roncamos Porque Podemos": Racialization, Redemption, and Mascu-latinidad.* PhD diss., University of Illinois at Chicago. ProQuest (Pub. No. 3327436).

Samponaro, Phillip. 2009. "Oye mi Canto (Listen to My Song): The History and Politics of Reggaeton." *Popular Music and Society* 32(4): 489–506.

Vidal-Ortiz, Salvador. 2006. "Sexuality Discussions in Santeria: A Case Study of Religion and Sexual Negotiation." *Sexuality Research and Social Policy* 3(3): 52–66.

chapter 6

"Te llevaste mi oro"

ChocQuibTown and Afro-Colombian Cultural Memory

Christopher Dennis

O ver the last few decades, perhaps no other manifestation of transnational popular culture has captured the attention of Latin American youth quite like Hip Hop and rap have done. Originating as a cultural and musical practice among African American, Caribbean (Jamaican), and Hispanic youth in the Bronx, Hip Hop has evolved into a global phenomenon providing new parameters of sociocultural meanings to youth groups all over the world. Partly owing to its associations with poor Black and Hispanic youth in U.S. inner cities, Hip Hop has circulated the globe as a cultural and musical practice primarily for marginalized urban youth. Of course, its class and racial undertones largely stem from the way in which multinational entertainment corporations have strategically marketed the street and ethnic gist of U.S. rap, and today's Latin American Hip Hop youth unquestionably represent a generation overwhelmed by mass-mediated, racialized, and gendered messages of African American commodified resistance. Whatever the reasons for Hip Hop's widespread circulation among certain social groups, marginalized youth from all stretches of Latin America now take part in Hip Hop as a cultural and musical medium for voicing their perspectives on a wide array of social and political issues (Dennis 2014).

In Colombia, Hip Hop and its many localized derivatives have been practiced since the 1980s as an easily accessible cultural and musical form through which youth construct positive identities, raise self-esteem, awaken social consciousness, and create a sense of belonging to their respective communities. While Hip Hop has motivated some young people to take part in various political activities, most Hip Hop artists and rappers choose not to participate in formal party politics. Nevertheless, through their musical productions, Colombian Hip Hop performers indeed articulate and spread their views on many of the social and political problems weighing on their communities while, at the same time, gauging and openly criticizing Colombia's ruling elites. Specifically for young Afro-Colombians, Hip Hop has provided an artistic outlet for voicing ethnic-racial perspectives that have historically been ignored by members of dominant culture. Various Black rappers, for instance, have successfully used Hip Hop as a medium for carrying their racial concerns to both national and international audiences. With this in mind, the main objective of this chapter is to demonstrate how the Afro-Colombian music group ChocQuibTown recovers and performs specific cultural memories through their own brand of Hip Hop as a strategy for preserving local history, defining Afro-Colombian identity, awakening ethnic-racial pride, and combating racial discrimination. In order to explore the relationship between their music and cultural memory, I focus on two songs: first, the Latin-Grammy-winning "De dónde vengo yo" (Where I come from), followed by a more in-depth consideration of "Oro" (gold), both tracks from the 2010 album also entitled *Oro*.

Cultural Memory

Though there is no universally accepted definition of cultural memory, this theoretical field owes a great deal to the contributions of several academics, most notably Maurice Halbwach and his work on collective memory (*La mémoire collective*, 1950), Pierre Nora and his notions on place of memory (*Les lieux de mémoire*, 1984–92), and especially Jan Assmann and his theories on cultural memory ("Collective Memory and Cultural Identity," 1995). It is essential to note, however, that the definition and application of cultural memory, particularly within the area of cultural studies, has evolved over the years.[1]

---

1. For Jan Assmann, cultural memory addresses events of a distant past rather than those of everyday life. According to him, cultural memory is recorded through cultural formations (texts, rites, monuments) and institutionalized communication. He views cultural memory as that which is established by means of official ceremony, and, therefore, its transmission depends

Accordingly, in this analysis, I turn to the theoretical concept most aligned with that of cultural studies in which cultural memory refers to the processes through which individuals and groups continuously recover, (re)construct, and perform identities based on a shared past, cultural norms, practices, and everyday lived experiences. Cultural memory, in other words, involves the methods by which individuals and social groups ensure cultural continuity via the preservation and transmission of collective knowledge through the use of mnemonic devices that facilitate the (re)construction and (re)presentation of cultural identity (Rodríguez and Fortier 2007, 1).

Before proceeding, it is first important to address some of the more common notions regarding different types or levels of cultural memory. According to Astrid Erll (2012), the first level is an individual one given that cultural memory often deals with the (re)presentation of daily experiences and personal or intimate memories. However, even personal memories are constantly activated, shaped, and even created in relation to one's sociocultural context. From interactions with community members and the different artifacts and media used, "we acquire schemata which help us recall the past and encode new experiences" (Erll 2011, 5). Erll (2011) also elaborates on a second level of cultural memory that is collective, pertaining to those memories that are more directly associated with the larger "symbolic order, the media, institutions and practices by which social groups construct a shared past" (5). Of course, the processes used to construct collective memories are quite similar to those used to create individual ones, such as the selectivity involved in crafting a particular version of the past. Furthermore, it is worth mentioning that this particular allusion to a second level of institutionalized and mediated cultural memories brings to mind what Abril Trigo (2003) refers to as both historical memory—reproduced by the ideological apparatuses of the state and thus guided by a nationalist teleology—and pop memory—produced and distributed by systems of mass communication under the logic of capital and merchandise (89).

Nonetheless, while on a purely theoretical plane it is possible to identify and define different types or levels of cultural memory, in practice they continuously overlap and interact. Collective and individual memories are mutually dependent, and all cultural memories are, to varying degrees, mediated and negotiated. In fact, cultural memories of oppressed groups often come

---

on specialized people and practices. As Astrid Erll indicates in her book *Memory in Culture* (2011), Assmann's theory does not include a broad definition of culture but instead is limited to the social constructs of "normative and formative versions of the past" (30). Thus, his use of the term "culture" is not entirely compatible with today's anthropological and sociological concepts that also include experiences and practices associated with everyday life and popular culture (ibid.).

into conflict with hegemonic cultural memories when marginalized individuals attempt to define group identities and local histories that counteract, challenge, or question dominant memorial discourses. Dominant culture reifies and normalizes hegemonic cultural memories through its institutions and media forms, while all too often disregarding those of marginalized groups. For this reason, a key part of present-day cultural memory studies is concerned with the dynamics behind the emergence, disappearance, and marginalization of memories. If cultural memories are no longer articulated and performed, they eventually fade away and become obsolete; they may be modified or completely abandoned. Thus, it is essential to identify those processes that enable particular cultural memories to become hegemonic (often excluding other memories) as well as those that make it possible for previously marginalized memories to become socially and politically significant in the public sphere (Erll and Rigney 2012). After all, the repeated representation of cultural memory frequently implies the survival of historically, politically, and socially marginalized groups (Rodríguez and Fortier 2007, 1).

Specifically in the case of ChocQuibTown and Afro-Colombian forms of Hip Hop, one of the factors that strongly influences the (re)construction and performance of cultural memory has to do with questions of race and ethnicity. Race offers a useful conceptual framework for studying cultural memory given that racial constructs (along with those of gender and socioeconomic class) nurture identities in very particular ways—due to cultural codes through which social groups build their identities—thereby determining how cultural memory is represented in specific milieus. Additionally, race and racial differences within any context imply unequal power relations, and cultural memory—as defined in this study—involves the "distribution of and contested claims to power. What a culture remembers and what it chooses to forget are intricately bound up with issues of power and hegemony" and, therefore, questions of race (Hirsch and Smith 2007, 225). Last, it is important to recognize that technology and expressive mediums not only serve as conduits for transmitting memories but also help mold them, which inevitably impacts the understanding of the past and its influence on present-day identity (ibid.). Put differently, the means used to (re)present and perform cultural memory also have a significant impact on the formation of identity constructs, collective aspirations, and future cultural agendas. In the end, cultural memory involves both a remembering and a remembrance. One side of cultural memory is the *traditio,* the process; who remembers, and how is it remembered? On the other side is the *traditium,* the product; what is actually remembered, and what feelings, aspirations, discourses, or modes of action does a specific memory evoke? (Rodríguez and Fortier 2007, 9–10).

The *Traditio*: Who? How?

Colombia's sizable Black population resulted from the African slave trade that took place primarily between the sixteenth and eighteenth centuries when European colonizers imported mass numbers of African slaves to New Granada (present-day countries of Colombia, Ecuador, Panama, and Venezuela). Slaves came from a multitude of ethnic groups primarily from Western Africa between Cape Verde and Angola. It was due to the declining Amerindian population that colonizers turned to African slave labor in their efforts to replace Indigenous workers on haciendas, within transportation networks, and especially in the region's gold and silver mines. For this reason, African slaves and their descendants would primarily come to occupy the tropical lowlands of Colombia's coastal regions (Uribe 2002, 32), and consequently, to this day, the population of the Pacific littoral is predominantly Afro-Colombian.

During much of the nation's history, the Pacific region—as a "Black" territory—was imagined as an inhospitable area of little economic and cultural value. Thus, the Pacific littoral and its inhabitants have tended to exist on the nation's margins, which in great part explains the region's low levels of economic development coupled with its high levels of poverty. With little capitalist investment or infrastructure, Afro-Colombians have historically carried out work that was previously assigned to slaves, such as mining, logging, and traditional methods of fishing and agriculture (Mosquera 2000, 25). Eventually, as a result of the country's neoliberal economic reform in the 1980s, the Pacific coastal region was identified as an ideal space for various projects of capitalist development. Nonetheless, the economic revalorization of the territory has done little to benefit local communities. Instead, it has produced a dramatic increase in violence as the nation-state, armed groups, and drug traffickers now compete for control over these highly coveted lands rich in mineral resources (Nubia Bello and Peña Frade 2004, 397–99).

Trapped between the interests of the various groups in conflict, over the last few decades, millions of Afro-Colombians sadly have been displaced from their ancestral lands toward large cities such as Medellín, Cali, and Bogotá, where they all too often join the ranks of the poor urban masses. Though constitutional reform and political recognition of the country's ethnic diversity have resulted in growing tolerance, Afro-Colombians continue to experience racial discrimination in the nation's cities, for example in the form of taxi drivers who refuse to stop for Black clients, police abuse, verbal insults, denial of access to certain public spaces (e.g., restaurants, clubs), and even landlords or property owners who refuse to rent or sale to Afro-Colombians (Dennis 2012, 80). In the end, Black Colombians—either on the nation's coasts or in its cities—endure the highest rates of poverty and unemployment while living in some of the most violent and insecure rural and urban areas in the country. There are noticeable disparities between Black and non-Black citizens with respect to access to proper nutrition, medical attention, and other public services. And naturally, difficulty in satisfying basic needs goes hand in hand with limited access to an adequate education. Unfortunately, the illiteracy rate among Black communities is much higher than the national average (Angel-Ajani 2008, 284; Murillo Urrutia 2001).

ChocQuibTown is composed of three Afro-Colombian performers, Tostao, Goyo, and Slow, along with the rest of the band members. These three artists are from the Department of Chocó, on the Pacific coast, which serves as the inspiration for the group's name; "Choc" comes from Chocó and "Quib" refers to Quibdó, the department's capital. Along with having to bear many of the challenges and hardships outlined above, these artists also represent a generation of Black Colombians who have come of age under the current context of globalization, as a socioeconomic and cultural phenomenon that, among other things, inundates the world's youth with U.S. cultural products. Accordingly, cultural memory, as much as cultural identity, now is constructed through the selection and adaptation of goods, images, and texts produced by the global cultural industries and the "collective cultural experiences to which the latter give rise" (Bennett 2010, 247). When considering today's diversity of media and the range of products that contribute to the making and framing of cultural memory and social identities, popular music undoubtedly has come to play a significant role.

Like many members of the African diaspora who historically have been excluded from literature as an expressive medium belonging almost solely to dominant (White) culture, Afro-Colombian artists have often turned to music as their chosen form of cultural expression.[2] Today, many young Afro-Colombian musicians look toward Hip Hop as an artistic medium for recovering and performing cultural memories and social identities. The Pacific littoral, in particular, is recognized for its musical wealth as demonstrated by the growing interest in its "traditional" music (e.g., *chirimía, currulao*) along with the national recognition now given to many of its rappers, especially those hailing from the region's major urban centers such as Cali, Buenaventura, and Quibdó. Although U.S. Hip Hop and rap arrived to the nation early in the 1980s through various entry points more or less simultaneously thanks to cross-cultural exchanges and international marketing campaigns, one of the

---

2. For more information on the obstacles that hinder Afro-Colombian literary expressions, see Dennis (2011).

most widely accepted explanations for Hip Hop's arrival to Colombia claims that it appeared for the first time in the port city of Buenaventura. In the documentary *Resistencia: Hip Hop in Colombia* (2002), produced by Tom Feiling, Dr. Ganja of Asilo 38 explains how Hip Hop and rap arrived through Buenaventura thanks to stowaways who traveled by boat to and from the United States, bringing with them Hip Hop magazines, styles, and music from the likes of the Fat Boys and Run-DMC. It is not surprising, therefore, that one of the nation's first recognized Hip Hop groups was Los Generales R&R from Buenaventura (Dennis 2012, 40).

In the end, U.S. Hip Hop and its commodified forms of "Black" resistance have come to provide key discursive strategies, aesthetic tools, and artistic frameworks within which many Afro-Colombian articulations of cultural memory are now embedded. ChocQuibTown, in particular, belongs to a generation of Afro-Colombian artists who have found inspiration in the music, rhetorical devices, and racial discourses of numerous U.S. rappers. Like many of their contemporaries, they reclaim dignity in their ethnicity, in part, based on their identification with Black U.S. Hip Hop artists such as Public Enemy, Lauryn Hill, Busta Rhymes, 50 Cent, Snoop Dogg, 2Pac, Jay-Z, Common, Kanye West, Mos Def, Talib Kweli, and Nas, among others (Dennis 2012, 40). In this sense, while Astrid Erll fittingly declares that the study of cultural memory requires an "exploration of unintentional and implicit ways of remembering . . . or of inherently non-narrative, for example visual or bodily, forms of memory" (Erll 2011, 2), I believe Hip Hop and popular music in general provide unique mediums for the (re)construction of cultural memory due to the ways in which they combine narrative (lyrics) and nonnarrative forms, such as music styles and sounds, video, images, and even the body, for instance, through dance.

The *Traditium*: The Product

ChocQuibTown's musical productions—from its forms to its narratives—evince not only the influence of their everyday lives within their sociocultural context (i.e., the Pacific littoral) but also the ways in which they necessarily negotiate with various external factors such as dominant discourse on race, personal experiences with racial discrimination, and the pejorative manner in which the media traditionally has represented Afro-Colombians. The racist behaviors and attitudes outlined above, for example, point to the continued impact of racial meanings inherited from a colonial nomenclature historically used to establish and maintain socio-racial hierarchies based on color codes that assign privilege to lighter skin color. In other words, despite any degree of social progress over the years, racial categories in Colombia are still largely organized in social hierarchies in which different phenotypic characteristics (specifically skin color) are assigned attributes of social status: Whiteness or lighter skin color signals beauty, wealth, purity, progress, and sophistication; Blackness denotes ugliness, poverty, impurity, and primitivism (Viveros Vigoya 2004, 84). Largely for this reason, ChocQuibTown produces music with the intention of awakening racial consciousness so as to inspire ethnic pride and greater acceptance of being Black in a country where darker skin color historically has implied inferiority. As a way of contributing to the construction of positive social identities, ChocQuibTown often creates music that manifests and celebrates memories based on daily experiences in their communities, such as those heard in the tracks "De dónde vengo yo" and "Oro." These songs, along with their videos (accessible on YouTube), illustrate how popular music provides a medium for performing marginalized cultural memories through a combination of sound, images, narrative, and dance.

Both tracks reveal a desire to recover and perform certain histories and lived experiences that are relevant to the cultural memory of Afro-Colombian communities of the Pacific coastal region. More precisely, in these two songs we discover a yearning to highlight specific memories that address the region's wealth of mineral resources along with its long history of racial exploitation, memories that many members of dominant culture would rather ignore if not forget. As previously mentioned, the album is also titled *Oro* (Gold), but not in the bling-bling sense associated with more contemporary, commercial Hip Hop from the United States. On the CD cover, for instance, the artists are bathed in gold dust not only as a tribute to the region's mineral wealth but also as a way to symbolize the human, cultural, and musical value of Afro-Colombian people. As Tostao affirmed in an interview, "We wanted to not only put the spotlight on the song but also the album itself by naming it *Oro,* as a way to say that we are people of gold—right?—people of value . . . and music of value too."[3]

As previously stated, the Pacific littoral is characterized by its predominantly Black population descended from slaves imported to the region primarily for working in the gold mines. Due to the inhospitable terrain and often-bellicose Indigenous communities, during the colonial period the small "White" or European population tended to remain in the region's urban mining centers. Furthermore, by the seventeenth century, Amerindians were outnumbered by

---

3. Tostao, in a discussion with the author via Skype, June 25, 2014. Translated into English by the author.

Afro-Colombians, a Black population composed of both slaves and *libres* who had purchased their freedom with earnings made from their mining activities during days of rest (Wade 2002, 4). Unfortunately, for most of the country's history, mining companies have exploited Afro-Colombian and Indigenous labor with the approval of both regional and national governments. A noteworthy example is that of the Compañía Minera Chocó Pacífico S. A., a subsidiary of the International Mining Corporation of New York, which obtained the right to mine Colombian territory from British, French, and Belgian companies that had been operating in the region since the 1880s. Sadly, these mining companies all too often have destroyed traditional economies, transformed local cultures, and devastated the environment (Mosquera Rentería 2009).

In the track "De dónde vengo yo," winner of a Latin Grammy, Choc-QuibTown raps about their identities strongly tied to their geographical region:

> De dónde vengo yo
> La cosa no es fácil pero siempre igual sobrevivimos
> Vengo yo
> De tanta lucha siempre con la nuestra nos salimos
> Vengo yo
> De aquí se habla mal pero todo está mucho mejor
> Vengo yo
> Tenemos la lluvia, el frío, el calor
>
> Where I come from
> It is not easy but we still survive
> I come
> From so much struggle but we find a way to move forward
> I come
> People speak poorly about this place but everything here is much better
> I come
> We have rain, cold, and heat.

ChocQuibTown admits that life in the Pacific coastal region is not easy due to various obstacles such as poverty, racial marginalization, and even self-discrimination. This track defines Black people of the Pacific littoral—particularly Chocó—not only as fighters and survivors but also as decent and cheerful people despite being surrounding by so much suffering. The tone of the track is surprisingly upbeat and celebratory, and there is even a comedic element, for example in the way they mock certain attitudes and behaviors allegedly common to the people of the region (alcohol consumption, gossip, etc.). Nevertheless, the song's humor is not meant to belittle anyone or down-play their community's plight; rather it represents a type of survival mechanism for overcoming the social and psychological effects caused by living under such precarious conditions. More relevant to the topic of this chapter, however, is that ChocQuibTown also raps about regional biodiversity and the displacement of Black communities as a consequence of the fight for control of these lands rich in natural resources:

Goyo:
Monte, culebra, máquina de guerra
Desplazamiento por intereses en la tierra
Subienda de pescaʼo, agua por toʼo laʼo
Selva espesa que ni el Discovery ha explotaʼo

Tostao:
¡Eh! ¡Oh! Minas llenas de oro y platino
¡Oh! Reyes en la biodiversidad
¡Eh! ¡Oh! Bochinche entre todos los vecinos
¡Eh! ¡Oh! Y en deportes ni hablar

Goyo:
Mountains, snakes, war machine
Displacement due to interests in the land
Schools of fish, water everywhere
Thick jungle that not even the Discovery Channel has exploited

Tostao:
Eh! Oh! Mines full of gold and platinum
Oh! Kings of biodiversity
Eh! Oh! Gossip among all the neighbors
Eh! Oh! And in sports, no need to comment

Despite the difficulties that these communities endure, this track applauds their capacity to (re)create and maintain cultural peculiarities that nurture their ethnic-racial identities (Dennis 2012, 140). Cultural memory here implies the (re)presentation of shared cultural norms, ethnic-racial idiosyncrasies, and daily lived experiences. Above all, the cultural identity elaborated in this song depicts social identities tightly bound to a region known for its mineral wealth and its long history of conflict, violence, and even displacement due to competing interests over its mineral-rich lands.

This specific history is more explicitly addressed in the music and video for the track "Oro." The video commences with a group of young Afro-Colombians mining a small river for gold under the watchful eye of the non-Black supervisor. Goyo stops working, turns to the camera, and narrates a local history about outsiders with strange accents who enter the region, promising prosperity in exchange for gold, only to later rob Afro-Colombians of their wealth. Slow likewise condemns the outsider's dishonest actions, defiantly demanding that he leave. Goyo then declares that despite her poverty and suffering, her cultural identity is intimately attached to this land on which she is determined to stay.

> Goyo:
> Con mi oro se ha acaba'o
> Los dueños son empleao's
> Más pobreza ha llega'o
> La inocencia se ha marcha'o
> Y de aquí no me voy, voy
> De esta tierra yo soy, soy
> Mi alma es como los ríos
> Camino recorri'o

> Goyo:
> With my gold, it's all come to an end
> The owners are now the workers
> More poverty has arrived
> Innocence has vanished
> I'm not leaving from here
> I'm from this land
> My soul is like the rivers
> Running through these parts

The subsequent scene of young Black workers revolting and marching out of the mine reinforces the track's message of resistance. On one hand, this performance serves as a way to remember these exploitative practices while challenging dominant versions of history that often attempt to gloss over the nation's ugly past of racial oppression. On the other hand, performing this memory also builds and preserves a link between the community's ancestral past and the present, for example through the images of young Afro-Colombians taking part in artisanal mining practices passed down through the generations along with the successive scenes of both young and old looking into the camera and reproaching those "outsiders" for having taken their gold.

The music and video's contribution to cultural memory is further strengthened through the incorporation of *currulao,* a traditional genre of music characterized by the sound of the marimba associated with Black communities of the Pacific littoral. According to Peter Wade (1993), *currulao* "is one of the most undiluted and independent black genres . . . Nowadays, the term refers exclusively to the Pacific coast genre, and its Africanness is quite apparent" (275). *Curralao*'s instrumentation consists of the marimba (wooden xylophone), the *bombo* (double-sided bass drum), two *cununos* (conical drums designated male and female), and the *guasá* (a cylindrical bamboo rattle). The video also includes scenes of young Afro-Colombians dressed in traditional garb participating in "folkloric" dance. The musical material, aesthetic styles, and forms of dance together evoke memories that link Afro-Colombian musical and cultural traditions to present-day ethnic identity. If an objective of cultural memory is the formation and preservation of social identities, this track and video emphasize certain cultural similarities and continuities as a way of showing that the Afro-Colombian ethnic group continues to exist. In fact, participation in these musical and cultural practices is a way for youth to establish and reaffirm their belonging to the community. However, in both the music and the video, the traditional elements are combined with Hip Hop, along with contemporary jazz and modern dance, which simultaneously place the performers' cultural memories and identities within a more contemporary and global scenario suggesting that the performers and their audiences also belong to the larger African diaspora.

Media and artistic forms constantly are evolving as a result of new technologies, "developments in the media landscape at large," and "the ever-growing repertoire of sense-making tools" (Erll and Rigney 2012, 3). Thus, "all representations of the past draw on available media technologies, on existent media products, on patterns of representation and medial aesthetics" (ibid.). Memorial media and artistic mediums borrow from, incorporate, critique, and refashion earlier forms, and under globalization there has been an intensified diversification of the ways in which the past is remembered and represented. People today have access to multiple mediums and frames of reference through which to reorganize and perform cultural memories (Bennett 2010, 246). Consequently, when interpreting the past through the use of more contemporary tools, artists inevitably contribute new meanings and nuances to cultural memory, which also influences the understanding of the present and the subsequent formation of social identities.

Due to the strong "folkloric" element of this particular song, some critics may argue that "Oro" is not a Hip Hop track. Without a doubt, this song sounds nothing like rap from the United States. Nevertheless, it serves as an example of how U.S. Hip Hop passes through a mode of transculturation, subjecting it to a type of transformation resulting from the incorporation of local Afro-Colombian cultural and musical material. At the same time, "Oro" also evinces the way in which U.S Hip Hop nurtures local Afro-Colombian music, for example through Slow's rapped verse in addition to certain styles and attitudes generally associated with Hip Hop. In the same interview, Tostao affirmed: "In a way, Hip Hop. . . in the beginning, had the intention of questioning certain things that were wrong with society." According to him, more than a specific musical style, "Hip Hop in itself was more about an attitude, and this song has that Hip Hop attitude . . . The element we used was traditional music, but that's an element that's always present in our music, in our way of making Hip Hop." Furthermore, Tostao explained, "the song's topic talks about a type of rebellion . . . The song has a background of anti-establishment music. It has a background of, let's say, rebellion music. The video couldn't be light . . . The subtext is a more political, more anti-status quo, rebellious theme."[4]

In this musical production, therefore, we observe that traditional music—as an essential part of daily life—provides young Afro-Colombians with certain schemata for evoking and articulating the past. However, global meanings of Hip Hop as "Black music" of resistance now also mediate, to a degree, the manner in which these artists perform Afro-Colombian cultural memories, thereby locating them in a much more transnational frame of reference. Their transcultural music exemplifies how they borrow from Hip Hop and other technologies, which are combined with local artifacts such as traditional music resulting in a distinct version of cultural memory that speaks to the lived experiences and emerging identities of today's Afro-Colombian youth of the Pacific littoral. In this way, ChocQuibTown's transcultural music not only traces connections made between past and present generations, but also maps cultural exchanges taking place among diasporic communities.

It also is worthwhile, at this point, to briefly consider the contributions of Pierre Nora to the studies of cultural memory given that one could argue that these two tracks also demonstrate the ways in which music and its performance (as symbolic actions) represent important places of cultural memory. This music and its traditional elements tied to the geographical location celebrated in these tracks—the Pacific littoral—awaken memories, images,

---

4. Tostao in a discussion with the author via Skype, June 25, 2014. Translated into English by the author.

and meanings related to Afro-Colombian identity. Although Nora's theories are limited to the nation, many academics have expanded his notions so as to analyze places of memory under diasporic and transnational perspectives that better signal complex transcultural networks of contemporary places of memory (Erll 2011, 26). Evidently, under present-day globalization and the deterritorialization that it produces, ChocQuibTown's transcultural music with its Hip Hop elements also denotes a fragmented image of both Afro-Colombian histories and identities. Globalization has generated the pluralization of cultural memories, places of memory, and social identities. Therefore, the construction of one coherent narrative has become much more complicated, if not impossible. In any case, this type of consideration regarding the selection and combination of artifacts, discourses, and symbols that Afro-Colombians now use to (re)construct their memories and identities reveals a great deal about the psyche of younger generations, along with their desires and apprehensions.

The Impetus of This Afro-Colombian Cultural Memory

With respect to the wishes and concerns of these artists and their audiences, it is vital to examine those factors that have provoked the recovery of this specific history. Cultural memories are often articulated based on a community's current needs, and this particular cultural memory has been recovered partly in response to Colombia's recent gold rush, spurred by the increase in the price of commodities after the recent global financial crisis. With the rise in the international price of gold, mining has become an even more lucrative business in Colombia. For this reason, President Juan Manuel Santos identified gold mining as one of the motors running Colombia's economy, and the recent free trade agreement (Tratado de Libre Comercio or TLC) with the United States will only intensify multinational and U.S. investments in the mining sector (Carabalí et al. 2012).

However, the rising value of gold has also generated new conflicts over land on which Afro-Colombians have subsisted for centuries through small-scale artisanal mining and agriculture. Additionally, one should keep in mind that the understanding of ethnic-racial identities in Colombia has undergone fundamental changes due to processes of constitutional reform that were initiated in the late 1980s when the country's leaders were trying to create a much more tolerant international image of the nation-state. Ironically, it was during that same period that national and multinational companies—motivated by neoliberal economic reform—intensified their efforts to exploit the mineral wealth of the Pacific littoral, thus invading many of the territories histori-cally occupied by Afro-Colombian and Indigenous inhabitants. These events, among others, encouraged the political mobilization of Afro-Colombian and Indigenous communities in their efforts to promote the rights of ethnic-racial minorities. Eventually, the negotiations that took place between Afro-Colombian groups and the nation-state influenced the Constitution of 1991 and Law 70 of 1993 (Law of the Black Communities), which recognizes Afro-Colombians as a distinct ethnic group while supposedly protecting Afro-Colombian and Indigenous ancestral lands of the Pacific littoral.

Nevertheless, Colombia's Constitutional Court has declared that the state is the rightful owner of all renewable and nonrenewable natural resources found in the land's soil and subsoil. Accordingly, in 2000 the Colombian gov-ernment accelerated the granting of mining concessions to national and inter-national investors without the consent of local Afro-Colombian or Indigenous residents. To make matters worse, paramilitary groups have invaded many of these areas, committing human rights abuses and displacing entire com-munities, which has led to the violent reorganization of economic activities throughout the region. Meanwhile, companies interested in exploiting the ter-ritory's mineral wealth have simply taken advantage of the region's instability as an opportunity to expand their mining operations (Carabalí et al. 2012). Put simply, the recovery of this cultural memory through popular music has been inspired by current events that now threaten artisanal gold mining, and with it, the livelihoods and cultural identities of the members of these partic-ular Afro-Colombian communities at a time when the national government is supposed to protect them.

Conclusion

Cultural memory is shaped by the social contexts in which it operates, while, at the same time, the mediums used—such as literature, cinema, or popu-lar music—offer frameworks or schemata that help give meaning to both the experience and the memories. Culture depends largely on memory and its symbols, and for the members of the African diaspora, music is one of the most valuable symbols through which cultural memory and ethnic identity have historically been recovered, constructed, performed, and maintained. Without a doubt, this chapter has highlighted the importance of the mate-rial dimension of culture and the manner in which artifacts and symbols—in this case, popular music—evoke memories, establish cultural continuity, and nourish social identities.

Cultural memory, in essence, can be understood as a field of struggle in which memories of different social groups compete for a place in History. Thus, the power of cultural memory is largely found within the conscious decision to select particular memories to be given importance in the public sphere (Rodríguez and Fortier 2007, 12). In the case of ChocQuibTown, these artists have decided to recover specific memories regarding the mineral wealth of their territories and the exploitation of Afro-Colombian labor. Tostao stated: "We wanted to call some attention to this topic that isn't taken into account . . . and it is political because one almost has to accept that Colombia allowed the gold to be taken."[5] Memories only become collective when they form part of a continuous process through which they "are shared with the help of symbolic artifacts that mediate between individuals" and, consequently, "create communality across both space and time" (Erll and Rigney 2012, 1). By way of their musical expressions, ChocQuibTown brings very specific memories into public consciousness in the same way that novels or films often spark public debates on historical topics that previously had been forgotten. Therefore, their music is more than a passive conveyor of information (Erll and Rigney 2012, 1). Their musical productions demonstrate that cultural memory represents an important "survival mechanism" for marginalized groups when it forms part of an artistic expression charged with emotions used to build collective identities (Rodríguez and Fortier 2007, 10). Additionally, it is through reiterations of cultural memories "across different platforms in the public arena (print, image, internet, commemorative rituals) that the topics takes root in the community," thereby setting the agenda for future collective remembrance (Erll and Rigney 2012, 2–3). Through songs like "De dónde vengo yo" and "Oro," ChocQuibTown contributes to a process through which "individuals understand how their selves in the past link with their selves in the present—and are also able to forge pathways that connect with their lives in the future" (Bennett 2010, 258). In other words, ChocQuibTown recovers and performs cultural memories and lived experiences that future generations will access in order to build and maintain their own cultural identities.

Last, for "those with power, memories can serve ideological purposes; while for those without, recollecting contrary memories can be a subversive act and one constitutive of class consciousness" (Mageo 2001, 3). Instead of basing their narratives and musical expressions solely on the country's master narratives, ChocQuibTown chooses to highlight specific memories and cultural expressions based on their own lived experiences within their local communities

---

5. Tostao in a discussion with the author via Skype, June 25, 2014. Translated into English by the author.

(though positioned, of course, within a transnational context and the fragmentation that it implies for "imagined communities"). Their articulation of marginalized cultural memories destabilizes the instrumental homogeneity of hegemonic cultural memory. For example, the musical forms and lyrical narratives found in ChocQuibTown's tracks "De dónde vengo yo" and "Oro" underline personal testimonies and cultural memories that indeed challenge hegemonic memories regarding both past and present-day racial relations in the country (Dennis 2011, 150). Above all, this music reveals some of the desires, needs, worries, and struggles of newer generations of Afro-Colombians. The cultural memories performed in this music indicate that, despite any degree of progress made as a result of constitutional reform and the country's move toward an officially sanctioned politics of multiculturalism, the promises of ethnic-racial tolerance and social equality have yet to be achieved, and consequently, Black communities must continue their fight for social justice.

Bibliography

Angel-Ajani, Asale. 2008. "Out of Chaos: Afro-Colombian Peace Communities and the Realities of War." In *Transnational Blackness: Navigating the Global Color Line,* edited by Manning Marable and Vanessa Agard-Jones. New York: Palgrave Macmillan. 281–90.

Bennett, Andy. 2010. "Popular Music, Cultural Memory and Everyday Aesthetics." In *The Philosophical and Cultural Theories of Music,* edited by Eduardo De La Fuente and Peter Murphy. Boston: Brill. 243–62.

Carabalí, Clemencia, Francia Márquz, Gimena Sánchez, Anthony Dest, and Charo Mina Rojas. 2012, January 25. "Illegal Mining and Paramilitary Violence in Afro-Colombian Territories: A Letter to the U.S. Congress on Continued Attacks on Afro-Colombians' Rights." Washington Office on Latin America: Promoting Human Rights, Democracy, and Social Justice. http://www.wola.org/publications/illegal_mining_and_paramilitary_violence_in_afro_colombian_territories.

Dennis, Christopher. 2011. "The Current and Future State of Afro-Colombian Prose Fiction." *Afro-Hispanic Review* 30(1): 81–100.

———. 2012. *Afro-Colombian Hip Hop: Globalization, Transcultural Music, and Ethnic Identities.* Lanham, MD: Lexington.

———. 2014. "Introduction: Locating Hip Hop's Place within Latin American Cultural Studies." *alter/nativas: Latin American Cultural Studies Journal* Spring 2. http://alternativas.osu.edu/en/issues/spring-2014/essays1/dennis.html.

Erll, Astrid. 2010. "Cultural Memory Studies: An Introduction." In *A Companion to Cultural Memory Studies,* edited by Astrid Erll and Ansgar Nünning. Berlin: De Gruyter. 1–18.

———. 2011. *Memory in Culture.* New York: Palgrave Macmillan.

Erll, Astrid, and Ann Rigney. 2012. "Introduction: Cultural Memory and Its Dynamics." In *Mediation, Remediation, and the Dynamics of Cultural Memory,* edited by Astrid Erll and Ann Rigney. Berlin: De Gruyter. 1–14.

Hirsch, Marianne, and Valerie Smith. 2007. "From Feminism and Cultural Memory: An Introduction." In *Theories of Memory: A Reader,* edited by Michael Rossington and Anne Whitehead. Baltimore: Johns Hopkins University Press. 223–29.

Mageo, Jeannette Marie. 2001. "Introduction." In *Cultural Memory: Reconfiguring History and Identity in the Postcolonial Pacific,* edited by Jeannette Marie Mageo. Honolulu: University of Hawai'i Press. 1–10.

Mosquera Mosquera, Juan de Dios. 2000. *Las comunidades negras de Colombia hacia el siglo XXI: Historia, realidad y organización.* Bogotá: Docentes Editores.

Mosquera Rentería, José Eulícer. 2009, February. "Exploitation of Natural Resources in Afro-Colombian Territories and the Free Trade Agreement (FTA)." Colombia Support Network (CSN). http://colombiasupport.net/2009/02/exploitation-of-natural-resources-in-afro-colombian-territories-and-the-free-trade-agreement-fta/.

Murillo Urrutia, Luis Gilberto. 2001, February 23. "El Choco: The African Heart of Colombia." Isla Information Services Latin America. http://isla.igc.org/SpecialRpts/SR2murillo.html.

Nubia Bello, Martha, and Nayibe Peña Frade. 2004. "Migración y desplazamiento forzado. De la exclusión a la desintegración de las comunidades indígenas, afrocolombianas y campesinas." In *Utopía para los excluidos: El multiculturalismo en África y América Latina,* edited by Jaime Arocha. Bogotá: Facultad de Ciencias Humanas UN. 395–410.

Resistencia: Hip Hop in Colombia. 2002. Directed by Tom Feiling. United Kingdom: Faction Films. Video Cassette.

Rodríguez, Jeanette, and Ted Fortier. 2007. *Cultural Memory: Resistance, Faith & Identity.* Austin: University of Texas Press.

Trigo, Abril. 2003. *Memorias migrantes: testimonios y ensayos sobre la diáspora uruguaya.* Montevideo, Uruguay: Ediciones Trilce.

Uribe, Jaime Jaramillo. 2002. "La población africana en el desarrollo económico de Colombia." In *Encuentros en la diversidad* (Tomo 1). Bogotá: Ministerio de Cultura. 31–38.

Viveros Vigoya, María. 2004. "Nuevas formas de representación y viejos estereotipos raciales en los comerciales publicitarios colombianos." In *Mouts Pour Nègres Maux Des Noir(e)s Enjeux Socio-Symboliques de la Nomination en Amérique Latine,* 83–99. Perpignan Cedex: Presses Universitaires de Perpignan, 2004.

Wade, Peter. 1993. *Blackness and Race Mixture: The Dynamics of Racial Identity in Colombia.* Baltimore: Johns Hopkins University Press, 1993.

———. 1999. "Trabajando con la cultura: grupos de rap e identidad negra en Cali." In *De montes, de ríos y ciudades: territorios e identidades de la gente negra en Colombia,* edited by J. Camacho and E. Restrepo. Bogotá: Natura-Ecofondo-Icanh. 263–86.

———. 2002. "Introduction: The Colombian Pacific in Perspective." *The Journal of Latin American Anthropology* 7(2): 2–33.

Discography

ChocQuibTown. 2010. *Oro.* Compact Disc. Nacional Records.

chapter 7

Now Let's Shake to This

Viral Power and Flow from Harlem to São Paulo

Honey Crawford

*¡C*on los terroristas!* A lone masked figure hovers in the midst of an otherwise orderly place of business. He performs an oddball dance that fails to faze the status quo. *¡Con los terroristas!* With the terrorists! He oscillates against an electro-synthesized track that chants of turmoil. *¡Terroris-ta! ¡Ta! ¡Ta! ¡Ta—ta—ta—ta!* Yet the bodies populating the space pay no mind. There is a booming call to motion. *And do the Harlem Shake!*[1]

Perhaps the most infectious in an ongoing thread of viral performance videos, *The Harlem Shake* meme shows groups of coworkers, strangers, and peers breaking order with a jump-cut to costumed pandemonium. In this 2013 trend that was credited with over 12,000 YouTube uploads per week, nonsensical zombie dances and furniture humping took on the title "Harlem Shake" and quickly came to represent a structured format for inciting chaos with acts of irreverent and absurd humor (Kaufman 2013). Festering under said absurdity were inklings of a legendary artistic community's misrepresentation and an

---

1. "Harlem Shake [BEST ONES!]," YouTube video, 5:29, posted by "GoodClipsDaily," February 11, 2013, https://www.youtube.com/watch?v=8f7wj_RcqYk.

unsettling hint of hipster racism.[2] Nonetheless, for roughly thirty seconds the meme begged its spectator to disregard history, context, or propriety and *shake!*

As if to affirm the suspicions of anyone familiar with the true Harlem Shake and its origins, man-on-the-street interviews followed shortly asking Harlem for her thoughts on the phenomenon. *That's not the Shake, B!* Harlem's residents found the meme less than comical, seeing through its layer of seemingly harmless play to uncover insult at the core of this viral sensation. Responses to the trend pinpointed the calculated disregard or what George Lipsitz might identify as strategic anti-essentialism[3] at play within the meme's given format. Harlem responded:

> That shit's kind of bugged out. That's definitely not the Harlem Shake . . . I feel like they're trying to disrespect us. They don't live in Harlem. They don't come from Harlem . . . It's an absolute mockery is what it was, because there's actually as sense of um . . . um . . . rhythm that goes along with it . . . It's actually an art form, a dance art form that doesn't have the respect that it should deserve . . . They're disrespecting Harlem's swag number one, because number one, Harlem wouldn't be dressing like this . . . They're basically taking what we do, like our dances, and making a joke of it . . . I feel this is really a violation towards Harlem and anybody that's in Harlem over something that we really take serious. This is not, you know, dancing. This is really a lifestyle . . . So this is another thing, another vehicle for America to take off on and make money on, and I'm sure there'll be some corporate person somewhere that's gonna capitalize on this and gonna be able to put money in it and it's gonna take off. . . That's not the Harlem shake, like we need our respect . . . Stop please . . . Find a new hobby. Stop ya bullshit . . . Stop that shit! . . . Do you know the history of Harlem? . . . Come to Harlem. Play some P Diddy with G-Depp, Harlem Shake routine throwback, you know, *Special Delivery,* you know. If you don't know that, then I don't know what to tell you my man, for real. Harlem's where it used to be, and it needs to come back.[4]

---

2. Here I reference Carmen van Kerckhove's 2006 *Racialicious* blog and ongoing discussion of liberal White artists using irony and satire to express overtly racist jokes, uses of blackface, and so forth.

3. Resistance to cultural identity through the adoption of another group's cultural form. This term is coined by the cultural theorist George Lipsitz.

4. "Harlem Reacts to Viral 'Harlem Shake' Videos—That Aint the Real Harlem Shake," YouTube video, 5:23, posted by "SchleppFilms," February 18, 2013, https://www.youtube.com /watch?v=IGH2HEgWppc. This citation shows selected responses from various individuals. Shifts from person to person are marked by an ellipse.

Fully conscious of the "practices that racialize space and spatialize race," this small cross-section of Harlem's collective voice, male and female, African and Latino/a American, ranging from teens to middle-age, recognized the position of safety and privilege their outside appropriators took in staging "mockeries" of their own lived experience (Lipsitz 2011, 6). *Do you know the history of Harlem? Come to Harlem*—an invitation to internet "shakers" to resituate themselves spatially, without the place-bound privilege that Whiteness, class, or cyber anonymity affords. This challenge recalled impositions on Harlem's physical and cultural space by a previous era of hipster irreverence, awakening Langston Hughes's "Note on Commercial Theater" in the reactions of residents. Hughes's words, forever entangled with Harlem's collective voice, chime in declaring, "You've taken my blues and gone—. . . and you've fixed 'em. They don't sound like me." Ironically, this cyber-era format found its material and geographic footing in White America's throwback source of inspiration—fixing, as Hughes put it, the music and dance of Harlem, fixing what was designed to *shake.*

As the meme publicly affirmed the virality of cultural appropriation, this snapshot of Harlem's residents zoomed in on local allegiance, testing the viewer's capacity to decipher coded language, gesture, and cultural references. Their words drew virtual borders situating their appropriators in imagined locales—*that's West 4th Street Dancing*—and excluding all who had never lived in Harlem—*If you're not from Harlem, don't do anything that's associated with it . . . Stick to your roots.* Uniformly rooted in language of location, these responses made no reference to the predictable social indicators of race and class, nor was the global scope of the meme addressed by claiming any identification with nationality. The integrity of a highly localized geographic identity was under attack, and the defense of this localized identity shaped a small and firmly unified front.

To be clear, the defense of locale in Hip Hop culture since its 1970s inception in the South Bronx has been a central theme and motivating force of rap scenes across the globe. An especially ingrained image of this impassioned territorialism would be the final verse of Naughty by Nature's 1991 track "Ghetto Bastards (Everything's Gonna Be Alright)," where the music video concludes with frontman Treach, Vinny Rock, and DJ Kay Gee pointing machetes at the camera outside East Orange, New Jersey's "Illtown" projects. Treach wraps up the song's grim narrative with a direct address to the spectator: "If you aint never been to the ghetto, don't ever come to the ghetto. 'Cause you wouldn't understand the ghetto, so stay the fuck out of the ghetto." Mincing no words, the group that epitomized early '90s crossover appeal with mainstream hits such as "Hip Hop Hooray" and "O. P. P." secured their street credibility by inscribing the boundary between outward interest in ghetto life and the reality of lived ghetto experience.

Some twenty-two years later and across the continental divide of North and South America, São Paulo, Brazil's wildly successful freestyle MC, Emicida, would offer a spin on the negotiation of spatialized privilege. With the hook of his 2013 track *"Gueto,"* Emicida and *funk*[5] artist Guime spell out alternate terms of inclusion, chanting *"O zé povinho só pode falar, mas o mundo todo pode ver, onde estiver onde pisar, nóis sempre vai ser gueto!"* Here the *zé-povinho,* the folkloric common man of Portugal, or colloquially the curious self-interested "hater" of everyday life, is put on notice. *O zé povinho* "can only *talk* about it, but the whole world can see—wherever we are, wherever we walk, we will always *be* ghetto." Emicida with Guime, like Treach and countless other MCs, stands guard against the trafficking of his cultural reality. Yet his defense of locale speaks on behalf of another population of marginalized Black youth of the Americas. Emicida's terms for performing *gueto,* while limiting the inclusion of outsiders, offers mobility to those who *are* ghetto. The ontological weight of this negotiation, *being* ghetto, is underscored in the final chant of his song "Bang!" from the same album, *O Glorioso Retorno de Quem Nunca Esteve Aqui (The Glorious Return of He Who Was Never Here).* Emicida again ponders the terms of ghetto existence against politics of location with the repeated verse *"nem todo mundo que tá é; nem todo mundo que é tá."* As if reassuring himself, he drills home his point by juxtaposing significations of Portuguese's two verbal forms of "being"—*ser* and *estar.* "Not everyone who is here *is*; not everyone who *is* is here." Read against Treach's warning to never come to the ghetto if you have never been, Emicida's concluding chant speaks to those who have in fact ventured to the ghettos, or *favelas,* of his city; it accounts for the inevitable inward and outward flow of cultural interests. You may come to the ghetto, but you may not be ghetto. Furthermore, those who *are* ghetto may traverse boundaries with the assurance that *being* ghetto moves with them—*nem todo mundo que é tá.*

Similar to Paul Gilroy's (1993b) turn to a Parliament Funkadelic sensibility, Emicida's perception of the marginalized Black experience is diasporic, not easily located, and open to the possibility that those who *are* ghetto may move as "one nation under a groove." A language of mobility, trafficking, and multidirectional flow reveals the potential for viral Hip Hop performance to press against and "shake" established compartmentalization and nationalist identity constructs between Black communities of the United States and Brazil. Such creative interplay across the Black American diaspora encourages the highly

---

5. *Funk* here refers to the Brazilian musical genre originating in *baile funk* parties of Rio de Janeiro. Also known as *funk carioca* or *favela funk,* this genre is not to be mistaken for funk music of the United States.

racialized spaces of the *favela* and the ghetto to engage in acts of reciprocity with a mutual harvesting of cultural and historical models of dissent.

I'll Show You How to Do This, Son!

A group of young Harlem dancers calling themselves "The Original Harlem Shakers" quickly joined the aforementioned virtual drama with an agenda to take their "blues" back. In a collaborative production with New York's Power 105 radio station titled "Harlem Reclaims the Shake," The Original Harlem Shakers physically clarified any misrepresentation of who and what Harlem is.[6] Their video adopted the format of the meme with Power 105's DJ Envy playing the role of an oddball instigator among a nonresponsive group of teens. Tipping their hand with the caption "This aint Harlem," the meme cuts to a frenzy of sharp rhythmic artistry boasting back at spectators with the unlikely proposition to give their talents a try. Kid the Wiz's original track underscores the laughable impossibility of this challenge with a repeated bridge, "I'll show you how to do this, son," as each dancer flaunts an impenetrable individuality framed by sporadic returns to the shake.

Showing their spectators how to "do this" is a well-played mockery in itself, and the potential power in reclaiming objects of appropriation is drilled into the spectator's consciousness with the repeated call "Now let's shake to this!" We could argue that "shaking to" one's own exploitation has marked the unpredictability, wit, and emboldened artistry of Black performances of resistance. Once again, the legacy of Harlem is invoked, and the spectator is reminded of Zora Neale Hurston's (2000) musings over the "Characteristics of Negro Expression." With drama positioned as "that thing" that permeates the Negro's "entire self," Hurston locates the great Negro Theater in the unsung performances of Harlem's jook joints. She writes, "The real Negro theatre is in the Jooks and the cabarets. Self-conscious individuals may turn away the eye and say, 'Let us search elsewhere for our dramatic art.' Let 'em search. They certainly won't find it" (43). If the jook sets the stage for Black expression, the great dramatists of the Black urban experience would certainly be its dancers. With choreographies both improvised and carefully timed, The Original Harlem Shakers use their viral reclamation to stage a resistance to the misrepresentation of yet another object of cultural history. They do not address the spectator with contempt, but rather use the playfulness and "dynamic

---

6. "Harlem Reclaims Back the Harlem Shake," YouTube video, 4:09, posted by "Kalablindings," February 28, 2013, https://www.youtube.com/watch?v=XdDUV97RlX4.

suggestion" of the Shake to protect their community's creative repertoire. The Original Harlem Shakers in their response shake what the meme format aimed to fix. More so, they shake the global audience's awareness, claiming what ground, tactile or virtual, is not to be tread upon.

When an oppressed body shakes, her unsettled and trembling emotions push the limits of confinement. Whether a reactionary spasm or an agitated muscular push for release, a shaking body is a body on the brink of explosion. When a collective body shakes, geographies, neighborhoods, and institutions unsettle, and the unregulated jerking motion threatens to dislodge deeply embedded structures of control. The viral reclamation of the Harlem Shake opens an entry to a discussion of Black urban protest that presses against spatialized oppression with the imminent threat to shatter psychologically and institutionally ingrained boundaries. The viral aspect of this phenomenon asks for a global look at an aesthetic of social unrest that tests the limits of creative interplay across the Black diaspora. Scholars and activists have rightfully defended marginalized communities against the impositions of cultural appropriation, but this essay hopes to offer a vocabulary of motion and viral exchange in negotiating the cultural currency between scattered and displaced African legacies across the Americas. When scholar, political commentator, and television host Melissa Harris-Perry took up the issue of the Harlem Shake on her weekly MSNBC broadcast, she educated her viewing public on the complexities involved in adopting the other's cultural property. Harris-Perry (2012) argued:

> It's about cultural appropriation. When communities create an original art they have a right to some creative control over its definition . . . This is especially true within the long history of voyeurism and appropriation of Harlem's artistic innovations. Harlem has given birth to some of the world's most distinctive art, music, and literature, and just as surely as Harlem has innovated it has been invaded by those who come to Harlem with no sense of history or social context, and no desire for political or economic solidarity.

Harris-Perry's (2012) direct address exemplifies prevalent discourse of the global appropriation of Black America's Hip Hop culture, sounding a protective need to prevent cavalier misuse and commercialization by employing language of property and conquest. However, in examining the adoption of Hip Hop performance by other Black communities of the Americas we may find a space to consider the power afforded by cultural appropriation in establishing the visibility and mobilization of similarly marginalized peoples of African descent. A comparative look at the youth cultures of Harlem and São Paulo, Brazil, for example, frames Hip Hop performance of the United States as a model of resistance, shouting "I'll show you how to do this" across hemispheres. Furthermore, a reflexive call for Black youth culture of the United States to reach across the diaspora, reclaiming what was mined, and sampling from what was gained, will nod towards more inclusive and thus more complete notions of Black aesthetics and protest.

Shout Out to São Paulo

The most direct method of reaching across spatial fractures in the Hip Hop lexicon is the shout-out. This simple tag phrase attached to the name of a person or location affirms the import of one's presence even in her absence, yet is often used with such deliberate excessiveness that significance and sincerity are lost in an endless trail of dropped names. An exception to this format is found in the works of São Paulo Hip Hop group Racionais MC's, where a prevalent and distinguishing feature is the heartfelt shout-out, both literal and metaphoric, to the Black experience of the United States. Arguably Brazil's most respected and commercially successful rap group, the Racionais have exemplified this practice throughout their career trajectory with steady references to influential African American artists and political figures, but their most notable shouts across the north–south divide directly address Black identity, claim transnational kinship, and demand Pan-African allegiance. In their 1992 hit record, "*Voz Ativa*," front man Mano Brown leads into his message of youth activism with a signature shout-out to his brothers, "*Eu tenho algo a dizer / e explicar pra você. / Mas não garanto porém / que engraçado eu serei dessa vez. / Para os manos daqui / para os manos de lá / se você se considera um negro / pra o negro será, mano!*" (Racionais MCs, Voz Ativa). With this verse Brown lays out a simple logic to the audience. "*Se voçe considera negro, pra negro será.*" In the ears of the brothers *de lá* (hinting towards the U.S.) his words "if you consider yourself black, then you'll be for the black man" might at first come across as a matter-of-fact, if not redundant, affirmation of racial consciousness. However, the verb "consider" attached to Blackness would also clash with an African American understanding of racial constructs by suggesting that Blackness is a state of volition. In the Afro-Brazilian context these words speak conversely to a pressing need for racial acknowledgment that, in this instance, is borrowed from African American sensibility. This deceptively simple notion of considering oneself Black and therefore embodying Blackness heralds an unsettling of two colonial methods of racial design.

Brown's shout-out to brothers across the hemispheric divide reminds African Americans of the imposition of a singular Black identity through the one-drop rule, while Afro-Brazilians are advised of their right to claim Blackness in a nation that historically denied racial division by scripting the myth of racial democracy. In *The Black Atlantic: Modernity and Double Consciousness,* Paul Gilroy (1993a) challenges oversimplified notions of racial identity that reduce the cultural consciousness of Blacks across the Atlantic to rigid dualisms in favor of nationalist ideology. As Gilroy uncovers the rich presence of hybridity and cultural reciprocity that entangles seemingly compartmentalized Black identities, he finds a powerful vehicle of creolization in the construction of Hip Hop music. Gilroy describes how music of the Black Atlantic evolved from expressions of cultural individuality to modes of adaptation and self-preservation under oppressive systems. Black music established what Gilroy identifies as "a distinct mode of lived blackness" evident in the "separate but converging musical traditions of the black Atlantic" (1993a, 82).

Hip Hop as a musical form enabled such convergences, allowing various displaced cultures to toy with hybridity using "styles of black America, as well as techniques like mixing, scratching, and sampling as part of their invention of a new mode of cultural production with an identity to match" (Gilroy 1993a, 82). Under Gilroy's lens Mano Brown, in appropriating the Hip Hop form as his mode of communication, assumes a Hip Hop identity that is hybridized, taking on an African American history and racial framework as an extension of himself. Therefore, when Brown shouts out to his brothers *daqui*—in Brazil—he assigns no privilege over his relation to his brothers *de lá*—across spatial or national boundaries. This hybridized identity is concretely performed in the Racionais' individual MC personas with Mano Brown, Ice Blue, Edi Rock, and DJ KL Jay all assuming distinctly Anglo names. On the same track the Racionais go so far as to assert direct pleas for Black Brazil to politicize itself under a Black American model when MC Edi Rock argues:

> Precisamos de um líder de crédito popular
> Como Malcolm X em outros tempos foi na América
> Que seja negro até os ossos, um dos nossos
> E reconstrua nosso orgulho que foi feito em destroços

> We need a credible leader of the people
> Like Malcolm X was in other times in America
> Who is black to the bone, one of ours
> And rebuilds our pride that was made in the wreckage

Such sentiments are underscored visually with imagery of Malcolm X, Tupac Shakur, and various icons of African American resistance prominently displayed in the group's numerous music videos. The appropriation of an African American Hip Hop identity is certainly not unique to Brazil and not especially profound in itself. As the Harlem Shake meme proved, Hip Hop and African American arts have historically laid fertile ground for outside creative and commercial interests in the United States as well as across the globe. Gilroy (1993a) acknowledges the complexity of non-African cultures appropriating Hip Hop, citing questions of the "authenticity of these hybrid cultural forms" (82). However, what is worth investigating in Black Brazilian appropriation of African American Hip Hop performance is the power this trope has afforded Brazil's massive Black population in renegotiating racial constructs while challenging the boundaries of spatial oppression.

In order to fully grasp Hip Hop's role in politicizing Black Brazilian communities, it is imperative to first examine Blackness as it has been framed historically through Portuguese colonization and slavery. The Afro-Brazilian playwright, scholar, and politician Abdias do Nascimento (1979), in his plea for Black Brazilian visibility, *Brazil: Mixture or Massacre,* describes Brazil's "special" brand of racism as such:

> a very special type of racism, an exclusive Luso-Brazilian creation. Subtle, diffuse, evasive, asymmetrical, but also persistent and so implacable that it is liquidating completely what is left of the Black race in Brazil. This type of racism has managed to deceive the world by masking itself in the ideology of racial utopia called "racial democracy," whose entrenchment has the power of confusing the Afro-Brazilian people, doping them, numbing them inside, frustrating them or barring almost definitively any possibility of their self-affirmation, integrity, or identity. (2)

Here Brazil's racial democracy, the argument that a slave system built on integration and miscegenation somehow blurred the lines of racial division and therefore released Brazil from any identifiable form of racism, is exposed as a covert tool of disempowerment. Per Nascimento (1979), the idea that slavery in Brazil was somehow less oppressive due to the *casa grande e senzala* plantation structure where the slave master's family inhabited the big house—*a casa grande*—and enslaved Africans lived in the close proximity of the barracks—*a senzala*—undermines the brutality endured by all African slaves in Brazil and specifically praises the institutionalized rape of African women as an admirable form of racial mixing. When Nascimento accuses the myth of racial democracy of "liquidating completely what is left of the Black race in Brazil" he does not speak in hyperbole. Indeed, the dilution of Brazil's massive Black population, second only to Nigeria, through compulsory miscegenation is defined by Nascimento and by cultural theorists such as Caio Prado Jr. and Florestan Fernandez as a strategic practice of cultural genocide. These "mechanisms of social lynching" include "forced miscegenation, color prejudice, racial discrimination, and an immigration policy designed for the explicit purpose of whitening the country and taking the means of survival away from Africans" (Nascimento 1979, 8).

The contextual backdrop of racial democracy shines light on affirmative statements of Blackness found in the lyrics of Racionais MCs and other popular Brazilian Hip Hop artists. Mano Brown's "*se voçe considera negra,*" or "if you consider yourself Black," aims to redistribute Brazil's highly color-coded list of racial designations—*preto, pardo, moreno, mulato, caboclo, negro*—under the unified signifier of negro. In this sense the appropriation of African American cultural performance shakes internal divisions between shades of Blackness, agitating and awakening a consciousness of activism with "*pra o negro será, mano!*" This shake of Brazil's Black consciousness through the peripheral communities of São Paulo takes on a pronounced radical urgency as it meets the deeply ingrained nationalist assumption that through racial democracy "negro" is an identity possessed by all and therefore owned by none. Mano Brown calls for Afro-Brazilians to turn to their *manos* in the United States, who ironically represent a unified Black political consciousness in the aftermath of America's segregation practices. His desire for a leader like Malcolm X who is "*negro até os ossos*" or "Black to the bone" pushes Brazil's highly epidermal understandings of race past the outer surface, suggesting an embodiment of Blackness that reaches to the core of one's being. The image of Malcolm X in this moment represents not only radical Black nationalism, but also a model of racial identification that complicates socially ingrained attachments to gradations of complexion. X's heightened sense of Blackness read against his fair complexion and auburn hair is an invitation to *morenos, mulatos, cabolcos, amarelos,* and all Brazilians of African descent to take an interest in Black liberation.

Mano a Mano

The greatest hurdle in establishing a transnational aesthetic of Black social mobility between the United States and Brazil will surely be developing a cultural exchange where Black American interest in the Afro-Brazilian experience reflects a balanced sense of reciprocity. Henry Louis Gates's 2011 documentary and corresponding text, *Black in Latin America,* made a notable move toward promoting African American explorations into the histories of Blacks in South

America, Central America, and the Caribbean, and in his dive into Brazil he describes idealized imaginings of Afro-Brazilian culture: "The pageantry and ecstasy of Carnaval; its syncretic mixtures of indigenous, African, and European cultural elements; the dancing to music and song born in Africa" (15). Gates's scope is representative of pervasive misconceptions of Brazil as a multicultural paradise, misconceptions that Brazilian scholars such as Caio Prado Jr. and Nascimento would argue were carefully crafted and presented globally to cover the most poisonous tactics of oppression. Gates opens his chapter on Brazil with an epigraph quoting W. E. B. Du Bois that reveals the degree to which Black Americans have been misled, believing that their brothers across continents experienced a raceless utopian existence. In Du Bois's words, "On the whole emancipation [in Brazil] was peaceful, and whites, Negroes, and Indians are to-day amalgamating into a new race" (Gates 2011, 12). Unfortunately, this 1915 misconception persists, and limited knowledge of the creative contributions of Afro-Brazilians maintains a flat and depoliticized image of the Black population of Brazil. Abdias do Nascimento (1979) notes the one-sided kinship between African American and Afro-Brazilian culture:

> When and which Black person of my country has transmitted to the North American reader directly, without intermediaries, the Afro-Brazilian version of our history, our vicissitudes, our creative efforts or our economic and socio-political battles? . . . I remember reading, also long ago and very moved, *The Big Sea,* by Langston Hughes, with whom I came to exchange sparse and fraternal correspondence. Another unforgettable was Richard Wright with *Native Son* and *Black Boy,* I also remember *Third Street* by Ann Perry and, more recently, *Giovanni's Room, Another Land,* and *The Fire Next Time* by James Baldwin. (1–2)

The contemporary analogy to this one-directional flow of cultural material is certainly represented in the "trafficking" of African American Hip Hop music to the slums of São Paulo, Salvador, and Rio de Janeiro. In *favelas* of these urban centers, Hip Hop imagery has come to represent resistance to confinement and reaching out from an extremely marginal existence. In the appropriation of Hip Hop throughout Brazil we find collective bodies shaking against the restrictions of living in compact and largely neglected communities. Anthropologist Jennifer Roth-Gordon (2009) offers her observations of Hip Hop's proliferation in the slums of São Paulo in her essay "Conversational Sampling, Race Trafficking, and the Invocation of the *Gueto* in Brazilian Hip Hop":

> The São Paulo based group Racionais MC's was on the verge of going plat-
> inum with their album *Sobrevivendo no Inferno* (Surviving Hell). Signs of
> Hip Hop culture were all over the *favela*: large murals and graffiti depicted
> album covers and song lyrics; U.S. sports teams and references to New York
> adorned the most coveted clothing items; and fans took on nicknames of
> popular rappers. Youth I met swapped, borrowed, and sometimes bought
> rap CDs to listen to on individual headphones and on boom boxes at nightly
> impromptu gatherings in the streets of their neighborhood. (63)

At the time of Roth-Gordon's research, Hip Hop culture had well reached
its global status, and in going global offered a transnational outlet for Black
culture of the *favela*. Where Abdias do Nascimento's cravings for African
American literature helped draft his Pan-African outlook in the 1970s, Afro-
Brazilian youth at the turn of the millennium were able to draw from a rich
palette of artists and performative trappings of the Hip Hop persona. Because
of the all-encompassing nature of Hip Hop performance, individual bodies
carrying this assumed identity into public spaces extended their performance
to the visuals, sounds, and commerce that filled their neighborhoods. Such is
the nature of Hip Hop, infectious and viral even before the viral era.

This viral flow, despite the increasing speed and accessibility of cybertech-
nology, continues to pass in one direction, outward from the United States,
with little interest or acceptance of the wealth of unmined cultural material
in the legacies of Black Brazil. Unfortunately, the degree of Black American
engagement with Brazilian Hip Hop aesthetics as of yet is limited to touris-
tic "on location" types of involvement. Snoop Dogg's 2003 hit track featuring Pharrell Williams, "Beautiful," encapsulates this approach with its "*favela*
chic" video directed by Chris Robinson. The video opens with a shirtless Black
youth looking out over Rio de Janeiro's Alto Vidigal *favela* onto Ipanema's
posh coastline. He answers a phone with "*Oi, fala comigo,*" and the voice of
Pharrell Williams responds to his greeting in English with "Yeah, let me talk
to Snoop." The remainder of the video follows suit, with images of sun-kissed
women in service of Snoop and Williams, braiding hair, lounging in bikinis,
and dancing before various iconic backdrops all for the pleasure of these two
apparent big shots on vacation. With the exception of an inserted flash of *bloco*
percussion, Afro-Brazilian music and culture are in no way connected to the
lyrics and instrumentation of the song. Furthermore, the notion that these
major figures of U.S. Hip Hop are just passing through is reinforced by a final
pan across Ipanema from Alto Vidigal with the message "*Obrigado Brasil*"
inscribed in postcard fashion.

A more balanced cultural interplay between the two largest Black popu-lations of the Western Hemisphere would naturally inform and broaden the sociopolitical perspectives of both communities. In the case of Black Brazil's assumption of Hip Hop performance, a shake to the individual and collec-tive negotiations of racial identity prompted a move away from racial democ-racy and a nostalgic look back to an earlier negritude movement. São Paulo rap groups such as Racionais MCs and Posse Mente Zulu drew a clear line between "marginal" rappers whose rhymes criticize subjugated slum existence and "positive" rappers who firmly believe that lyrical criticism of injustice not partnered with activism falls short of the understood goal. Derek Pardue's (2008) *Ideologies of Marginalities in Brazilian Hip Hop* explains, "The com-mon ground among 'positive' Hip Hoppers is the belief that denouncements of the *periferia* daily life are not enough. They argue that Hip Hop needs to provide concrete solutions beginning with sharper strategies of collectivity built on education and entertainment" (115). This commitment to social action partnered with the commercial appeal of Hip Hop music led to measurable community development projects in São Paulo specifically where the hugely successful Racionais MCs married musical endeavors to community develop-ment projects such as *ARAPensando e Educação* (Rap Thinking and Educa-tion) and *Musica Negra em Ação* (Black Music in Action), serving São Paulo schools, youth athletics, juvenile detention centers, and health clinics.

While the appropriation of Hip Hop culture in Brazilian slums opened a door to self-determinist thought and practice, the originators of Hip Hop, New York's Bronx and Harlem communities, saw artists detach from the social realities of the ghetto in favor of performing extreme opulence. At the height of Racionais MCs' philanthropic endeavors, Harlem's Sean "Puffy" Combs and Bad Boy Entertainment ushered in the "bling-bling" aesthetic, promoting shameless displays of material excess as a badge of having escaped Harlem. It was during this bling-bling era in rap music that Combs and artist GDep (Ghetto Dependent) introduced the mainstream audience to the Harlem Shake dance in the 2001 video for GDep's "Let's Get It." The video, which is formulaic of ghetto-fabulous productions of the time, shows boastful rappers leaning into the camera with heavy platinum and diamond jewelry promi-nently displayed to the lens. Young dancers perform the Shake intermittently while Puffy and GDep deliver unapologetic verses about money, cars, sexual exploits, and crime. However, in the midst of such materialism Combs makes a point of affirming his allegiance to Harlem, stating "make raps and tracks and go Harlem." Combs, in this shout-out to Harlem, exemplifies a dilemma that many successful African American Hip Hop artists face, an allegiance to their poor communities of origin that is compromised by the alienation of their larger-than-life personas. If Black American Hip Hop artists were to look toward their Brazilian counterparts, they would find a fair share of purely commercial material, but they would also undoubtedly happen upon a unique throwback to the origins of Black and Latino/a Hip Hop aesthetics in the United States. A reclamation of Hip Hop with Harlem artists taking back "conscious" rap and applying the Brazilian format of public service combined with creative exploration might result in São Paulo showing Harlem "how to do this"—how to allow the community that nurtured early inspirations to maintain direct and purposeful engagement with your artistic journey. Street credibility would be redefined with the added aspect of accountability to the hometown, and shout-outs to that community would regain sincerity and significance. Most importantly, a reciprocal practice of appropriation between the creative communities of Harlem and São Paulo, or African Americans and Afro-Brazilians, would introduce African American communities to a new set of folk heroes and an alternate history of resistance. If an image of Malcolm X wielding a firearm beside his window can shake Brazil's understanding and commitment to Blackness, then an image of Rei Zumbi[7] defending the maroon colony of Palmares against repeated Portuguese invasions might shake African American notions of intracommunal sustainability.

Representing

Accountability to one's community plays out in Hip Hop culture through the act of "representing." At any level of critical or commercial success, Hip Hop artists are expected to "represent" on behalf of the masses who psychologically ride along on their journey. How an artist chooses to represent is a matter of personal ethics and creative choice. However, the everyday performance of Hip Hop aesthetics in cultural centers such as Harlem and São Paulo also carries the responsibility of representing and maintaining a sense of collective pride in one's block, one's hood, one's people. The viral misrepresentation of Harlem's artistry carelessly threatened a legacy that is fiercely guarded in the quotidian acts of Harlem's residents. Moreover, global and viral representations of Harlem and African American youth culture carry the weight of "reppin'" for marginalized Black communities worldwide. Consciously or unconsciously, the widely marketed "Harlem World" concept takes on a

7. Zumbi dos Palmares, leader of the maroon colony Quilombo dos Palmares, is the most visible figure of Black resistance in Brazil; his birthday, November 20, is celebrated as the Day of Black Consciousness.

literal responsibility in positioning Harlem as the great Black microcosm and, as seen in the *favelas* of Brazil, the adoption of these global Hip Hop aesthetics can serve to shake restrictive concepts of self as well as restrictive social systems. Progressive moves toward a viral Hip Hop flow between Africans of the Americas have the potential to shake nationalist identification, breaking open the possibility for newly drawn allegiances. Where culture is utilized as political currency, the mutual exchange and appropriation of cultural sensibilities might clear a channel for the exchange of power.

Bibliography

Gates, Henry Louis Jr. 2011. *Black in Latin America*. New York and London: New York University Press.

Gilroy, Paul. 1993a. *The Black Atlantic: Modernity and Double Consciousness*. Cambridge: Harvard University Press, 1993.

———. 1993b. *Small Acts: Thoughts on the Politics of Black Culture*. London and New York: Serpent's Tail.

Harris-Perry, Melissa. 2012. *Introducing the Real Harlem Shake*. MSNBC, April 19. http://www.msnbc.com/melissa-harris-perry/watch/introducing-the-real-harlem-shake-20497987791

Hughes, Langston. 2000. "The Negro Artist and the Racial Mountain." In *African American Literary Theory: A Reader,* edited by Winston Napier. New York: New York University Press. 27–30.

Hurston, Zora Neale. 2000. "Characteristics of Negro Expression." In *African American Literary Theory: A Reader,* edited by Winston Napier. New York: New York University Press. 31–44.

Kaufman, Sarah. 2013. "Is It Any Wonder the Harlem Shake Went Viral?" *Washington Post,* February 14. https://www.washingtonpost.com/news/arts-and-entertainment/wp/2013/02/14/is-it-any-wonder-the-harlem-shake-went-viral/.

Lipsitz, George. 2011. *How Racism Takes Place*. Philadelphia: Temple University Press.

Nascimento, Abdias do. 1979. *Brazil: Mixture or Massacre? Essays in the Genocide of a Black People*. Dover, MA: Majority.

Pardue, Derek. 2008. *Ideologies of Marginality in Brazilian Hip Hop*. New York: Palgrave Macmillan.

Roth-Gordon, Jennifer. 2009. "Conversational Sampling, Race Trafficking, and the Invocation of the *Gueto* in Brazilian Hip Hop." In *Global Linguistic Flows: Hip Hop Linguistic Flows, Youth Identities, and the Politics of Language,* edited by Sammy H. Alim, Awad Ibrahim, and Alastair Pennycook. New York: Routledge. 63.

PART III

CHICANO? MEXICAN?

On the Borderlands of Mexican and Mexican American Hip Hop

Collective Amnesia

Bocafloja

A wide gap exists between the phenomenon of cultural appropriation and historical reclamation. How do you justify when you are twelve and at that age you have been programmed by an information structure and culture that has determined all features of your identity?

The phenomenon of migration, the informal market, and the constant flow between the idealization of the First World in the northern corner and the underworld in the backyard made it possible for me one day, while walking with my grandmother in a street market in Mexico, to stumble across a cassette tape with Ice Cube's face on it that said "Amerikkkas Most Wanted." My understanding of English, at that time, was quite limited, but I managed to understand the imagery and vaguely grasp the sentiment of what I read on the cover, which piqued my interest.

The models of success, beauty, progress, popularity, and respect in Mexico are always linked to White/European images, and the most visible leaders in the media, political, religious, and cultural realms have never hesitated in referring to Spain as the motherland of all Mexicans, or at least of the Mexicans they protect and defend. We grew up with King Juan Carlos the First and Queen Sophia of Spain as the exemplary model of good taste for families.

The popular culture role models that are heard on the radio or that take up space on television always praise elements that are clearly Anglo-Saxon in their phenotype as virtues of beauty. All that which boasts of the honorability of a family makes a necessary reference to Spanish, French, or Portuguese ancestors, depending on the region of Mexico in which they are encountered.

We do not have worthy role models. The majority of people who look even slightly like me always appear in denigrating roles and positions in the media. One of the most popular television personalities of the seventies and eighties was "La India Maria," or "Indian Mary," an Indigenous woman who arrives in the city from the countryside without full command of the Spanish language and suffers all types of hazing and mistreatment that, when displayed onscreen, is intended to invoke humor.

"Submissiveness," "naivety," and "good heart," a few phrases the first conquistadors used to narrate their initial experiences upon interacting with the Indigenous peoples of New Spain, continue to serve as characteristics that qualify as virtues in the framework of the "civilized oppressor and good savage." The continued repetition of this identifying index ends up naturalizing and confirming the process almost as though it were an automatic part of the Mexican psyche.

A similar case is that of "El negro Tomas," or "Black Thomas," a television personality who was an eleven-year-old Black boy from the coast of Veracruz, Mexico, played by an adult male who wore a stereotypical Sambo mask. He is constantly reprimanding his mother in a hypersexualized double entendre and play on words, and has an apparent lack of interest or capacity for memory in the school activities his mother suggests, which takes us again back to the registry of the colonial narrative that never ceased highlighting negative traits, such as laziness, apathy, and libidinous behavior, as a part of a continuum of vices in the personality of Black men on the American continent.

It is important to note that the mother's character is played by a man portrayed as a Black woman in stereotypical nanny costume who demonstrated an incessant fervor for spiritual practices, all of which was addressed through this rough, superficial, and disrespectful representation. It is not too much to mention that the linguistic form in which these characters are expressed is already charged with a series of values that historically affirm centuries of manipulation, exclusion, and erasure. I am a firm believer that humor is an acute symptom of a specific and well-outlined agenda. So, in this case, to give credit to this type of despicable spectacle would only make me complicit in my own abuse.

It is in this way, seeing Ice Cube on the cover of the cassette, in a pose which in one way or another suggested a type of empowerment and strength, that I was allowed to establish direct contact with the manifestation and exercise of historical reclamation, even though the hegemonies and geopolitics of that time would argue the contrary. To have deciphered, in totality, the lyrics of the album would have been nearly impossible for me, but it was more than clear that the Black man, in whichever country he lived, did not represent a sector of the population which had been privileged by or benefited from history. I knew very well that his words, merely by their intention and the force in which they resonated, were aimed at sharing a different version of history, one much closer to my reality, even though thousands of miles separated us.

Historically, in Mexico, racial stratification has been concealed within a false discourse of harmonious miscegenation, with the aim of destroying any possibility of questioning race within the fabric of an apparently homogenous society. As a young boy, when looking at my father, I always knew that we were somehow different, physically and culturally. The ancestral memory manifested. The physiognomic remnants of thousands of African slaves, brought to Mexico to work the sugar cane fields and mines, renounced the possibility of forcing their dispersal throughout the collective amnesia of this neocolonial fabric.

Let's travel back to the seventeenth century: at some point around 1645 the African population in New Spain (Mexico as we know it today) represented the second largest assemblage of Africans in the Americas, right behind Brazil. At many points during this century the Black population in Mexico was larger than the White and creole Spaniards.

We could develop an extremely extensive summary of the many peculiarities of this diasporic process, spanning from the smallest linguistic detail, in which African contributions permeate our daily lexicon, to a full review of every cultural manifestation that occurs through elements that stem from Africa; food, oral tradition, religious practices, an endless number of elements that are fascinating to discover and analyze, owing especially to the fact that these elements have been strategically erased and minimized by official history.

Currently liberalism in a country like Mexico has begun to capitalize on its own historical abuses in a very punctuated manner. What better propagandistic strategy to enrich an ostensibly inclusive state than to make a case for ethnic and cultural diversity that exclusively focuses on the folkloric and exotic aspects of the Black experience? The state makes visible the Black presence as part of the origins of the country; however, it is presented in a form that seems to be a far-away, distant history or dream. The goal, then, is really to eliminate any possibility of creating a Black consciousness or identity that would put at risk the construction of a Mexican ideology manufactured in a crossbreeding imaginary.

Under this premise, the state and hegemonic culture in Mexico obstructs the possibility of generating Pan-African and diasporic ties of solidarity with other communities of the World. This is most exemplified when the state promotes an annual African cultural festival in which one of Bob Marley's sons will perform, and have to "alternate," with a *Son Jarocho* group from Veracruz. In this setting, the ideas of Black world leaders are discussed as though the relevance of their struggles was not part of our condition as citizens born in Mexico.

Even if we limit the example to local Mexican history, the recognition and estimation that the state has for Gaspar Yanga is minimal in comparison to the official registry of the country's colonial history, which describes his contributions as brief, almost insignificant, passages in terms of their historical impact. Gaspar Yanga founded San Lorenzo de los Negros, one of the first free towns on the American continent, through an uprising of marooned slaves and later a negotiation that secured their transition to autonomy under the authority of the colonial Spanish regime in 1618 in the state of Veracruz.

We understand that convenient heroes will always be those who never challenged the normalized morality of the powers that be, the ones who obeyed the harsh guidelines of ecclesiastic powers even though, on paper, they affirmed a secular state. It is no accident that few in Mexico know of Gaspar Yanga. His condition as a free Black man with organizing, negotiating, and honorable skills still raises doubts about the fantasy of progress and the baroque sense of aesthetic harmony that prevails in a Mexico that calls itself independent. It is in this way that the recognition of a Black consciousness or respect for cultural, organizational, and economic expressions of Indigenous peoples represents a real attack against Mexican hegemonic stability, in many cases regardless of the political affiliations that they represent.

Mexican independence from Spain birthed a new model of internal colonialism in which the children of Spaniards and their direct descendants born in Mexico, clearly White Mexicans, with all the privileges of race and class that their historic condition granted them, became the new lords who would benefit from the exploitation of the people. The great wealth generated from the exploitation of local resources may not have been sent to the Spanish crown, but it wasn't distributed to benefit the social welfare of the people, either. The wealth stayed in the country, but solely accumulated in the chests of a few privileged families, who to this day continue to be in control of the majority of the nation's resources. The poorest areas and people affected by exclusion and systemic marginalization were and continue to be visibly darkest, with respect to skin color of the settlers.

Twenty years have passed since I came across that Ice Cube cassette. I never imagined at that time that at some point in my life I would find myself on the other side of the equation. Through a string of near logical events, I became part of one of the first generations of young people to affirm themselves as a community connected by Hip Hop. Years later, in the blink of an eye, I found myself rapping professionally and touring Mexico, other countries in Latin America, and the United States. On this journey, I have discovered that art has the capacity for both impact and power, which goes beyond the individual satisfaction of a creative exercise.

Walter Rodney, a prominent Guyenese historian and the author of *How Europe Underdeveloped Africa* ([1972] 2012) knew very well that his role in academia was always strategic. One of his fundamental priorities was that of sharing his thinking with people that had no opportunity to expose themselves to certain types of knowledge who were restricted by the systemic conditions reserved for a select group of people. Rodney was aware that a Black man in prison or without housing potentially had a greater chance of development and survival in this state of extermination if he had an enhanced awareness of his history and the reasons for his current state.

Rooted in this learning, and taking advantage of the power of influence that artistic visibility provides, I accepted the responsibility of sharing and producing counterhegemonic knowledge. Swimming in a cultural industry where Hip Hop has been co-opted by a system as one more tool in the processes of submission and normalization, it was more than important to generate a project that broke the traditional modes of communication between artist and cultural consumer, which in the majority of cases lacks exchange or interaction, but rather exists as a unilateral expression directed from the part of the artist to the audience without any real feedback. This is how the "Quilomboarte Collective" emerged, of which I am the founder.

Quilomboarte is an organization that produces multidisciplinary cultural events in which rap and spoken word function as a nonorthodox educational tool and an essential collaborative adjunct to social and political movements in the process of transformation throughout the Americas. The organization derives its name from the communities in resistance, "Quilombos," which during the colonial period on the American continent were established by fugitive Black slaves (also known as maroons and cimarrones), Indigenous peoples, and others who rejected colonialism's domination, who preferred to live as free people in communal form. Quilombos (also known as mocambos in Mexico and Palenques in Colombia) were founded as independent and self-sustaining collectives that rejected the state of slavery and its oppressive nature.

We believe in decolonization as a fundamental step in the process of understanding and establishing the meaning of self-determination in our communities. Our way of communicating with youth is through this project, which, in the majority of cases, is the first time many of these young individuals are exposed to a source of information that questions and is critical of accepted history and, furthermore, is imparted by a group of people with whom they can identify immediately. In the great majority of events we hold in Mexico, we try to invite artists from the African diaspora that share a congruent discourse with the emancipatory needs of our people, offering a platform of exchange and interaction with youth in Mexico. One of the first steps to take in order to establish these platforms of solidarity is to recognize the fact that historically the system was designed to created animosity between Black and Brown people.

It is worth remembering that in some cases the colonial regime in the Americas utilized African slaves as overseers of Indigenous slaves, a divisive strategy between oppressed subjects that would naturally prevent any type of integrated uprising between Black and Brown. We are speaking of the first strokes of induced hate. The analogy could easily be applied to many of the present-day ghettos in the United States where the enemy doesn't appear to be a mercenary and exclusive system but rather the neighbor with a skin tone slightly lighter or darker.

It is crucial that we solidify connections between different communities of the diaspora outside of the traditional circuits of development, which in many cases are found to be permeated by bureaucratic thinking which defends the interests of the liberal agenda, and more when the vehicle itself questions the framework of the "safe," of what is considered high art, high culture, or "ethnic" culture, as they love to say.

Decolonize, self-manage, transgress, emancipate. Our redefined version of Hip Hop's four elements.

There is a long way ahead of us, and this is the time in which we are witnessing the first and incipient drafts of an affirmative process related to Black identity within the Mexican population. The responsibility to facilitate the platforms that can open dialogues and continue a production of culture that demystifies national identity, race relations, and self-determination needs by consensus is fundamental to our project and agenda.

Gonzalo Aguirre Beltran (1946, 1967), a Mexican anthropologist whose continuous contributions to Afro-Mexican studies brought him recognition as one of the most relevant academics and researchers on the subject, plays a dual role in this historical processes. On one hand, he was the first researcher to create a path toward the visibilization and exposure of the subject within highbrow academia through the publication of several books and the entailment with state agencies. Ironically, Beltran was also the one who, due to personal perceptions and expectations, halted the strengthening of and continued research on the Afro-Mexican legacy based on a myopic argument. Beltran thought that the miscegenation between Indigenous, Black, and Mestizo communities would end up diluting the African presence in Mexico by the end of the seventies, when the Pan-American highway was being built, and displace the towns of the Guerrero coasts, which, he argued, would entirely disaggregate the communities without leaving any trace of its existence.

The truth of the matter is that Aguirre Beltran's expectations had always revolved around the exoticism of finding a faithful reproduction of a sixteenth-century community from Gabon or Guinea recreated in the Mexican state of Guerrero or the Veracruz coast in the 1950s. What Aguirre Beltran never fully understood is that the specific characteristics of the Black population in Mexico wouldn't be "less Black" because of their communal contextualization within Indigenous communities. Also, Aguirre Beltran was never interested in the process of politicization of Black towns, and he was even less interested in the development of solidarity bridges that would link the Black experience in Mexico with others along the Diaspora with the intention of stimulating a sense of self-determination toward the states and nations that demarcate those communities.

Under this framework, I am reminded of Walter Rodney's (1979) contributions, in which he once mentioned, "No one today can afford to be misled by the myths of race." In that sense I would say that we've lived sedated under the placebo of inclusion in national projects to the point where we defend with our own lives the interests of our main oppressors in the name of patriotic fervor, which has never ensured our interests within this political, social, and economic model that is nothing else but neo-slavery in practice. We've learned to naturalize our apparent failure, assuming the entire responsibility of our conditions without questioning causes and origins. We have imported and perpetuated an irrational hate for "the other," when "the other" is, in this instance, a reflection of ourselves.

I still have that old Ice Cube cassette that unleashed a whole series of events in my life. Ice Cube is probably not Amerikkkas most wanted anymore, or maybe never was; perhaps it was just a mirage that cast the silhouette of a powerful conjuncture in the marginalized communities of South Central L.A., with the capability to impact and reproduce itself all over the world, which in itself is a huge achievement.

What remains clear to me is the fact that Amerikkka—written and spelled with three k's, no matter how sophisticated in its oppression and operation techniques, despite its subjective bubble of inclusion, racial democracy, and public policies falsely inclusive—is still walking on our backs, capitalizing our subjugated condition in order to keep satisfying mercenary interests in which you, me, and millions of people outside of this room play a perpetual secondary role.

Today more than ever, Rodney's words continue to resonate in constant reminder that true social victories must have the capability to permeate the masses. For this reason it is fundamental that we assume our responsibilities to the extent possible and establish bridges connecting academic discourse with organizing in our communities.

The people are waiting for us outside.

Bibliography

Aguirre Beltran, Gonzalo. 1946. *La población negra de México 1519–1810*. Mexico DF: Ediciones Fuente Cultural.

———. 1967. *Regiones de Refugio: El Desarrollo de La Comunidad y el Proceso Dominical en Mestizo América*. México: Instituto Indigenista Interamericano, 1967.

Rodney, Walter. [1972] 2012. *How Europe Underdeveloped Africa*. Nairobi: Pambazuka.

———. 1979. "History Is a Weapon." http://www.historyisaweapon.com/defcon1/rodneystrspe .html (accessed March 8, 2014).

chapter 9

"Yo soy Hip Hop"

Transnationalism and Authenticity in Mexican New York

Melissa Castillo-Garsow

In their 2012 video "Recesión," or Recession,[1] the New York–based Mexican Hip Hop group Hispanos Causando Pániko (HCP) consciously claims Hip Hop's history as part of their call for a music-based Latino movement, as well as an authentic "rap en español." Incorporating Hip Hop's four elements—MC, DJ, graffiti, and breakdance—and decked out in Yankees caps, the group demonstrates their allegiance to NYC traditions. From the old-school sound, to their choice of lettering, to the scratchy style of the video, their work is more reminiscent of classic Hip Hop videos from the 1980s and early '90s than most work produced today. Moreover, their incorporation of both a sense of crew and multigenre style is clearly meant to invoke a sense of Hip Hop culture's origins as a community-based event. And yet, HCP's brand of Hip Hop would have been entirely unrecognizable ten years ago and is still completely unrecognizable to many today. First of all, its classic New York sound is achieved almost entirely in Spanish; second, it is produced and performed by Mexicans based outside of both the Southwest and Mexico; and

---

1. All translations in this article are mine and are meant to be the most literal possible. They do not attempt to translate or mimic the rhythms, rhymes, and wordplays present in the music.

third, their themes are grounded in a New York Mexican experience that is both relatively new and largely unexpressed.

Formed in Corona, Queens, in 2005, Hispanos Causando Pániko—composed of Enrique "Demente" Trejo, 31; Raúl "Meck" Hernández, 30; and Daniel "Nemesis" Gil, 31—consider themselves the pioneers of Mexican Hip Hop in New York. Taking their name from Latino Hip Hop groundbreaker Kid Frost's debut album, HCP features Spanish-language lyrics that describe the immigrant struggle in New York City with a sound inspired by the beats of Big Pun and Wu-Tang. HCP has performed from NYC to L.A., opening for bands such as Kinto Sol, Awkid, Delinquent Habits, and Jae P, and their fans follow them from as far away as Mexico City, Ecuador, and Russia. HCP independently sold 15,000 units of their 2007 mixtape and are currently in the final stages of completing their debut album, *De Las Calles, Para Las Calles.*[2]

Significantly, the basis of their Hip Hop identity is a unique blend of authenticity, representing, and *mexicanidad* that can only be understood within a particular contemporary New York City Mexican context. However, they also highlight an important and emerging direction in the genre. HCP provides a lens to examine the ways that Mexican identities are negotiated and performed in spaces—in this case both Hip Hop and New York—that have little to no recognition of them. Their declaration "Yo soy Hip Hop" (I am Hip Hop) is in many ways a revolutionary statement within a genre that has become a "constitutive part of black popular culture as well as American popular culture more generally," where "American" largely excludes those of Mexican descent (Dimitriadis 2009, 2). Through a discussion of their transnational sense of location, their global music sense, and their community-based practices, this chapter explores how Hispanos Causando Pániko, a group composed of 1.5- and second-generation Mexican immigrants, were able to realize, negotiate, and authenticate a Hip Hop identity that both empowered them as Mexican men and helped them carve out a place of belonging in a city and genre that did not initially accept them. In this way, HCP reveals the origins of a growing Mexican American presence within an increasing global Hip Hop community.

Mexican New York: A New Nueva York

New York City is one of the most iconic immigrant cities and yet a city which is rarely seen in relation to this country's most iconic immigrant group,

---

2. This biographical information is sourced from the Hispanos Causando Pániko website (http://www.hispanoscausandopaniko.com)—a collaboration between the author of this chapter and the group members.

Mexicans. Sociologist Robert Smith (2006) outlines stages of Mexican immigration in New York ranging from the 1940s to 1980s in which there was only a small but tight-knit network of Mexicans, to the third stage in the late 1980s when New York City saw an explosion of Mexicans, mostly from the state of Puebla in south central Mexico. A number of these immigrants were able to gain amnesty and eventually become eligible for permanent resident status through the 1986 Immigration Reform and Control Act (ibid., 22), allowing for many of the transnational links Smith and others have documented (such as frequent visits to Mexico and involvement in hometown politics).[3] Since Smith's writing, New York City is witnessing a fourth flow of Mexican migrants from increasingly diverse areas of origin,[4] most notably Mexico City and its surrounding areas (Risomena and Massey 2012, 9–10).

Today, the Mexican-origin population is New York City's fastest-growing Latino national group, growing from a population of 6,700 Mexicans in 1980, to 55,587 in 1990, to 183,792 in 2000, and 342,699 in 2010 (Bergad 2011, 23). Fueled by both escalating immigration and rates of reproduction, by 2005 Mexicans became the third largest Latino nationality in NYC, behind Dominicans (747,473), who surpassed Puerto Ricans (719,444) in 2014. According to Laird Bergad (2011) of the Latino Data Project, if these rates continue, Mexicans will comprise the region's largest Latino national subgroup sometime in the early 2020s. Moreover as a significant portion of the Mexican population in the United States is undocumented (57% of undocumented migrants in

---

3. See for example Nancy Foner (2001, 2005). Likewise, Alex Rivera's 2003 PBS documentary *The Sixth Section* captures the experience of "Grupo Unión," a New York City–area hometown organization of immigrants from Puebla.

4. As Risomena and Massey (2012) have outlined, in recent years the spatial distribution of Mexican-migrant-sending regions has also shifted away from its traditional heartland in the Central-West Region (the states of Durango, Zacatecas, San Luis Potosí, Aguascalientes, Guanajuato, Jalisco, Nayarit, Colima, and Michoacán), which from the 1920s until recently has composed at least 50 percent of the total outflow to the United States but has declined to just below 40 percent. Until the mid-1990s, the second most important sending region was the Border Region (20–28%), which includes the states of Baja California, Baja California Sur, Sonora, Sinaloa, Chihuahua, Coahuila, Nuevo León, and Tamaulipas. However, after the mid-1990s this share fell below 20 percent and then dipped to 11 percent by 2000 as the region came to house the most rapidly growing sector of the Mexican economy and now attracts a large number of internal migrants. As a result, two new sending regions have come online: the Central Region (Querétaro, Mexico, Distrito Federal, Hidalgo, Tlaxcala, Morelos, Puebla, Guerrero, and Oaxaca) and the Southeastern Region (Veracruz, Tabasco, Chiapas, Campeche, Quintana Roo, and Yucatán). The Central Region was relatively unimportant until 1980, accounting for no more than 10 percent of migrants to the United States, but rose steadily thereafter to just over 30 percent by century's end, while Mexico's Southeastern Region remained insignificant as a migration source until recently, contributing fewer than 2 percent of migrants through the early 1990s. By the end of the millennium, however, migrants from this region composed 7 percent of the total; more recently, this figure has increased to 13 percent (9–10).

NYC), the precise number of Mexicans living in New York City is difficult to ascertain. While conservative estimates range from an additional 300,000 to 450,000 in 2010 for the greater New York City region (Bergad 2011, 1–2), the Mexican Consulate in New York, for example, estimates that there are approximately 1.2 million Mexicans in the region (Semple 2010, A018).

This last phase of migration as represented by Mexican Hip Hop aficionados, which is much more diverse in terms of regions of origin, has added great diversity to both Mexican expression and experiences in the region that thus far have not been studied. At the oldest, these families represent three generations of life in New York, while others have only a couple of years in the country. Upon arrival, Mexicans concentrate in Brooklyn, Queens, and the Bronx, where they face harsh housing and work conditions. Mexican immigrant households are more likely to experience overcrowding and to spend more than half their income on rent than those of any other immigrant group or the native-born population.[5] Mexicans also have among the lowest household incomes and education rates due to the large number of new migrants, many of whom arrive as teenagers or as young adults and so did not or do not complete high school (Bergad 2011, 29–38). Because of these higher birth rates, and despite the fact that the migration to the New York City metropolitan region was composed mainly of adults, Mexicans had the youngest population of any of the major Latino nationalities, with an average age of twenty-five. This fosters a Mexican youth culture that is multicultural and transnationally tech-savvy (Bergad 2011, 19–20). As such, despite the challenges Mexican migrants and their children face, New York is home to an increasingly diverse young Mexican population that is mainly male (61%) and yearning for creative outlets to add meaning and create community beyond their often limited work options. For many, this is the appeal of Hip Hop.

The New Authenticity Debates: Creating Space for Mexican Hip Hop in NYC

In terms of Hip Hop studies, little discussion exists about Mexican Americans in New York,[6] and as both Raquel Rivera and Juan Flores note, even the little that has been written about Latinos in Hip Hop's birthplace largely represents

---

5. For more on housing conditions of Mexicans, see Debbie Nathan, "David and His 26 Roommates," *New York Magazine*, May 16, 2005, http://nymag.com/nymetro/news/features /1869.

6. The only research I know of on this topic to date is my article in *Words Beats & Life: The Global Journal of Hip-Hop Studies* 6 (Spring 2015) and this volume.

an erasure. Yet as Mark Naison (2016) describes the scene, "Hip Hop was born multicultural" (*La Verdad* ix). Born in the Bronx, its invention came out of the sound system and culture of the anglophone Caribbean, traditions of English-language vernacular improvisation by African Americans and West Indians, mambo dancing, capoeira, African drumming, the movements of James Brown and Bruce Lee movies, and much more. As Rivera's (2003) work has demonstrated, Puerto Ricans have been present since the first days of Hip Hop, especially in the visual and movement aspects; however, as English-language rappers came to define Hip Hop's public profile globally as well as in the United States, these contributions were often pushed to the side.

If, as Flores (2004) states, to speak of Puerto Ricans in rap means to "defy the sense of instant amnesia" (70), then the history of Mexicans in Hip Hop is even more invisible. Nevertheless, since the early to mid-1980s, Chicano artists like Kid Frost were participating in the creation of a unique West Coast Hip Hop scene and were soon followed in the early '90s by groups like ALT, A Lighter Shade of Brown, and Cypress Hill. In addition, the huge dance parties of Chicano L.A.'s '70s dance scene were primed to embrace Hip Hop.[7] Despite the spread of Hip Hop to Mexican groups like the largely successful and well-known Control Machete, Cartel de Santa, and Molotov, in the United States, Chicano rappers are almost exclusively located in California, with a few groups representing Arizona, Texas, and occasionally the Midwest. Nevertheless, this regional affiliation has not changed the perception of rap as an exercise that is authentically "Black." According to Pancho McFarland (2008), "With some exceptions, Chicano rap acts have received very little airplay or national recognition. Most Chicano rap acts are known and supported in their hometowns and regions and work in small concert venues within a limited circuit that primarily encompasses the southwestern United States, though may have taken their acts to other countries" (4). Thus, despite McFarland's (2008) perception of *Chicano* rap as a "new millennial mestizaje/mulataje consisting of Mexican/Chicana/o, African (American) and European (American) elements" (3), Mexicans are not necessarily embraced in this Hip Hop history, especially outside certain regions. More common are conclusions like those of Alan Light (2004), who writes, "rap is about giving voice to a black community otherwise underrepresented" (144).

Mexican Hip Hop in New York represents the opportunity to re-emphasize Hip Hop's multicultural and Afro-diasporic roots, while also exploring Spanish as a new frontier for rapping. In his classic study *The Black Atlantic,* Paul

---

7. For a more comprehensive history on Chicano rap, see Pancho McFarland (2008), Raegan Kelley (2004), and Josh Kun (2010).

Gilroy (1993) has problematized the notion of Black authenticity. As he points out, Hip Hop is significant for the Black Atlantic because of its unique history of "cross fertilization of African-American vernacular cultures with their Caribbean equivalents" (103) in spite of the reality that "black music is so often the principal symbol of racial authenticity" (34). As such, while Hip Hop's popularization as the authentic Black American culture is a powerful one, it is also a clear reflection of the status of nationality and national cultures in a postmodern era (Gilroy 1993, 34). Here we face a clear conundrum. If, as Gilroy argues, Black music reflects a certain type of national authenticity, then the perception of Hip Hop as authentically Black American is problematic. It certainly does not reflect Hip Hop's history, nor its present, but instead is an act of erasure on the part of White America to streamline U.S. culture into something racially categorizable.

Nevertheless, the significance of "authenticity" debates to Hip Hop in particular and to Black music in general cannot be overlooked, as they also play an important role in concepts of nationhood. As foundational Hip Hop scholars Mark Anthony Neal and Murray Forman (2004) explore in *That's the Joint*, questions of "authenticity" in Hip Hop emerged with its commercial success. These debates have ranged from a West Coast to East Coast feud,[8] and an essentializing of Black culture as "hood," "poor," and "ghetto" in what Ronald A. T. Judy has termed "nigga authenticity" (2004, 58). Yet, as Raquel Rivera (2003) and others have demonstrated, this is a Hip Hop nation that not only essentializes Blackness but pushes out those who helped build it. As a result, today, conversations about authenticity begin with a false premise that Hip Hop is and always has been exclusively Black American (despite its massive consumption by middle-class White youth), while Mexicans are migrants who refuse to assimilate to American culture. Not only do Mexican migrants to the United States disrupt this narrow concept of the Hip Hop nation, these debates don't even take into consideration that they might want to or why.

Unfortunately, this concept of Hip Hop nation does not reflect Hip Hop's very real presence south of the border. For the past several decades visual artists, music producers, MCs, vocalists, and dancers from Latin America have created localized art combining their surrounding culture with influences

---

8. At the core of the East Coast versus West Coast conflict was a fundamental belief that the experiences of those on one coast marked them as more authentic—more gangsta, more ghetto, more hardcore—than those on the other. In other words, one 'hood was deemed more authentically Hip Hop, and, by extension, more authentically black, than the other (Neal 2004, 57).

from north of the U.S. border.[9] Hip Hop in Latin America has grown to the point where Latin American artists are now major influences for some U.S. Latino and non-Latino artists, traveling around the world and performing in large non-English-language showcases. One excellent example of this is the Mexican poet, rap artist, scholar, cultural ambassador, and founder of the Quilomboarte Collective, Bocafloja. One of the most revered icons in Spanish-speaking Hip Hop communities, Bocafloja travels widely and collaborates with numerous U.S. Latino artists, encouraging and spreading his redefined version of Hip Hop's four elements: "Decolonize, self-manage, transgress, emancipate" (*La Verdad*, 130). Significantly, his Hip Hop collective is named "Quilomboarte" to recognize the Quilombos, which during the colonial period on the American continent were established by fugitive Black slaves (also known as maroons and cimarrones), Indigenous peoples, and others who rejected colonialism's domination, who preferred to live as free people in communal form.

Mexican New York serves, then, to expand the Hip Hop nation not just beyond the borders of the continental United States but beyond the borders of an essentialized "nigga authenticity." They encompass not just Bocafloja's physical travels between Mexico City and New York City (and beyond) but his historical and musical travels as well. In it, for example, is Bocafloja's (2016) recognition of Hip Hop's widespread acceptance in Mexico despite its own "collective amnesia"—as he terms it—of Mexico's African roots (*La Verdad* 125) and a recuperation of that history from a Hip Hop sensibility. It is also a new borderlands where tracks like "El Día de Mi Suerte," a song in which Bocafloja criticizes U.S. imperialist tactics over one of Hector Lavoe's most famous salsa songs, is no longer an outlier but an important reflection of these new Mexican and New York stories. Instead, it demonstrates how New York as the newest Mexican city cannot be fully examined without a longer view of history, one in which today's immigrant markets overlay former slave economies as well as past and present Black and Caribbean expressions.

As such, although all-Spanish-language or even all-Mexican shows are no longer a fantasy for Hip Hop aficionados in Mexican Nueva York, outside the Spanish-speaking Hip Hop community Mexican rappers are still considered an oddity, especially in the Northeast. Yet, given this history and the global spread of Hip Hop in general, that young Mexicans who have migrated to or grown up in New York would participate in this youth culture should not be surprising. And yet, as HCP finds, outside the West Coast and that community,

---

9. Unfortunately, very little work exists (at least in English) on Latin American Hip Hop as well.

it often raises eyebrows. Perhaps this is because Mexicans experience an invisibility not only in Hip Hop but also, until recently (as previously described), in New York City. Mexicans are both the largest and the fastest-growing Hispanic subgroup in the United States. They are simultaneously an old and new group—nationally they account for 77 percent of third-generation, 68 percent of second-generation, and 58 percent of first-generation Hispanics (Rumbaut 2006, 34). Yet, despite this large presence and long history in the country,[10] Mexicans are still a relatively new and largely overlooked population in New York.[11] This is also in spite of the fact that the Mexican population growth is no longer due to migration to the United States (more Mexicans are leaving the U.S. than entering at this point) but due to childbirth and the creation of new settled families and communities (Passel, Cohn, and Gonzalez-Barrera 2012). Instead of the invisibility of Mexicans due to their perceived illegality, this new generation experiences what Nicholas P. De Genova (2002) called "deportability in everyday life" (419).

As HCP's story reveals, for the Mexican population who largely immigrated after the 1986 Immigration Law, the inability to return as well as the increased militarization of the border is palpable in their daily lives. They have to decide where they can travel to perform and who can and can't represent their music outside of New York. In the case of HCP, for example, the undocumented status of two the members signifies that travel within the United States is a risk they must heavily weigh, while travel to their fan base in Mexico and Latin America is thus far an impossibility (June 18, 2013).[12] For them, three major aspects of the Immigration Reform and Control Act of 1986 greatly affect them and other Mexicans in New York. First, the pathway to legal status is not and has never been available to the majority of this population. Second, new surveillance technology and increased staff at the border has meant that Mexican migrants in New York are largely cut off from their families and communities in their home countries. Finally, penalties on businesses that knowingly hire or employ unauthorized immigrants have meant greater exploitation and less protections for undocumented Mexican workers. This reality has

---

10. See Tellez and Ortiz (2008) for a comprehensive history of Mexican Americans in the United States from the mid-nineteenth century to the present.

11. As Salamon (2004) reports for the *New York Times*: "Mexicans are the fastest-growing immigrant population in New York. But they say they often feel invisible in a city where the word Chicano is far more likely to evoke the streets of Los Angeles, or border towns in Texas, than Queens, Brooklyn or the Bronx" (E101).

12. Dates reference information from personal interviews conducted with the author either in Spanish, English, or Spanglish. These interviews are the following: Daniel Gil, April 10, 2011; Raúl Hernández, January 31, 2011, April 12, 2011, and June 18, 2013; Hispanos Causando Pániko, February 7, 2011; Enrique Trejo, April 12, 2011.

only become more poignant for the young MCs of this chapter who, in the aftermath of the events of September 11, 2001, have watched the United States' proclamation of a planetary "War on Terrorism" turn into a war on Mexican immigration through the creation of the Department of Homeland Security (De Genova 2007, 421).

This is significant, musically, because the limited though important research done on Chicano rap, mainly of the West Coast by Pancho McFarland, reflects neither the experiences nor the perspectives of Mexican rappers in New York. It is a new Mexican identity that they are representing. Their production of Hip Hop in New York embodies a different type of cultural creation than the *mestizaje* described by McFarland (2006) or Kelley (2006) for Chicano rap on the West Coast. As Gómez Peña (2003) states, "The mestizaje model was originally created to try to grapple with the fusion between the Spanish and the Indigenous. But what do you do with the Post-Mexicanos? We're the product of several racial mixtures and many overlapping subcultures. . . . We're an expression of a double process; the Chicanoization and Americanization of Mexico and the Mexicanization of the United States" (para. 29). HCP and others, then, demonstrate the Mexicanization of New York, the Mexicanization of East Coast rap. It is two undocumented migrants and a Mexican American forming a group called Hispanos Causando Pániko named in honor of a legendary West Coast Chicano rapper, spitting "Viva México" over a classic Otis Redding sample.

Desde Queens Para El Mundo: Hispanos Causando Pániko

In "De Corazón," from their forthcoming album *De Las Calles Para Las Calles,* New York–based Hispanos Causando Pániko (HCP) claim authority as rap artists in two sites: their Mexican identity and their *pasión.* These spaces overlap constantly throughout the song as the lyrics swing back and forth between representing themselves as skilled and sincere artists and as Mexicans. This stance is clear from the song's opening and refrain:

> Cuando entro en la cabina soy la verdad
> No me importa lo que te dijeron
> Yo soy Hip Hop y no creo en la autoridad
> Pero esta es oficial, real.
> Reconoce real mi carnal y Yo
> vamos a rockanrolear hasta el final

y soy leal a lo que represento
Hispanos Causando Pániko y
Mexicanos 100% de Corazón . . .
Esto es lo que es holmes,
Yo no hago reggaeton
Solo hago Hip Hop en español de corazón

When I enter the booth I am the truth
It doesn't matter what they've said
I am Hip Hop and I don't believe in authority
But this is official, real
Recognize real my friends and
We will rock and roll until the end
And I'm loyal to what I represent
Hispanics Causing Panic and
Mexicans 100% from the heart
This is what it is holmes
I don't do reggaeton
I only do Hip Hop in Spanish from the heart

This self-representation is just one indicator of the complex way HCP's per-formance of a Mexicanidad alongside a New York Hip Hop style is begin-ning to speak to a growing population of Mexican-migrant, 1.5- and second-generation youth in New York City. As Ignacio Corona and Alejandro Madrid (2008) indicate in *Postnational Musical Identities*, "music has always been linked to the construction of regional and national identities" (ix); however, the simultaneous representation as "*Mexicano 100%*" and "*Yo soy Hip Hop*" indicates a unique construction of identity in New York that works on mul-tiple levels. In this song, HCP clearly align themselves immediately outside of what has become considered the Latino realm of Hip Hop, Reggaeton, and instead differentiates it as an authentic Hip Hop. As their discography demon-strates, it is a specific style of Hip Hop that associates itself with conscious evocation of New York's early history, as opposed to the more commercial sounds of Reggaeton or the gangsta style currently popular in Chicano West Coast rap. Nevertheless, the nods to Chicano rap (i.e., slang "holmes" as well as their name) demonstrate a complex layering of a particular regional iden-tity that functions within a larger ethnic Hip Hop nation history. Importantly, it indicates how Hip Hop serves some Mexican youths like the members of HCP, to both maintain a sense of pride in their Mexican identity and demand a form of cultural citizenship via a claim to an "authentic" Hip Hop based in

New York. It is in fact, to use Nicholas De Genova's (2010) term, "a politics of anti-identity" in their refusal to be Mexican on anything but their own terms.

HCP's intervention in Hip Hop's authenticity debates highlights several aspects of *mexicanidad* in New York. First, they affiliate themselves with the East Coast while nevertheless celebrating their Chicano rap predecessors as pioneers of Mexican Hip Hop in the United States. They recognize their significance and influence as pioneers and even collaborate[13] with other pioneering Chicano artists such as Sick Jacken,[14] although they view their lives as very different. At the same time, in the conflict between what is "the real" of Hip Hop in commercial versus politically conscious rap,[15] their affiliations are clearly with the latter, especially in their rejection of the highly popular Reggaeton. Their highly personal lyrics demonstrate their practice of "nigga authenticity," an integral component of which is to "know yourself" and is most evident in their choice to rap in Spanish. As Alastair Pennycock (2007) describes it, "Hip-hop forces us to confront some of the conflictual discourses of authenticity and locality, from those that insist that African American Hip Hop is the real variety and that all other forms are inauthentic deviations . . . to those who insist that to be authentic one needs to stick to one's 'own' cultural and linguistic domain, to draw on one's own traditions, to be overtly local" (103). Thus, what examining HCP provides is a new lens to understand the way an increasingly globalized form of authenticity has returned to New York roots and evolved.

HCP's story begins with the last phase of Mexican migration documented by Robert Smith (2006), a migration which is much more diverse in terms of regions of origin (additionally, more migrants come from urban areas).

---

13. One example of this collaboration is the song *La Verdad,* recorded in 2010 when Sick Jacken was visiting NYC and heard some lyrics he couldn't resist. That very day Jacken would record a verse for HCP's new song, "La Verdad." A classic Hip Hop tale of survival and street life, "La Verdad" is significant because it represents both the history and future of Latino Hip Hop in the United States. A member of Psycho Realm and frequent collaborator of Cypress Hill, Sick Jacken has been an important member of the West Coast Hip Hop scene since the early '90s.

14. For more on Sick Jacken, see McFarland (2008), pp. 40–45, 118–27.

15. In his chapter in *That's the Joint* (2004), Alan Light suggests that Hip Hop was often driven by two divergent camps, whether they be the hardcore versus the pop-lite, or the ghetto surreal versus the politically conscious. According to Light, "Hip-hop is first and foremost a pop form, seeking to make people dance and laugh and think. To make them listen and feel, and to sell records, by doing so," but hip-hop also "by definition has a political content . . . rap is about giving voice to a black community otherwise underrepresented, if not silent, in the mass media." Light admits that "these differences are irreconcilable . . . the two strains have been forced to move further apart and to work, in many ways, at cross purposes." Light's comments highlight the diversity inherent in any popular form, but that is largely denied to the African American purveyors of Hip Hop music and culture (59).

Moreover, many of these recent migrants plan to remain permanently in New York, especially the numerous cohort who arrived as children and have now spent the majority of their lives outside of Mexico. Both of these characteristics are reflected in the backgrounds of HCP. Demente, who immigrated from Mexico City at age twelve, arrived in East Harlem on 116th Street (before later moving to Corona, Queens) in the heyday of Hip Hop and quickly started doing graffiti. He met Nemesis, who was born in Queens to parents from Mexico City, in Flushing High School in the eleventh grade, and they used to live near each other in Corona, Queens. There they faced isolation in the 1990s as Mexicans. For example, as Nemesis recalls, everyone thought he was Colombian and Asian. Ironically, the pair didn't even recognize each other as Mexicans (Demente says he thought Nemesis was Arab; Nemesis thought Demente was Dominican) until Nemesis saw Demente with a *Lowrider* magazine. Meck arrived to the birthplace of Hip Hop, the South Bronx, from Puebla, Mexico, at age ten and experienced taunts and racial epithets when attending a predominantly Colombian high school in Jackson Heights, Queens (April 10, 2011). For example, Meck describes meeting about ten Mexican friends with flags in his high school cafeteria on Mexican Independence day, September 16. Immediately, the security guards warned them that they were going to get jumped: "It was tough when I was growing up. A lot of Mexicans formed gangs to protect themselves. I remember at one point there were like sixty Mexican gangs—and that's just the ones that were known . . . I used to avoid hanging out with Mexicans because if they saw three of you walking together—you were a gang . . . I was never in a gang but even so I used to get into a lot of fights" (April 12, 2011). Ironically, he even got his MC name as a result of being one of the only Mexicans in a then Colombian neighborhood. They used to call him "Mexican," which got shortened to "Mex" and then transformed into "Meck" (February 7, 2011).

This combination of proximity to the centers of Hip Hop culture as well as their experiences of marginalization led all three to explore Hip Hop as a way to identify with their surroundings (February 7, 2011). For Meck, Hip Hop at first was a way to learn English and a way to make friends. It was also a way to identify with the tough streets around him: "It was real. They talked about problems that happen in the neighborhood, school, streets, home, drugs" (January 31, 2011). Yet what inspired them to take their music seriously was more than just a love of Hip Hop; it was their need for a version of the music that represented them. As Meck describes it: "I like Wu-Tang, I like Nas, I like to listen to Biggie . . . I wanted to listen to someone like this in Spanish." Likewise, Demente states that the only Spanish-language rap music of the time, Reggaeton—which tends more toward club-style music about partying and women[16]—didn't fit with their musical interests or experiences. According to Meck, "They talk about girls shaking their ass, about bling which I don't have, money I don't have, cars I don't have" (June 18, 2013). This is their form of "nigga authenticity." The music is a reflection of their personal experience, and it was the personal experience that made them turn to Hip Hop.

Significantly, the East Coast rappers (not reggaetoneros) referenced by HCP are not just African American but Latinos, although Latinos who rapped predominately in English, like Big Pun. At the same time, though all three describe listening to West Coast Chicano rap such as Kid Frost (generally considered the grandfather of Latin Hip Hop), Psycho Realm, and The Mexicans while they were growing up, and even take their name "Hispanos Causando Pániko" from Kid Frost's debut album of the same name, they see their sound and style as distinct. "We sound like New York because we grew up listening to East Coast rap," Demente says (February 7, 2011).[17] Thus, HCP's Hip Hop biography is very distinct from both Chicano rappers and Puerto Rican MCs. The Nuyorican experience—the navigation between distinct Puerto Rican sensibilities and those derived from life in New York City—that marked so many of the first generation of Puerto Rican Hip Hop artists is very different than those of "La Raza" rappers like Kid Frost and the Aztlan Underground or Cuban-American MC Mellow Man Ace. According to Raegan Kelley, "To call yourself Chicano is to claim La Raza, to locate your origin within the struggle of a people for land and for cultural, political and economic self-determination" (101). On the other hand, neither HCP nor any other Mexican rapper in New York makes claims to Aztlan—they claim their neighborhood(s) in New York and Mexico. Thus, while they listen to, respect, and even collaborate with West Coast rappers, their perspective and lyrics are those of a recent migrant struggling to find work and respect as an undocumented person or one that is most often viewed and treated

---

16. For more about Reggaeton, see Raquel Rivera, Wayne Marshall, and Deborah Pacini Hernandez (2009).

17. Members of HCP clearly distinguish themselves from "Chicano rap" even though they often collaborate with artists on the West Coast. They also separate what they see as older Chicano rap from the gangsta rap that they see as more predominant today (Gil, April 10, 2011). Meck elaborates: "When Chicano Rap started, it was full of pride of being Mexican-American, but now it's changed, it's more like gangster rap . . . I don't consider myself Chicano, but me and those old school rappers shared that Mexican pride. A Chicano is someone that was born in the U.S. and has Mexican blood. They don't call themselves Mexicans or Americans because in some ways they feel rejected from both races. Our Hip Hop is definitely different from the Hip Hop in the West Coast. We have different struggles, we are just learning how to get respect from everyone else, we jumped the border meanwhile the border jumped the West Coast" (April 12, 2011). Thus, while HCP members clearly share a respect for and knowledge of the history and importance of Chicano rap and the importance of that identity, they clearly see their music, struggles, and identity as separate.

as such. Rather than enter into the East Coast–West Coast authenticity debates, they recognize the significance of the Chicano call for solidarity with "La Raza" and create their own call for Mexican pride in New York.

As just this small piece of HCP's experience attests, their identities in New York are influenced both by a particular time in Hip Hop history and by their migration experiences as Mexicans and their reception in New York. Regardless of their actual immigration status, as Mexicans in New York, HCP and others like them have largely been viewed as "illegal immigrants" with all the negative connotations associated with that term. HCP's claim to an authentic Hip Hop, thus, is also crucial as a way to navigate their new, often unwelcoming surroundings, by embracing their own Hip Hop identity. It is a Hip Hop authenticity, grounded in New York's historically central role, as well as in their Queens upbringing and their identity as Mexicans. It is an effort to make a lack of citizenship into a form of membership in an alternative transnational Hip Hop nation. As such, their Hip Hop identity is more than just a claim to an authentic NYC Hip Hop; it is also the representation of a particular culture and community found within Mexico's newest Borderlands.

As such, HCP reflects a new chapter in studies of Mexican migration. While Mexican scholars of Mexican migration to the United States have tended to approach the topic from an analysis of U.S. capitalism and demands for low wage labor, U.S. scholars have often approached the study via questions of "settlement" and "assimilation" (De Genova 2002, 434). For example, while Robert Smith has researched "Black Mexicans" in New York; that is, phenotypically "Mexican-looking" youth who identified as Black during adolescence and used this identity to become upwardly mobile, this is not HCP's story ("Black Mexicans" 517). Theirs is an act of neither assimilation nor rebellion but a form of "politics of anti-identity" (De Genova 2010, 110). Rather than apologetic or accommodationist, it is instead a profound statement of self-acceptance. Like the slogans "We are here and we're not leaving" in the wake of the 2006 mobilization, HCP's brand of Hip Hop is instead anti-assimilationist. As De Genova (2010) writes:

> The bold and fearless character of this posture, furthermore, was only surpassed by its uncompromising intransigence and *incorrigibility*: this was a profoundly *anti-assimilationist* gesture. *We are here,* they proclaimed, and by implication, they insisted: *We are who we are, and what we are.* The millions who literally put their deportable bodies on the line in this struggle—at least, when they chanted *this* slogan—were not begging anyone for their putative civil or human "rights," were not asking any authorities for permission or pardon, and did not seek anyone's approval or acceptance. (103)

In a similar way, HCP refuse to either assimilate to what is seen as the stereo-typical Latino's place in Hip Hop (Reggaeton) or to become "Black Mexicans." From their sound to their lyrics, their music is an unapologetic explanation of who they are. It is one, for example, that does not apologize for undocu-mented status. For example, "Desde Los Ojos de un Inmigrante" ("From the Eyes of an Immigrant"), written by Meck, relates the experience of crossing the border: from meeting the coyote, to trekking across the border, to losing connections to family members. He also turns the personal experience into a challenge, naming himself as "sólo uno de millones que han cruzado la fron-tera" ("I'm just one of millions who have crossed the border") and challenging his listeners to "ve la vida desde los ojos de un inmigrante" ("view life through the eyes of an immigrant").

HCP's lyrics similarly demonstrate their negotiation of their Mexican identity within a diverse New York that has never been receptive. This New York also includes a Hip Hop nation that was not initially welcoming and is still often skeptical. Meck's Hip Hop "biography," "Así Comencé" ("This Is How I Started"), demonstrates this experience of isolation within New York's Hip Hop community as well as his sense of marginalization as a migrant.

> Todo comenzó en Corona como una broma
> Y en poco tiempo en la zona me decían que mi letra era cabrona
> Comencé a pensar que tenía talento
> Y en aquel tiempo en Nueva York
> no había nadie con quien compartir ese sentimiento
>
> el sueño americano no es como se cree
> hay humillación y injusticia mucha malicia
> solo un por ciento que se ve en noticias
> quería que el mundo supiera mi verdad
> quería que vieran la realidad
>
> Everything started in Corona like a joke
> And in a little time in the area
> They told me my lyrics were tight
> I started to think that I had talent
> But in that time in New York
> There was no one to share this feeling
>
> The American dream is not what you believe
> There's humiliation injustice lots of malice

> It's only one percent you see in the news
> I wanted to world to know my reality
> It's not stubbornness
> I wanted them to see my reality

In this song, Meck describes the loneliness and isolation of pursuing Hip Hop as a Mexican in New York during a time when there was no one with whom to share his interests. His decision, however, to pursue this chosen medium despite hardship is "for his family" and "his race." In particular, he describes the need to express "his reality," which had very little to do with some fanciful "American Dream" but instead was full of "humiliations" and "injustice." Meck, in describing the inspiration for HCP's lyrics, adds: "I think of what we went through. Everything we saw, all the suffering, crossing the border, living with twenty people in one apartment. My father used to make $200 a week as a dishwasher" (February 7, 2011). Instead, their choice of Hip Hop in Spanish, establishing close connections to artists across the United States and Mexico, and making use of international artists in sampling, demonstrate their emphasis on strengthening a Mexican identity in New York via a new aesthetic. Meanwhile, their large Latin American following points to the power of transnationalism in the way their Mexican-themed music is impacting a global Hip Hop and forging new and wider connections.

HCP's lyrics represent a powerful form of autohistoria in the tradition of Gloria Anzaldúa. It is a technique of spoken-word-art-performance-activism via Hip Hop music by Mexicans in New York City employed to narrate both personal and collective stories. As Anzaldúa (2007) explains, "*Autohistoria* is a term I use to describe the genre of writing about one's personal and collective history using fictive elements, a sort of fictionalized autobiography or memoir: an autohistoria-teoría is a personal essay that theorizes" (6). Composed of personal stories as well as observations, HCP's lyrics reflect an attempt to both experience their story and build community connections. Similarly, Mexican MCs' autohistorias reflect their experience in multiple worlds and contact zones within New York, Hip Hop, and questions of Mexicanidad. For HCP, then, it is East Coast and West Coast rap history, the trauma of Mexican migration, and the realities of surveillance in a post-9/11 world laid down over classic anglophone-Caribbean-inspired beats.

The basis of HCP's Hip Hop identity is a unique blend of authenticity and community representation that can only be understood within a particular contemporary New York context that also highlights important and emerging directions in the genre. HCP provides a lens to examine the ways that Mexican identities are negotiated and performed in spaces—in this case both

Hip Hop and New York—that have little to no recognition of them. Like the 2006 migrant activists who refused to be defined by discourses of illegality, HCP's claim to an authentic Mexican identity through Hip Hop is also similar to earlier responses to essentialized identities articulated by Stuart Hall (2003) and Paul Gilroy (2000).[18] As Hall points out, "Perhaps instead of thinking of identity as an already accomplished fact, which the new cultural practices then represent, we should think, instead, of identity as a 'production' which is never complete, always in process, and always constituted within, not outside, representation. This view problematizes the very authority and authenticity to which the term 'cultural identity' lays claim" (234). In this way, HCP's insistence on their authenticity is an important intervention against charges of "assimilation" or cultural appropriation, terms that have been used to dismiss Latino artists who were seen to privilege Hip Hop over Latinidad in the 1990s (Rivera 2003, 152–63). They are authentic to Hip Hop's New York traditions and history but not to its more recent racialized inflections.

As scholars of contemporary transnationalism such as Saskia Sassen (2014) and Arjun Appadurai (1996) have observed, an emphasis on movement also requires an engagement with the particularities of place and location (or locatedness). For this reason, while Meck grounds his Hip Hop origins in Corona, where he largely grew up and still lives, it is from the particular that the global occurs. While the song "De Corazón" legitimizes them as 100 percent Mexican and 100 percent authentically Hip Hop, the concept of "Hispanos" spreads their voice "desde Queens para todo el mundo" and declares "Soy hispano soy latino 100%." Here they expand the meaning of "raza" from Mexicans to Latinos, whom they are equally proud to represent, because "en NY los latinos hablan español" (in New York Latinos speak Spanish). Though their stories are New York Mexican–based,[19] they see the plight of their gente (Mexicanos)

---

18. According to Gilroy (2000), "Though largely ignored by recent debates over modernity and its discontents, these ideas about nationality, ethnicity, authenticity, and cultural integrity are characteristically modern phenomena that have profound implications for cultural criticism and cultural history" (44).

19. In songs like "Recesión" ("Recession"), "Sacrificio" ("Sacrifice"), and "Medidas drásticas" ("Drastic Measures"), they describe both the socioeconomic hardships and lack of opportunities that cause despair. For example, in "Recesión" they describe the difficulties of upward mobility: "El sueño americano nos sale caro / desperdiciamos años fumando, tomando, culeando / atrapados en el barrio sin salida" (The American dream costs us a lot / We waste years drinking, smoking, fucking / we're trapped in the barrio without exit). Meanwhile, in "Sacrificio" they describe the costs of underemployment experienced by many Mexican men—from taking risks for the hope of some benefit, to working so much they hardly see their children. This feeling of living a trapped life as a result of their immigrant status comes through full force in "Medidas Drásticas," in which they rap "A veces me siento que estoy entre la espada y la pared / y la seria infrared me tiene apuntado en la frente / y una gente me tiene la migra me quiere acabar con

as irrefutably connected to the question of Latinos in the United States, adding yet another layer to their sources of identification. Thus, at the same time that HCP uses Hip Hop to legitimize their Mexican identity (and vice versa) as a powerful source of ethnic pride, this pride and music exists on an unapologetically transnational plane. Their Spanish-language music is diffused throughout Latin America, and they regularly perform with artists from other countries. In a New York context in which "Latino" has largely meant Puerto Rican, or more generally Caribbean, these links also indicate a Mexicanization of East Coast Latinidad not often recognized in current studies of Mexican transnational flows, since those studies tend to focus on the borderlands and on Mexican–U.S. relations.[20] While clearly Mexico for HCP is an imagined community they draw on for ethnic social capital in New York, their participation in a global Spanish-language "Hip Hop" and larger U.S. Latino communities demonstrates a much more complex formation of cultural identity.

HCP, like their Hip Hop music, find themselves in a very particular in-between place. In not having chosen their own immigration, they were made transnational, while their choices in music reflect a struggle to adapt and survive in the United States. Their negative reception in New York, and their use of Hip Hop to emphasize Mexicanidad, indicates that their continued expression of a transnational Mexican identity is a choice, a "deportable" identity they have chosen to embrace. For HCP, "Yo soy Hip Hop" allows them to move in and out of multiple identities through which they can connect to multiple audiences. It is a political identity, a method of community building, and a form of musical expression. It is Mexican and Latino and Latin American. It is old-school Hip Hop and reflects new media platforms (YouTube, Facebook). "Yo soy Hip Hop" is more than just a statement; it is also a

---

la vida" (sometimes I feel like I am between a rock and a hard place / and the infrared rangefinder is pointing at my forehead / some people have me, ICE wants to end my life). In songs like these, HCP paints a grim vision of what it means to be a Mexican immigrant in the United States. Rather than emphasize their Queens experience, they privilege a Mexican one, and let their sound give their listeners a sense of New York's streets by evoking the style of Big Pun and Wu-Tang. What makes their rap authentic, they feel, is not just the sound, but also the storytelling tradition. According to Meck: "Hip Hop is like the newspaper of the streets. We tell the stories you can't find anywhere else" (personal communication, June 18, 2013).

20. For example, the important work of Robert Smith (2006) on Mexican immigration to New York focuses on transnational linkages between immigrants and their hometowns. I would argue that equally important are the linkages formed and maintained not just between Latino immigrants and their home countries but across national and ethnic borders. Equally significant, especially in a New York context, are the transnational linkages that Mexican immigrants are forming with other immigrant groups as well as across Latin America and the Caribbean. These are significant, understudied circuits of influence that have increasing impacts on cultural identity formation.

complex, ever-shifting identity dependent on situation, audience, context, surroundings. But it is a Mexican identity that could not exist without Hip Hop. Here, the medium and the message intertwine to represent a new expression of Mexicanidad, from the streets of Corona, Queens, "para el mundo."

Bibliography

Anzaldúa, Gloria. 2007. *Borderlands / La Frontera: The New Mestiza*, 3rd ed. San Francisco: Ann Lute Books.

Appadurai, Arjun. 1996. *Modernity at Large: Cultural Dimensions of Globalization.* Minneapolis: University of Minnesota Press.

Bergad, Laird. 2011. *Mexicans in New York 1990–2005.* Latino Data Project. Center for Latin American, Caribbean, and Latino Studies Graduate Center. http://clacls.gc.cuny.edu/files /2013/10/Mexicans-in-New-York-City-1990-2005.pdf.

Corona, Ignacio, and Alejandro Madrid. 2008. *Postnational Musical Identities.* Lanham, MD: Lexington Books.

De Genova, Nicholas. 2002. "Migrant 'Illegality' and Deportability in Everyday Life." *Annual Review of Anthropology* 31: 419–47.

———. 2007. "The Production of Culprits: From Deportability to Detainability in the Aftermath of 'Homeland Security.'" *Citizenship Studies* 11(5): 421–48.

———. 2010. "The Queer Politics of Migration: Reflections on 'Illegality' and Incorrigibility." *Studies in Social Justice* 4(2): 101–26.

Department of City Planning of New York City. 2012. "NYC 2010: Results from the Census." http://www.nyc.gov/html/dcp/pdf/census/census_brief2_051012.pdf (accessed June 24, 2013).

Dimitriadis, Greg. 2009. *Performing Identity/Performing Culture: Hip Hop as Text, Pedagogy, and Lived Practice.* New York: Peter Lang.

Flores, Juan. 2000. *From Bomba to Hip Hop: Puerto Rican Culture and Latino Identity.* New York: Columbia University Press.

———. 2004. "Puerto Rocks: Rap, Roots and Amnesia." In Forman and Neal, 69–96.

Foner, Nancy. 2001. *New Immigrants in New York.* New York: Columbia University Press.

———. 2005. *In the New Land: A Comparative View of Immigration.* New York: New York University Press.

Forman, Murray, and Mark Anthony Neal, eds. *That's the Joint: The Hip Hop Studies Reader.* New York: Routledge, 2004.

George, Nelson. 1998. *Hip Hop America.* New York: Penguin Books.

Gilroy, Paul. 1993. *The Black Atlantic: Modernity and Double-Consciousness.* Cambridge: Harvard University Press.

———. 2000. "The Black Atlantic as Counter Culture Modernity." In *Black British Culture and Society: A Text-Reader,* edited by Kwesi Owusu. London: Routledge. 439–52.

Gómez Peña, Guillermo. 2003. "Interview by Gabrielle Banks—Culture Tracfficking for the 21st Century." *Colorlines,* June 15. http://colorlines.com/archives/2003/06/culturetracfficking_for _the_21st_century.html.

Hall, Stuart. 2003. "Cultural Identity and Diaspora." In *Theorizing Diaspora: A Reader,* edited by Jana Evans Braziel and Anita Mannur. Malden, MA: Blackwell. 233–46.

Judy, R. A. T. 2004. "On the Question of Nigga Authenticity." In Forman and Neal, 105–17.

Kelley, Raegan. 2004. "Hip Hop Chicano: A Separate but Parallel Story." In Forman and Neal, 95–103.

Kun, Josh. 2010. "Hecho in El Lay." *Los Angeles Magazine* 55(9): 100–102.

Light, Alan. 2004. "About a Salary or Reality? Rap's Recurrent Conflict." In Forman and Neal, 137–45.

McFarland, Pancho. 2006. "Chicano Rap Roots: Black-Brown Cultural Exchange and the Making of a Genre." *Callaloo* 39(3): 939–57.

———. 2008. *Chicano Rap: Gender and Violence in the Postindustrial Barrio.* Austin: University of Texas Press.

Passel, Jeffrey S., D'Vera Cohn, and Ana Gonzalez-Barrera. 2012. "Net Migration from Mexico Falls to Zero—and Perhaps Less." Pew Research Center, April 23.

Pennycock, Alastair. 2007. *Global English and Transcultural Flows.* London: Routledge.

Risomena, Fernando, and Douglas S. Massey. 2012. "Pathways to El Norte: Origins, Destinations, and Characteristics of Mexican Migrants to the United States." *International Migration Review* 46(1): 3–36.

Rivera, Raquel. 2003. *New York Ricans from the Hip Hop Zone.* New York: Palgrave Macmillan.

Rivera, Raquel, Wayne Marshall, and Deborah Pacini Hernandez. 2009. *Reggaeton.* Durham, NC: Duke University Press.

Rumbaut, Ruben. 2006. "The Making of a People." In *Hispanics and the Future of America,* edited by Marta Tienda and Faith Mitchell. Committee on Transforming Our Common Destiny, National Research Council. Washington, DC: National Academies Press. 16–65.

Salamon, Julie. 2004. "Celebrating Mexican Life in New York." *New York Times,* December 8, late ed., E101.

Sassen, Saskia. 2014. "Nomadic Territories and Times." August 5, 2015.

Semple, Kirk. 2010. "Immigrants Sets Sights On the Mayor's Office, Back Home in Mexico." *New York Times,* June 2, late ed., A018.

Smith, Robert Courtney. 2006. *Mexican New York: Transnational Lives of New Immigrants.* Berkley: University of California Press.

———. 2014. "Black Mexicans, Conjunctural Ethnicity, and Operating Identities: Long-Term Ethnographic Analysis." *American Sociological Review* 79(3): 517–48.

Solis, Jocelyn. 2001. "Immigration Status and Identity: Undocumented Mexicans in New York." In *Mambo Montage: The Latinization of New York,* edited by Agustin Laos-Montes and Arlene Dávila. New York: Columbia University Press. 337–62.

Tellez, Edward, and Vilma Ortiz. 2008. *Generations of Exclusion: Mexican Americans, Assimilation, and Race.* New York: Russell Sage Foundation.

Discography

Hispanos Causando Pániko. Forthcoming. *De Las Calles Para Las Calles.*

Hispanos Causando Pániko. 2007. Mixtape.

chapter 10

Graffiti and Rap on Mexico's Northern Border

Observing Two Youth Practices— Transgressions or Reproductions of Social Order?

Lisset Anahí Jiménez Estudillo

Translated by Janelle Gondar

In Baja California, Mexico, Tijuana is the smallest municipality with respect to territorial size; however, it contains more than 1,559,683 inhabitants according to the 2010 census performed by the National Institute of Statistics and Geography. Over the last decades, the city has experienced an overflowing and uncontrolled population growth, always to the south and to the east, never to the west—because of its proximity to the Pacific Ocean—and much less to the "northside," as there is an old and rusted wall there that reminds the inhabitants of Tijuana that they are excluded by those on the other side. In other words, there exists an international borderline that divides the urban patch that extends from one side of the boundary to the other. Nevertheless, the daily actions of thousands of people who inhabit these border cities prompts us to consider that the great *trans*borderline urban space can be better understood as a "border zone," since within these areas there is a dialectical relationship between the processes of national differentiation, migratory control, economic separation, police surveillance, and identity conflict; yet, there are also processes of demographic convergence, cultural hybridization, and social articulation.

Tijuana's geographic position makes it a border city, a fact that needs to be understood and studied in a way that is both particular and precise (Grimson 2011, 116). Border zones, and this one in particular, combine and mix social, economic, and cultural elements, as well as political ones, with their neighboring country, which, in this case, is the United States. This does not make Tijuana less Mexican or more American. Instead, the young people have managed to develop interesting and unique *trans*borderline social phenomena, although they are not isolated from this global system.

Graffiti is something undeniable in this city; while traversing it, one can observe that it is covered by said phenomenon, since every flat, round, smooth, or rough surface can have graffiti painted on it. Truth be told, one can even come to appreciate the diverse types of markings, be they legible calligraphy with local neighborhood references, simple *throw-ups* or *tags,* more elaborate *pieces* and *burners,* legal walls, or sanctioned artistic murals. But Tijuana did not emerge like this, with painted walls; someone gave this idea to its inhabitants. Mainly because of the close relationship between Baja California and California, and more specifically, Tijuana–Los Angeles, people in Tijuana adopted graffiti in the late 1980s and early 1990s. The same thing began to happen in the entire border zone, and it is for this reason that "Tijuana is one of Mexico's pioneer metropolises with regard to presenting the symptoms of graffiti on its walls"[1] (Anaya Cortés 2002, 66).

However, graffiti neither traveled nor arrived alone. In an interview I did in 2010 with one of Tijuana's most veteran practitioners of the medium, he states that Hip Hop dancing was one of the first activities that gained popularity during the early '90s. Shente, a Tijuanan graffiti artist, recalls that during his childhood he would see McDonald's ads on the television in which there were children breakdancing in different parts of the world. According to Shente, it was so contagious that, at the age of nine, he and his friends from the block began breakdancing. Along with that came rap music, as well as playing with turntables.

At present, the four elements that compose Hip Hop culture—which was born in the 1970s in the Bronx and then moved across the country from the East Coast until it boomed on the West Coast—allowed the close and historical relationship between Baja California and California, particularly that of Tijuana–Los Angeles, to forge a pathway for this movement to also become ingrained in this Mexican city. While rap music is one of the most popular genres among present-day Tijuanan youth, graffiti is the most visible element of Hip Hop culture in the city.

---

1. All quotes originally in Spanish. Translation of quotes by Janelle Gondar.

As such, Tijuana has functioned as a bridge for the consolidation of the Hip Hop movement, at least in Mexico, facilitating the transition of these cultural and youth movements from *trans*borderline to transnational. But none of this would have been possible without the constant cultural migratory flows of the zone due to the migratory mobility among people—in other words, the sociocultural connections that already existed and continue to exist between communities on both sides of the border, in addition to cultural industries and mass media. It was all of these factors that pushed and fostered the reproduction of graffiti and rap on this south side of the borderland.

After the acknowledgment and presence of new youth identities, graffiti and rap artists had to search for and establish certain criteria that, first, would correspond to their *trans*borderline context and, second, did not distance them from what was happening in the rest of the world, and much less from what was originally established in New York. There was no better way to do this than to begin to incorporate these new identities into their daily lives. Faced with this challenge, the Tijuanan youth, conscious of their border situation, on one hand considered their geographic position to be privileged. They believed that they had greater access to information, merchandise, and a connection to other similar young people from other countries since "at the borders peculiar socio-cultural frameworks from either country come into contact" (Grimson 2011, 116). According to the Tijuanan youth, this puts them in a geographically favorable position, as their proximity to the United States has promoted a greater development of their practices in comparison to other young people in the rest of the country.

On the other hand, these young people also see themselves at a disadvantage, and in various conversations they mention having experienced situations of exclusion, for being outside the center. Tijuanan youth are constantly situated in the periphery in two ways: first, because they feel and see themselves as distanced from the center of their country, Mexico—this has led them to describe themselves as "different" and "strange" with respect to certain habits and customs of the "Mexican citizen"—and second, because they feel exposed to a position of subordination, in the presence of youth from the United States. Though at times they are considered allies with their U.S. counterparts, they are simultaneously seen as opponents, as "in terms of identity, nationality is the primary mode of interpolation and self-affiliation in this zone" (Grimson 2011, 125).

Nevertheless, they highly tout their privilege of easily being able to cross the San Ysidro Land Port of Entry for the purchase of materials and/or the acquisition of books, magazines, music, or clothes, or simply to admire the urban landscapes filled with graffiti that the others, those in the southern part of the country, cannot access so easily. According to Shente (35 years old):

> Imagine, someone that goes to another country to steal paint and bring it back to his/her own country; to be bringing back ideas from there and to also infiltrate the area in order to do a little vandalism on that side; but HEM [Made in Mexico "*Hecho en México*"] had to happen, it was created with the notion that "we're going to hit 'em where it hurts, we're going to show 'em that we also have graffiti in Tijuana," because we weren't thinking so much about down there in the center of Mexico, we were thinking "how can we hit 'em where it hurts up there in the U.S.? How can we leave a mark that they'll never forget? Let 'em know that HEM was in their house." Then later we became cool with them, but all we wanted was to receive the kind of respect that you show someone that is on your same level.

Their situation of inclusion and exclusion puts them in a constant back and forth between an "us" and a "them." And in conversations among themselves, it is common to find a certain level of rejection or conflict with young people who assume the role of or identify with their U.S. counterparts. It is in this contact that "transborderline cultural relationships and elements are a key area of production and reproduction of symbolic borders, both on the level of personal and group identification as well as in their practices" (Grimson 2011, 126), thus contributing to the construction of a borderline identity within a context in which national identities are often pitted against one another.

New and Old Youth Identities

Although graffiti and rap gained ground in the border zone, it is not clear exactly how many young people began to actively pursue rap, since there was not (and there still is not) a way to detain or criminalize them, unlike in the case of graffiti, simply for rhyming. For example, a civil association from the United States called "Graffiti Busters" "in 2001, published a record of at least 25 groups of young people that painted graffiti. Later, in 2003, they warned that there were 2,500 active graffiti artists in Tijuana" (Sánchez López 2010, 45). Thus, new youth forms of organization and expression, like graffiti and rap, continue to search for a certain distinction and acceptance within the larger society.

When Hip Hop culture invaded the city in the early 1990s, many young people who today are involved in the art of painting and rhyming belonged to other youth identities. During the in-depth interviews I had in the field, many of the interviewees mentioned that, before, they would affiliate themselves with such identity groups known as *cholos,* expressing that at that time they represented a certain neighborhood—generally that of the colony in which they resided—and not a crew.

Mode, a graffiti artist who has been painting for more than ten years, recounts that in his adolescence, when he lived in the Libertad colony, which is located in the eastern part of the city and close to the border, he belonged to a clique (*clica*) known as *Liber 13* in which he participated in assaults, fights, and robberies. Robs and Nube, both of whom are relatively new on the Tijuana scene, state that the first experience they had after becoming part of a crew of *taggers* was in collectives that continued to preserve this neighborhood way of identifying. However, in all three cases, there was a decision to abandon these types of collectives in order to find another type of social space. They all expressed having felt a need to do something different, to find a place to develop what they loved to do most: drawing.

In the case of rap music, the first tracks to which these young people had access were made by Afro-descendents and, almost equally, by Chicanos. Therefore, rap in English was their first influence, but it was soon followed by rap in Spanish. With this, they affirm that among their first influences were groups like Wu-Tang Clan, KRS-One, El Dyablo, El Tecolete, and Cypress Hill, to name just a few. Despite the difference in language, the topics discussed were very similar, since the majority rapped about murder, drugs, money, and women, very much in the style of what is called *gangsta rap*: "I thought that the language of rap was English since it was the only kind that would get to us, but when we heard Chicanos rapping in Spanish in the United States, we identified with them and we would say 'Yo, dude, it's rap, but I understand it! I don't have to kill myself with a stupid dictionary to see what these guys are saying'" (interview with Danger, 24 years old).

Danger, who nowadays dedicates his life to rap, admits that at one point he identified as a *cholo,* but it was because that is what he saw and what there was in his neighborhood, *Mata 13*—which references his place of residence, Ejido Matamoros. According to Danger, at that time, rap was associated with one's neighborhood and with extreme violence. However, he also confesses that he never felt comfortable making this type of rap music, since *cholo* or *chicano* rap, as he calls it, only closed doors for him as young people from other neighborhoods refused to listen to it. Despite feeling a strong attraction to Anglo-Saxon music, various Tijuana rappers expressed that they did not identify with it entirely; they stated that while the subject matter of the songs had a certain resemblance to their own context, it wasn't something they themselves experienced, but above all, it was something they wanted to talk about. However, with the arrival of groups like Control Machete, Cartel de Santa, Akwid, and others, they discovered a way to rap in their own language. As such, it was mainly through Spanish and Latin American groups that they found new themes, rhythms, meters, and flows.

The transformation occurred when young *Tijuanenses* found the way to move themselves toward new arenas, making music and painting walls in their own unique style. Despite their determination to create something new, they still had to walk through uncharted territory, as they did not have a clear idea and were not yet familiar with certain organizational logics that these new identities to which they were affiliating themselves required. They had to confront a very complex process of transition. As Danger describes, "Although we were no longer a neighborhood group, we still kept the same essence. I know that we didn't represent the neighborhood anymore, that now we defended a *crew,* but even though we were not cholos anymore, we still had those habits because that's where almost all of us had come from, from a neighborhood group. Now, we don't do any of those things."

In this way, new tendencies began to emerge, and the participating artists began to talk about new social themes through aerosol art and lyrical rap, in addition to purchasing specific brands and a whole new set of accessories that the movements required: caps, baggy pants, Hip Hop– or graffiti-themed T-shirts, while primarily wearing hoodies and sneakers. Brands from the United States like Adidas, Ecko Unltd, and Tribal Gear began to take off and reach such high sales so as to position themselves as the favorites among young people in Tijuana and all over the world.

With these new products, the young people who had joined the new movements of rap and graffiti began to differentiate themselves from previous youth identities such as *cholos,* the thirteens (*treces*), and the eighteens (*dieciochos*). But, as I have stated before, the change was not easy, since they all occupied a shared space: the streets. Even though young people who belonged to both identities were neighbors, at one point they had to confront one another in order to understand what was happening and, therefore, reach an acknowledgment and understanding of one another.

Spaces of Transnational Sociability

Graffiti and rap as movements are transnational cultural phenomena that were able to migrate and become established in almost any place in the world while preserving a constant dialogue with the men and women who assume these identities at the moment of reproducing these practices; these artists are thus responsible for the construction of networks and flows that guarantee an articulation among various points and people in the world. The networks that these participants have constructed have multiple levels, which could be categorized as local, national, and transnational.

Tijuana is no exception. During my field research, I found information that demonstrated how the young people have defined these networks and, more importantly, at what level they have inserted themselves. In both cases, graffiti and rap artists alike have managed to insert themselves in all of the previously mentioned ones, and have also created an additional level, which I will call *trans*local or *trans*borderline, which is supported by institutional, territorial, and technological elements.

Social spaces, understood as "a symbolic issue of meanings, of representations, of collective imaginations, of practices and actions, where one constructs a sense of place" (Soto Villagrán 2006, 9) and, at the same time, a sense of subjects, can be of two kinds: physical and virtual. In other words, first the subjects involved have managed to construct a physical social space as a result of being located in the same social environment, such as school, work, the block, the colony, and even kinship. This could primarily correspond with a certain level of local and *trans*local interaction, since by moving about from one side of the border to the other they have been able to establish these types of connections, uniting a physical transnational social space that shifts between the institutional and the territorial.

Later on, with the arrival and opening of the internet, youth socialization through this medium became popularized with increased access. According to the National Survey of Young People conducted in 2010, in Baja California 48 percent of young people had access to the internet from home. Therefore, rappers and writers began using platforms like Myspace to show their work, socialize with their friends, and meet people with similar interests at the same time that they were able to connect with people who lived in the interior of Mexico, in the United States, or in any part of the world. While working on this ethnography, I noticed that they used Messenger, and more recently Facebook, to create local, translocal, national, and transnational social spaces.

When young people began to use these types of platforms, they expanded both their physical and their virtual social spaces, and this also allowed them to be informed about what was going on in other cities. And it was there that they saw the opportunity to generate spaces in which to circulate their cultural production, since operating in an independent and underground territory— in comparison to major cultural industries—was the only way, besides the streets, to be their own agents in disseminating their talents. For example, the young female rapper Pyyeza believes that it was due to her use of MSN, and later Myspace, that she was able to position her rap music in Tijuana.

Through these networks, these young artists manage to leave their city and get to know others. Spel, thanks to his connections and virtual expositions on the internet, was able to show his work in cities like San Diego, Los Angeles, Mexico City, and Oaxaca. The young artists also began to experiment with processes to expand their collectives, as in the case of HEM crew. At first, the members formed part of a local and translocal (Tijuana–San Diego) scene; however, today they are considered to be a transnational crew with members in Switzerland, Spain, Canada, Arizona, San Francisco, Mexico City, Queretaro, Guadalajara, and Rosarito, among others.

In the case of rap music, the crossing over of these young rappers and their productions to other places is a recent event. First of all, their principal connection was established in California—Los Angeles to be exact—and later throughout all of Mexico, since nowadays the cultural creations of these young musicians travel with greater speed, arriving in places with which even they are not familiar.

> In 2002, 2004 unfortunately, we didn't have as much access to the Internet like we do now. For me, it was an incredible increase. I didn't have Internet, I didn't have MSN, and when I did go on MSN, I didn't have a computer at home, so I would go online whenever I would go over to someone's house or whenever I went to the Internet cafe, but little by little this "*mediosity*" [*sic*] has grown and has helped us to move out music. There are moments in which I realize that outside of my city people know what I do or recognize what I do; I remember that one day on messenger they said to me, "hey dude, here in San Luis Potosi some guy passed by in his car with your track playing"—"San Luis Potosi? I have no idea where that is, man; you must be joking! What the fuck??" (interview with Danger, 24 years old)

A Sense of Belonging

As we have seen, the presence of both movements in the city is both real and existent, a movement that is articulated within and outside of itself. This has led some young people who are involved in graffiti and rap to read and document one another in depth: to find out where what they love to do comes from. Others, while less interested in its history, find knowing about and searching for issues related to these practices to be fundamental; in other words, they show an interest in learning about and researching what is new and what is not so new with respect to what is being done in each discipline. During their conversations, they always mention current information or information from a few years back regarding collaborations among rappers, places, walls, and other graffiti artists' content.

In this way, the young people express feeling part of a community on a small and large scale; that is, outside of their social circles and within them. It is precisely this sense of belonging that has given their lives meaning, seeing in them a hope and an opportunity to feel like someone, to be someone. Moreover, for many it is seen as the only way, or at least the way they chose to express themselves. As Serieh says: "Graffiti is my opportunity to stand out somehow." Shente adds that, in fact, it does not matter who did it first; what she cares about is that it exists and that it gave a lot of hope to other young people who might not have been good at other socially acceptable activities such as soccer or baseball.

For some young people, living in Tijuana represents a crude and complicated reality, as is the case of Fernando—he is eighteen, and, at this early age, he had already been obligated to abandon his studies to go work in construction, and he currently works in a television factory with David, who goes by the alias RS (*Revolución Subterránea* or "Underground Revolution"). The two are neighbors, and a couple of years ago they decided to write rap songs. Now, they have decided to invest money and time in order to record tracks in a semiprofessional studio at the modest rate of 100 *pesos* per track. Both young men admit that they like to play their music while working at the plant, since they feel a sense of satisfaction in hearing themselves and in showing off their music to their co-workers, especially when their colleagues show disbelief that they are really the ones they are listening to on the headphones.

Another example is that of Suker, a member of the Alto Kalibre crew, who, in the last few years, gave up rap to sell vegetables out of a wheeled cart since now he has a family to support. He is aware of the fact that, for the time being, it is complicated for him to return to making music, but he is hopeful that he will find the time to do so since, even though he is not trying to make a career out of it or much less earn any money from it, he does plan on obtaining some recognition, as he sees rap music as the only way to gain recognition from other young people in society.

Nevertheless, there are other reasons why young people are motivated to rap or paint graffiti, since not all young people who do so live in conditions of poverty or marginalization, although the majority of them do have precarious employment situations. One example is Esraes, a young university student who considers himself to be middle class but who, unable to find work as a graphic designer, works at a call center thanks to his ability to speak English well. He states that it was thanks to a severe depressive crisis that he found in writing rhymes a new way to live, and now he is looking to take his passion to the professional level. He is so serious about this that in 2010 he was working on the mockup of his first solo album, *11x18,* which is currently available on the internet and as a CD.

By feeling as though they are a part of something—a movement—and upon finding a social space that offers them security and recognition, these young people feel the need, not just individually, but collectively, to carry graffiti and rap "24/7," as they say; they are convinced that their practices, aside from being a way of life in order to inhabit the city, serve as a personal satisfaction, as they can contribute to the improvement of their surroundings in addition to the construction of an atmosphere of social transformation. In other words, they believe that, depending on the case, music and/or art is the channel through which they can give people a taste of what has kept them alive, despite the fact that many people will ignore it and others will not understand it: "I know that I am not going to change the world by painting a wall, but perhaps just the act of someone passing by it and saying 'Oh, that's funny!' and smiling; it could be the start of a positive day for that person or I don't know'" (interview with Spel, 23 years old).

However, for them, the message has not been transmitted or received the way they would have liked; they believe that society has taken it upon itself to question their practices and stigmatize them in an erroneous way. They argue that it is this same society that has never approached them to start a dialogue or to understand them, so now it is they who are trying to bridge that gap. From their perspective, it seems as though they have not had a very positive outcome, seeing as how the state continuously responds with more and more laws and regulations against letters and images. Instead, graffiti and rap are increasingly associated with delinquency and the consumption of illicit substances—and while some people are, in fact, involved in these dynamics, it is definitely not the norm and is much less a valid label to describe them since it creates a stigma. And, in truth, what these young people have created is a different way of making culture, a culture that has been devalued and stigmatized.

From the experience and narratives of these young people, we can deduce that the first obstacle that they have to face, oftentimes, is at home; the majority of those interviewed stated that their families were not in favor of their activities right away. However, their families had to accept these activities once they saw that the young people refused to stop doing them and stood firm in the face of opposition, demonstrating to their families that graffiti or rap had become a part of their life plan:

> My father was very disappointed because rap music absorbed my school and work. Because I have always known that in the moment that I enter the

university, I will not have time to do what I want to do. And my mom, well, she is a lovely person who says, "soon you will get over it, it's only a phase," but I wrote a rhyme for her that says: "Mom, this rap thing is a passing phase, don't worry, I plan on stopping when I die." (interview with Danger, 24 years old)

Contrary to what society thinks by saying that these activities are passing fads or hobbies, for many young people it's a lifestyle, and they see it as an extension of their bodies. Also, it is worth mentioning that, for them, graffiti and rap are not only fingerprints that one leaves on a wall or on a recording of a song: they are practices that bring a feeling of community and belonging, where the root is in the sociability that they generate and not in how to handle an aerosol can or a microphone; as Mode says, "to paint a wall with spray paint doesn't make you a graffiti artist." Therefore, graffiti and rap go beyond that; they are practices that transcend and are formulated in the social spaces that these young people construct and articulate.

Incomprehension and a lack of understanding on the part of the families, as well as the rest of society and the state, have not deterred these youngsters. Instead, these barriers have served as motivators, although they do not deny or dismiss having received some support, understanding, and approval of their actions by the same. However, they would like for the rest to be able to know and understand what it really means to stain your hands with aerosol spray or to spend hours with a pen and paper until the ideas finally appear. "To me, graffiti is as if it were an organ in my body, it's there to make something else work, if it were removed, I wouldn't feel alive" (interview with Sabes, 25 years old).

For young people, graffiti and rap represent hope, a sense of belonging and of protest, and even a form of relief. It is true that they do it because they love it and use it as a mechanism to talk about their realities and about how they see the world. Nonetheless, they also find pleasure in being a model for their community, given that they express that it feels good to walk down the street and be recognized; that is, to feel like they are not just one more body passing through the city, but instead to be filled with satisfaction from receiving comments on their work from others, often strangers.

Masculine and *Masculinizing* Identities

Graffiti and rap are characterized by the implication of activities that demand a skill set that includes agility, intelligence, leadership, bravery, and physical and mental ability, as well as other elements for the competitiveness that the mediums require. Socially, these characteristics are associated with masculinity, which would be the first point in explaining why there are more men than women in these circles. Nonetheless, they are practices and spaces that, in theory, are not exclusively *for* men, but are frequently *of* men. Note that belonging to one of these social spaces does not mean that the subjects involved isolate themselves or stop being a part of other social groups like family, school, work; in fact, it is just the opposite. And despite the fact that the actors have learned to manage a certain performativity in order to move in and out of one group or another, they are not detached from sociocultural elements that have been learned in the hegemonic culture to which they belong. In other words, in their socialities, youth blur what they learned at home with what it means to be a man or a woman.

Therefore, one of these elements is the gender order whereby, according to Connel (1997), masculinity is a social norm for male conduct, and the same could be said in the case of women and femininity. Although it is important to point out that gender "is a social practice that constantly refers to the bodies and to what the bodies do," it is not a social practice that is solely reduced to the body (ibid., 109). In that sense, we could talk about spaces and practices with a gender connotation based on their characteristics. In this case, graffiti and rap are associated with what is socially called masculine, since they are high-risk practices that demand the presence of "rough bodies."

In either case, the idea of men as brave, strong, and heterosexual conquerors is fundamental, and all of these factors are considered when trying to find, or better yet obtain, the respect of other men. Moreover, this masculinity dictates that they should show loyalty to those closest to them, keep their word, and maintain a sharp image—that is, never show any signs of weakness. At the same time, they should demonstrate an air of superiority in front of everyone else, which implies that not just anyone can receive their level of recognition.

Although these elements are very visible and noticeable within both identities, it must be said that this is not an image that they have constructed alone, but a stereotype that has been socially imposed. However, these young people have legitimized it and established it as a code within their socializations that responds to the hegemonic and the heteronormative; they find in it, and in its practices, a way to conquer the ladies through the reinforcement of their masculinity.

> Man has always wanted to be, the boys not the girls, we have always wanted to be bad because they have taught us that girls like bad boys, like in the movies. So you say "I'm going to smoke, I'm going to use slang, and I'm going to dress in baggy clothes" and I don't know if that's it or not, but you begin

to dress in baggy clothes ever since your mom stops buying your clothes and you begin to buy your own. (interview with Danger, 24 years old)

Before I was a graffiti artist, I noticed that even the ugliest dudes had a bunch of chicks all over them, or that they were very nice to them, or that they were leading because they had good tags/pieces, and that motivated me to want to have the same benefits. (interview with Serieh, 23 years old)

For those involved, what is transmitted on the walls or through the music also corresponds to a gender order, and when what is expressed goes outside of that norm of masculinity and falls back into something that is seen as being tied to femininity, it could be the cause of jokes and discredit, despite the work being good and worthy of praise. For example, we have the case of Sabes, a graffiti artist who decided to replace letters with ladybugs in order to paint the city walls; when I asked him why, he answered that he had simply allowed himself to follow what he felt and wanted to paint without caring whether or not they branded him a "faggot."

What is more, within both practices the existence of subjects that characterize themselves as passive actors is very common; in other words, despite being a part of the circle with which they interact, they do not necessarily carry out any activity while the active ones, those in constant movement, are producing. Most of the time, in a very essentialist way, the women are associated with passivity, and they are seen as companions and nothing more, although, ironically, some men express a desire to have a partner who does the same thing they do, in the hopes of being understood.

Nonetheless, even though they are a minority, there are women taking part in both activities, but the process of incorporation into these groups tends to be slower and longer term, mainly due to their gender. These women's entry into crews as well as the rap or graffiti scenes is done one of two ways: one, through a romantic relationship with a male artist in the group; and two, through persistence. In both cases the women are subject to a double effort: first, to win a spot, and second, to gain recognition from the rest of the group. Such is the case of Nube, who despite having been a part of graffiti crews since she was fifteen years old has had a tough time joining them, since most made excuses for her exclusion with comments like "women don't even tag." Even she admits that it was not until two years ago, when she was twenty, that she began to paint; before then, the male crew members would put her name up on walls around the city.

Luisa Hernández Herse (2012) states that, within the crews, and I would add within the scene since not all women belong to a crew, "norms or regulations that prohibit access to women are nonexistent; however, they operate in subtle ways in order to avoid their permanence, stunt their development, or relegate them to marginal positions" (137). And it is very complicated for the women who are involved and interested in maintaining their presence in these public spaces to easily rid themselves of the labels that place them in a position of partner or as someone who needs to be taught; this implies that these women need to search for strategies that go against passivity and, with difficulty, against mentoring.

Nevertheless, not everything is so different; women also experience similar processes of incorporation. Within the graffiti and rap communities, there are no processes that are distinctly for one sex or the other; instead, both sexes are immersed in pre-established rules from which neither sex can be excused— although they could be through other rationales. One of these is the battle for a nickname or tag: when women find another woman who uses the same tag they do, they submit to a showdown for the rights to the tag, just as the men do. However, since many of the women in graffiti crews do not actually do their own tagging (spray painting), they look for other ways, like violence, to contend for their tag.

> There was also this other chick who tagged "*Misma*" [which means "same"], and I remember that one day I passed by, I was with my sister and with another friend from Calimax, and there was a KP party and this guy yelled out to me "Hey Misma, the other Misma is talking to you!" and I said something like "What the hell! Where is she?" There was a handful of guys and chicks, and I told my sister "They're about to kick my ass" and my sister said to me "Well, if they do something to you, I will get involved." But I stayed there waiting for this chick to come out, but I never found out who she was so we left. The truth is that I gave up the name Misma; I didn't want any problems. (interview with Nube, 22 years old)

When the work and dedication of women tend to be consistent, and they begin to demonstrate that "despite their condition of being women" (as seen by the men) they can take rap or graffiti seriously, the relationships between men and women become closer, and one could say that the women begin to gain space "on their own merits." However, upon observing this relationship, the gender roles, feminine/masculine, are exacerbated, and men assume roles that place them in the positions of provider and protector at the same time that they feel obligated to take certain considerations into account that would not normally happen with other men, like worrying about whether female members get home safely due to the danger to which they are exposed by being out in the streets late at night. The young women involved in both of these practices, even while conscious of the violent context in which they live and of the vulnerability to which their bodies are exposed in the public sphere, primarily in dark and isolated places, still decide to take on the risks.

Pyyeza, Nube, and Monse are three young women who live in the eastern zone of the city, a zone in which the rate of sexual assaults on young women is recurrent. In spite of their awareness of this, they choose to move around and express their art on public streets, although they are regularly accompanied by men who offer them more security, according to the young women. Nonetheless, all three of them walk around alone at times, but this apparently does not cause them any fear or anxiety; instead they reaffirm the idea that they will not stop doing so even though they have previously experienced assaults or have been chased by men; they accept the responsibility that if something were to happen to them, it was a risk they took.

> Before, it was common to see dead people. Now, we hardly do. It's a bad thing for me because I'm no longer scared to cross through there at night. The problem is that when I go home I have to go down through a Waldos [mart] and walk in the dark and this is a problem. That's why sometimes I prefer to stay in the studio, but my mom gets angry because sometimes I don't arrive home. So, I have to return to my home and tell my mom that I was dropped off, but sometimes the guys can't drive me home. I think that until something happens to me I will be ok, but the problem is that I can't walk comfortably through the streets with no fear of anything happening to me, but that's what I have to do. (interview with Nube, 22 years old)

Due to the existence of these additional risks for women, society looks down on their moving through public spaces unaccompanied by a masculine figure as well as their not being "in their rightful place." This has marginalized them in such a way that they cannot experience Hip Hop development similar to that of their male counterparts, for fear of being detained, of the dangers of the streets, or of their parents finding out what they are doing.

Thus these women often decide to carry out these practices under the frame of legality or in the private sphere, in addition to searching for ways to modify the stigmatized imaginary that exists with respect to being a female graffiti or rap artist, to acquire social and, more importantly, parental acceptance in order to later express themselves openly. For example, Nube admits to feeling "envious" of her male crew members, as she would have liked to go out to paint at night and to write graffiti illegally, but does not do so for fear of getting arrested. Also, there is the case of Pyyeza, who began rapping in high school; she says that she and her friend, with whom she had a group called *Locas con estilo* [crazy girls with style], were very much *under* so that "not even her parents knew about it." Their first songs were about love; then, they decided to write songs that broke with the image that their family members had about rap music. But their songs were written in a diary and were for their eyes only. In fact, it was not until 2010 that their work became public, since from the beginning it was never about "being famous," it was about venting.

Still, for them, graffiti and rap or creating artistic interventions in the public sphere, as in Monse's case, are areas to which they are nevertheless drawn, as they state that traditional feminine spaces are boring and do not appeal to them in the least. In addition, they say that they have a better "coexistence with men than with women," associated with the fact that in their interactions, they find it more appealing to make plans with friends to go paint a wall than to go get their nails done with their girlfriends. Therefore, in ways that are not necessarily conscious, they question and transgress what has been socially imposed upon them by being women.

The acknowledgment of female work is an issue that is practically nonexistent. Within these cultural practices, as Nancy Macdonald argues, the men "are considered competent, in other words, capable of doing graffiti 'well' and they have the opportunity to be recognized according to the development of their work, which is in sharp contrast to the women, whose capabilities, presence, and unlikely successes are not recognized" (Hernández Herse 2012, 138). Throughout various conversations I had with the men with whom I did my fieldwork, I suggested talking about their admiration for other people in that medium; all of them quickly responded with a great number of works by male artists. However, when I asked if there was any woman for whom they could offer any recognition, I was able to put them in a real predicament, and they took a long time to give me at least one name.

For many men, the work done by women can only be compared to the work of other women, and often many female artists end up accepting this, even if they do not agree with it. Nube comments that there was a time when her work was often compared to the work of another woman who, at that time, also did graffiti; however, this other female graffiti artist had to move to another city, so Nube, seeing as how she was now alone, opted for comparing her work to that of her male counterparts, who, in turn, did not see her as any competition. Nonetheless, she has received much praise after encountering men who are shocked to see a woman painting, and for her the best acknowledgment has been: "No way! You paint better than other guys I know. Seriously, I can't believe that you paint better than another guy."

Since receiving admiration for their work, they have realized that this recognition is either fleeting or superficial, and that it is still the men who continue to dominate this space, given that socially they are the ones who receive the most respect and who are considered to do the most professional work. As a result, men have greater access, and at events, they are the ones who are given all the spots or are hired for special jobs.

Conclusion

Without a doubt, the arrival of graffiti and rap to Tijuana brought with it new organizational logics and youth sociability, giving young people in this border zone new ways of *being young* and, of course, of occupying public space. However, social stigmatization has created societal views that consider them to be a social threat as well as violent youths who only sully the city. Still, these young people formed social spaces that impacted areas beyond the borders, thus converting themselves into *trans*borderline and transnational subjects, as well as social transgressors. Given that youth identities are not entities that are created out of nothing or that operate in socially isolated spaces, but instead are articulated in other aspects of social reality, the young people who were the bearers of these new identities learned to use the constructed images that have been attributed to them, be they negative or positive, in order to talk about social problems.

Little by little they have conquered spaces within the city, and with this, they have managed to obtain mobility in hegemonic and subaltern spaces such as galleries and, more specifically, on the streets. As such, Tijuana's rappers and graffiti artists have been able to transgress the social order in these multiple spaces, demonstrating that it is not the illegality that breaks the social order, but what is expressed in the space. And although their work for institutions or the private sector is different, arriving at that level represents for them the achievement of recognition and greater mobility in order to be understood, so that society might change its perspective of them; it is also a way to professionalize and live off of their practices. According to Castiblanco Lemus (2005), youth cultural practices, as those in this case, are practices of resistance with "an enormous potential to transform one's way of thinking and one's identity, as well as to construct autonomies of subjectivity; in the same way, there is potential in the processes of construction and reconstruction of social realities" (261).

These spaces are considered to be very open and plural, but in reality they are heteronormative places with a masculine nature, which presents an obstacle for young women as well as homosexual men. What is viewed as feminine is considered to be negative, something for which there is no place, even though according to the men, the women are not seen as competition or as threats. As such, the women, the few who are able to enter and become a part of these circles, undergo processes of masculinization.

Undoubtedly, the reproduction of gender roles places women in a subordinate situation to that of the men, which limits their ability to experience certain processes that their male counterparts do, like walking through the streets at night or committing illegal acts, since "the scared thoughts, the risk, and the fear take on multiple forms in the gender experience, and what is more important still is that oftentimes it restricts the practices of female mobility" (Soto Villagran 2006, 361). While the incorporation of these young women in said practices apparently places them in a situation of double subjugation, they in fact find themselves situated in paradoxical spaces. One might say that in the areas where they are considered to be transgressors, like those of graffiti and rap, they actually continue to occupy a subordinate space; and yet, in culturally hegemonic and institutionalized spaces like school or family, these women appear, paradoxically, to have a higher degree of empowerment than other women and men.

I share with you Morgan's idea (2009); she finds in her research that the women within these practices are not naive and idealistic, and they consider these spaces to be freeing compared to other social spaces; they see in graffiti and rap a potential for parity, since there it is impossible not to be recognized when one has skills. In this case, the three young women interviewed expressed that they felt and behaved differently than other young people with whom they shared a classroom, a workspace, and even a roof. And despite the fact that the research does not produce precise information about the degree to which both practices and their permanence in the public space have influenced and allowed these women to have different ideas and actions than other young people who are similar to them—especially since there could be other factors that have contributed to the changes—these practices have been a tool for transforming their social relationships in other spaces; even though their subordinate situation has not been erased, they have noticed small changes in their everyday life.

Consequently, we could say that painting walls and writing rhymes manages to achieve a social transformation—it makes social problems that are experienced by these young people, like poverty, social inequality, violence, and more, visible. However, these practices have unfortunately been unable to change or question the gender regime in which they are immersed, although one can imagine that with the participation of more women and men who are conscious of these issues, a change is possible.

Bibliography

Anaya Cortés, Ricardo. 2002. *El Graffiti en México ¿Arte o desastre?* México: Universidad Autónoma de Querétaro.

Castiblanco Lemus, Gladys. 2005. "Rap y prácticas de resistencia: Una forma de ser joven. Reflexiones preliminares a partir de la interacción con algunas agrupaciones bogotanas." *Tabula Rasa* 3 (enero–diciembre): 253–70.

Connel, Robert. 1997. "La organización social de la masculinidad." In *Masculinidad/es: Poder y crisis*, edited by Teresa Valdés and José Olavarría. Santiago de Chile: ISIS-FLACSO. 103–29.

Grimson, Alegandro, 2011. *Los límites de la cultura: Crítica de las teorías de la identidad.* Buenos Aires: Siglo XXI.

Hernández Herse, Luisa F. 2012. "Aproximaciones al análisis sobre graffti y género en México." *URBS* 2(2): 133–41.

Jiménez Estudillo, Lisset Anahí. 2013. *¡Aquí es el borderland! El graffiti y el rap como prácticas juveniles en la ciudad transnacional.* Tesis de licenciatura. México: UAM.

Morgan, Marcyliena. 2009. *The Real Hip Hop: Battling for Knowledge, Power, and Respect in the LA Underground.* Durham, NC: Duke University Press.

Sánchez López, Jorge Francisco. 2010. *La construcción simbólica del paisaje urbano: La disputa por la significación del graffiti en Tijuana.* Tesis de maestría. México: COLEF.

Soto Villagran, Paula. 2006. *Prácticas, significados e imágenes genéricas de la ciudad: Mujeres, lugares y espacios urbanos en la comuna de Concepción. Octava Región. Chile,* Tesis de doctorado. México: UAM.

chapter 11

Somos pocos pero somos locos

Chicano Hip Hop Finds a Small but Captive Audience in Taipei

Daniel D. Zarazua

After at least four years of sporadically looking, I had finally tracked down the mythical DJ Chicano. It had started from a mixtape, which I don't even remember how I came across. The mix was basic, mostly '90s R&B hits, yet I was determined to find him. Whenever I could, I sought out more information, even enlisting my mother for help, and dragging my grandfather along on my quest. I finally tracked Chicano down to the Doobiest Hip Hop shop on Taipei's west side, but he wasn't working that day, and it was nearly another full year before I finally met him.

So what was so special about a Mexican American DJ spinning urban music? As a long-time Hip Hop fan, DJ, and of mixed Chicano[1] heritage myself, I had heard my share of mixtapes. The difference was that Chicano was based in Taiwan, a small island country, but a large cultural hub of Asia. I wanted to meet my *compañero*,[2] who I figured was probably from East L.A.,

---

1. The term Chicano is a term for people of the United States of Mexican ancestry. It often has political connotations as a self-identifier to signify political awareness and pride in one's culture. A variation of the term is spelled Xicano, in reference to Mexico's strong Indigenous heritage.

2. A Spanish word for friend or comrade.

based not only on his name, but also on the name of his store, which I associated with the Los Angeles Hip Hop group Funkdoobiest, as well as the fliers I saw referencing clothing labels from Southern California and fonts that harked back to Chicano culture. I just knew I was going to see a muscle-bound, tank-top-wearing, bald-headed *cholo*,[3] tatted up with Mexican art. Nope. He was a slight, bespectacled, Taipei-born-and-raised local! I was surprised but quickly learned that he knew his music and was well respected on the scene. One of his contemporaries even called him the "Kool Herc" of Taiwanese Hip Hop, a reference to one of the founders of Hip Hop culture. But what took me to Taiwan in the first place?

Taipei was the place of my birth, where my Chicano father met my Taiwanese mother. We ended up leaving Taiwan when I was three and my father's career in the U.S. military had us moving to places as disparate as Reese, Michigan, and Desenzano, Italy, very few of which had thriving Latino or Asian communities to connect with. We finally settled down in the United States when I was nine years old, in Montgomery, Alabama. In junior high I began to attend a predominately African American school at the dawn of Hip Hop's "Golden Age." I loved watching MC Hammer dance, listening to the wordplay of Rakim, being politicized by Public Enemy, and watching Sinead O'Conner jam in MC Lyte's "Lyte as a Rock" video. More than just music, Hip Hop shaped my worldview, including valuing improvisation, challenging the status quo, and having pride in oneself. The latter inspired me to learn more about African American activism and to seek out information about Asian American and Latino activists. However, I began to realize that my blending of Hip Hop, African American, pan-Latino, and pan-Asian influences was not the norm.

In my efforts to find a community, I explored many places, including my birthplace, and would often return to visit family. As I had yet to meet others in Taiwan who had shared similar experiences, even in hindsight my excitement about the mysterious Kuang-Ting "DJ Chicano" Chien made sense. He came to symbolize a hybridity of my worlds, although my nearly non-existent Mandarin skills and sporadic visits to Taiwan made the search drag out. Along the way I've seen the impact of technology on local culture and identity, as well as learned things about life in Taiwan that are not reflected in textbooks or travel magazines.

---

3. *Cholo* is a Spanish-language term of varying meanings, but in this context it is a reference to a Mexican American who favors the street life and is often associated with gangs. It is a hybrid Mexican and American culture expressed in ways such as tattoo art, slang, "oldies" soul music, customized cars and bikes, Catholic imagery, and Aztec or Mayan cultural references.

Chicano was not the first local to practice Hip Hop, and a few artists, namely the L.A. Boyz and MC Hot Dog, achieved a fair amount of commercial success, but Chicano has probably been the most consistent at pushing Hip Hop's more traditional elements, including playing vinyl records, working with local dancers, and influencing countless other DJs, graffiti writers, and music enthusiasts. When I spoke to younger DJs, his name nearly always came up.

While in junior high school in the early '90s, Chicano started DJing, greatly influenced by the Hip Hop videos that started showing up on MTV and local Taiwanese music shows. During one of our conversations he had to stifle a chuckle when he said that Young MC's "The Principal's Office" video is what turned him on to Hip Hop. Chicano was part of a DJ crew called Def Soul, a collective that played other forms of urban music, including house and even southern Hip Hop, as one of the members was from Texas. They weren't focused on a particular style, and he's quick to add that his interest in music broadly encompasses soul, funk, and Hip Hop in general. When he got his first official gig at a place called Mickey Star Disco Pub he actually played Top 40 American music. So with this wide range of influence, how did he come to the DJ name of Chicano?

The origin is quite simple, really. Like many other Taiwanese youth, Chicano listened to ICRT (International Community Radio Taipei), Taiwan's only English-language radio station. The late '80s and early '90s featured a charismatic Haitian American on-air personality from Chicago who built up a sizable following, due in no small part to his ability to interact with fans through his fluency in Mandarin and Taiwanese, Taiwan's two most popular languages. One night this DJ, Patrick Steele, played Mellow Man Ace's "Mentirosa," a bilingual Hip Hop track about love gone awry that sampled Santana's "Oye Como Va," unwittingly setting the stage for an entire music scene. For Chicano, hearing the integration of Spanish, as well as the smooth sounds of Santana, hooked him and led to exploration for other music drawing on this aesthetic, including Cypress Hill and A Lighter Shade of Brown. Soon after, he heard East L.A.'s Kid Frost's release, "This Is for La Raza," which included the line "Chicano, and I'm Brown and Proud." As Chicano loved the song, was drawn to this style, and found the name easy to pronounce, he began using it at parties. However, he only played music on vinyl records, of which very little Chicano Hip Hop[4] was available. Thus what proved to be a key step in

---

4. Chicano Hip Hop commonly refers to a style that heavily draws upon Chicano culture, including the sampling of "oldies" music, the usage of localized slang, and often, but not always, references to gang life.

the establishment of the scene was the Doobiest store, which was a partial outgrowth of Def Soul.

Chicano and his friends had been holding Hip Hop events and workshops and were finally able to secure a site as a base for their activities in 1999. Doobiest was started by Chicano and his friends Chung-Ho "Sam" Liu and Chao-Jung "Goldie" Chang to sell Hip Hop related clothing, music, and videos. Having only later learned that Doobiest could be seen as a reference to marijuana, Chicano says he originally thought it was slang for "do best." However, as it referenced one of their favorite groups, Funkdoobiest, they stuck with the name. Another friend, dancer, and record store owner, Chung-Yi "Al" Chang, suggested that they carry the Tribal clothing line, a southern California line that blended Mexican, Hip Hop, and urban influences. Doobiest soon added similar companies such as Joker and Dyse One. Despite their love for all styles of Hip Hop, the influence of these lines was enormous, and countless Taiwanese youth began emulating Chicano-styled Hip Hop, particularly the clothing and art. Doobiest continued to be a center for Hip Hop culture, drawing foreigners and locals alike. Among the locals was Hsiao-Shan "Berry" Chen, a mover and shaker behind the scenes, who served as an interpreter for many of my interactions, and Chi Chang Yang, who went on to build a name for himself as DJ Vicar.

Vicar's introduction to Hip Hop was through the L.A. Boyz, a Taiwanese American pop group who excited the Taiwanese dance with their choreography and presence in a genre that was predominately African American.[5] While attending parties and dance workshops, he began watching Chicano DJ, studying his technique and the music being played. Sporting the Chicano-style clothing popularized by Doobiest, Vicar began researching the music on his own, quickly developing an interest in soul, R&B, and funk, as well as Hip Hop at large. Like Chicano, he began collecting vinyl records, making multiple trips to Japan, and spending thousands of dollars amassing a collection that has earned him international acclaim. He continues to play vinyl-only events in Taiwan and Japan, collaborating with Chicano, Japan's DJ Honda, and expats such as DJ Zulu of Barcelona.

Although there's a thriving graffiti scene in Taipei and Chicano culture has a strong visual element, the Chicano influence on local street art appears to be minimal. However, a small number of Taipei-based tattoo artists are clearly influenced by the likes of celebrated artists such as Mr. Cartoon, who has done work for various celebrities including Eminem and who founded

---

5. While their impact on Taiwan's music scene was immense, the L.A. Boyz were largely unknown in American Hip Hop circles and are considered by many to be more of a pop group.

Joker Brand Clothing. Yen-Chi "Mr. Chino" Chu was the first Taiwanese tattoo artist I met, and stepping into his studio was like walking into the heart of L.A.'s Mexican community, complete with lowrider model cars, *Dia de los Muertos*[6] trinkets, and even a little street sign for Olvera Street, one of the oldest streets in Los Angeles. Furthermore, he carried a small selection of Chicano rap CDs. Because he spoke little English or Spanish, my friend Mike translated, and I pushed Chino on his attraction to the music and why he draped himself in Chicano culture. As with others, he iterated that "Chicano style" was just one of his interests, and as he really enjoyed soul music he liked the samples used in Chicano rap. When pressed, he said that he preferred a lot of the Chicano rappers; he felt that they were more "real" than a lot of African American rappers who, in his opinion, had gone commercial. "Josh" of Surface Art Tattoo was also known for incorporating Chicano-inspired culture into his pieces, but who exactly was the receptor of their work?

By far the most famous is Wei-Ting "Oldies" Chung, the owner of "Oldie's Burger" and a budding tattoo model. I first met Oldies about five years ago when he was working at Doobiest and had no visible tats. Now, in 2014, he was nearly covered from the waist up, including the back, sides, and top of his head. Over the years Doobiest has often partnered with their clothing lines to bring Chicano rappers such as Psycho Realm, Funkdoobiest member DJ Ralph M, and Delinquent Habits. Among Psycho Realm's entourage was Alan "Big Tiny" Ayala, a tattoo artist whose clients include producer DJ Muggs of Cypress Hill and House of Pain fame. Big Tiny gave Oldies his first tat, which opened the door to increased experimentation by Oldies, who worked with Josh on a number of pieces, including a giant Virgin Mary and baby Jesus piece that covers his entire back. The dozens of tattoos now covering his body include a textbook of Chicano Hip Hop staples such as Al Pacino's *Scarface* character, Marlon Brando's Don Corleone from *The Godfather* movie, various references to Los Angeles, and even a cross with three dots, which in some circles is a gang reference.[7]

This leads to the next obvious question: since much of Chicano Hip Hop is gang-affiliated, are any of these Taiwan fans claiming gang membership? In addition to Doobiest and Mr. Chino's shop, I visited a few other businesses that carried Chicano Hip Hop related items, and they favored the Sureño umbrella of Chicano gangs. Roughly speaking, Chicano gangs in California fall under two large umbrellas, the blue-wearing Sureños and the red-wearing

---

6. A popular Mexican celebration commemorating deceased loved ones.

7. There many interpretations of this symbol across the globe, but in Chicano culture it often means *Mi Vida Loca* (My Crazy Life) or allegiance to a *Sureño* gang set.

Norteños, with a number of localized cliques, or sets, under each umbrella, plus a number of smaller unaffiliated ones as well. Granted, gang affiliation can be widely interpreted, and not every "gang member" is a criminal. While gang culture and Chicano culture cannot be used interchangeably, the life-style promoted in Chicano rap is layered and comes from a historical context. I knew that the Chicano scene in Japan was much larger than Taiwan's, and I had seen Japanese fans claiming gang affiliations, including tattoos and nick-names. Was the same thing happening in Taiwan?

Every person I spoke with expressed surprise that I had this impression, and even the ornately inked Oldies was adamant about abhorring criminal activity. All said they were drawn to the laidback vibe shown in the videos from the West Coast in contrast to the busy, fast-paced feel of New York's Hip Hop scene.

I asked Berry if people were scared when they saw Oldies walking around. She said that a lot of little kids and older people love talking to him and that people always want to take pictures. I can see that. Oldies is very friendly and does walk around with a smile on his face. He has traveled overseas, includ-ing to London for tattoo conventions, and never had problems. However, as I thought about places I lived, not only would I be wary if I saw him, I wouldn't even want to be seen in certain neighborhoods *with* him. His tats would be too much of a liability and draw the wrong attention from gang members, the police, and community at large. Heavily tattooed people are negatively stereo-typed in general, but in the wrong neighborhood, with the wrong tats, there are real life-and-death consequences.

But, quite frankly, how would local Taiwanese who take on these styles know better? There's very little information about Hip Hop or Chicano culture available in Taiwan that's not in English, and no one I spoke with had an ongo-ing relationship with Chicanos, even if they had traveled to the United States. Unlike neighboring countries such as Japan, there are fewer opportunities for Chicanos to come to Taiwan, as the United States shut down its military bases there in 1979.[8] While Taiwan has seen a growing number of students and immigrants from Latin America, including Mexico, very few have ties to the United States; thus Chicano culture is just as foreign to them. There are a handful of restaurants in Taipei that serve Mexican food, including Eddie's Cantina, whose proprietor has roots in Chihuahua and Monterrey, Mexico, but none of the Taiwanese I spoke to had ever eaten there. Similarly, I spoke

8. The U.S. government broke formal diplomatic ties with Taiwan's de facto ruling gov-ernment, the Republic of China, in 1979. Taiwan's history is a complicated one, and in just the past few decades Taiwan has been called an independent country, the home of the true Chinese government, and a renegade Chinese territory, depending on who you ask.

with a number of Latinos in Taiwan, including a Salvadoran from Los Angeles, and none even knew that there was a Chicano scene in Taiwan. Raby Doo, a Belizean of partial Mexican heritage, has been an undergraduate and graduate student in Taiwan for six years, and despite being an avid music lover and hobbyist DJ had heard of DJ Chicano but never attended one of his events.

By 2014 the Chicano scene in Taipei had definitely seen better days. Stores that used to push "Chicano style" have moved on to other lines or shut down, although Doobiest remains open and even added a shop in Taiwan's second largest city of Kaohsiung. However, many of the original members of Def Soul and Doobiest have moved on to other crews or professions. Oldies, Berry, and Chicano, all former employees at Doobiest, have started their own organizations—Oldies with his restaurant and Chicano with his monthly Beat Square Hip Hop event, of which Berry is a main supporter and volunteer. Chicano now performs as Mr. Swing in homage to the "New Jack Swing" style of his youth, a sound created by producer Teddy Riley and popularized by the likes of R&B singers Bobby Brown and Guy. Now considered "OGs"[9] or part of the old school, fans such as Berry and Vicar say that the new generation of fans have moved on. Even at Chicano Hip Hop's peak, according to Berry, touring performers such as Psycho Realm didn't pull big numbers, even if those in attendance said that the performances were great. Vicar added that many Taiwanese young people are into Korean pop music, EDM (electronic dance music), or more commercial Hip Hop and R&B. Berry adds that teens will dance to anything that has a good beat and follows trends, a fact I can attest to, as during my own DJ sets in Taiwan the floor stayed busy whether I was playing Detroit techno or Latin music. That doesn't mean that the influence of Chicano Hip Hop isn't alive, though.

The dance scene remains strong, with dancers still draped in Tribal Gear and similar styles while practicing West Coast–inspired dance moves. Doobiest still carries hats sporting "Brown and Proud." Although there isn't a lowrider scene, there is a dedicated group of aficionados who modify their cars with Chicano influence, and even DJ Chicano owned a Cadillac El Dorado, a model favored by many Chicanos back in the States. Young DJs such as DJ Wright have a vinyl record collection of soul and funk that many collectors back in the United States would envy, inspired by Chicano and Vicar's music digging obsessions. While I was told that there no MCs who mimicked Chicano styles, the number of Taiwanese rappers has certainly grown, although they mainly model themselves after mainstream American artists.

---

9. OG literally means "original gangster," but it has evolved in most circles to generically mean "original" or is used as a term of respect for an older person.

As I learned more about the Chicano influence in Taiwan, I went through a number of emotions. The first was curiosity, mixed with excitement. Then, I was a bit insulted; I felt as if it were a mockery of a community I am part of, thinking of the saying "I'm a culture, not a costume." However, as I got to know some of the key practitioners, we engaged in serious dialogue about music, culture, and identity. Over the years I've shared my Taiwan experience with friends and students I taught back in the States. Reactions ranged from pride to wonderment to disdain. Oakland resident Martin Rochin appreciates the interest but is worried about Chicanos being turned into caricatures, while his friend Eric Romero, a former gang member and former college student at UC Santa Cruz, said that the gang life was not something to emulate. If someone got too self-righteous, I pointed out the tendencies of Americans getting tattoos of Asian symbols, having geisha-themed parties, or listen to violently homophobic reggae songs because they don't understand the lyrics but like the beat.

Ultimately I hope that Chicano Hip Hop and other forms of pop culture open the door for more dialogue and inspire locals to create their own culture. Over the years of talking to people, one of the standout comments was by a young woman listening to my conversation with Mr. Chino. When I asked her about the interest in Chicano Hip Hop, she said it was stupid and she was against any trend, whether it was Taiwanese or foreign. Although I'm a Hip Hop lover, one of its tenets is originality and creating something new out of the old. A positive side I see of the "Chicano Style" losing steam in Taiwan is that it symbolizes the scene's maturation into taking pride of its local heritage.

Despite laying much of their early foundation in music, Chicano and Vicar have clearly outgrown the Chicano scene, with Vicar saying that it always had limited appeal as he simply wasn't a gangster. In his hunt for obscure records, Vicar has been documenting Taiwanese music, and along with Chicano, continues to spin vinyl in an effort to expose young listeners to Hip Hop's roots. Tattoo artist Fallen B chose the name Mr. Oriental to emphasize his focus on Asian-style art. Dancer Ruby Red synthesizes indigenous Taiwanese music, dress, and music with Jamaican dancehall culture in her choreography, while members of the politicized Hip Hop group Kou Chou Ching have teamed up with other MCs to form a new group called Community Service that continues to address social justice issues as they rhyme in different Taiwanese dialects.

There are challenges, of course, and like underground scenes everywhere, these torchbearers struggle with small crowds, constant efforts to educate their audience, and limited financial rewards. Witnessing their passion, I think of the Chicano saying *somos pocos, pero somos locos,* which means "we're few, but we're crazy." In a gang context, it conveys courage but can also be interpreted to mean that one will succeed, no matter the obstacles. As I think about the money and sweat they invest to promote the cultures they love, I appreciate all their work to push Taiwanese culture forward by developing the music scene, promoting Taiwanese pride, and encouraging locals to look beyond the music and learn more about Chicano and African American culture.[10]

As I spent so many years away from Taiwan, I began to feel a growing disconnect. Finding this small but vibrant scene helped me feel like there was still a place for me, and it's empowering to see how a series of small events, in this case sparked by a silly song from L.A., could impact a culture nearly 7,000 miles away and continue to generate dialogue two decades later. *Siempre pa'lante.*[11]

---

10. As one example, Chang Jui-chuan is a Hip Hop MC, musician, and professor who's used lyrics by Tupac and excerpts from the *Autobiography of Malcolm X* in his college classes.

11. Slang for "always moving forward."

PART IV

SOMOS MUJERES, SOMOS HIP HOP

chapter 12

Chicana Hip Hop

Expanding Knowledge in the L.A. Barrio

Diana Carolina Peláez Rodríguez

Translated by Adriana Onita

The Latino population in Los Angeles County is a little over five million people, 66 percent of whom have Mexican roots. Hip Hop in this area is quite popular, and Latino Hip Hop production has grown exponentially since the nineties, when the movement went global and different cultures began appropriating and diversifying its style. This chapter presents a facet of this production, focusing on females who express themselves on the microphone.

Mexican American female rappers in L.A. have been part of the movement since its birth, but they have not been documented in the same way as their male counterparts. In fact, scholarly interest in Latino Hip Hop in the United States is still quite recent. Even though the influence of the Puerto Rican community in the development of breakdancing has been demonstrated, and Chicano graffiti artists have been acknowledged, Hip Hop studies have focused primarily on the experience of the African diaspora in this country.

As a collective, Chicana rappers contextualize the complex experience of growing up Chicana in a global U.S. city with high sociocultural contrasts. Their autobiographical songs are packed with stories, complaints, and criticisms that reveal the everyday stresses of triple oppression by class, ethnicity, and gender, as well as conflicts and differences that arise between family generations. Furthermore, their work not only provides us with a glimpse of the conditions in the postindustrial *barrio* but accompanies us through journeys of a shared struggle: the vindication of the feminine as a place of power from which they can enunciate differences and renegotiate social relationships that subordinate them.

Throughout this chapter, the concept of Chicana Hip Hop is offered as a contribution to studies on this cultural movement and third-wave feminism. Chicana Hip Hop is a dialogic platform producing a powerful feminine presence that creatively intervenes in the organization of the world through all of Hip Hop's artistic forms yet is still rooted in *el barrio*. Thus, key to Chicana Hip Hop is the position of the postindustrial *barrio* as a starting point for sharing life experiences, ideas, desires, opinions, criticism, and conflicts through Hip Hop. In this way, Chicana rappers are able to represent the multiple migrations and displacements of Mexican American women in the United States. Their artistic production can be in English, Spanish, or Spanglish, representing the multiplicity of codes that they use and embrace as their own. Each language carries inherent power relations; thus, to position oneself in either language is to acknowledge this fact.

This study delves into the Hip Hop world to illustrate Chicana rappers' motivations, strategies, and struggles. The chapter begins with a discussion of Chicano/a Hip Hop in the city of Los Angeles, focusing on its importance for the youth in this postindustrial *barrio,* and female production as the missing element for a more comprehensive representation of the culture. The second section considers the conflicts and strategies that these women experience and use within the movement, and, finally, Chicana Hip Hop is presented as activism. The analysis is accompanied by lyrics and interviews with five Chicana rappers from L.A. who participated in a qualitative study from 2010 to 2012.

Chicano Beats in *Lost* Angeles

> Don't take my block lightly
> We're screwed up like everybody in the world might be
> Born into Union and 17th
> Out of the womb in the 70's
> Repping Lost Angeles through musical melodies
>
> —Sick Jacken, "Born in L.A."

The postindustrial era in the United States developed in the seventies and matured with the neoliberal reforms implemented since Ronald Reagan's presidency. Throughout this process, urban centers have experienced a unique and complex set of global forces that have contributed to the economic and social restructuring of American cities: the growth of multinational telecommunications networks, global economic competition, an unprecedented technological revolution, the formation of new international divisions of labor, the increasing power of finance relative to production, and new patterns of migration from developing countries (Rose 1994, 27).

But this process of globalization also has adverse effects on the human experience of time/space. While for some, globalization is a process of mobility, simultaneity, speed, and spatial liberation, for others it is closer to stagnation, immobility, and localization (Bauman 2001, 28). In this polarization, "segmented local networks, often ethnically based, rely on their identity as the most valuable resource to defend their interests and ultimately their being" (Castells 1989, 228).

In the 1980s, thanks to the flow of Japanese and Canadian capital, the city of Los Angeles became the second most powerful financial center in the Pacific Rim, after Tokyo. The city began exhibiting a new "geography of power" with emblematic cultural monuments that converted it into a global city (Davis 1990, 74). However, drastic cuts in public resources were implemented in the so-called *inner city*. Ana Castillo (1994) points out that the achievements of the Chicano/Latino movement were almost all drowned out because initiatives seeking to preserve Mexican Amerindian culture through community projects, rehabilitation, alternative education, youth counseling, women's shelters, and so forth were all financed by the government (31) . Thus, with this economic reconfiguration, spaces inhabited by the Mexican and Chicano communities became postindustrial *barrios* whose main characteristics are increased levels of poverty, unemployment, imprisonment, violence, drugs, gangs, and lack of access to good schools and social service programs (McFarland 2008, 22).

In these neighborhoods, African and Hispanic diasporas, especially Mexican and Central American communities, have been in constant interaction. These groups have shared similar struggles in terms of civil rights and labor activism, while also competing over housing and employment (Johnson 2002, 316). In the streets and schools of postindustrial *barrios* or ghettos, young people share knowledge and practices that identify them as part of a racialized and segregated group, but that also give them the ability to creatively resist and defy the prejudices and racial stereotypes that devalue and disempower them. However, this complex cultural exchange does not occur in a space free of conflict. Indeed, the daily tension between these two communities comprises high levels of hostility epitomized by the competition for scarce resources and the uncritical acceptance of racist stereotypes imposed by the dominant culture. Nevertheless, during the process of deindustrialization in the late twentieth century, this cultural exchange gave rise to a Chicano rap style that travels over funk and soul beats, and an Afro Hip Hop that appropriates lowrider Chicano culture from the streets of L.A. (McFarland 2006, 943).

Los Angeles is internationally known for being the birthplace of gangsta rap. In 1988 NWA (Niggas With Attitude) released their album *Straight Outta Compton,* a discursive construction that focuses on a specific neighborhood, contrasting the abstraction of the Queensbridge/Bronx/Harlem ghetto that was being championed in New York. The "hood" or neighborhood is built in terms of "home," and representing the hood means constructing its territory and condition with everyday scenes and sights. In practice, the lyrics and rhymes of the artist must be recognized by the locals from the hood, who must relate to the experience. The style and images must resonate significantly with them to endorse it as true, otherwise known as "keeping it real" (Forman 2004, 207–8).

> Mi disco cuenta sobre cómo crecí en la ciudad de Los Ángeles. Crecí por la tercera y la Rampart [Rampart District]. Es un área donde hay muchas pandillas y casi todas las noches había helicópteros. A veces toda la noche . . . [1]But it was really explosive, because you would go down one street and you are in "18 neighborhood." And then you go down one more street and then you are in "MS territory" [*Mara Salvatrucha*]. So a lot of the Hip Hop coming out of this area was Gangsta rap. (Tenochtitlán, personal interview 2011)[2]

Rap on the West Coast has its anchor in the specifics of the immediate environment: what distinguishes a neighborhood or street from another within the same ghetto. This is often exemplified by gangs that take over specific streets in the same neighborhood. Legendary gangs in Los Angeles are the Bloods and the Crips, which are African American, and the self-identified *Cholos* in the barrio of east L.A., Chicanos whose fight for city territory has become increasingly violent since the eighties, specifically for control of transnational distribution of cocaine and "crack" (Davis 1990, 270). In the eighties, new gangs formed in L.A., representing new Latino migrations: the Mara Salvatrucha (MS-13) and Barrio 18, with men and women from El Salvador, Guatemala, and Honduras sharing similar characteristics with the Mexican cholos (Nateras Domínguez 2007, 151).

---

1. "My album talks about growing up in the city of Los Angeles. I grew up on 3rd Street and Rampart. It's an area filled with gangs; there are helicopters there every night."

2. Tenochtitlán was twenty-nine when this interview took place. She is a single mother. Her ethnic self-identification is Mexican American, Chicana, and Latina. Her music falls under the subgenre of hardcore underground Hip Hop.

It took nearly a decade for Chicano Hip Hop to enter into the consciousness of national popular culture, despite the fact that Chicanas and Chicanos have been participating in Hip Hop culture since the early eighties, helping to write the *barrio* language with rap, graffiti, DJing, and breakdancing. In 1990 the album *Hispanic Causing Panic* by Kid Frost and his hit song "La Raza" became iconic, epitomizing the Mexican American youth experience in that period. In this song, Frost combines the slang (or *caló*) and street knowledge of the *barrio* with Chicano cultural nationalism, political critique, and a hypermasculine heterosexual identity, resulting in a locus of cultural, racial, and gender characteristics that strongly resonate with the androcentric Chicano audience in the lowrider and *cholo* scene (Pérez-Torres 2006, 326). This image remains one of the most reinforced in the city even today.

In the same year, A Lighter Shade of Brown (LSOB) released their album *Brown and Proud,* and just a year later Cypress Hill published its homonymous work, starting a trend for groups located in the L.A. postindustrial barrio to enter the mainstream market, such as Psycho Realm and Delinquent Habits. Cypress Hill, unlike Frost, offers not a nationalist discourse but a barriocentric one: a discourse that showcases and takes pride in its multiethnic underclass urban roots.

> Cypress Hill reflects the realities of inner-city life for many people of color as one of cultural exchange, borrowing, transformation, and common struggle. They, as well as Chicano and other rappers, appeal to our youth of color because they acknowledge a multiethnic, multiracial, post-industrial, inner-city experience that political leaders from an older generation rarely engage. (McFarland 2006, 951)

The diversity of Hip Hop in Los Angeles is expanding according to the different representational needs of its inhabitants. Tired of gangsta rap, whose misogyny, violence, and aggressive language left out much of the experience of being a young person of color in the hood, a group of people created a café named The Good Life in Crenshaw in the early nineties. This café offered a space every Thursday for young people to develop their creative talents, especially in freestyle rap. This is how *Project Blowed* was born, as a place to share and compete, turning into the most influential space in the development of the L.A. underground Hip Hop scene. And although it was a distinctly African American space, some artists of the Mexican diaspora built their careers there, like 2Mex and Olmeca.

> When I first went to Project Blowed, I saw the female group Figures of Speech. Those sisters had a song that was all like bashing on the system! You know! like basically talking about decolonization, and this is when I am

17, 18 and holy shit! There is a different Hip Hop? What is going on! I am like awake to a whole different world I did not know about! That is, to me, "decolonizing Hip Hop." (Eyerie, personal interview 2012)

When we trace the most representative female Hip Hop artists in L.A., the group Figures of Speech and the artist Medusa stand out. Both are of African American descent, and both developed their talents in *Project Blowed*. On the other hand, when investigating Chicana female artists of the nineties, not one name emerges. This is not because they did not exist, but because they were not an active part of the local scene until independent labels started representing them or women themselves began to produce their own work and participate more actively in the movement.

In the twenty-first century, the diversity of Chicano Hip Hop can be seen in distinct new characteristics, for example the explicit mix of traditional Mexican music and *corridos* or banda music. Among the best known groups for this is Akwid, composed of two Mexicans who grew up in Los Angeles and who went on to win a Grammy and two Billboard awards. Indigenous and Xicanista projects also arise in rap, as exemplified by El Vuh, who emphasizes Indigenous roots, spirituality, and politics of the Indigenous struggle (McFarland 2008, 55).

Hip Hop scholar Pancho McFarland has rigorously studied the Hip Hop movement, especially Chicano rap. His analysis goes from the appropriation and transformation of Hip Hop by young Chicanos and Mexicans in the southern cities of the United States, identifying a myriad of voices in the struggle for self-determination, to a thorough analysis of their relationship with history, territory, and violence. He also analyzes their resources and strategies, and even the gender ideologies that permeate their political representation. McFarland (2013) acknowledges that Chicano Hip Hop has developed a unique epistemology and ontology through the lived experience in the *barrio* streets, "an experience of dislocation *and* empowerment, criminalization *and* liberation" (32).

In his book-length work *Chicano Rap: Gender and Violence in the Postindustrial Barrio,* McFarland (2008) found that the objectification of women and violence are recurring themes of manifestation of power. He proposes three types of cultural products that contribute to this phenomenon: mainstream media controlled by large corporations that naturalize androcentric and ethnic reductionist stereotypes and values, aspects of African American manhood which have influenced and have been highly marketed in cinema, and Mexican and Chicano patriarchal culture. The latter often reduces the role of a woman to a *virgen/puta* binary, which finds fertile ground in Chicano rap, where representations of femininity are one-dimensional and fail to grasp or appreciate female complexity. In male rap songs, the two possible female roles are summarized in this binary discourse of reproduction/eroticism, and this occurs as much in *cholo* Chicano rap, as in the multiethnic *barrio*.

On the other hand, Indigenous or Xicanista Hip Hop seeks to empower the female subject, but often falls short because it only highlights feminine virtues such as reproduction or the power to unite a community. Moreover, when it comes to giving women the space to become Hip Hop intellectuals on the same level as men, by collaborating on songs with men or being invited to feature in their concerts, relations continue to be excluding.

The heteronormative patriarchal root is so deep that reflections on this topic will take a long time. Although Indigenous/Mexica Hip Hop provides a fine rhetoric of resistance and critique of capitalism, colonialism and racism persist:

> Their claims to developing a more equitable society with superior nature–society relations will fall short as women and their ideas are marginalized and made into passive spectators of male warrior action. The patriarchal heteronormative understanding of the world, and especially of gender, severely limits the possibilities that the neo-indigenist cultural and political movement can lead to a more equitable, open, and just world. (McFarland 2013, 79)

However, women themselves are responsible for producing a complex and powerful feminine presence in Hip Hop. Usually, women tend to insert themselves in youth groups, thereby making their differences "invisible" (Reguillo 2003, 375). However, although considered minorities, there are always women who refuse to be invisible and represented, and they creatively rush to offer their own worldview. The next section offers an analysis of Chicana participation in the L.A. rap scene based on the experiences of five rappers from the underground scene: Eyerie and Centzi from the group Guerrilla Queenz, Tenochtitlán, Fe, and Cihuatl Ce. The analysis includes struggles that they encounter within their local movement, their strategies for empowerment, as well as the practical aspects of their work, which will allow for a more complete picture of the Los Angeles postindustrial *barrio*.

Guerrera Beats: Chicana Hip Hop and *Barrio* Knowledge

Since the redrawing of U.S.–Mexico borders in the nineteenth century, Mexican migration to the United States has been constant and has changed in nature with the policies between the two countries and historical changes. Until 1980 the migratory flow from Mexico was primarily male, temporary, and of rural origin (Massey et al. 1987). Since the eighties, studies have found that migration is now undocumented, involving the whole family, and flows have become feminized (Leite, Angoa, and Rodriguez 2009).

Economic reconfiguration has had "differential impacts on women and men, on male-typed and female-typed work cultures, on male and female centered forms of power and empowerment" (Sassen 2005, 110). While men of color and immigrants have seen their employment opportunities diminish in primary sectors, which for Latinos are normally gardening, food preparation, and construction (Davis 2000, 96), immigrant women have seen increased work opportunities as they represent cheaper labor than men and they reflect the growth of alternative global circuits.

> Las mujeres lloran
> Dejando sus niños en el otro lado
> Trabajando como esclavas día y noche
> Por un peso, que ya no vale nada
>
> En el norte Juárez–mis hermanas, las mujeres de las maquiladoras
> Por el sur, sureños peleando con los de la otra calle
> Eastside—Westside
> Somos de la misma tribu
> Una nación debajo de la represión, de la policía, de la migra . . .
>
> (Fe, "Las Mujeres Lloran")

> The women weep,
> Leaving their children on the other side
> Working like slaves, day and night
> For a peso that's worth nothing
>
> In the north, Juárez—my sisters, women of the maquiladoras
> In the south, sureños fighting with those across the street
> Eastside—Westside
> We are from the same tribe
> One nation under repression, by police, by the migra . . .
>
> (Fe, "The Women Weep")

In this song, Fe identifies a system of exploitation in which women feel trapped. She recognizes not only the sacrifices that migrant women make and the fact that they are undervalued in society, but also the domination exercised over the female body on both sides of the border. She encourages unity and understanding of the strength of these women and the community itself. She manages to portray what Sassen (2000) describes as the era of the "feminization of survival," where both homes and communities and even governments are increasingly depending on women to survive (520). It is a system where undocumented migrant women represent "an advantage to an employer insofar as they can exploit socially ingrained values of submissiveness" (Kittay 2010, 62). Chicana women are among the most excluded groups in the United States. They are constant victims of discrimination, with some of the lowest incomes and least access to education. Faced with the realities of triple oppression, some Chicanas find rap as a way to express themselves creatively and articulate possibilities of liberation.

Out of all the aesthetic forms of Hip Hop, the Chicanas interviewed chose rap because of its lyrical and poetic quality, the veracity in the stories, and the ability to create new words: "Hip Hop is great storytelling, and it's all about how we grew up in the streets. There's a lot of wordplay, it's very clever, there's humor, there's really dry mood and I love it!" (Tenochtitlán, personal interview 2012). As for the accompanying music, the power of the beat is what channels emotional connections related to the place or territory, be it the *barrio,* a specific street, the city, the *pachamama.*

> Hip Hop is definitely alter-native; it has that native way wherever it's coming from. Understanding the indigenous beat, the heartbeat, the *tambor* that cultures come from, wherever you come from in the world, there is that indigenous ancestry, there's a beat, usually. There's a heartbeat, and youth are connected to that, feel that, and move to it. (Fe, personal interview 2012)[3]

Simon Frith (2003) reveals that "rap is a voice-based form with an exceptionally strong sense of presence" (194). As a musical genre, it offers a unique, intense perception of the "I," from the subjective to the collective. Rap is "identity produced in performance" (194). It is an aesthetic means to produce presence, recognize the place where one is from, and celebrate it by articulating the struggle for the right to be there.

The themes of Chicana rap songs vary according to the emotions and thoughts that each artist has to share. Usually, their stories are full of frustration, trauma, and pain but also hope, positivity, and communal unity. Something that is never lacking in their message is where they are from. They make

---

3. Fe was thirty-five when this interview took place. She does not have children and lives with her partner in a civil union. Her ethnic self-description is Xicana, or Indigenous Chicana. Her musical production is called Floetry Hip Hop.

explicit the place and imagined community being represented: East Coast, West Coast, Los Angeles, a specific district, barrio, gang, Afro, Chicano, cholo, Indigenous, and so forth, always describing the conditions of oppression from a viewpoint of a subaltern living there.

Indeed, it is not easy for a female to creatively intervene in a cultural and musical movement where the performance of a strong masculine identity has set the framework to judge talent by the ability of an artist to excite and agitate the public, or "get the crowd hyped." Since both the performance and audience of Hip Hop are predominantly male, women do not typically participate actively in the movement, except as companions of men. Therefore, Hip Hop has been a platform for reproducing a powerful male presence in which talent depends on how much the audience identifies with this discourse while simultaneously enjoying the style and rhythm of the beat.

One interesting aspect in the types of attitudes and energies unconsciously used by women to focus their talent is aggressiveness, which has been associated historically with the masculine.

> But also, I think that all of us here, as women, get really aggressive on the mic. It's very rare that we do a really soft song. It is almost kinda as to prove our skill level or that we can do it just as good as men, we tend to get aggressive on the mic. (Cihuatl Ce, personal interview 2012)[4]

If the dominant expressions in Hip Hop are male and within this matrix of meaning there exists the drive to compete and differentiate talent from mediocrity, women who enter this field assume facets of masculinity not only to compete but because it makes sense to them. From a human perspective, they also feel frustration, anger, and pain about what they experience in their city, their streets, their families, and their bodies; thus they have to develop aggressive attitudes to assertively position themselves in this power structure. Hip Hop is a medium that allows them to act this way. In doing so, they both break with and transform normalized ways of being portrayed as arbitrary feminine artifices, and move toward a balance in the creative production of knowledge about the reality of a global city from a female perspective.

> We're going to speak about our reality, we're going to speak our lives, we're going to speak about our truths, what affects us! And what affects us as

---

4. Cihuatl Ce was thirty-two at the time of this interview. She is a single mother. Her ethnic self-description is Mexican or Urban Indigenous. Her music can be categorized as Indigenous Hip Hop.

women is different from what affects us as men. A male might talk about a domestic violence song, they might!—a few of them have!—*pero siempre va a ser desde* la perspective of a male, not a perspective of a female. So in that sense is where I see the difference. (Centzi, personal interview 2012)[5]

For the five participants, it is not just the violence exercised by the police against locals, or violence from the organized crime that invades daily life, but violence against women, which is a constant problem in families and on the neighborhood streets. Many of these abuses are lived in silence, and many go unpunished because no one dares to accuse anyone or take it to the police.

As Cihuatl Ce expresses in the song "Not Another Ever Again!" there seems to be no positive sense of worth related to females in this society. Instead, disrespect is evident in the signifiers that capture women as sexual objects, disposable after use.

> She was only 24 when she was found face down on the beach
> dead from a beat down
> No one but the waves still hear the sound of the scream of her pain
> And it's going on all around
> Tears falling like the rain (. . .)
> How many females would be ignored!
> How many funerals! How many burials!
> Before the hardcore man and women warriors begin a dialogue!
> (Cihuatl Ce, "Not Another Ever Again!")

To grow up Chicana in the *barrio* means to construct one's identity among often conflicting meanings and messages: traditional ideals of Mexican women transmitted by family, feminine ideals of the dominant group transmitted by the media, the influence of feminist discourse of the middle class and women of color (or second- and third-wave feminism), and the reality that they experience in their daily lives.

To grow up and become Chicana in conditions of being constantly undervalued requires continuous confrontations. Chicanas constantly encounter one-dimensional views that their bodies are "natural" mediators of satisfaction for others, and they endlessly search to redefine these views and to renegotiate their representation. They consciously revise symbols from their environment

---

5. Centzi was thirty-three when this interview took place. She is a mother of four and lives with her partner. She is a rapper in the revolutionary Indigenous Hip Hop group Guerrilla Queenz.

and reimagine how these translate into the meanings of their bodies as devalued subjects.

> In today's society, women have been devalued, disrespected, sexually objectified or represented as someone who lives to serve others. We must restore the sacred value of women. She is not only the creator/mother but also a warrior, always fighting for her family, her community, her future. She is a woman who is self-empowered, who has power over herself and power inside of herself, and who does not need validation from anyone else because she has her self-worth. And nobody can steal that from her! (Eyerie, personal interview 2012)

This is one thing that all interviewed rappers had in common: they all agreed that there is a disrespect and devaluation of females in their society, from inherited history to the present moment. There is also a common desire to change this. They often refer to their Indigenous history to find powerful female archetypes in order to deconstruct those traditional images.

There have even been attempts to seek a pre-patriarchal memory of themselves, if this ever existed. This path offers the possibility of decolonizing the meanings that have disciplined, objectified, and exploited their bodies. The archetypes of powerful goddesses relieve them of their "natural impotence" and offer them other terms for renegotiating their historical condition of subordination. Thus the recovery and appropriation of the feminine from the great *Diosa Madre,* or Mother Goddess, in opposition to the *Madre de Dios,* or Mother of God, comes into play.[6] In this vein, women are presented in a different way, as they are associated with Mother Earth, highlighting their creative and destructive powers.

> A temple statue hits the ground. It cracks and crumbles.
> It is la Diosa Azteca, I emerge from the rubble
> Awakened from ages of a deep state of slumber.
> Drop, hit the deck, seek refuge, take cover.

---

6. In the cosmology of the Toltecs, Coatlicue, who wore a serpent skirt, was the *Gran Diosa Madre,* or Great Mother Goddess. She contained and balanced the dualities of male and female, light and dark, life and death, creation and destruction. In those days, women could own property and they could become priestesses. The loss of the balanced oppositions began after the pilgrimage to Aztlán, when eventually they adopted Tetzauhteotl Huitzilopochtli, the god of the sun, as the great god of their religious system, and the power of Coatlicue was reduced to that of being the mother of the god (Anzaldúa 1999, 54–56), thus forming the Mexica androcentric female archetype which reveres the mother but subordinates them to men. This archetype is further advanced with Catholic colonization and the imposition of the Virgin as the mother of God.

I'm more deadly vicious than a pack of velociraptor.
With the target on-lock, and it's the rap game I'm after.
I spit acid that causes lethal, mental erosion.
Your dumb-founded can't take it, causing cerebral implosion.
Like ceremonial skulls, I put dunces on skewers.
Pseudo-Hip Hop's the plague,
Fear not, cause Teno's the cure!

(Tenochtitlán, "1519")

The *Diosa Madre,* creator and taker of life, nurturing and terrible, all-powerful, autonomous, and sovereign, owns her body and her sexuality (Maier 2001). She offers a range of terms that give meaning to the reality of women in the postindustrial *barrio,* in a way that is more coherent than the *Madre de Dios* image. She also offers Chicanas a spiritual dimension distinct from the Catholic religion, since they are looking to connect with internal and universal duality in order to know themselves and how to balance this duality. Thus, terms such as "warrior," "creator," "balanced," and "independent" confirm the qualities of the ideal woman of these rappers.

Chicana Hip Hop as Activism

I see Hip Hop as a driving force within the youth throughout the whole world to express their reality of what's going on! Hip Hop is very effective. So that's why we entered into all this Hip Hop world, because there is power behind Hip Hop. Capitalism took it over. Look at what it is now! They reproduce an idea that best gives them money. But the root is there! It's still talking. It still exists in the underground! We have to use those media as well to push it in! There's been a rise of Hip Hop being used as activism as well. (Centzi 2012)

There are many important elements in this comment from Centzi that need to be unpacked in order to understand the complexity of the Chicana Hip Hop phenomenon in the global city of L.A. First, she speaks about the power of Hip Hop as an aesthetic medium that can capture the attention of people and compete in the dispute over meanings that take place in the city. Recognizing this power of Hip Hop pushes her to express her interests through this medium. Second, she states that this power has also been recognized by capitalism, which has seized it and has privileged consumption, violence, and sex as elements that translate into money, over the discourses of social criticism and communal unity. However, as she explains, young people of the ghetto, the *barrio*, continue to represent their experiences in ways that are meaningful for them and that represent their realities. This is a simple way to note the differences between mainstream Hip Hop and underground Hip Hop. All of the participants in this study would be part of the latter group.

They also recognize two ways of positioning themselves in the underground scene: as storytellers of the *barrio* reality, or as those who tell stories but who also take part in the community to bring about change. Within this division it could be argued that the five participants are part of the underground scene, because their main interests are not commercial but rather communal, uniting their efforts to transform their realities: "When you want to get heard in the streets you have to use the vernacular of the streets and in order to do so, that includes a lot of Hip Hop!" (Eyerie, personal interview 2012).

This activism is practiced on two levels: the objective and the symbolic. The first, according to those interviewed, is recognized as a community venture that tries to innovate and develop ideas and actions that come from the community itself. These communities know that depending on government resources is something temporary, because as soon as an economic situation arises, the first budget cuts occur in their *barrios*. This aspect was found to be a crucial reason for which these women were drawn to activism: because it is a way of being active in the community and in the city.

Tenochtitlán, for example, realizes that she cannot solve the problems of her *barrio,* nor can she fix district bureaucracy. Therefore, people must get together to pick up trash in their neighborhood, paint the streets, collect mattresses that are left lying on the streets for months, and so on. She sees that underground Hip Hop artists talk a lot about the great difficulties they had growing up in their *barrios,* but they do not act to improve things in order for local children to grow up with more opportunities. For example, in response to this lack of action, and understanding the convening power of many artists in the city, Tenochtitlán decided to organize Hip Hop for Humanity, an event that sought to collect canned food for the L.A. Food Bank. Local artists donated CDs, T-shirts, posters, and other products, and whoever brought their food donation would receive a gift bag with these products. The event was a success and provoked much admiration of local artists, who applauded her initiative, confirming the necessity of community involvement in Hip Hop.

Another way to use Hip Hop as a form of activism is by channeling rap's own power, not only by offering stories about the difficulties of living in the postindustrial *barrio*, but also by trying to change the status quo by imagining a community with dignity. The five interviewed women shared a belief that their action through Hip Hop can translate into a way of exercising power to transform history. The ways in which this occurs has two components: *decolonization* and *healing*.

Decolonization is a way to dismantle ahistorical and essentialist notions that dominant discourses have used to create gender, ethnic, class, and generational differences. Its aim is to expose power structures and historical oppression that place some at a disadvantage and in positions of nonpower. Healing creates new meanings for the fragmentations that individuals and groups have experienced which have generated trauma, damage, and pain.

> Decolonization means being part of a process where you are willing to look at yourself to see the parts that have been affected by White supremacy and check them. [. . .] We are walking contradictions [. . .] If we are willing to look at them and to create spaces where this other world is possible, then you are in that process of decolonizing. (Cihuatl Ce, introduction to the song "Femi- 9mm")

The interviewed rappers are working to build a countermemory. Blackwell (2011) calls this "retrofitted memories"—a process of restoring deleted information in the common memory by reappropriating and editing lost or fragmented knowledge. Thus, they can perform a historicized identity that creates cracks in the "stable" dominant representation system, and therefore opens up the possibility for unknowing. For this reason, they overlap historical aspects from different time periods in their songs, which are part of the collective memory, where women were more in a position of power. Thus, the capacity for self-representation is recovered, allowing for the production and reproduction of new meanings.

> Nuestra gente no vivía con divisiones
> No más un pueblo compartiendo la cultura, los valores, las tradiciones
> De cada cuatro puntos, cada cuatro direcciones
> We were on this land once before united
> 'till the devil got us all caught up
> Now we're divided
> Norteños, sureños, crips, bloods,
> Africanos, mexicanos, salvadoreños, pandilleros
>
> But first we gotta unite, before we could fight
> Eastside, Westside, Southside, no side, all sides, all one side!
> 'cause it's all about the unity
> Starting with our own communities
> Understanding who's your enemy [. . .]
>
> (Cihuatl Ce, "All Sides")

In Xicanista Theory, the methodology used to decolonize knowledge and bodies is done by positioning the Indigenous—ethnic and genderwise—as the core of the identification process. In this way, a space opens up to reclaim a historicized gender and ethnic identity that results in a political subject. This methodology was evident in all participants, some explicitly in interviews, and some more explicitly in their songs. When performing the imaginary of a feminine root that is sacred and a warrior, such as *la Diosa Madre,* this group of women seeks to honor the feminine from perspectives that recuperate and recognize knowledge that both belongs to them and legitimizes them and their right to sovereignty over their body, mind, spirit, community, and city. The notion of honoring should be understood as the recognition of a continuous historical oppression, exploitation, and devaluation of the feminine, by offering—and for some "offering up"—new meanings to rename themselves, to reconcile and to resolve dehumanizing colonial dualities, meanings that empower and vindicate.

By honoring "natural" feminine values emerging from these imagined cultural roots, such as connections to Mother Earth, and an appreciation of the sacred and creative power of women, this symbolic efficiency translates into confidence, security, and a sense of empowerment for other women. The impact that this message has for girls, young ladies, and older women would be another research project: what is clear is that this activism is one of the main objectives of the artists interviewed in this study.

In male Hip Hop, the same objective is met, but from a male perspective—female rappers are aware of these discursive failures and realize that no one else will produce experiences of the *barrio* from a female perspective if women themselves do not. This gives them the strength to carry on and keep fighting to reach the microphone and be heard. The contents of their songs, within the dynamic of honoring themselves and others, deal with personal stories, family, daily life in the *barrio,* violence, poverty, but also hope and wishes for a united community struggling to improve.

In terms of violence from a female perspective, they deal with sexual abuse, femicide, and domestic violence. While stories of violence in male Hip Hop are mainly about territorial dynamics in the *barrio,* these women focus on the household, on relationships, and the abuse of masculine power over women when symbolic or psychological violence seems not to be enough.[7]

---

7. "Most of my music is my perspective as a female. That's why I try to talk about those issues of domestic violence, and the abuse of children, because I want that cycle to end with me and my daughter. That's also why I do the music, to give voice to young girls or women who have experienced that in their own homes! So that we begin to talk about it, 'cause when we can talk about it, we can begin to heal" (Cihuatl Ce, personal interview 2012).

In the ongoing process of identity formation, cities, as well as the people and movements that form them, are subject to history and its transformations. Hip Hop has represented a historic moment in the postindustrial process of global cities and has become a safe space for young people to produce a presence and demand their right to be there in the city, to be part of the construction of meaning and to make changes. But Hip Hop has also been a process of reconfiguration: making mistakes and correcting itself.

> We are using Hip Hop as it has never been used before, because we are identifying ourselves with our indigenous roots, we are talking about indigenismo or reclaiming what is ours, and talking about the social struggles going on! We help to change the face of Hip Hop as well! (Centzi, personal interview 2012)

Rapping requires the courage to speak, to come to the microphone and make the most of that moment. It calls for constant work to develop skills, find your own style, and pave your own way. The continued participation of women like these five rappers shifts the frontiers of sexual differentiation. This contributes not only to the transformation of gender identity but to the cultural movement itself. As such, it is a real contribution to strengthening Hip Hop as a forum for discussion and dialogue.

Conclusion

Women who have grown up in the postindustrial L.A. *barrio* have been in constant contact with Hip Hop—whether they like it or not, it has been one of the dominant languages used by youth to express themselves for the last thirty years. Those who are interested in actively participating in the movement can represent and contextualize the complexity of their experience as observers and storytellers of their community. Through rap they articulate different stories, complaints, and criticisms that reveal everyday struggles of triple oppression of class, ethnicity, and gender, but also hope for social change.

Moreover, they refer to the contrasts and tensions that arise between family generations, allowing for a glimpse into the conditions of life in the *barrio*. They embody a shared struggle: the vindication of the feminine as a place of power from which to assert differences and to renegotiate the various social relationships that subordinate them. The strategies they have developed include recognizing, revising, and appropriating knowledge from their profound cultural imagined roots. In doing so they redefine what it means to be female, reconsider who they are, and transform their practices. The cultural nationalism of Chicana rappers bestows new meanings upon inherited female identity and thus displaces notions of traditional gender relations.

In an androcentric regime, female silence is a positive quality: a virtue, an enigma shaped by male fantasy, a symbol of beauty that, when materialized, turns the female body into an object. If the silence is broken, this coherence is interrupted, and all of a sudden women become agents with the power to disturb and rearrange their habitus. By denying women the word, we also deny women the ability to be themselves, to be creative and to creatively intervene in the world.

Female rap challenges and defies this way of thinking. It harnesses the power of the word to produce female knowledge, addressing symbolic and geographic borders in order to move them and gain ground in a creative world that has "naturally" been denied to them. Thus, the dichotomies that fragment human experience into mind/body, active/passive, strong/weak, courage/cowardice, public/private, terms that have historically tried to define male and female, are revealed as an arbitrary artifice that can and must be redefined. Chicana rappers fight for gender equality in a field where talent, courage, and creativity also belong to them; they perform the search for a new feminine identity.

While the initial interest is to capture and keep the attention of their community in order to tell stories that youth can relate to, Chicana rappers' main motivation comes in the form of activism. Their Hip Hop production encourages social change in their community, exercising power for the transformation of history. This transformation is constructed in terms of decolonizing and healing. Through decolonization they seek to dismantle ahistorical and essentialist notions that dominant groups have used to create gender, ethnic, class, and generational differences. The process of healing creates new meanings for the fragmentations that individuals and groups have experienced which have generated trauma, damage, and pain. The path toward transformation begins with speaking from an ethnic and Indigenous center, reclaiming a historicized experience that honors the Chicana female and her knowledge, and that legitimizes her presence as a worthy citizen.

Therefore we can say that rap offers Chicanas a space to harness their creative power to initiate change, and that Chicanas offer rap a female perspective on life in the *barrio* and city. The subjects they communicate in their songs range from honoring women and men in their community, personal and family stories, caring for the land and its resources, everyday city life, poverty, migration, and violence; but also they speak of hope for a better future and communal unity.

As for the reflections on the violence they experience, it is one of the issues that differentiates male and female rap, as the former concentrates on state and street violence in a kind of territoriality of the neighborhood, while the second speaks of domestic and sexual violence, and frames misogynistic acts of aggression as femicide. This is consistent with the views of Sassen (2006) when she says that being present and becoming visible to one another means recognizing the place as central to the claims for the right to be there. In this case, men concentrated their recognition in public places as their space for meaning, while women, despite a presence in the public domain, focus their attention on reclaiming private spaces—places that historically have "belonged" to them, but in silence.

Bibliography

Anzaldúa, Gloria. 1999. *Borderlands / La Frontera. The New Mestiza,* 2nd ed. San Francisco: Aunt Lute Books.

Ayala, Jennifer, Patricia Herrera, Laura Jimenez, and Irene Lara. 2006. "Fiera, Guambra, Y Karichina! Transgressing the Borders of Community and Academy." In *Chicana/Latina Education in Everyday Life: Femenista Perspectives on Pedagogy and Epistemology,* edited by Dolores Delgado Bernal, C. Alejandra Elenes, Francisca E. Godinez, and Sofia Villenas. Albany: State University of New York Press. 261–80.

Bauman, Zygmunt. 2001. *La globalización: Sus consecuencias humanas.* México: FCE.

Blackwell, Maylei. 2011. *¡Chicana Power! Contested Histories of Feminism in the Chicano Movement.* Austin: University of Texas Press.

Castells, Manuel. 1989. *The Informational City.* Oxford-Cambridge: Blackwell.

Castillo, Ana. 1994. *Massacre of the Dreamers: Essays on Xicanisma.* Albuquerque: New Mexico University Press.

Cross, Brian. 1993. *It's Not About a Salary: Rap, Race and Resistance in Los Angeles.* London: Verso.

Davis, Mike. 1990. *City of Quartz: Excavating the Future of Los Angeles.* Berkeley: University Press Books.

———. 2000. *Magical Urbanism: Latinos Reinvent the US City.* London: Verso.

Forman, Murray. 2004. "'Represent': Race, Space, and Place in Rap Music." In *That's the Joint: The Hip Hop Studies Reader,* edited by Murray Forman and Mark Anthony McNeal. New York: Routledge. 201–23.

Frith, Simon. 2003. "Música e identidad." In *Cuestiones de identidad cultural,* edited by Stuart Hall and Paul du Gay. Buenos Aires-Madrid: Amorrortu Ediciones. 181–203.

Johnson, Gaye T. 2002. "A Sifting of Centuries: Afro-Chicano Interaction and Popular Musical Cultura in California, 1960–2000." In *Decolonial Voices: Chicano and Chicana Cultural Studies in the 21st Century,* edited by Arturo Aldama and Naomi Quiñonez. Bloomington: Indiana University Press. 316–29.

Kittay, Eva. 2010. "The Moral Harm of Migrant Carework: Realizing a Global Right to Care." *Philosophical Topics* 37(1): 53–73.

Leite, Paula, Adela Angoa, and Mauricio Rodríguez. 2009. "Emigración mexicana a Estados Unidos: Balance de las últimas décadas." In *La situación demográfica de México 2009.* México: Consejo Nacional de Población. 103–23.

Lévi-Strauss, Claude. 1949. *Antropología Estructural*. Buenos Aires: Eudeba.

Maier, Elizabeth. 2001. *Las madres de los desaparecidos ¿un nuevo mito materno en América Latina?* Mexico: UAM.

Massey, Douglas S., Rafael Alarcon, Jorge Durand, and Humberto Gonzalez. 1987. *Return to Aztlan: The Social Process of International Migration from Western Mexico*. Berkeley: University of California Press.

McFarland, Pancho. 2006. "Chicano Rap Roots: Black-Brown Cultural Exchange and the Making of a Genre." *Callaloo* 29(3): 939–55.

———. 2008. *Chicano Rap: Gender and Violence in the Postindustrial Barrio*. Austin: University of Texas Press.

———. 2013. *The Chican@ Hip Hop Nation. Politics of a New Millennial Mestizaje*. East Lansing: Michigan State University Press.

Morgan, Marcyliena H. 2009. *The Real Hip Hop: Battling for Knowledge, Power, and Respect in the L.A. Underground*. Durham, NC: Duke University Press.

Nateras Domínguez, Alfredo. 2007. "Adscripciones juveniles y violencias transnacionales: cholos y maras." In *Las Maras, Identidades Juveniles al Límite*, edited by José Manuel Valenzuela Arce, Alfredo Nateras Domínguez, and Rossana Reguillo Cruz. UAM Iztapalapa y Colegio de la Frontera Norte.

Pérez-Torres, Rafael. 2006. "Chicano Hip Hop and Postmodern Mestizaje." In *The Chicano/a Cultural Studies Reader*, edited by Angie Chabram-Dernersesian. London: Routledge. 324–39.

Reguillo, Rossana. 2003. "Jóvenes y Estudios Culturales. Notas para un balance reflexivo." In *Los Estudios Culturales en México*, edited by José Manuel Valenzuela Arce. Mexico: Fondo de Cultura Económica. 354–79.

Ríos, Francisco. 2008. *From Chicano-a to Xicana*. Online. http://files.eric.ed.gov/fulltext/EJ809068.pdf (accessed January 16, 2012).

Rose, Tricia. 1994. *Black Noise: Rap Music and Black Culture in Contemporary America*. Middletown, CT: Wesleyan University Press.

Sassen, Saskia. 1997. *Whose City Is It? Globalization and the Formation of New Claims*. http://www.asu.edu/courses/pos445/Sassen—Whose%20city%20is%20it%3F.pdf (accessed Feb 18, 2012).

———. 2000. "Women's Burden: Counter-Geographies of Globalization and the Feminization of Survival." *Journal of International Affairs* 53(2): 503–24.

———. 2005. *Global City: Introducing a Concept*. Columbia University. http://www.columbia.edu/~sjs2/PDFs/globalcity.introconcept.2005.pdf (accessed February 18, 2012).

———. 2006. *Territory, Authority, Rights: From Medieval to Global Assemblages*. Princeton, NJ: Princeton University Press.

Velasco, Juan. 2006. "The X in Race and Gender: Rethinking Chicano/a Cultural Production Through the Paradigms of Xicanisma and Me(x)icaness." In *The Chicano/a Cultural Studies Reader*, edited by Angie Chabram-Dernersesian. London: Routledge. 203–10.

Discography

Cihuatl Ce. 2010. *Femi-9mm*. (Demo).

Fe. 2010. "The Women Weep." (Demo).

Guerrilla Queenz, with Krudas Kubensi. 2011. "Mucho Amor." (Demo).

Sick Jacken. 2009. "Born in L.A." *Stray Bullets*. Whittier: Rebel Music Group, Track number 17.

Tenochtitlán. 2010. "1519." In *Obsidian Rapture*. (Demo).

chapter 13

Daring to Be "Mujeres Libres, Lindas, Locas"

An Interview with the Ladies Destroying Crew of Nicaragua and Costa Rica

Jessica N. Pabón

L adies Destroying Crew (LDC) is a group of Central American graffiti
grrlz[1] founded in 2010 by La Kyd (a.k.a Kyd; www.facebook.com/lakyd).
At the time of this writing, the members of LDC are Moxxa, Tash (San José,
Costa Rica), La Kyd, Eliz, Miky, and Pia (Managua, Nicaragua).[2] Though they
paint in a crew, and learn from one another, their aesthetics vary by member,
which is not unusual especially for younger crews still developing their artistry, skill with the medium, and cohesiveness as a group. Moxxa paints legibly
with basic 3D elements; her letters tend to dance across the wall in a looped

---

1. "Graffiti grrlz" is an umbrella term I use in my writing and research to designate the
various individuals, mostly cisgendered and heterosexual, who practice Hip Hop graffiti. I use
the term for multiple reasons: it is common within the subculture to mark, connect, and build
archives on social media using the hashtag #graffgirlz or #graffgrrlz; illegal graffiti-writing is still
a youth-led subculture encouraging writers to resist "growing up," which of course has particular
meaning for girls; and the minor adaption to "girlz" calls upon and contributes to a lineage of
feminist linguistic revisions in mainstream and subcultural discourse, such as "Riot Grrl" instead
of Riot Girl. I also use the term "graffitera" when referring to Latina and Latin American grrlz.

2. As I prepared the final version of this essay for the volume's editors, Rachel Cassandra
and Lauren Gucik published the photobook *Women Street Artists of Latin America: Art Without
Fear*; the introductory essay for the section on LDC takes place in Pia's home.

ribbon style to match the X in her name. Tash's letters—also highly legible with basic 3D work—combine sharp edges and soft curves with a muted palette, forcing the eye to focus on shape rather than color composition. La Kyd's letters, purposefully illegible, as she considers herself a wildstyle[3] writer, are tightly woven together, often with a pattern reminiscent of a piece of fabric— camouflage, polka dot, gingham. Miky favors a blockbuster style (block letters executed to cover as much space in as little time as possible, often with a paint roller), focusing her efforts on size and visibility rather than intricate elements, complex layers, or vibrant colors. Each in her early twenties, these graffiteras grew up in the '90s—a decade marked by the established presence of women fighting for their rights, from various standpoints, in the public sphere for at least a century;[4] a decade marked by the acceptance and adaptation of Hip Hop's cultural elements, originally centered in New York City.[5] *Las destructoras* (the destructors) are part of a larger nonstructured subcultural "feminist" movement happening crew by crew across the globe, most visibly in Latin America, that is changing the gendered landscape of Hip Hop graffiti subculture through aesthetics with inherent, but not obvious, politics.

I place feminist in scare quotes because, unlike the formal feminist or women's rights organizations in both countries and across Latin America,[6] more often than not these graffiteras do not identify as feminist/women's rights activists whether they are in agreement with the social policy goals of the movements or not—their "feminism" comes into being through action.[7] By developing all-grrl crews, graffiteras are actively resisting the prevalent sexist notions that girls lack "real" interest in Hip Hop graffiti, can't handle the pressure of a sometimes illegal, sometimes "dirty" act, or are categorically "weaker" artists/writers stylistically.[8] The crew's founder, La Kyd, explained

---

3. Wildstyle is a genre of Hip Hop graffiti art characterized by letters that are both deconstructed and reconstructed in order to be illegible to most spectators—the letters are "wild."

4. See Karen Kampwirth (2006).

5. See Christopher Dennis (2014). The issue includes essays on Hip Hop in Brazil, Chile, Colombia, Cuba, El Salvador, Panama, Peru, Puerto Rico, and the United States.

6. For more on feminist activism in both countries and across Latin America, see González-Rivera and Kampwirth (2001).

7. See Ilse Abshagen Leitinger's (1997) explanation of "*investigación-acción*," or action-oriented feminism, in the introduction to *The Costa Rican Women's Movement: A Reader*. Also worth noting is the difference between movements distinguished as "feminist" or "women's": the former are generally understood to refer to activists who strive to change social and political structures of oppression (class difference, gender roles, etc.); the latter refer to activists whose primary interest is not altering institutions per se, but rather gaining equality within them (González-Rivera 2012, 176).

8. Nancy Macdonald (2001) advanced the observation (made perfunctorily by other graffiti scholars) that these stereotypes are informed by a sense of threatened male masculinity.

in an interview for the blog *Women Street Artists* (2015) that these ideological and material barriers motivate her work:

> Just being a graffiti artist is harder for a woman than a man, because the graffiti scene is dominated by men, at least that's the case in Nicaragua and so I try to encourage other girls who want to be part of this world, to grow the women's movement in my country.

As part of her efforts, in 2012 Kyd (joined by Sak) led a community-based graffiti workshop for roughly twenty eager participants, ranging in age from ten to forty, in Managua. By the end of the workshop, participants (newly armed with their own tag names) filled in letters outlined by Kyd and Sak that spelled out the "fierce message '*mujeres libres, lindas, locas*' or 'liberated, beautiful, crazy women'" (Saravannote 2012). Crews like LDC paint together and are very public about their actions; they are informal urban art collectives that "do feminism" with their graffiti through various forms of advocacy: apprenticeship, community organizing, mentorship, emotional support, and network building (Pabón 2013a).

Despite the important social and political cultural work these young women are accomplishing, documentation has been limited primarily to Facebook (www.facebook.com/lasdestructoras), Tumblr (http://lasdestructoras .tumblr.com), and minor random blogs—digital places that are inherently ephemeral (in a way that mirrors the art form itself) and subject to being "lost." In fact, I first learned about LDC in early 2012 when Kyd shared an image of their crew name in a throw-up (a quickly done, usually two-toned and bubbled piece), "LD," dated July 23, 2011, with the Facebook group "Female International Graffiti"—a private group that intends to be international, but that is mostly frequented by Latin American graffiteras. I returned to the group to locate that original post recently, with no luck; it disappeared.

On August 2, 2014, I instant-messaged with Kyd on Facebook, trying to pin down some pending follow-up questions with crew members.[9] She emphasized that she had contacted everyone and that three of the original

---

9. After sending, and resending, the interview questions, I realized that not all of the members have constant or reliable access to the internet or to a computer. Nor do they necessarily have the desire, or the leisure time, to sit down and respond. These are the pitfalls of digital ethnography when Skype is not an option. However, I have interviewed plenty of graffiti grrlz face-to-face who respond with limited words as well. Generally I attribute these abridged responses to at least two related factors: they are, after all, participants in a criminal subculture, and for all intents and purposes we are strangers (when we first meet). For my research with LDC in particular, add to this dynamic the physical and linguistic distance between these grrlz and myself, a Puerto Rican academic from the United States with a limited ability to speak

members had retired. LDC is a relatively new crew composed of graffiteras who have been painting for less than five years; the members fluctuate, and the crew is still very much in a process of becoming (it is worth noting that the crew began as a group of teenage grrlz teaching themselves and each other how to paint). In addition to the up-front reality that graffiti is an ephemeral subculture and art form (with a great deal of participant "turnover"), and the difficulty of forming a specifically all-grrl crew, Kyd is also confronted with maintaining cohesiveness in a crew composed of members in two countries. "It is a very big challenge," Kyd noted, "but at least I dared to form the first group of graffiteras in my country." Indeed. If this group—that dared to be the first—should fade or retire entirely, we should wonder about the circumstances of that retirement in terms of the environmental, social, political, economic, and gendered consequences of girls becoming "liberated, beautiful, crazy women."

As readers, scholars, and lovers of Latinx and Latin American Hip Hop, we should keep our eyes open for how *las destructoras* mature as graffiti artists and how their maturity contributes to the aesthetic and social advancement of street art and graffiti art culture in the cities of Managua and San José, and beyond.[10]

> JP: If you feel comfortable, please tell me your: age, class, race and/or ethnicity, gender, sexuality, religion?[11]
>
> LA KYD: I am 22 years old.
>
> MOXXA: I am 22 years old, middle class, of African descent, heterosexual, and I have no religious affiliation.
>
> ELIZ: 21 years old, woman, heterosexual, I am a member of Latter Day Saints of the last days, better known as the Mormons.
>
> MIKY: I am 20 years old, I consider myself comfortable social class (that is where there is plenty of food, no ambition of making it big), probably mestiza race, mixed like an MP3, because I love rock, Hip Hop, bolero

---

Spanish fluently (and a different dialect of Spanish at that). Our original email exchanges took place in May.

10. Since July 2011, there has been a regularly updated Facebook page dedicated to documenting the Costa Rican graffiti scene. See https://www.facebook.com/pages/Graffiti-Costa-Rica/251780478172115. Two years later, in July 2013, someone launched a community Facebook page dedicated to graffiti in Nicaragua. See "Graffiti Battle Zone Nicaragua" at https://www.facebook.com/gbznicaragua.

11. The following interviews were conducted via email and Facebook chat from 3 May to 9 May 2014 in Spanish and then translated to English in part with assistance from Elena Bolorin. Their interviews were conducted individually and not collectively, although La Kyd circulated the questions and answers.

(slow tempo latin music) and above all dance hall music. When it comes to my sexuality I am 100% partial to men, my religion is Christ and that's it.

JP: When did you join LDC? Why do you paint graffiti in an all-female crew?

LA KYD: It was in 2010 that I founded the group LDC in conjunction with Day and Eliz. Ladies Destroying was the first group of female graffiti artists in my country of Nicaragua. I like the fact that I can share with other females on the same wall, it's like family.

MOXXA: When I met Tash she was part of the group already, and talked to me about it. She asked if I wanted to be part of the group and I said yes, Kyd welcomed me. I sense that there's lots of support even though we are in different countries I feel very close to the other girls.

ELIZ: November 2010. I believe that painting with other females gives me confidence and support it's not that I reject the support of men, but with the females it's different because of we are of the same gender.

MIKY: I joined the group in 2011, but by that time the group have been active awhile. First of all, not only because we are a graffiti group but also because we are friends, I feel very comfortable with these ladies, I have their support and sisterhood.

JP: How did graffiteras from Nicaragua and Costa Rica meet?

LA KYD: It was all due to the social media that we have been contacting one another to make our group grow.

MOXXA: We found each other through Facebook and a while back we met in person.

ELIZ: The head and leader of the group, La Kyd always wanted to make a group of female artists, because this didn't exist in Nicaragua, so she called several females that wanted to paint and show off their talent, then she got in touch with females from Costa Rica and they loved the idea of painting together.

MIKY: Actually we have 2 Costa Ricans graffiteras, the group began to grow as time went on and new talent that wanted to be part of the culture showed interest, loyalty and unity to the crew and to graffiti.

JP: The name of your crew is Ladies Destroying—what are you "destroying"? Can you explain the crew name?

LA KYD: We needed a name with a combination between the rough and the subtle of a woman to describe our group. Since seeing graffiti made by a group of girls was not customary here, we formed the first group of graffiteras, it was the beginning of a new movement of female graffiti. And as the scene was dominated only by men, then the name of our group had to have a strong sound but that at the same time communicate that the group was only comprised of girls. And that is when "Ladies Destroyers" was born, but then I liked "Ladies Destroying."

JP: What year did you start painting graffiti and how did you discover it?

LA KYD: I've seen the walls of my city full of color forever, but I didn't know what this art was called and so I began to do a little research. I've always liked to draw then in 2010 I started to do graffiti in the streets of my city.

MOXXA: I became aware of it back in 2001 and it always had my attention. But it wasn't until 2008 when I met other painters and I began to paint.

ELIZ: December 2010.

MIKY: I started unconsciously without knowing what graffiti was in my infancy when I saw the gangs in our neighborhood doing graffiti near my house, people used to call them "lazy." While I watched in silence I was wishing to be with them. I tried to do letters in paper with lots of colors and details but had no specific technique, until years later when I met people that were already established in this world and began having conversations with these people, little by little I started to immerse myself in the culture until I created my first piece in 2011.

JP: Why do you continue to paint graffiti? How does it make you feel?

LA KYD: Because painting graffiti is one of my life's passions. When I paint there's a connection between the can, the wall, and me. Every piece gives me a new experience and above all having a great time that is incomparable with all the moments of my life.

MOXXA: Lots of times I'm not fulfilled, I put too much pressure on myself.

ELIZ: I have always enjoyed painting and drawing, but until 2010 that's when I experimented with aerosols and I like it a lot, it's something that fills me and makes me happy. Every chance I get I like to paint. In the beginning I was a little shy because I felt sorry for myself thinking that the experienced ones would laugh at my work. As I paint more and more I've come to the realization that no painting will look like any other, every artist has their own unique style, when you see a painting you can identify the artist. This is how I feel right now, I love doing this, it really makes me happy, I believe that even if I have kids I would never stop doing it.

MIKY: Because the moment I had that can in my hand, I knew that this is what I wanted to do the rest of my life, I am happy, free, fulfilled every time I do graffiti. I just enjoy it, it's as simple as that. It's not a hobby it's a lifestyle. This is me, my own world, my own space, like I said before: I am happy, free and fulfilled.

JP: Is graffiti illegal in your city? What are the penalties for getting caught?

LA KYD: That depends on the point of view of the population, for a lot of people it's an act of vandalism but graffiti will always be illegal; but on the contrary if you ask for a permit then it's ok. There is not an enacted law that says it's illegal to paint on public or private walls. But, yes you can end up incarcerated for acts of vandalism.

MOXXA: Yes, really there are no sanctions per se, but if you get caught they would take your paint and at times keep you locked up for some time.

ELIZ: No, but if you paint on a wall without a permit obviously I would be scared and would leave running.

MIKY: Graffiti is legal as long as it doesn't turn into vandalism.

JP: Describe your graffiti style. Do you think your graffiti is political?

LA KYD: Above all I like to do wild style letters, but this doesn't mean that I won't dabble in characters also. I do graffiti because I love doing it and while I do not get paid for doing so, I am expressing myself freely. On occasion I have touched upon social issues, but I have never done graffiti that has to do with politics.

MOXXA: I like letters of only one line and I do blocks, lately I've done simple letters. Don't like to do the same thing all the time, I guess I don't have a definite style.

ELIZ: A little bit of everything, but I lean towards characters.

MIKY: My style in graffiti is super simple, I like bomba [bombing] style, these are letters that are legible; Block Buster, gigantic letters that are kind of square and legible as well. I always tried to make my letters have a mix of femininity and aggressiveness.

JP: Do you know when Hip Hop culture became popular in your countries? Do you think that graffiti is part of Hip Hop culture where you live? Can you tell me when people started writing graffiti and who they were?

LA KYD: Yes, graffiti is one of the 4 elements of the Hip Hop culture. Graffiti is part of the history of how Hip Hop culture was born. DJ Afria Bambaataa is known for giving birth to this new movement with the name Hip Hop that describes how members are part of the four elements: DJs, MCs, Breaking and Graffiti. In Nicaragua, Hip Hop culture began in the '90s—and graffiti was born on the streets of Managua at the same time. Pioneers like Chuck, Fly, Dog, Thief, and Meak were among others who joined the movement, but the first girl to do graffiti in my country was LUCHA.[12]

MOXXA: For sure, graffiti has always been tied to Hip Hop culture. It's growing rapidly, it's not rare to see BBoys frequently and everywhere at rap events.

ELIZ: For sure graffiti as is it's one of the 4 pillars of the Hip Hop culture, it relates to everything. Growing up in Managua graffiti culture was very poor, there were some graffiteers and bboys and because of my lack of knowledge I was not fully into it, but now I could say that I have evolved because it's well known everywhere due to all the support of lots of organizations that help the young to develop as artists.

MIKY: Of course I believe it! We all know that graffiti is an element of the Hip Hop culture. Well, in my neighborhood it was done in a very informal way, boys and girls practicing something they knew nothing about. The rest of the city is just as bad, lots of people rapping, graffiting, disc jockeying and break dancing without having an idea that all those elements have a history and lots of basic techniques, the same way there are people that have all the necessary or deep knowledge about this culture. In some regions there has been an ongoing revolution in each of these elements compared to years before, even though ignorance on this subject still prevails intensely.

JP: Tell me what you know about the history of graffiteras. Do you know about other Latin American all-female graffiti crews?

LA KYD: I always like to see the work of female graffiti artists all over the world, and I admire all female graffiti artists. I know the girls of Turronas Crew. I admire their work. As women who do graffiti, we are interested in knowing the work of other girls who are dedicated to the same thing. Personally, I like to know the work of other graffiteras.

MOXXA: Really I don't know who was the first graffitera, all I know is there are lots of them making history, personally I admire MadC, Stick Up Girls, and Few and Far; for me these are the best.[13]

ELIZ: The first and only pioneer woman of graffiti in Nicaragua is Christian Dugan better known as Lucha inside the culture. After 2009 or 2010

---

12. See *Lucha Graffiti*, 2007, http://youtu.be/dLBccz59kSc; "Photo by Toxoulogy," July 24, 2014, *Instagram*, http://instagram.com/p/q1g5wzhkMN/; and Jonathan Jackson, "Noche de Lucha," *Hecho Magazine*, March 2009, http://hechomagazine.com/culture/noche-de-lucha/lang/en/.

13. MadC, the Stick Up Girls, and Few and Far all have a strong digital presence. The Stick Up Girls and Few and Far are both international crews. See Pabón (2013b).

more and more women started coming up and expressing ourselves through graffiti.

MIKY: Truthfully, I don't have a broad knowledge about them, but in my country the pioneer is LUCHA.

JP: How and why do you use the Internet to share your graffiti?

LA KYD: It's a way of spreading my art without borders.

MOXXA: I like to share what I paint with everyone especially with people from other countries via Instagram, Tumblr, or Facebook.

ELIZ: First to make a name for myself and be known as an artist and people know my work. Also is a great tool to know more of the Hip Hop culture and share with the other females that paint graffiti.

MIKY: We use whatever is available on the internet that's at our disposal to promote us as crew from the artistic point of view.

JP: In 2012, Kyd and Sak trained people in the community to paint graffiti in a workshop. Do you still host workshops and teach other people how to paint?

LA KYD: On two occasions we have offered workshops to women, one session was in Managua and another in Matagalpa. We also did a workshop where the participants were girls and boys from semi-rural neighborhoods in the capital. Soon, I'm going to teach a graffiti workshop to other girls in my sister country Honduras.[14] As a crew, we have plans to continue doing these workshops in order to educate others about Hip Hop culture and encourage new girls to do graffiti.

JP: Do you think of yourself (and your crew) as feminist? What is feminism?

LA KYD: In my group the only thing I'm in search of is the empowerment of females in graffiti.

MOXXA: In a sense yes, I like when I see the work of a graffitera and give her support because I know how hard it is for women to make it due to stereotypes. Support each other and make a difference, we are women and we are strong. We have the same rights as men.

ELIZ: Of course it's always good to support women, and above all learn to respect them for what they want to do. For me feminism is more than a

14. Here, Kyd is referring to the *Taller de Graffiti Feminas en el HipHop Honduras* (workshop on women in graffiti for Hip Hop Honduras) event that took place in October 2014, where she lectured on some of her favorite women in graffiti and facilitated a graffiti-writing skills training. You can see images on a public Facebook post here: https://www.facebook.com /rebecalane6/posts/801902713204764.

movement is a way of life, of making your rights be valued as a woman and not allow anyone to reject you because of your gender and allow society to impose a roll established just for women.

MIKY: To tell you the truth I have a very impartial thought because I don't support injustice either from men or women, I try to stay out of all that and do my part. To me it's an organization that promotes women rights in the absolute, equality between women and men and the rejection of discrimination of women.

JP: What do you hope to contribute to the subculture (in your country)?

LA KYD: Currently, I organize an event with my friends from Chacuatol called "Hall of Femme"[15] where we invite all girls belonging to Hip Hop from Central America (Graffiteras, Bgirls, rappers and Djs). All gather at this event, which is held annually, and participate in educational workshops and talks in order to continue encouraging the participation and empowerment of women within the culture.

Bibliography

Cassandra, Rachel, and Lauren Gucik. 2015. *Women Street Artists of Latin America: Art Without Fear.* San Francisco: Manic D.

Dennis, Christopher. 2014. "Locating Hip Hop's Place within Latin American Cultural Studies." *Alter/nativas: Latin American Cultural Studies Journal* 2(Spring): 1–20.

González-Rivera, Victoria. 2012. *Before the Revolution: Women's Rights and Right-Wing Politics in Nicaragua, 1821–1979.* University Park: Pennsylvania State University Press.

González-Rivera, Victoria, and Karen Kampwirth, eds. 2001. *Radical Women in Latin America: Left and Right.* University Park: Pennsylvania State University Press.

Kampwirth, Karen. 2006. "Resisting the Feminist Threat: Antifeminist Politics in Post-Sandinista Nicaragua." *NWSA Journal* 18(2): 73–100.

Leitinger, Ilse Abshagen, ed. and trans. 1997. *The Costa Rican Women's Movement: A Reader.* Pittsburgh, PA: University of Pittsburgh Press.

Macdonald, Nancy. 2001. *The Graffiti Subculture: Youth, Masculinity, and Identity in London and New York.* Basingstoke, Hampshire; New York: Palgrave Macmillan.

Pabón, Jessica. 2013a. "Be About It: Graffiteras Performing Feminist Community." *TDR: The Journal of Performance Studies* 59(219): 88–116.

---

15. La Kyd is an organizer-participant for the annual "Hall of Femme" event founded in 2013 that takes places in Nicaragua (www.facebook.com/halloffemmenicaragua). The title is a bit of feminist wordplay citing the widespread practice of having a place (a rooftop, an alley, an abandoned building)—called a "Hall of Fame"—where the best of the best showcase their graffiti work. The difference is that the Hall of Femme event calls specifically on Central American *women* in any of Hip Hop's cultural forms to participate.

———. 2013b. "Shifting Aesthetics: The Stick Up Girlz Perform Crew in a Virtual World." Edited by John Lennon and Matthew Burns. *Rhizomes* 25. http://rhizomes.net/issue25/pabon/index .html.

Saravannote. 2012. "Girls + Graffiti = Ladies Destroying Crew." *Vagabonde*, May 7. http://saravannote .wordpress.com/2012/05/07/girls-graffiti-ladies-destroying-crew/ (accessed July 2014).

WomenStreetArtists.com. 2015. "LA KYD—Women Street Artists." http://www.womenstreetartists .com/la-kyd (accessed November 16).

chapter 14

"Conscious Cuban Rap"

Krudas Cubensi and Supercrónica Obsesión

Sandra Abd'Allah-Álvarez Ramírez

Translated by Janelle Gondar

The contributions that Cuba has made to the global Hip Hop movement, at this point in the twenty-first century, are undeniable, above all with respect to rap music, which has found recognition in the Caribbean, as well as in Latin America and internationally.

The context has thus been an island with a renowned musical history that has provided rhythms like *son,* salsa, mambo, and cha-cha-cha, among others. To this list, one can add rap, which has been nourished by the rhythmic bases of Cuban music, like other musical trends have, and that, as is typical of the genre, has been focused on tackling the principal issues of Cuban society in a rebellious way and providing solutions whenever possible. In this work, I analyze some of the contributions that Cuba has made to the Latin American Hip Hop movement, especially by systematically and incisively making visible problems like racial discrimination, violence against women, and the imposition of a hetero-patriarchal system that oppresses the "different" and converts it into the "inferior." With this goal in mind, and based on lyrical analyses, I review the performance and work of two of the most well-known

Cuban rap groups: Krudas Cubensi and Supercrónica Obsesión, both of which have also become known for the existing coherence between their members' personal lives and their artistic production. In this sense, we are talking about two groups that sustain an indisputable promise to their communities and that have sparked activism through their own work and beyond it.

The first of these groups, Krudas Cubensi, has favored themes of a social character related to sexual diversity, feminism, violence against women, femicide, and sorority, among others, tied to enriching experiences like migration. Supercrónica Obsesión, on the other hand, has made it a point to tackle, among other issues, discourses related to racial identity, national identity, and race relations within Cuban society. The intersections between these groups allow one to talk about a "conscious Cuban rap" that deals with diverse topics of Cuba's reality in a profound way.

Krudas Cubensi: *Pero nosotras siempre representando*[1]

Wanda (Odalys Cuesta), Pasa Kruda (Odaymara Cuesta), and Pelusa (Olivia Prendes) come from a long history of rebellious cultural projects. One in particular that stands out is the formation, along with Llane Alexis Domínguez, of the first queer and vegan art group in Cuba in 1996. Later, in 1999, Krudas Cubensi is born. Another year after that, they would found the theater collectives *Gigantería* and *Tropazancos Cubensi.*

The Krudas arrived to break with traditional modes of making rap music and, above all, to do away with the male dominance of the Cuban rap scene. According to Ariel Fernández Díaz, interviewed in the documentary *Queen of Myself: Las Krudas d' Cuba,* by Celiany Rivera-Velázquez, "The Krudas arrive at a certain time to tell us, your discourse is incomplete, there are certain ingredients in this discourse that are missing, and we are going to provide them, we are going to bring it and we are going to be alongside you in this battle, but you have to listen to us"[2] (2010).

During the Krudas's first phase, they would focus on *afrocubanness,* which was clearly visible from their appearance as women with dreadlocks and clothing reminiscent of the mother continent, as well as in their lyrics. At that

---

1. "but we always representing"
2. All translations in this chapter are by Janelle Gondar.

time, they also had strong creative connections with intellectuals like Alfredo Hernández, a.k.a. "Punta de Laza,"[3] and Pablo Herrera.[4]

These sage Cuban women manage to add rhythm and flow to their thoughts in such a way that in their songs they narrate the experience of women who combine physical and intellectual freedom, and love through music mixed with an inevitable desire to dance and enjoy oneself:

No terrenal, amor verdadero, descomunal, dominical
vamos a jugar hasta el amanecer en espiral, mira, yo, me monto en camello
toco tus cabellos,
te envuelvo en destello, estallo,
te subo la dosis,
me tienes, te excito, educo, palpito,
el orificio calentico, el sabor dulzón salaíto
y el cielo azulito,
con brillo infinito, temblando de a poco, de a muchito,
y luego te digo te quiero y tu me dices: ¡Ke rico!

Not earthly, but real love, colossal, Sabbath,
We are going to play until the dawn in a spiral, look, I will ride the camel
I touch your hair,
I surround you in sparkles, I burst,
I up your dosage,
you have me, I excite you, educate you, I throb,
the hot orifice, the sweet salty flavor
and the blue sky,
with infinite shine, trembling from a little, from a lot,
and later I tell you I love you and you tell me: Mmm yummy!

I am not aware of any cultural studies that reveal how other female Cuban musicians have addressed the topic of sexual-erotic relations between women, but at first glance, there do not seem to be many examples of the aforementioned. Singing about lesbian relations has not been a central theme in the

---

3. Alfredo Hernández Gómez (deceased) is a well-known Cuban percussionist, an autodidact who worked within the Cuban Hip Hop movement connected to groups like Krudas Cubensi, Obsesión, and Ogguere.

4. Pablo Herrera is a Cuban intellectual of major prominence within the Cuban Hip Hop movement and an agent for groups that would later become real landmarks of Cuban music, as is the case with the group Orishas.

work of these Cuban singer-songwriters, not even for the ones who are lesbians. To this effect, the reporter Joaquín Borges-Triana (2012) states:

> Among the typical order of associations that the Krudas generate for me is the invocation of María Teresa Vera, a very distinguished representative of the best of our traditional *trova* [song]. This mulatto woman, known among the group as a lesbian, is the perfect example of the composer who avoided incorporating into her work phrases or verses that could have served as a marker of gender, race, or sexual orientation that would distinguish and identify her.

Krudas Cubensi, then, belongs to a very limited group of Cuban artists who favor radical feminist discourse about the politics of the body and eroticism. As survivor-dissidents of Cuban Hip Hop's "machanguería" (Cuban slang for male-dominated-hegemonic-machismo), The Krudas amplified their truly revolutionary and progressive style of rap to the point of having to emigrate: the "musical island" was too small for their interests and passions.

One cannot be exceedingly politically "incorrect" in a society that preconceives order and categorization as what is valid. Even less so in a movement that, for all its rebelliousness, does not cease to be male chauvinist, sexist, and, in some cases, misogynist. As Tanya Saunders (2009), author of the recently released book-length study *Cuban Underground Hip Hop: Black Thoughts, Black Revolution and Black Modernity,* describes,

> Krudas' politics of a linguistic and ideological intervention into hegemonic discourses surrounding race, gender, and sexuality, problematizes oppression through the critique of individual experiences that they link to systemic forms of social oppression. Their work centers on changing the minds of fellow citizens as a means of spurring grassroots social change. (2)

The Krudas left complaints, laments, and rivalries behind a long time ago. That was a necessary phase of a Cuban rap movement in which women were made invisible and misogyny made waves—and still does, surely. Now, these female rappers, both global and Cuban, have found and are building a positive path towards the enjoyment of their own existence and ours, too. As The Krudas say, "No victimization"; the result is then a profoundly rebellious discourse, inclusive and progressive, that, at least in Cuba, has no comparison.

> It is through their usage of tools such as poetry (hip-hop lyrics) and street theater performance that Las Krudas has been able to work within Cuba's cultural sphere, a key component of Cuba's public sphere. In this sphere, they

> have been able to challenge the hegemony of the sexist, racist, and homopho-
> bic discourses that continue to circulate within Cuban society. They do so by
> educating their peers and communities about social inequality, particularly
> racial, gender, and sexual inequalities. (ibid.)

With various years of artistic involvement outside of Cuba, the group members have presented themselves in circuits that represent the diversity of contemporary society. Rhythmically, the beats that currently back up The Krudas's verses stand out for including Latin American genres like *cumbia,* for
instance. The experience of touring across various parts of the United States,
as well as visiting Mexico, for example, has left its mark on their contemporary
compositions. Their track "*Cumbia para Oshun*" from the album *Levántate,*
which was produced in Austin, Texas, in 2012, is a perfect example of this.

However, upon returning to the island, they always find a scene that considers them to be a part of the best of Cuban rap, which implies that, in addition to their lyrics, their improvisation and work as activists emphasizes their
intention to offer a meaning and a path for the still fledgling movement of
female Cuban rappers to follow. In the words of the Cuban activist and historian Logbona Olukonee (2014),

> Positioning themselves as queer, feminist, afro-descendant, Caribbean
> women, defenders of Pacha Mama's rights and of raw vegan food, Pasita and
> Pelusa are changing the hetero-patriarchal face of Cuban Hip Hop, not only
> by their presence, but also with the formative and spiritual support of the
> rest of the female rappers and activists that surround them.

For that reason, The Krudas continue to be ours, that is to say, Cuban, because
they continue dealing with those topics that, while also universal—like afro-
descendance—are particular to Cuba. They also sing about our mothers,
a theme that, although uncommon in Hip Hop, does not lose its relevance for
this group:

> Gracias por brindarme la primera mano
> gracias por coser tanto pa' comprarme el piano
> gracias por inculcarme to' este orgullo cubano
> gracias mamá por querer a este ser profano.
> Gracias por las jabas y la luz mi santa
> aunque muy lejos estoy mi voz en tu oído canta,
> aunque un nudo se haga en esta mi garganta
> cuando pienso en ud me convierto en giganta.

Thank you for being the first to offer me your hand
thank you for sewing so much to buy me a piano
thank you for instilling in me all of this Cuban pride
Thank you, Mom, for loving this profane being
Thank you for the bags and the light, my saint
Although I'm very far away, my voice sings in your ear
although I might get a lump in this here throat of mine
When I think of you, I become a giant.

I can assert, then, that the existence of a group like Krudas Cubensi has legiti-mized an "alternative"[5] artistic scene in Cuba that implicitly carries those val-ues that these "artivists"[6] defend:

To love. Justice in this world. Nature. Equilibrix[7]. Respectx.
Horizontality = Circularity.
Art as a way of life that empowers us and improves existence. Change,
    emigration.
The attention to the body as a temple = Vegetariansimx + Krudismx.
Caring for the planet, its resources and the species that inhabit it.
Happiness. Autonomy. AfroCuba. A celebration of oxr bodies. Self-esteem.

(Álvarez Ramírez 2013)

Supercrónica Obsesión: *Afrocubano pensamiento*

The group Supercrónica Obsesión was founded on June 26, 1996. Attracted to the inviting and reformist influences of rap, its members Alexey Rodríguez, a.k.a. Eltipoeste ["the eastern guy"], and Magia López quickly fell in line with the vanguard that was responsible for the genre's appropriation and definition within Cuban culture.

Since then, and to this very day, its members have been loyal and proud representatives of Afro-descendance, which is present beyond their origins, in their aesthetic and in the art they produce daily. This group especially

---

5. I use the word "alternative" discreetly in order to promote understanding, but in reality I am not in favor of its indiscriminate use, as it legitimizes the idea that there is a center, a par-adigm, when in reality there are several, but some are just hegemonic and shared by a majority.

6. The term "artivism" is a recent creation used by those artists and intellectuals that participate in social movements, protests, etc. In it the words art and activism are combined.

7. The use of *x* is from the original Spanish interview and is a way in which the subjects express themselves in a gender neutral form.

stands out for its rising trajectory dedicated to what they call "*afrocubano pensamiento*" or "Afro-Cuban thought" (Álvarez Ramírez 2011).

Obsesión's music reflects an interesting generic equilibrium and a stylistic and musical diversity that flow from working with elements of jazz, Cuban music, and a whole array of musical currents from Cuba and Latin America with latent African origins to the creation of very dissimilar lyrics where the message, always in the form of a chronicle, proposes changes to stereotypical behaviors and attitudes. Additionally, throughout their vast career, Obsesión has always known how to combine good art, humor, and reformist desires with activism, community service, and the struggle to create a better world. Not only have they amassed important awards and prizes at festivals, but they have also performed, nationally and internationally, alongside leading figures of the music world; in addition, they have been linked to the work of renowned Cuban artists like the audiovisual director Roberto Chile and the visual artists Alexis Leyva (Kcho) and Eduardo Roca (Choco).

Eltipoeste states that the first Obsesión track that dealt with racial themes was a strange spoken-word track in the form of a "sworn statement" where, according to its director, "rage, rebellion, mockery, and pride were all mixed in; in those lyrics we made it clear that when we finally did get the opportunity to make a video, we would do so demonstrating the diversity among Black people." Since then, there have been many tracks created by Obsesión that address negritude and the complex world of racial relations in Cuba. For example, in 2011 the group released the album *El disco negro de Obsesión* as both an MP3 and a special edition CD with a singular and creative physical appearance.

Just as Obsesión's director, Alexey Rodríguez, declared during the volume's presentation, Obsesión began its journey in the fight against racial discrimination and racism a long time ago, when the Cuban historiographer Tomás Fernández Robaina—whom Rodríguez considers to be his mentor—invited the group to understand the depth of some of the historical events that impact the identity of Black people in Cuban society.[8] The achievement and presentation of this album is done intentionally, according to Magia López, in 2011, within the framework designated by the United Nations as the International Year for People of African Descent.[9] In a note for this special edition, the Cuban intellectual Marcel Loueiro wrote:

---

8. Words of . . . Eltipoeste . . . during the concert presentation of *El disco negro de Obsesión* on March 17, 2012, in Covarrubias Hall at the Teatro Nacional of Havana, Cuba.

9. Magia López, during the concert presentation of *El disco negro de Obsesión* on March 17, 2012, in Covarrubias Hall at the Teatro Nacional of Havana, Cuba.

You have in your hands a luminous and minuscule fragment (immense due to its *futurity*) of Cuban culture; the synthesis of a concept; a way to take on life, memory, and politics that shimmers in the mirror of the living dead like Aponte, Plácido, Maceo, Banderas, and Ivonet, but, above all, in the mirror of so many anonymous Blacks that make Cuban nationality possible with their perennial presence (from the remote fields of the sugar cane plantations and the wars for independence to the humble neighborhoods of today's Cuba).

The concert that was conceived for the presentation of *El disco negro* confirmed the group's intention to treat the subject of anti-Black racism in the country with seriousness but, at the same time, stood out for the newness of the volume's conception.

The album in question, produced independently, consists of twelve tracks: eight rap songs and four interludes. This was the group's second album, and, that same year, it was entered into the country's national discography contest, CUBADISCO, where it won the grand prize in its category. One of the tracks included on this album, "*Calle G,*" fostered the debate about how racism is currently perpetuated in Cuba, particularly with respect to certain symbols associated with specific incidents that took place on the island and that have been skirted by official accounts. Such is the case of the statue of the Cuban general José Miguel Gómez, part of a lavish mausoleum located in one of Havana's most important intersections: Avenida de los Presidentes or Calle G—an avenue where the statues of Latin American dignitaries like Eloy Alfaro, Simón Bolívar, and Benito Juárez can also be found.

I must briefly mention that under José Miguel Gómez's presidency, thousands of Blacks and mestizos were massacred in 1912. The incident, wrongly called the "*guerrita del 12*" or "little war of 1912," has been erased by official historical accounts. With the track "Calle G," Obsesión situates itself inside the vortex of the debate about racism in Cuban. The lyrics are a denunciation of the statue's presence:

> En la mismísima Calle G o Avenida de los Presidentes hay
> Una gran estatua de José Miguel Gómez que si la ve Pedro Ivonet (¡ay!)
> No entiendo que hace ese tipo ahí, después de una Revolución que se hizo aquí.
> ¿Que fue lo que pasó con la memoria de este país?
> ¡No se a ti, a nosotros no nos representa!
> (¡Que no me den muela!)
> Que para mí está claro que está glorificando el racismo al descaro

On the very same street, Calle G or Avenida de los Presidentes, there is
A great statue of José Miguel Gómez that, should Pedro Ivonet see it . . .
    (Ah!!)
I don't know what that guy is doing there, after we had a Revolution here.
What happened to this country's memory?
I don't know about you, but we are not represented!
(Don't give me any lip service!)
To me, it's clear that they are shamelessly glorifying racism

At the same time, they offer a solution based on Hip Hop's own culture:

Hago un llamado al graffiti cubano
¡Si no la tumban vamo' y la graffiteamo'!

I call upon the Cuban graffiti community
If they don't knock it down, let's go tag it up!

In the email debate that took place as a result of the song,[10] several intellectuals offered their opinions on the matter and, as one might expect, some were in favor of the statue, while others were against it. Nevertheless, what was truly significant was the exposure of such a delicate issue like the legitimacy that is granted (or not) to distressing incidents of national history since the Cuban Revolution. With respect to the concept of rap as a creator of social consciousness, Eltipoeste expressed the following during the debate:

> We are very happy that our track "Calle G" has provoked this polemic, which accomplishes our goal of denouncing first and debating the topic afterwards. If our song was able to do that, then one part of the process has been completed. They say that there is not just one truth, but we have our own, and that's the one that we put forward.

Obsesivas Krudas and Cubensi Supercrónica: Inescapable Proximities

Between Obsesión and The Krudas, beyond being in the same geographical zone and common social scene, there are explicit points of convergence.

---

10. See the entire debate regarding "José Miguel Gómez en Calle G" available at http://negracubanateniaqueser.wordpress.com/el-ciberdebate/jose-mig/.

In particular, these points become clear with a discussion of two tracks: "*Mi belleza*"—a spoken-word track on *El disco negro de Obsesión* (2011)—and "*Eres bella,*" from the album *Cubensi Hip Hop* (2003).

As one might infer from the titles, both tracks address the issue of beauty standards that later become everyday routines and that also function as ideals, which are then shared socially and become more and more difficult to avoid as society continuously emphasizes them and the media constantly reproduce them. These paradigms of beauty, about which there is a general consensus,[11] also establish hierarchies of values where the positive corresponds with "the white/light" and the negative with "the black/dark," at least in Cuba's case.

In general, the diverse movements of Cuban music have favored essentialist views of women in such a way that it is commonplace to hear songs that exalt their femininity based on tenderness, fragility, delicateness, weakness, and so forth. At the same time, however, songs often criticize women for not fulfilling such paradigms. As with other branches of culture, Black women have been excluded from said representations. In the words of the Cuban researcher Inés María Martiatu (2009):

> The Black woman has been insulted by the discourse of those who have historically boasted economic and cultural power in our country, a White minority, masculine and heterosexual, that, from positions of indisputable power, has imposed its vision in which beauty, the aesthetic, cultural, and religious projections of the Black woman have been systematically disregarded, discounted, and disqualified. (301)

Nonetheless, even within Hip Hop culture, those stereotypes that support White supremacy have been reproduced or Black women have simply been newly marginalized. The Krudas describe how their bodies are generally referred to as their "only virtue." In short, male rappers, barring a few exceptions, have not made it very easy for the Black women represented in their lyrics nor the female rappers on the scene.

> We Black women are left, then, in a state of defenselessness. Subaltern to a subaltern subject, discriminated by gender and by race, we have been historically obligated to correspond to the social construct that denies the Black and mestizo woman's intellectual capacity. Corralled by extreme assessments of our sensuality to the detriment of our intellectual production and contributions as women of the 21st century, we are invisible within a conflictive

---

11. For a more in-depth analysis of this aspect, see Junco (2009).

society that changes daily, disfiguring our social roles in literature, music, and the collective imaginary. (González 2009, 272)

On the other hand, the White hegemony's control of the Black body also includes the subjugation of Black people's hair, be it via a shaved head, chemical straightening,[12] extensions, or other methods. Regarding this, The Krudas tell us:

> Chardas, mecate,
> juguemos nuestro papel,
> es nuestro tiempo,
> artificios desrices y postizos son
> continuación del cuento colonialista
> no te cojas pa' eso,
> deja esa falsa vista."

> Black women, ropes
> let us play our part,
> it's our time,
> artificial straighteners and (wigs/extensions) are
> a continuation of the colonialist story,
> don't get caught up in that,
> leave that false view behind.

The recurrence of this theme in Obsesión's lyrics is notable. In fact, the issue is astutely exposed in "*Los pelos*,"[13] a track that crystalizes the group's antiracist militancy. However, because "*Mi belleza*" is a spoken-word track, it changes the tone from a complaint to a subtle, dramatically structured speech. In this way, it lays out the following ideas:

> Mi belleza es punto de partida para cada hazaña.
> Es limpia, no se disfraza, no se engaña
> Mi belleza afronta mis desafíos, ahuyenta mis titubeos. (. . .)
> No es la de revista, no es la que estás imaginando.
> No es la clásica belleza eurocéntricamente hablando.

---

12. Regarding the connections that exist between gender identity and hair straightening, see del Valle (2009).

13. In 2010 the video for the track "*Los pelos*" received the grand prize in the rap–Hip Hop category of the "Lucas" national competition, the only one in the country. The track was written in 1999, and Melissa Rivière made the video in 2005.

My beauty is the starting point for every great deed.
It's clean, it's not disguised, and it doesn't fool itself
My beauty confronts my challenges, it banishes my hesitations (. . .)
It's not the kind from magazines, it's not the one you're imagining.
It's not the classic beauty, eurocentrically speaking.

At the same time, the stereotypical treatment of Black women's bodies is very present in the representations that comic strips, the media, and so forth usually make of them. In fact, the country's most famous representation of Black or mestizo women is a cartoon known as "*las criollitas de Wilson*" ("Wilson's Little Creole Women"), hypersexualized women presented as objects of masculine pleasure that stand out because of their voluminous rumps.[14] Cubensi's track "*Eres bella*" then provides a complementary social critique about the reduction of women to physical appearance. Thus, against a Cuban popular speech filled with marked derogatory connotations for the facial features of Black people—"*bemba*" for thick lips, "*pasa*" for very curly or kinky hair, and "*ñata*" for a flattened nose—these two groups demand a re-evaluation of Blackness and female beauty on different terms, terms that both highlight and critique racialized hierarchies of appearance and worthiness.

Conclusion

In the Cuban Hip Hop scene Supercrónica Obsesión and Krudas Cubensi both stand out because of their swift insertion into the Cuban rap movement and their longevity despite the passage of time and the eventual exits of some of their members. At the same time, the incisive work that both groups have contributed to the discussion of these issues of race, gender, sexuality as well as the evolution and revision of their own ideas on the subject cannot be overlooked. One example of this is increased focus on the topic of prostitution in the case of Obsesión and emmigration for The Krudas, which can be observed in songs recorded after the group left Cuba and created a new mix of Cuban rhythms with music from various Latin American countries.

Clearly, the discourse of both groups is evidence of a "conscious Cuban rap" buttressed by a complex knowledge of the complex structures of power both nationally and globally based in the subordination of women, White hegemony, heteronormativity, and so on—as well as their role as rappers in the deconstruction of those mechanisms that support and reproduce said

---

14. For more on this topic, see Álvarez Ramírez (2009).

oppressions. Luckily, both groups are still "alive and kicking," or, as they say in Cuba, *"vivitas y coleando,"* which means that they are out there "doing their thing," participating actively with their art in the communities that they have chosen as their own, regardless of geographical ties.

Bibliography

Álvarez Ramírez, Sandra. 2008. "Esclavitud y cuerpos al desnudo. La sexualidad y la belleza de la mujer negra." *Revista Sexología y Sociedad* 14 (August): 36–39.

———. 2009. "La sexualidad y la belleza de la mujer negra, una aproximación desde Cuba." *CubaDebate,* August 23. http://www.cubadebate.cu/especiales/2009/08/23/la-sexualidad-y-la-belleza-de-la-mujer-negra-una-aproximacion-desde-cuba/.

———. 2011. "El rap y el 'afrocubano pensamiento': Entrevistando a Obsesión." *Otras modernidades* 6(11): 277–80. http://riviste.unimi.it/index.php/AMonline/article/viewFile/1609/1808.

———. 2013. "Krudas Cubensi, rap desde las trompas de Falopio." *Pikara Magazine,* May 24. http://www.pikaramagazine.com/2013/05/krudas-cubensi-rap-desde-las-trompas-de-falopio/#more-11505.

Borges-Triana, Joaquín. 2012. "¡Vivan las gordas sin domesticar!" *Caimán Barbudo,* September 7. http://www.caimanbarbudo.cu/musica/2012/09/vivan-las-gordas-sin-domesticar/.

del Valle, Sandra. 2009. "Pasar por blanca." *La Gaceta* 3 (May–June).

González, Carmen. 2009. "Alzar la voz. Quebrar el margen. Rap y discurso femenino." *Syllabus afrocubano.* Kingston: Ediciones La Ceiba. https://afrocubanas.wordpress.com/2015/02/12/alzar-la-voz-quebrar-el-margen-rap-y-discurso-femenino-2/.

Junco, Yulexiz Almeida. 2009. "Género y racialidad. Un estudio de representaciones sociales en el barrio La Timba." Master's thesis. Habana: Universidad de La Habana.

Martiatu, Inés María. 2009. "Discurso femenino en el Hip Hop cubano. Nuevas voces, nuevos reclamos en la cancionística cubana." *Syllabus afrocubano.* Kingston: Ediciones La Ceiba.

Olukonee, Logbona. 2014. "Krudas Cubensi: timón del nuevo afro-feminismo queer cubano." *Negra cubana tenía que ser,* February 24. http://negracubanateniaqueser.wordpress.com/2014/02/24/krudas-cubensi-timon-del-nuevo-afro-feminismo-queer-cubano/.

Rivera-Velázquez, Celiany. 2010. *Reina de mi Misma, Queen of Myself: Las Krudas d' Cuba.* Documentary.

Saunders, Tanya. 2009. "La Lucha Mujerista: Krudas CUBENSI and Black Feminist Sexual Politics in Cuba." *Caribbean Review of Gender Studies* 3. Mona: University of the West Indies. http://sta.uwi.edu/crgs/november2009/journals/CRGS%20Las%20Krudas.pdf.

Discography

Cuesta, Odaymara, and Olivia Prendes. 2012. "Punto G." On *Levántate.* Austin, TX. Compact Disc.

Krudas Cubensi and Sound Sister. 2012. "Madrecita." On *Levántate.* Austin, TX. Compact Disc.

PART V

RAP CONSCIENTE: HIP HOP'S ROLE IN ACTIVISM

chapter 15

Ethnicity, Race, Nation, and the Male Voice in Alteño Hip Hop in Bolivia

María Angela Riveros Pinto

Translated by Jocelyn Langer, Manuela Borzone, and Alexander Ponomareff

In memory of Abraham Bojorquez, who gave strength and vital energy to Alteño Hip Hop

L ocated in the heart of South America, Bolivia is a country with a diverse geography composed of a variety of eco-regions, which run from plateaus and mesothermal valleys to the plains and the Amazon. Its salient feature is its broad cultural diversity, made up of thirty-six ethnic groups; one of these important populations is, without a doubt, the Aymara, who make up 25 percent of the country's total population.[1] In Bolivia, the Indigenous populations have historically been marginalized by the White elites, excluded from places of power and discriminated against. However, since the end of the 1990s there has been a series of historic transformations for these groups.

El Alto is an Aymara city situated almost 4,000 meters above sea level, with a population of over 700,000, of which 74 percent are Aymara, 60 percent of whom are under the age of twenty-five.[2] El Alto was part of the city of La Paz, the current seat of the government, until the 1980s, when it became an independent city due to its growing migrant population. This first generation

---

1. 2001 Census Data, Bolivian National Institute of Statistics (Instituto Nacional de Estadistica, INE).
2. Ibid.

of migrants arrived in the 1980s, mostly from rural towns of the department of La Paz, in search of better opportunities in which to live, work, and study. These migrants and their families have settled in El Alto, and while they consider themselves Alteño, the vast majority of them are Aymara or have a strong Aymara cultural tradition, which shapes the dominant identity of El Alto.

Much of the Alteño population lives in conditions of poverty; many neighborhoods still lack basic amenities such as potable water and electricity. In these conditions, many young people don't have access to basic education, much less higher education, or health care. By the 1990s these conditions of poverty and discontent led to the establishment of an important platform for a variety of social movements. In 2003 a series of protests culminated in the Gas War. During its final days, in which the entire Alteño population stood up against the possible sale of gas to Chile, Alteño residents emerged as the defenders of their natural resources. The citizens of El Alto, a city with a significant Aymara population, became key actors in this revolutionary force; the women and youth stood out as protagonists during the defense of their gas, a natural resource of national importance. As a result of these events, which mark the contemporary history of Bolivia, Evo Morales, an Indigenous president, is currently serving his third consecutive term in the Plurinational State.

In recent years the country has undergone a series of fundamental changes, including a new Constitution, which, after many years, is inclusive of the Indigenous people who were marginalized for so long by the old Republic, and which today shapes the present Plurinational State. Another important advance has been the adoption of Law 45, against racism and all forms of discrimination, which, although it remains to be fully implemented, has raised a series of issues related to racism and the exclusion of the Indigenous people, which had previously not been discussed in Bolivia.

At the start of this century, these changes in the country were the backdrop for the Alteño Hip Hop movement, which, through its songs and activity, inspired the issues discussed in this chapter. These issues include important advances made by the current government, such as the inclusion of the Indigenous people, the denouncement of racism and of the exclusion of Indigenous groups, and the recovery of the Aymara identity, in particular their symbols, history, and culture. Even though the Alteño Hip Hop artists did not and do not consider themselves to be political, they have nonetheless, on many occasions, demonstrated that politics are "filthy and corrupt," and their proposals had a markedly political content at a time when Evo Morales's first mandate had not yet begun.

The political and social transformations that Bolivia has undergone in recent years have had an impact on the daily life of the people, through cultural practices and also youth identities, as exemplified by the case of Hip Hop. In the 1980s Hip Hop became popular among the youth of La Paz, just as it did in many other countries around the world. In the late '90s, Hip Hop began to gain momentum in El Alto, circulating among groups of youth who pirated Hip Hop records. Later the production of Hip Hop would be influenced by the events of the October 2003 Gas War, and this marked it as having local content.

Hip Hop is undoubtedly an expression of global youth culture of the late twentieth and early twenty-first centuries, and tends to concentrate on social criticism generated by young people who live in marginalized neighborhoods and feel excluded from society. Authors such as Pillai (1999), Yúdice (2002), and Rodríguez (2005) agree that it is the Afro and Mestizo youth from these marginalized neighborhoods who enjoy and practice Hip Hop in countries such as Ecuador, Brazil, and Cuba, respectively. In Bolivia, in the particular case of El Alto, those who identify with Hip Hop are the Indigenous youth, who live in this city with a high rate of poverty.

In the Bolivian case, this fact has caught the attention of the national and international press, especially in the early years of the twenty-first century (Samanamud et al. 2007, Mollericona 2008). In general, what has been reported on is Alteño Hip Hop as a form of political expression, used to affirm Aymara identity. However, this cultural movement is not only a political expression of ethnic identity; there exist other lesser-known aspects of its social commentary, such as discrimination for being young or poor, or the conception of movement around the ethnic–national relationship. Even less studied are the forms of exclusion within the movement, such as gender, since Hip Hop generally consists of subaltern voices, but voices which are still male.

This chapter is the result of fieldwork that began in the late 1990s among the youth of El Alto and that continued until 2006, after the impact of the Gas War of 2003. Since then, the content of Hip Hop songs in El Alto has changed, and some groups have even disappeared, such as Ukamau y Ke, the group that wrote the most political lyrics in the first decade of the twenty-first century. Thus, this research reflects not only the construction of the Hip Hop cultural movement in El Alto but also the political and social processes in Bolivia in recent years.

The Bolivian Hip Hop movement also arises from the global culture that is Hip Hop and thus demonstrates how these youth manage to articulate not only ethnicity and nationality but also the current age itself. These young Alteños, through their familiarity with technology as well as their access to media, use this global forum to express their demands, to present their local struggles.

From a global perspective, the worldwide youth culture that is Hip Hop acquires a counterhegemonic[3] sense, both in the past and in the present.

"La Raza": A Counterhegemonic Concept

In Bolivia the issue of racism is very much linked to the history of colonialism. Since colonial times, Indigenous groups have been discriminated against by social groups who consider themselves to be of Spanish descent: the Whites and the Mestizos. Although this form of racism has long existed as a sort of silent racism, it has been pervasive. Until the election of Evo Morales in 2005, Indigenous groups existed at the margins of political and economic spaces and were routinely discriminated against because of their skin color, their language, their clothing, and their cultural practices.

In general, the term "raza"[4] is not very popular among Bolivians, and it is not often used, even in academic spheres; instead, it is preferable to speak of racial discrimination, which is linked to social inequality. When they do refer to "raza," it is immediately associated with physical aspects (phenotypes) such as skin color or hair color; in other words, it is related more to the biological-physical than to a sense of the social construction of the concept, so it has a negative connotation because it is seen as a matter that should have been overcome by now. This is how the members of Llajuas interpret the term:

> Those who use "raza": it's to discriminate, it's like an insult, I'm not calling you brother, you're insulting me, right? I mean, this is my way of thinking about it, foreign people say "I don't like this race" but it bothers me when there are people who say "hey, I'm White" or "you're from El Alto," that is, with dark skin, that race. I was in the Bolívar School and I always heard that, that which is race: racism . . . (group interview with Grupo Llajuas, March 2005)

They also refer to "raza" as a concept that is not recognized as their own, and they view it as foreign, so they prefer to use other terms that refer to cultural

---

3. Ari (2007a, 136) discusses a democratic globalism "that is more of an oppositional force that comes from the base and is promoted by transnational movements and coalitions." In other words, globalism carries an encapsulated counterglobalism within its own hegemonic discourse.

4. A cognate of the term "race" in English, "raza" has a different historical and academic trajectory. For more, see Debra J. Rosenthal, 2004, *Race Mixture in Nineteenth-Century U.S. and Spanish American Fictions: Gender, Culture, and Nation Building* (Chapel Hill: University of North Carolina Press) [Translator's note].

differences such as ethnicity and ethnic groups, trying to avoid the negative connotation of the concept of race and its associated connection to the
phenotypical characteristics (color of the skin, eyes, hair, etc.). According to
MC Choclo (2005), "I think that the concept of race was brought by the Spanish, this race, that word is not ours, ours is something like ethnic, or I don't
know, *suyu*.⁵"

According to Ari (2007b), in countries like Bolivia the history and the
present of the race factor are related to the repercussions of colonialism and
the practices of imperial domination. The term race is used to express social
hierarchies, and even subaltern groups have developed their own internal and
to some extent external discourses, although for Ari the counterhegemonic
ideas of "raza" are still less effective than the racialized hegemonic discourses.
In this way Hip Hop artists, and in particular the Alteño group Ukamau y Ke,
take up the discussion around "raza" and subvert its negative connotation,
proposing one of their own.

While in the opinion of some Hip Hop artists "raza" has a negative connotation, in the productions of some groups like Ukamau y Ke I find they use
the term "raza" but subvert its meaning. In their album *Para la Raza,* in the
song "La Raza," they talk about the Aymara race as a suppressed group that
is rising. In particular, they highlight their values, mention the *wiphala,* and
refer to Tiwanaku and to the sacred lake as symbols that represent the force
of the "Aymara race." Ukamau y Ke describe their decision to use "La Raza" as
follows:

> Eh, I have a song, I am Ukamau y Ke, and the song is titled "We're with the
> Race," that influence is foreign, specifically, like you say, Mexican, that term
> is Chicano, that is, that's the resemblance, that is, the indigenous peoples
> of Mexico are just like us, just like the Aymaras, I think that's the source,
> because when I say "we're with the race," I say I'm with my people, not with
> my indigenous population, that is, more or less, that's the idea I want to
> focus on, but I think it's been just an influence, nothing more. (Llajuas 2005)

Thus "Raza" appears in material produced by an Alteño Hip Hop group
because they redefine the meaning of the term, talking of race in the sense
of a group of people, of an "us." Through their songs, this group transforms
the meaning of "raza" for many Bolivians from a pejorative sense to a force

---

5. This term refers to the Aymara dominions before the conquest of the Incas. Collasuyo,
señorio of the north of the country, which means the region (suyu-portion) of the medicines
(colla-medicines) (Bouysse Cassagne, 1987).

of collective identity, and they do this, according to a member of the group Ukamau y Ke, based on inspiration from Chicano culture such as the film *Blood In, Blood Out.*

In the 1990s various youth from the city of El Alto were influenced by the film *Blood In, Blood Out.* The plot of the movie centers on the life of a young Chicano[6] who enters San Quentin Prison to kill a member of a gang. In the prison, the gangs are divided up by race: the "Mojados" are the Mexicans, the "Osos Polares" are the Whites, and the BGS are the Blacks.[7] Among Chicanos, the use of the term "race" is based on brotherly bonds of friendship and ethnic origin.[8] Race, in this case, composes an "us," a sense that has been adopted by the Alteño Hip Hop group, for whom "race" means "my nation, my group, my people."

It is well known that this movie has inspired young people to form youth gangs; however, here we see that it has also influenced youth in other ways, in this case through inspiring a rebellious discourse against discrimination and racism. According to Zolov (1999), for Mexican Americans, "Chicano" connotes a rejection of colonial values, the search for a collective identity based on the notion of race, cultural attributes, and language. "Chicano" and "raza," then, take on important meanings among the young people of El Alto, in which they reinterpret the term for their own purposes. In the case of these Alteño rappers, "raza" is made up of a term that takes on the sense of a group, a community, in order to respond in a rebellious way to the racism and discrimination they endure daily for being the children of Aymara migrants. In this way, these youth develop their own discourse on race and subvert its negative connotations in a counterhegemonic sense, thus developing their own versions of racial discourse.

Asserting Aymara Identity

Another trait that these young Aymara Hip Hop artists subvert in their discourse on race and ethnicity is the traditional skirts, or *polleras,* worn by Indigenous women, who are discriminated against for wearing this type of

---

6. A child of Mexicans born in the United States.

7. In the U.S. version of the movie in English, the names of the gangs are "La Onda," "Aryan Vanguard," and BGS respectively [translator's note].

8. According to Wade (2000), after the Second World War, the term "race" was replaced by "ethnicity," so that there would be no reason to think of superior or inferior races; thus people began to talk about ethnicity in reference to Blacks and Indians. For this author, the concept of race, like ethnicity, is constructed socially.

clothing. The *pollera,* a skirt of Spanish origin, has been worn by Indigenous women since the eighteenth century. The skirt and the dress instituted a system of ethnic hierarchies starting in the eighteenth century, and since then the *pollera* has gone out of style among the elites and has been worn by Mestiza and Indigenous women. The signs that distinguish the men of different social groups became variations of the same model, while women's outfits maintain the Spanish/Indigenous duality in the dress/*pollera* distinction. (Guaygua et al. 2000).

Women in *polleras* are discriminated against daily in public places, but following the social movements of 2003 some things have changed in the country. For example, when I conducted my research for this study of youth in El Alto in 1999, parents didn't want their daughters to be seen in *polleras* because of the history of discrimination associated with this type of clothing. Parents preferred their daughters to wear jeans or a dress because this improved their chances of entering the spaces of the dominant class. However, in March 2005 a group of young people were gathered at a breakdancing event in El Alto, when the Alteño group Ukamau y Ke took the stage "to represent" their art, wearing fatigues and baggy jackets, along with black wool hats with "Bolivia" written in red, yellow, and green letters. Before beginning to rap, they made the following statement: "We are proud to be children of the *pollera.*" This remark was immediately met with applause from their audience, which was composed entirely of young people.

Ukamau y Ke seized the opportunity to express their pride in their *pollera*-wearing mothers, anticipating the changes that would take place in the country in the coming years. In Bolivia, particularly in the Andean regions like La Paz and El Alto, the *pollera* has regained popularity in recent years as a symbol of Indigenous pride. Since Evo Morales's first term in office, Indigenous women in *polleras* have been incorporated into the country's political life, so we find that women wearing *polleras* have become deputies,[9] senators, ministers, and public officials in the Plurinational State, which before would have been unthinkable. However, racism and discrimination continue to exist in everyday life in subtle ways as a form of resistance by the elite and privileged classes, who feel invaded in the spaces they have traditionally occupied.

Another important way that ethnic identities are asserted is by bringing back Native languages, especially in the instance of these Indigenous urban youth, who, like many others, had ceased to learn the language of their parents and grandparents in order to avoid being discriminated against. This is how one of the members of the Waynarap collective describes his experience:

---

9. A type of elected representative in Bolivia (translator's note).

> We speak Aymara at home and all of that, and I've seen in all this time that before when I was little I would go to my hometown and everyone spoke in Aymara but with time this is getting lost and now many are ashamed to speak it and they say that Aymara this and that. But what we wanted to do is to highlight through Hip Hop that Aymara, that there's nothing to be ashamed of, that, on the contrary, they should be proud to have our culture and our essence, that we shouldn't let our essence get lost. (MC Grover 2006)

It is in this context that these young people appropriate a global style of music: Hip Hop is used to recast their urban Indigenous identities in a positive light, bringing back the Aymara language, and regaining a sense of pride in their roots, a situation that would have been unlikely a few years ago in Bolivia. Just as they were for wearing the *pollera,* the Aymara were discriminated against for speaking the Aymara language. It was their own parents that didn't speak to their children in Aymara in order to avoid discrimination.

Although Hip Hop could be seen as an alienating style of music, a group of young people in El Alto have appropriated it in order to make their own mark on it. In El Alto, the cultural movement of Hip Hop is changing to include particular characteristics that, due to their form and content, have been referred to as an Aymara or Andean Hip Hop. In 2005 a group of young people from "Klanes de El Alto" traveled to the sixteenth youth festival in Venezuela, where they met with people from more than twenty-five countries. At this event, the particularity of this type of Aymara Hip Hop became evident:

> So when I ran into some of them and they'd ask where are you from and why are you here, [I'd respond] I've come to do Hip Hop, yeah, like there's Hip Hop in Bolivia. Then it was time to be on the stage and to show these lyrics, this Aymara essence and a lot of people were surprised. I've had the chance to speak with a few rappers and they'd say boy that's sweet that at least you recognize you're Aymara. Look bro, I'm from Puerto Rico and my dad is from the United States, and my mom is from Puerto Rico, and it's cool that you guys feel proud to be descendants of the Aymara, of the Quechua, right? (MC Toriño 2006)

On this occasion of exchange among various countries through the common language of Hip Hop, the unique approach of Bolivian Hip Hop can be observed, and specifically Alteño Hip Hop, which is characterized not only by the fusion of the Andean and modern rhythms and lyrical content but also by the interpretation of songs in the Aymara language. Although in other Latin American countries like Brazil (Yúdice 2002), Ecuador (Pillai 1999), and Cuba (Rodríguez 2005) the youth who practice Hip Hop are Afro or Mestizo, in none of these cases have these scholars spoken of a Hip Hop that is Indigenous, Andean, or Aymara, as in the Bolivian case.

The Hip Hop groups that use the Aymara language have mixed it with Spanish—it is hard to find songs only in Aymara. In other cases they use Aymara only for the chorus:

Wacas,[10] achachilas
Apus,[11] apachetas[12]
Pachamamas yanaptajeta
Chajwañataqui
Janirinakaru atipjañataqui
Jisa taqueni
Jiska jacha
nayraru sarañañi

wacas, achachilas
apus, apachetas
pachamamas help us
we'll fight
they won't defeat us
yes all
young, old
we'll make it

(Ukamau y ke, "Para la Raza" / Wilamasis mayacht'asiñani)

This is one of the clearest examples of the use of Aymara in Hip Hop, from which I highlight a part of the lyrics that ask the Andean deities for strength in order to fight for the unity of the Aymara people. It is interesting that in this case the example of the Aymara language is restricted to short, individual words, and not used to express ideas that are too elaborate in that language, which permits them to maintain the rhythm of Hip Hop that is characterized by the use of short phrases.

---

10. *Wacas* are sacred places, objects, or elements in the framework of the Andean worldview.

11. *Apus* and *Achachilas* have the same sense and meaning in the context of the Andean beliefs; they are the protective and sacred mountains that offer their gifts to those who pay homage to them.

12. In the Andes, *pachetas* function as piles of stones that mark the path, much like sacred points at which one must make an offering before continuing on course to a specific destination. It is also common to find these manmade piles of stones at the tops of many sacred mountains (Apus or Achachilas).

To Be Bolivian and Aymara

The discourse about "the national" is linked to the Bolivian Hip Hop groups' understanding of Bolivia. The Hip Hop cultural movement, not only from El Alto but also from La Paz, has hosted a variety of events at which Hip Hop artists have raised the Bolivian flag during their live performances. Another element that stands out is how, in their song lyrics, many Hip Hop groups in Bolivia emphasize a feeling of belonging to a country, "our homeland," Bolivia:

> Boliviano hermano debemos avanzar y se caes hoy
> Tu no debes desmayar
> Por nuestra patria todos debemos luchar

> Bolivian brother we must move forward and if you fall today
> You shouldn't suffer
> We must all fight for our homeland
> > (MC Invisible, Klanes de El Alto Waynarap, "Bolivian Brother")

The focus of the Alteño Hip Hop artists, in relation to their sense of belonging to Bolivia, is strengthened by the idea of asserting an Indigenous Aymara identity. The message of the Hip Hop cultural movement of El Alto is one of belonging to a unique country. Bolivia is a country that recognizes its pluriculture and diversity, as these artists express it, but one in which the Indigenous roots of the movement's members are not denied. One example can be found in the song "Mi cultura," or "My Culture":

> Bolivia patria mía
> hoy día para ti mi rima
> desde el fondo de mi corazón
> te entrego esta canción para tu cordillera nevada
> los andes cuatro mil cien de altura
> por siempre en el altiplano
> cerros y montañas cumbres nevadas
> Tiwanaku ruinas
> sin saber sin conocer
> amo a mi patria para poder crecer
> no rechazo mi raíz indígena

> Bolivia my homeland
> today my rhymes

from the bottom of my heart
I give you this song for your snowy mountains
the Andes four thousand one hundred in height
forever in the altiplano
hills and mountains snowy peaks
Tiwanaku ruins
without knowing without learning
I love my homeland so I can grow
I don't reject my indigenous roots

(MC Grafo, Seven Clan D-Calle, "Mi cultura")

In the cultural expressions, and in particular in the Hip Hop cultural movement of El Alto, this unique aspect has been continually present, most prominently in the oral expression through the songs. We find this assertion of identity, particularly the Indigenous identity, in a series of symbolic elements in these young people's productions and presentations, as in the case of the *wiphala,*[13] the red or green *ponchos,* the coca leaves, the *pollera,* and the multicolored *awayus.*[14] In Bolivia between 1980 and 2003, the social movements made prominent this set of symbols of indigenous power (Mamani 2004), and the Hip Hop movement has also included these elements in the affirmation of its Aymara identity.

One symbolic element frequently used at Hip Hop concerts, festivals, or gatherings is the *wiphala.* The groups and MCs take the stage waving this flag, which has become an alternative to the customary national symbols. In the case of the Hip Hop movement this is not necessarily a substitute, as many times both the *wiphala* and the Bolivian flag can be seen flying on stage. On the other hand, *ponchos,*[15] *awayus,* and *coca*[16] appear on album covers, in videos, and in other media used by Hip Hop artists to express their artistic movement. The group Ukamau y Ke's CD *Para la Raza* contains a video including important symbols of various social movements, such as the *wiphala,* as well as men in *ponchos* and women wearing their *aguayos.* These symbols are present in the songs of the groups and MCs, as we see in this example:

---

13. The *wiphala* is a square, checkered flag of pre-Hispanic origin, which bears the colors of the rainbow and is recognized as another symbol of the Estado Plurinacional de Bolivia.

14. *Awayu* is a traditional cloth, sometimes woven by hand, which preserves the canons of pre-Hispanic design and has many functions: it is used to carry cargo or babies on the back and is also part of the shroud-style dress or is used for ritual purposes.

15. This is a traditional Andean men's outfit.

16. Similarly, at different Hip Hop events, gatherings, or talks that we attended in the cultural center Waynatambo, they always had coca to chew.

Aquí está presente mi raza aymara
Con mucho corazón
Traigo los colores del arco iris
De la wiphala de mi nación
Collas, cambas los mismos paisanos bolivianos
Nacidos en las tierras aymaras
Amadas de mi Pachamama
Tierras sagradas

Here is my Aymara race
With a lot of love
I bring the colors of the rainbow
From the wiphala of my nation
Collas,[17] cambas[18] the same Bolivian peasants
Born in the Aymara land
Loved lands of my Pachamama.[19]
Holy Lands

(Ukamau y Ke, "Wilamasis I")

This song makes reference to the *wiphala,* which has become a very clear signifier of Indigenous identity. For this reason, this symbol represents the Aymara nation. However, it is also significant that in the song they also refer to "Collas" and "Cambas," in the sense that both are Bolivian. In Bolivia, the people who live in the Andean region are called "Collas." The three Indigenous groups within this region are the Aymara, the Quechua, and the Urus. Those who live in the Amazon region are called "Cambas," and in this region there are thirty-three other ethnic groups. In this song as well as in others, the Indigenous identity is centered on what is Andean and what is Aymara, as demonstrated when they say that both *collas* and *cambas* have been born on Aymara land.

The lyrics of their songs also reflect certain symbols of the past, such as the pre-Hispanic culture of Tiwanaku. In the present, these Tiwanaku ruins are central to their representation of the distant past of their Aymara ancestors, and are recognized as such. These youth incorporate not only the name Tiwanaku in their songs but also icons like the *estelas* (monoliths of Tiwanaku) or the great buildings of the city, without omitting some references to the Inca

17. Native to the Andean mountain region of Bolivia, specifically of the departments of La Paz, Oruro, and Potosi.

18. Native to the tropical region in eastern Bolivia, specifically of the departments of Santa Cruz, Beni, and Pando.

19. Pachamama is a female Andean deity associated with the earth and fertility.

culture like the Collasuyo and Tawantinsuyo. Similarly, these symbols appear on the covers of the CDs they have produced.

In the same way, they refer to rebel leaders like Tupac Katari[20] and Bartolina Sisa, protagonists of the Indian uprisings and the 1781 siege of La Paz. Both were important figures in social movements and represent symbols of Indigenous power. For example, Katari was often mentioned in the speeches of Felipe Quispe, "el Mallku," who led the social uprisings of 2003. Currently, Tupac Katari and Bartolina Sisa are recognized as important influences on the contemporary Plurinational State. This is clear in the following song:

> Duro y fuerte como el Monolito de Ponce
> Manifiesto y represento a mi raza de bronce
> Rápido y ágil como el inesperado wanako
> Yo defiendo las tierras del gran Tiwanaku
> Con agallas de mi gente, los aymaras
> Soy descendiente de Tupak Katari
> Soy su pariente, su ideología en mi mente
> Preparando la raza estuvo
> Durante siglos inconsciente

> Hard and strong like the Ponce Monolith
> I manifest and represent my bronze race
> Agile and fast like the unexpected guanaco
> I defend the Great Tiwanaku's lands
> With the guts of my people, the Aymara
> I am a descendant of Tupac Katari
> I am his relative, his ideology in my mind
> He has been preparing the race
> Unconscious all this time

(Ukamau y Ke, "Wilamasis I")

The use of Indigenous Aymara symbols and elements in the artistic expression of Alteño Hip Hop has been what has caught the most attention in the national and international press and among social scientists; however, this is not new to the history of youth culture movements. The *Jipitecas* (Zolov 1999) and the *Raztecas* (Reguillo 2000) of Mexico are an antecedent to the youth culture movement in Bolivia that now seeks to return to its origins and recover its roots.[21]

---

20. An Aymara word meaning "serpent."

21. The *jipitecas* were young people who identified with rock and roll and who went to live in Mexico in 1962 in the Huahuatla region, with the goal of learning about the Indigenous

At different moments in history, youth cultures have had this tendency to recover Indigenous values, and Alteño Hip Hop is doing so again today. As opposed to an assertion of a national identity which has existed in other youth cultural movements such as Mexican rock music, which acquired a nationalistic tinge in the 1970s, El Alto Hip Hop artists make it clear to assert Indigenous identities, like the Aymara. At the same time, they also make clear that this Indigenous identity does not in any way exclude or contradict the assertion of national identity, since both work together and coexist harmoniously. In Bolivia both identities, the ethnic and the national, compose an "interculture," which is deeply historicized in the Bolivian consciousness (Abercrombie 2006). Therefore, the Alteño Hip Hop cultural movement expresses that in Bolivia it is possible to be Bolivian and to be Aymara.

Women in Hip Hop

At the time I was conducting my research, few women were involved in the Alteño Hip Hop scene. However, since then, Nina Uma and La Imilla have become well-known female Hip Hop artists. Likewise, in breakdance in recent years (from 2008 to 2014), some women have been incorporated into the dance groups that practice in various places in La Paz. It is very unusual to find female graffiti artists, much less DJs, but what women are striving for is to rap, although with qualities different from those of their male counterparts.

In late 2005 groups of female rappers did not exist in El Alto—soloists were men, and groups were made up of men. In addition, the "movidas," or events that Hip Hop artists perform, such as concerts, gatherings, or workshops, had a mostly male audience. Few women attended these events, and some of those who did were accompanying their boyfriends or other male friends. After a time, some young women in El Alto were inspired to enter the Hip Hop scene, and then it became much easier for me to access information about Hip Hop through them. This also gave me a chance to gain a deeper understanding of gender constructs in Alteño Hip Hop.

Few women have an interest in Hip Hop—they prefer romantic music or Reggaeton, and above all, they enjoy dancing rather than singing. It's less common for women to take up composing or singing or, more specifically in this case, rapping. As already mentioned, in the case of Hip Hop in El Alto in 2005,

---

experience. Followers of reggae, the *raztecas*, take the name from the portmanteau of Rastafarians and *Azteca*. Rastafarianism is a religious and political movement in Jamaica, whose main focus is the proposal of the return to Africa and their roots, in the way that the Aztec is the recovery of the Mexican Indigenous tradition.

all the Hip Hop groups were made up of men, although later the following year, some Hip Hop groups made up of women began to appear. However, to this day the appearance of some women has not meant significant female participation in the Hip Hop scene in El Alto, and the same is true in other cities around the country in general.

For many women, despite their attraction to what the Hip Hop movement represents, it is somewhat challenging to participate in this mostly masculine world. One of the members of a female rap group commented that it was very difficult to follow the rhythm of the Hip Hop scene: "Everything is at night and so I come home late; my mom is about to kick me out" (group interview, August 26, 2006). However, this young woman said that her family was proud that she had a music group and that she sang, especially in a sphere where there is little participation from women.

The female rap group "Hermandad Fémina," or "Female Sisterhood," appeared on February 20, 2005, and gained prominence in 2006, only to practically disappear in 2007. The group was made up of four young women, of whom three lived in El Alto and one in La Paz. This group came together through the members' participation in the Hip Hop scenes of El Alto and La Paz. In the words of one of their members, many of their male peers considered them "feminists" because of the name of their group.

Another aspect that has motivated these young women to do Hip Hop is that, according to them, it permits them to be themselves. In the words of Noelia (group interview, August 26, 2006), one of the members of the group: "This is what I like about Hip Hop, that you are who you are and you don't need to change, or be a stereotypical woman." Also, the female Hip Hop artists wear loose, baggy clothing, a type of unisex uniform for Hip Hop artists; they don't wear tight clothing, which is the usual style for young women. Therefore, for some women to do Hip Hop is a form of rebellion against society's stereotypes of women.

Groups like "Hermandad Fémina" have been an example of women rappers' short-lived participation in the Hip Hop movement. The group didn't manage to release an album, and they were lost among so many male groups and rappers. Nevertheless, the uniqueness of a female group should be noted. Adding their own flavor, they have participated in a variety of activities organized by institutions and NGOs that support women's rights, because their compositions have emphasized topics of interest to women, such as abortion and rape.

For young women Alteños who do Hip Hop, their music is a form of expression and social criticism, in a society in which women in general are not supposed to show a great interest in social issues. For example, the interviewees claim that most women prefer songs that talk about love.

> Women don't care much about social stuff. . . I mean, girls who are in school. We range from 26 to about 28 years old for all of us, right? I am 27 and I'm one of the oldest, I think, right, I mean, girls don't care much about what people in that age group care about. They're in school, they're about to start college, and they care little about social, protest, stuff, the Manifesto, and all of that. (Llajuas 2005)

This is how a young Hip Hop artist responded to the question of why there were hardly any women rappers in the movement by 2005. More than twenty young people participated in the group interview, only one of whom was a woman. Furthermore, when this MC responded to the question, he appeared to feel somewhat uncomfortable in my presence because I was a woman, and he even addressed me directly, stating that older women can develop an interest in the political, and that younger, school-age girls are not the least bit interested in political issues.

For their part, the women who do participate in Hip Hop don't deny their preference for writing songs that refer to love; however, this doesn't mean that they necessarily have no interest in social and political issues. In recent years some female Hip Hop artists have emphasized more social content, as Nina Uma has done. Nonetheless, the content of songs by female rappers touches on aspects beyond life on the street, poverty, or discrimination that also interest them but that are also frequently found in the lyrics of the songs of male rappers. The female rappers are also interested in issues that affect them as women, such as abortion and rape.

Thus, there is a clear difference between male and female rappers in their interests and interpretation of the Hip Hop movement. In 2003 the men placed a stronger emphasis on political issues in their lyrics. In their songs they discuss issues such as discrimination and racism, they recover certain ethnic and national values, or they sing about what happened back in October 2003. In contrast, the songs that women compose can have a markedly different content because of their own experiences as women: for them, to be a woman poses another type of complaint against society because they experience problems that their male counterparts do not. Although the political problems of the country are not completely absent from their songs, they still focus more on their own lives as women, which is political, although not always conceptualized as such.

Despite the fact that this youth cultural movement of El Alto had inclusive citizenship at the center of its struggle, it is also clear that the movement was not without its own internal exclusions. With few exceptions, those who make up this movement, not only in El Alto but on a global level, are men.

Therefore, their structure has had a predominantly male configuration, and for this reason Alteño Hip Hop, in spite of its demands and discourse with regard to ethnic and national issues, still often overlooks female issues, which have remained marginalized or tangential.

Bibliography

Abercrombie, Thomas. 2006. *Caminos de la memoria y del poder: Etnografía e historia en una comunidad andina.* La Paz, Bolivia: IFEA, IEB, ASDI.

Agustín, José. 1996. *La Contra Cultura en México: La historia y el significado de los rebeldes sin causa, los jipitecas, los punks y las bandas.* México: Grijalbo.

Alarcón, Oscar. 2005. *Vivir el Hip Hop: La emergente identidad político-cultural en jóvenes de clases populares en La Paz y El Alto.* La Paz, Bolivia: XIX Reunión Anual de Etnología, Autonomías Regionales. (CD)

Albo, Xavier. 2000. *Iguales aunque diferentes.* La Paz, Bolivia: CIPCA—UNICEF.

Ari, Waskar. 2007a. "Globalismo Democrático y el Futuro del Pueblo Aymara." In *Aruskipasipxañasataki,* edited by Waskar Ari Chachaki. La Paz, Bolivia: Editorial Anmuyañataki.

———. 2007b. "Historia y presente del factor raza en Bolivia." *Fé y Pueblo* 2(10): 4–18.

Bouysse-Cassagne, Thérèse. 1987. *La identidad aymara: aproximación histórica.* La Paz, Lima: HISBOL/IFEA

Calatayud, Jacqueline. 2001. *La rima unitaria.* La Paz, Bolivia: La Prensa.

Grover & Toriño. 2006. "Que es pues siempre el Hip Hop." *Tertulias con Sabor a Coca.* April 29. (Event).

Guaygua, Germán, Daniel Bogado Egüez, Ángela Riveros, Arnaldo Lijerón Casanovas, Cristhian Vaca Zelada, and Máximo Quisbert. 2000. *Ser Joven en El Alto.* La Paz, Bolivia: PIEB.

Guaygua, Germán, Ángela Riveros, and Máximo Quisbert. 1999. "Ecografía de la juventud alteña." *Tinkazos* 5: 59–74.

Mamani, Pablo. 2004. *El rugir de las multitudes: La fuerza de los levantamientos indígenas en Bolivia/Qullasuyu.* La Paz, Bolivia: Ediciones Yachaywasi.

Mcbride, James. 2007. "Cultura Hip Hop: Cómo se apoderó del mundo." *Nacional Geographic (En español)* 20 (April).

Mollericona, Juan. 2008. *Jóvenes hiphoppers aymaras en la ciudad de El Alto y sus luchas por una ciudadanía intercultural.* La Paz, Bolivia: UPIEB, IBASE.

Nelson, Diane. 1999. *A Finger in the Wound: Body Politics in Quincentennial Guatemala.* Berkley and Los Angeles: University of California Press.

Pillai, Shanti. 1999. "Hip-Hop Guayaquil: Culturas Viajeras e identidades locales." New York: *Bulletin de l'Institute français d'études andines* 28(3): 485–99.

Riveros, Angela. 2000. "Conflictos generacionales: Los dilemas de la juventud alteña." La Paz, Bolivia: XIII Reunión Anual de Etnología. MUSEF, Tomo II.

———. 2009. "Prácticas interculturales del movimiento cultural de Hip Hop en la ciudad de La Paz." *Dinámicas interculturales en contextos (trans) andinos,* CEPA, VLIR, Ministerio de Relaciones Exteriores y Cultos del Estado Plurinacional de Bolivia, La Paz.

———. 2010. "Raza etnicidad y nación a través del Hip Hop alteño." *XXIII Reunión Anual de Etnología.* Repensando el mestizaje, Tomo II, MUSEF, La Paz.

Reguillo, Rossana. 2000. *Emergencias de las culturas juveniles: Estrategias del desencanto.* Bogotá, Colombia: Grupo Editorial Norma.

————. 2003. "Las culturas juveniles: Un campo de estudio; breve agenda para la discusión." *Aproximaciones a la diversidad juvenil*. México: Colegio de México, Bolivia. 103–18.

Rodríguez, Lázaro. 2005. "¿Todos los negros toman café? Políticas públicas de cultura, equidad, raza y pobreza como condición cultural." *Pobreza, exclusión social y discriminación étnico-racial en América Latina y el Caribe*. Seminario Internacional Universidad del Valle, Cali, Colombia, 23 al 25 de noviembre.

Samanamud, Jiovany, Cleverth Cardenas, and Patricia Prieto. 2007. *Jóvenes y política en El Alto: La subjetividad de los otros*. La Paz, Bolivia: PIEB.

Stephenson, Marcia. 1999. *Gender and Modernity in Andean Bolivia*. Austin: University of Texas Press.

Wade, Peter. 2000. *Music, Race and Nation: Música Tropical in Colombia*. Chicago: University of Chicago Press.

Yúdice, George. 2002. *El recurso de la cultura*. Barcelona, Spain: Gedisa.

Zolov, Eric. 1999. *Refried Elvis: The Rise of the Mexican Counterculture*. Berkley: University of California Press.

Discography

Ukamau y Ke. 2006. *Para la Raza*.

chapter 16

Homosexuals, Hemophiliacs, Heroin Addicts, and Haitians

How Hip Hop Transformed Haitian Stigmatization into a Source of Pride

Stéphanie Melyon-Reinette

U ndoubtedly, Wyclef Jean is the best-known Haitian Hip Hop artist to date. At least, he was recognized as such since he began to brandish and wave his flag and his native tongue and to overtly invest money in Haitian artistry. And yet, many others have been involved in this movement, stuck to its credo, values, culture, codes since the 1980s in Haiti. Since the 2000s a new wave of Haitian Hip Hop artists has been breaking out on stage and has gained visibility on the internet. From the native country to the diasporic settlements, new MCs have been appearing; some either inspired by Wyclef Jean, who has mentored a number of young Haitian artists, or who emulate Black American rappers. This latest Haitian Hip Hop movement is quite nascent in the United States and in the world with regard to its achievements, development, and broadcasting. It has also developed in the lineage of a broader spectrum of Latin American or Latino Hip Hop trends and artists, and even on a larger scale, among worldwide movements fed from the African diaspora.

Hip Hop in reality belongs to a vast and long-lasting phenomenon which I coined the "Blackstream" (Melyon-Reinette 2008, 2009b) and which encompasses series of political movements, artistic trends, and musical currents that mirror—roughly speaking—the full span of the Blackness spirit fed with discourses of the oppressed against oppression. I define "Blackstream"[1] as the negative—in photographic terms—of the mainstream or dominant identity and cultural trends that overwhelm the United States and that have defined its predominant cultural patterns. The Blackstream has inspired some oppressed peoples and even given way to both emulators and critics (Melyon-Reinette 2009b). A few examples include Bob Marley's Rastafarian reggae, jazz music, and the multicultural, multilingual, multiethnic, global spread of Hip Hop. And yet, despite the globalization effect, the Blackstream's very origins remain rooted in ghetto counterculture. This is why marginalized people—or those who feel marginalized—adopt this modus vivendi.

In other words, Blackstreaming could be defined as the permeation of Black cultural moods globally. This is easily observable in that the music most extensively promoted abroad is Black. Internationally, the best-known artists—Rihanna, Beyoncé, 50 Cent, and others—are African Americans. Their music is Black and mainstream. And it has been so for decades. The codes of those musical trends have been adopted, reused, retrained, recycled, and rethought throughout the world. At its best, Hip Hop culture has spread without losing the substance which is ghetto-centric, counterculture, anti-xenophobic, of and about struggling, and based in the global underground. In this arena, Hip Hop is about freedom, ethnic-racial pride, and recognition. Today's Haitian Hip Hop is a very reflection of the Hip Hop spirit.

The starting point of this reflection develops from an analysis of the diachronic, historical development of the Haitian community in the United States through the lens of the Blackstream. In particular, I explore the range of experiences lived by Haitians in the United States, from severe discrimination to a demonstration of pride. This transition is reflected in the title of this chapter. In the 1980s the 4Hs meant homosexuals, hemophiliacs, heroin addicts and haitians." Those were the populations pointed out by the Center of Health Studies as being at risk of HIV infection. Although not the sole aspect used to discriminate against and stigmatize this community, it was a major aspect of the period. Thus, it is important to understand how this phenomenon was transformed through Hip Hop. As such, in this chapter I first outline the stigmatization of the Haitian community as highlighted and bound to the dynamic of the Blackstream, first by apprehending the identity energies that pass each other, notably through the terms of indigeneity, and the stigmas of poverty. Second, I make an incursion into the Haitian identities which have broadly branched off the so-called pure Haitianness towards the paradigmatic

---

1. "Blackstream" is a concept introduced in my PhD dissertation that I am further developing in forthcoming work.

African Americanness, in order to depict the semiotics linked to them. Last, I explore the Haitian heritage Hip Hop movement through its protagonists, developments, raison d'être, and heirs.

Indigeneity, Stigmas, and the Blackstream

How can indigeneity and the Blackstream be reconciled? In other words, how could rootedness and globalization be compatible? How could they conjugate? This is an essential point to make since they seem to be contradictory movements. The first one seems to be fixed to a certain territory, whether geographical, cultural, or philosophical. And the second sounds like a multidimensional movement, referring to dispersion and revolution—in the astronomical meaning, still in a motionlike acception.

Indigenous Haiti has long appeared—and still appears—to be fixed. This is the perspective that most populations alienated from Haitian history have adopted in order to consider the nation and its people. This is also the vision of them that is exported, transmitted, passed down through generations until this very core of Haitian cultures is all that is shown to the world. Haitians are Black, and have long been considered to be a social illness, since they are poor and their country is cursed. Since its independence, Haiti has been seen as a plague, a leper among nations (Melyon-Reinette 2011a). Keith Wailoo (2006) wrote that "the early 20th century saw one kind of convergence between disease stigma and racial stigma. In an era when infectious disease predominated, African Americans were often portrayed as a key disease vector, capable of infecting other parts of the American population" (531). A similar phenomenon is the 1980s' "4Hs" policy of the Center of Health Security, which presented the Haitians as one of the four groups at risk of HIV infection in the United States. This led to huge campaigns and discrimination against Haitians in employment, education, and health establishments. Haitian children have been viewed as HIV carriers or AIDS carriers, to name only two abuses they have suffered. Some of them were harassed or molested, notably by Anglo-Caribbeans—reproducing xenophobic and antagonistic patterns being imported through emigrations and discriminatory behaviors toward Haitian people (Melyon-Reinette 2009b, 2011b).

At the same time, various evils have plundered Haiti's economy and undermined its political life: dictatorship, coups, *Macoutism*, 1950s' *Duvalierism*, and so forth. These few details demonstrate the antagonistic forces that existed inside and outside of Haiti. Prejudice against the practice of vodou coexists with the romanticization of Haiti as the world's first independent Black nation.

Additionally, the country's degradation is only heightened due to forced payment to France after independence and the various dictatorships that have plundered the economy and terrorized the population, and successive waves of migration have emptied the country of its strengths. As a result of Haiti's history, intellectuals were the first to flee the country, and the peasants followed in the 1980s. They wanted to "chèché lavi" (find a better life elsewhere), creating an emigration flow that was ill-welcomed along the Floridian shores, as the so-called boat people were seen as parasites on U.S. society as well as the Caribbean. These media misrepresentations of Haitian migrants still contribute to their undermining in U.S. society and are supported by U.S. government actions. In addition to policies of the Center for Health Security, Haitian migrants have never been welcomed by the U.S. government when they have tried to reach its borders and shores. The most significant illustration is the CHE Act (Cuban Haitian Entrants), which allowed Cuban entrants to benefit from asylum once they had stepped on U.S. shores (under the dry foot–wet foot principle) but denied the same rights to Haitians.

Photographs of Haitians in rags, tired, and sick are published and broadcast, with only the sad, bloody, ugly, and disqualifying face of Haiti shown. This image of Haiti was yet again reinforced after the 2010 earthquake. Today, Haiti is known more for those horrific images than for its intellectuals, writers, and artists.

The massive settlements of Haitians in the United States date back to the late 1950s, with a skyrocketing peak in the 1980s, and spread to the early 2000s, where they have slowed tremendously because of specific measures taken by the government. In roughly two generations, the identifications have varied in the Haitian communities. The first generation was *Ayisyèn* (Haitian), and the second generation was already partly assimilated or bicultural. However, Haitian identities in the United States cannot be explained exclusively by immigration. Globalization and the arrival of many strangers in Haiti have provoked both Francophilia and Anglophilia since postcolonial times. Additionally, Haiti is not monocultural as many perceive, and it has always been influenced and permeated by other cultures.

Haiti is not a monolith. It has long been multicultural, with Francophilic, Christian cultures coexisting alongside African-based, vodoo-based, rural communities. Haiti has always bathed in European influences, both French and English. As of today, the Haitian schools are modeled on the French system (from elementary school to the baccalaureate), and the various political regimes that have succeeded one another over the centuries were pastiches of the French government patterns. Haiti has had emperors (Jean-Jacques Dessalines), kings (Henri Christophe), and presidents (Pétion, Boyer). French has been and still is the status language, especially for the Mulatto "caste," as it was in the Black petite bourgeoisie. Nevertheless, we cannot forget the tremendous impact of the "indigenism" literary current, which marked a backlash movement of the intellectuals to their African roots and the dense use of Creole in their writings. To struggle against the Jim Crow laws the Americans wanted to impose on them during their occupation (1915–34), intellectuals had to resort to what was at the bottom of their hearts: their roots. In Haiti there coexists today literary excellence and identity in both the Creole and the French languages.

Haitian Heritage Hip Hop

Haitians have suffered severe discrimination, especially from the Anglo-Caribbean. On one hand, via the transposition of xenophobic patterns which overwhelmed the English-speaking Caribbean societies, they tended to reproduce their discriminatory behaviors toward Haitian people (Melyon-Reinette 2009b) in the United States. On the other hand, first-generation Haitians tended to differentiate themselves from both African Americans and Anglo Caribbean identities, through their Frenchness/Creoleness and their behaviors concerning racial relationships. They are seen as not affected by racialized relationships. Their Caribbean French culture and the fact that they had evolved in an all-Black society resulted in their differentiation towards racism and their place in society. Nevertheless, their U.S.-born offspring have faced a very different racial situation as well as specific stigmatized views of Haitians generated in the 1980s as boat people and HIV carriers. Thus, the identity strategies they have developed are distinct: some assimilate into the closest dominant group they live near, African Americans, by imitating their ghettocentric cultural codes and creating hyphenated artistic expressions. Through the portrait of Wyclef Jean we will see that his evolution was patterned on the Afro-Americanization process. Finally, we will illustrate the Haitian Hip Hop movement and demonstrate how far it has developed as a reflection of Haitian inheritance.

Blackstream is all at once about *globalization* and *glocalization*—concepts derived from localization and globalization that explain that in a global market, something is more likely to be successful when customized for or through the local culture in which it is sold. So, the former indicates a process of spreading a trend, culture, or movement beyond its original borders, while the latter indicates the process of adapting this culture to fit local codes and expectations. Factually, Haitian Hip Hop is designed according to this twofold pattern.

In 1980s Haiti, Hip Hop had already planted its first seeds. Ragamuffin—meaning hustler, and coined after the social character of the outcast—defines a movement in which the protagonists express their desires to be unconformed to the society they live in. So there are definitely acquaintances with the Hip Hop philosophy. And, actually, we consider 1980s early Haitian Hip Hop to be far closer to Raggamuffin than U.S. Hip Hop strictly speaking, with regard to its instrumentation: the riddim looks more like local carnival or mizik rasin orchestrations and rhythms, while scandering is either slower or close to rapping.[2] Of that period, one of the best known—recognized by the Haitian community as the Father of Haitian Hip Hop—is George Lys Herard (May 30, 1961–May 21, 1994), better known as Master DJI who is acknowledged as one of the first rappers and Hip Hop artists in Haiti. He was the DJ of the Haiti Rap'N Ragga crew. His first *Rap Kreyol* eponymous album made him very famous. He imposed himself as one of the deepest Haitian lyricists, with a most poetical signature. He somewhat pioneered this trend, as he brought to his artistic generation a real renewal with a style that infringed the frontiers between rara,[3] rasin,[4] konpa,[5] and reggae. His songs were often filled with romantic themes. For instance, the title "Manmzel" that he performed in a great dancehall with Supa Deno is an ode to the sensualness of women. He released three other albums: *Politik pam* (1990, Bwa Patat records, Haiti); *Match la rèd* (1990, Declic Communication, France), in a collaboration with his crew Haiti Rap'N Ragga; and *Maximum Respect* (1996, Crossover Records, Florida, US). This final record made clear moves toward transnational and diasporic connections to the U.S. Haitian community. Additionally, the more he moved forward, the more he seemed to politicize his music. For example,

---

2. Both scandering and rapping refer to the artist's flow (rhythm and rhyme, or cadence and rhyming): the way one delivers the lyrics. Scandering refers to a slow flow, as in spoken word performed in time to the beat, with a few or quite the same number of syllables per bar, whereas rapping doesn't work systematically on the beat. Plus, rappers develop their styles, among other terminology: the syncopated bounce (Bone Thugs-n-Harmony), the straight forward style (2Pac, Dr. Dre, Jay-Z), the chant (Project Pat), the Rubik's Cube style (Lauryn Hill, Common, The Roots), etc. Progressively, rappers' rhythmic styles will become faster and faster, by putting as many syllables as possible in a bar (Busta Rhymes), making them more syncopated, percussive, and effusive.

3. "Rara" is a traditional form of carnival music used during processions, especially during Easter week. The instruments used are vaksen (cynlindrical bamboo trumpets), drums, maracas, güiros, and metal bells. A repeating rhythm is played by the vaksen in a monotonous, trance-like way. Its pattern is called hocket.

4. "Rasin" (or "Mizik Rasin") is a modern style of music from Haiti that emerged in the 1970s, mixing elements of traditional Vodou ceremonial or folkloric music with rock and roll.

5. "Konpa" is Haitian modern music that appeared and was made popular by Jean-Baptiste Nemours in 1955. It is inspired from the high-tempo Haitian meringue, affiliated with Latin American music. The meringue's rhythm was slowed down and gave birth to Konpa.

his song "Match-la Rèd" explains the harshness of living in Haiti and includes a slight evocation of the boat people phenomenon.

Along the same musical lines, we can find in the 2000s new Hip Hop artists mixing altogether carnival rhythms—recalling the Trinidadian soca—rara and rap scandering. Barikad Crew (Port-au-Prince) is one of those. But it was also in this era that Haitian Hip Hop became quite diverse, reflecting the global developments of the music. For example, other Haitian rappers were inspired by the Blackstream U.S. artists. In their YouTube videos, the scenarios and gimmicks are copies of African American artists. Izolan (of Barikad Crew, Haiti) and Boz La identify more with the R&B African American artists in their attitude, scandering flow, and topics, such as complaining about a woman's unfaithfulness. Wendy Traka (Haiti) explores another style: the ego-trip stance. As if his MC name, "Majeste," weren't clear enough, he sings in "A. B. M.":

Yo vlé stope'm me yo pa réyisi
Yo vinn'pou bézé'm me yo pa réyisi
Yo fè asosyasyon pou yo étenn mwen . . .

They want to stope'm but they failed
They came to fuck me up but they could not
They gathered to smoke me . . .

His egotistical lyrics remain a gimmick of the contemporary gangsta rap movement. This artist even hand-signs his name, shaping a "W" with his two hands joined together. All the ghetto-centric signs are present in his videos. Transnationalism is also significant here, as he scanders in three languages: Creole, English, and French. In the same vein, G Shine Zion, a young female Rap Kreyòl artist in Haiti who sings in "Kisa Pou'm fè anko" (What else can I do), performs her ego in an aggressive manner, laying claim to her position in the Rap Kreyòl industry.

Recently, a second wave of Haitian Hip Hoppers has recently emerged who are both more political and more nationalistic. They have benefited both from Haiti's frightening reputation for gangs and the positivity of Wyclef Jean's artistic, political aura. They display this shift in specific dress codes—the Haitian flag is omnipresent, and its two main colors (blue and red) are the colors of the Haitian Hip Hop movement. The Haitian rappers—even those of the Zoe Pound gang—assert that they sing for the Haitian flag to be honored. Finally, they believe in the recognition of their cultures and consider themselves true sons of Haiti. Rapper Mecca a.k.a. Grimo—whose name is a Creole term for mulatto skin color and is often considered offensive—sings "Rouge et Bleu—Haitian Flag Tribute" just as Wyclef did.

> On konn ki es ki la
> Fo nou te fè'l
> Ou konn' sa li yé
> Rouge et bleu, Rouge et Bleu, Rouge et Bleu!
> Pa bliye se nou ki te premye
> Rouge et bleu, Rouge et Bleu, Rouge et Bleu!
> Non la riya, se nou yo respèkte
> Konyéya tout' moun vle di se ayisyen yo ye
> Sa se pa on jwet
> Sa se kase tèt
> Se kole tèt . . .

> Do you know who is there
> We had to do it
> You know how it is
> Red and Blue, Red and Blue, Red and Blue!
> Don't forget we were the first ones
> Red and Blue, Red and Blue, Red and Blue!
> In the streets, they respect us
> Now everyone wants to say they are Haitian
> This is not a game
> It breaks your head
> It's about gathering . . .

Another Hip Hop artist worth highlighting is Suicide (NYC), who sings brandishing his flag, and Benchoumy (Haiti), who is so emulative of Wyclef Jean that he sang "Nou la (we're here)" on a sample of "Ready or Not" by the Fugees. "Menm si Beat-la pa nèf, sé pa Wyclef" (even though the beat is not new, this is not Wyclef), he sings. A number of other Haitian Hip Hop MCs can be found between Haiti and Florida: Rockfam, Baly (Florida), MaxFlo (Florida), Black Dada (Florida, Haitian American), and Haitian Fresh (born in Haiti and migrated to Florida as a youth), VooDoo Child (New Jersey), Sesa Konza, 5Kob Penich, Spark Flame, Stichiz (a Hip Hop MC born in Canada to parents of Haitian descent and raised in South Florida), and so on.

Through this influence of Wyclef Jean, it is clear that Haitian identity has become important as opposed to a Hip Hop which purely attempts to imitate

African American ghetto-centric culture. At his beginnings, Wyclef[6] didn't express his Haitianness ostentatiously, although he claimed the Haitian American reggae artist Charles Andre Dorismond, a.k.a. Bigga Haitian,[7] as one of his influences. In his time with the Tranzlator Crew (1980s), the former name of The Fugees, they present themselves via clearly marked African American Hip Hop styles, gestures, and speech. Later, with the change of name to "Fugees" (a shortening of refugees), however, Wyclef began to address Haitian struggles, such as immigration issues. Even though not overtly obvious, in certain songs, his Haitianness appears. For example, in "Fu-Gee-La," Wyclef's lyrics read:

> Damn, Another dead pigeon
> If your mafiosos then I'm bringin' on Haitian Sicilians
> Nobody's shootin,' my body's made of hand grenade
> Girl bled to death while she was tongue-kissing a razor blade . . .

Thus, amidst Hip Hop's ego-trip, dirty-dozen-style lyrics, his roots are pointed out. Plus, as his remixes went by the name of Refugee Camp, the sign is clearly sent. Still, it was not until he began his solo career in 1997 with his album *The Carnival featuring the Refugee AllStars* that his Haitianness went on full display. This is clear from songs like "Guantanamera" (with Celia Cruz and Lauryn Hill):

> Yo, I wrote this in Haiti, overlooking Cuba
> I asked her what's her name, she said, "Guantanamera"
> Remind me of an old latin song, my uncle used to play
> On his old forty-five when he used to be alive . . .

Likewise, other songs are explicitly written and delivered in Haitian Creole— while on his previous albums a few exclamations in Creole were heard. In "Sang Fézi" featuring Lauryn Hill, he seems to celebrate "Haitian gangsters":

> Ki ayisien kap di'm map mache new-york san fezi
> Mwen di ou messie nou menti

---

6. Wyclef Jean, born Wyclef Jeanelle Jean, October 17, 1969, is one of the charismatic leaders and MCs of the well-known trio The Fugees. He was born in Croix-des-Bouquets in Haiti. His father was a Nazarene pastor. They moved to New Jersey in 1982; Wyclef was then thirteen. He studied music at the Berklee College of Music from 2009 onward. Regarding Haitian music, it is relevant to speak about Wyclef Jean, as he sort of pioneered the Haitian-identified Hip Hop movement.

7. The first Haitian singer to break into the Jamaican reggae scene.

Lè bum yo kenbe ou yo devore ou se lè ou mouri police vini
Mwen di ou messie nou menti

which haitian says I walk in New York without a gun
I tell you man y'all lying
when the bum catches you they eat you up it's when you die the police comes
I tell you man y'all lying . . .

Finally, with the song "President," on *Welcome to Haiti: Creole 101* (2004), his lyrics remind us of the unstable political turmoil in which Haiti has rotted decade after decade since its independence: "If I was president, I'd get elected on Friday, assassinated on Saturday, and buried on Sunday." Moreover, the albums which Wyclef would release after show even more and more Haitian colors, tones, shades, and expressions: the shining of the carnival show in the album titles (*Masquerade, Carnival vol. I and II*), the accents of Creole add authenticity with tracks like "Lavi Nouyok," "Fanm Kreyol," "24 è tan pou-viv," and "Lè ou marye" on the *Welcome to Haiti: Creole 101* album. When he doesn't use the Creole language, Wyclef introduces rasin music and specific Haitian rhythms such as konpa, for example, in his latest, "Bagay Nef" (New Things), melting konpa and Hip Hop beats and sung in Krenglish (the fusion of Kreyòl and English).

Thus, the more Wyclef gained momentum in the Hip Hop world, the more he displayed his Haitianness and contributed to the restoration of his community's image, helping it to regain prestige after the harshness of almost two decades of discrimination. He also got involved in nonprofit organizations by founding his own, *Yélé Ayiti* (the Wyclef Jean Foundation), providing funds, financing schools and scholarships for Haitian children, and raising funds after natural disasters such as 2004's Hurricane Jeanne and the 2010 earthquake. He is the quintessence of the Haitian Hip Hop identity, a landmark, a point of reference.

In this environment, Haitian American women are also making their mark. Sabine Blaizin is an acupressure healer and a DJ who, when we met, had never gone to Haiti. For a while, she had embraced the African American Hip Hop movement, having grown up with African American music and culture. After her grandmother died, she went to Haiti for the first time, a trip which would forever change her perspective. Exploring her roots consisted in a revolution against her insipid education deprived of ethnic pride:

I wasn't celebrating Haitian culture, again it wasn't until I graduated college, when I was in college I sort of explored that, but it was more like a political thing to me, like a sociopolitical thing for me to do that. But when I was younger I was in rock music. That sounds more "White" than African American, you know. I was in punk, grunge, you know heavy metal. Then I went to like Hip Hop, everything like Hip Hop in the 90s, like A Tribe Called Quest, De la Soul, you know, stuff like that. And I got to house music, which sounds more . . . you know it seems more African American, or Latino . . . so, yeah I think that even I didn't identify myself with African Americans, I was Haitian American, but I think that just my culture was African American. You know. . . . (Sabine Blaizin, interview with author, 2008)

Upon her return, Sabine looked for her Haitian identity in several sociopolitical and ethnocultural contexts once she entered the house music and DJing worlds. Here, she met Jephté Guillaume—a Haitian American house music DJ—who opens a new music world at the thresholds of two semiotic cultures. According to Sabine, "I, in fact, DJ with Jephté Guillaume, and he's my main influence in terms of DJ because he's the only Haitian producer that I know, that combines the sounds of house music with traditional Haitian music" (interview with author, 2008).

As a result of these experiences, she finally understood how both worlds interconnected. There were parallels, although she had evolved in both of them without ever finding the connection.

Because I grew up in an environment where . . . okay I'm American, and I was exposed to house music [. . .] At that time, I wasn't thinking of house music, I wasn't very conscious to be connected to like the rhythm, the associates they do come from the African history, like the percussion, and the drum. So that was my American upbringing. And then also when I came to the Haitian culture and learnt about the music and things like the dance, I meant I always too want to bring those two worlds together, because they are the two halves of myself, that make up who I am, right. Like the American and the Haitian part. (ibid.)

Sabine mixes her Haitian roots and house or electronic music. Exploring their universes demonstrates clearly the processes of mixing, crossbreeding influences and the mutation the Haitian identities experiment. They are transformed through the various milieus visited, crossed by the subjects, the protagonists. The African American influence is quite indubitable here. But the Haitian identity clearly emerges as well.

The Haitian Hip Hop movement has been built through transnational links. First, the languages they use are various and reflect the transnationality of the movement: French/Creole in Haiti; English, Creole, and Krenglish in Florida. Second, collaborations are frequent between Haiti-based artists and Floridian Haitian artists—such as Barikad Crew's and Mecca aka Grimo's collaborations. Thus, today there is a true Haitian Hip Hop network which crosses the borders of both Haiti and the United States (in particular, Florida). Moreover, their networking is enabled by the multiple websites and YouTube channels (Rap Lakay, Kreyòl Remix, and Creolemagazine.com) they have developed.

The Haitian Americans' performances are further achieved from their roots in African American cultural traditions as they often have technical means to develop their musical projects. But in Haiti, Hip Hop is also improving visually and musically. In Haiti, Jerry Moïse Rosembert draws on walls to campaign against the abuses inflicted on the people. He denounces mischief, crimes, and injustice. Meanwhile, the Haitian Hip Hop movement in the United States has grown tremendously from reproducing the African American moves to fully appropriating them for itself and embodying the soul of Hip Hop. This is a very Haitian lifestyle, way of thinking, way of living. Just as Haitian emblems are often infused into their ghetto-centric identities, there is also a real pride in both the Haitians' and Haitian Americans' claims as Hip Hop artists. Necessarily, this part of the Haitian diaspora had to find its place in the struggle for recognition in the marginalized part of American society. As in education, politics, and diplomacy, Haitian immigrants and their descendants have found their spot in the Blackstream, which is, indubitably, one of the economic and political strengths of U.S. culture abroad. For Haitian Hip Hoppers, the once derogatory 4Hs of HIV stigma, homosexuals, hemophiliacs, heroin-addicts and haitians now stand for "Haitian Heritage Hip Hop" movement.

Bibliography

Melyon-Reinette, Stéphanie. 2008. "De la Diaspora haïtienne à la communauté haïtiano-américaine: Modèle d'une intégration réussie?" PhD thesis, Université des Antilles et de la Guyane.

———. 2009a. "Afro-Américanisation: d'Haïti à New York City." Cahiers Sens Public, Un Monde en Noir et Blanc. *Amitiés Postcoloniales* 10:57–67.

———. 2009b. *Haïtiens à New York City—entre Amérique noire et Amérique Multiculturelle*. Paris: L'Harmattan, Coll.

———. 2010. "De la dédiasporisation des jeunes Haïtiens à New-York," *Études caribéennes*, August 16. Available at: http://etudescaribeennes.revues.org/4628.

———. 2011a. "Une Lépreuse parmi les Nations—Essai sur l'antihaïtianisme caribo/Nord-Américain." Joint, L.-A. & Julien Mérion (ed.), *L'immigration haïtienne dans la Caraïbe—quel défi pour l'unité des peuples*. Guadeloupe: Éditions Nestor. 111–36.

———. 2011b. *Mémoires de Jaspora—Voix intimes d'Haïtiens enracinés en Amérique du Nord*. Paris: Éditions Persée.

———, ed. 2012. *Marronnage and Arts—Revolts in Bodies and Voices*. Oxford: Cambridge Scholars Publishing.

Stepick, Alex. 1998. *Pride against Prejudice: Haitians in the United States*. Boston: Allyn & Bacon.

Turino, Thomas, and James Lea. 2004. *Identity and the Arts in Diaspora Communities*. Warren, MI: Harmonie Park.

Wailoo, Keith. 2006. "Stigma, Race and Disease in 20th Century America." *Lancet* 367 (9509): 531–33.

Zéphir, Flore. 2001. *Trends in Ethnic Identification among Second-Generation Haitian Immigrants in New York City*. Westport, CT; London: Bergin & Garvey.

———. 2004. *The Haitian Americans*. Westport, CT; London: Greenwood.

Discography

Jean, Wyclef. 1997. *The Carnival* (featuring Refugee Allstars).

———. 2000. *The Eclefic Side—2 Sides II A Book*. Columbia Records.

———. 2004. *Welcome to Haiti Creole 101*. Sak Pasé Records.

———. 2007. *Carnival II—Memoirs of an Immigrant*. Columbia Records.

Mecca aka Grimo. 2007. *Ayisyen*. Mixtape Vol. 2.

The Fugees. 1994. *Blunted on Reality*. Columbia Records.

———. 1996. *Bootleg Versions*. Columbia Records.

———. 1996. *The Score*. Columbia Records.

———. 2003. *Greatest Hits*. Columbia Records.

chapter 17

Hip Hop Culture Bridges Gaps Between Young Caribbean Citizens

Steve Gadet

The Caribbean region is known for its political and cultural diversity in spite of a common colonial past. However, its colonial heritage gave birth to similarities as well as deep divisions. It is still hard and very expensive sometimes for French nationals to travel throughout the region. In the same way, it is hard for Jamaican or Trinidadian nationals to travel and do business in those French territories. For years, many cultural associations, some cities, and some activists have tried on both sides to bridge the gaps between these different territories. Guadeloupe and Martinique are two French overseas departments. Politically, they're attached to France and the European community. Trinidad is an independent republic and a full member of the CARICOM (Caribbean Community Market) as well as the Commonwealth. Jamaica is an independent nation trying to sever its ties with England completely by becoming a republic. Jamaica is also a full member of the CARICOM and the Commonwealth. Because of these two different political statuses, French territories and independent Caribbean nations have been unable to fully implement regional integration. Major steps have been taken since 2012 by Martinique and Guadeloupe. They are progressively being accepted as members of some regional organizations.[1] Nevertheless, most young people are educated and grow up in these countries unaware of their regional neighbors. After several decades of major regional ignorance, it is a challenge to educate the young generations to live their lives in ways that include their neighboring territories. To face that challenge, Hip Hop culture has become a channel of communication among young Caribbean citizens. It helps them travel, meet, build lasting relationships, and become more aware of one another.

This chapter is divided into two parts. In the first, I document the introduction of Hip Hop culture to Guadeloupe, Trinidad, Martinique, and Jamaica. Since 2005 I have had the opportunity to travel and interview participants in these four territories. In the second part, I discuss the capacity of Hip Hop culture to increase the awareness of young Caribbean people of the notion of citizenship in the region as a whole.

Hip Hop Culture in the Caribbean

Emergence of Hip Hop Culture in the French Territories of Guadeloupe and Martinique

Even though Hip Hop culture arrived in Guadeloupe and Martinique around 1984, no studies have been written about it. For this reason I had to meet local actors in order to obtain factual information. These two islands have been overseas French departments since 1946. I interviewed graffiti writers, rappers (also known as MCs), and record label executives. My principal informants were two MCs/beatmakers from Guadeloupe and Martinique who witnessed the first manifestations of Hip Hop in their island. Both Christophe Sophy, also known as Exxos, and Richefal Rodolphe, also known as Nèg Lyrical, have fully participated in Hip Hop culture since the 1980s.[2] Hip Hop culture spread in France, then in Guadeloupe, thanks to a television show launched in 1984 on the French channel TF1. The weekly show, *Hip-Hop*, was hosted by Sydney Duteil, the first Black man in France to hold such a position. French television shows were broadcast in Guadeloupe, so *Hip-Hop* became very pivotal in the involvement of Guadeloupean youth in Hip Hop culture. The appearance of

---

1. On April 14, 2014, Martinique and Guadeloupe became Associate Members of the Association of Caribbean States (ACS) in their own right. They have also applied to join the CARICOM, but their applications need further deliberation.

2. Interviews for this chapter were conducted in New-Kingston, Jamaica in May 2007; Trinidad, October 2005; Guadeloupe and Paris, 2005; Martinique, 2012 and 2013.

independent radio stations such as Kadans FM, Radyo Tambou, and Radio Bis (formerly known as Sun FM and known today as Trace FM) facilitated the diffusion of rap music from France and America. These radio stations provided spaces for local rappers to express themselves, first in Martinique, another French department located next to Guadeloupe. Ever since 1989 there have been special Hip Hop radio programs devoted to the culture and rap music in Guadeloupe with a rapper named Trafyk Jam. In Martinique during these gatherings, or *krazé-gòj*[3] in Creole, rappers would express themselves freely over North American beats. According to Rodolphe Richefal, one of the first Martinican pioneers in Hip Hop Creole culture, these radio programs were being heard in Guadeloupe. The performances of these young Martinican rappers hosted on "Sunshine Mix" by Shakima and DJ Patpo are the first affirmations of Creolity in Martinican Hip Hop. The show lasted from 1990 to 1994. For the very first time, young Hip Hoppers were using Creole, their own language, to paint pictures of their West Indian reality.

The same modus operandi was at work at the University of Shoelcher in Martinique on Campus FM between 1995 and 1998. This inspired Guadeloupean rappers to use Creole as a mean of expression to paint pictures of their reality. Many rappers in Guadeloupe had chosen to ape their American or French comrades and rapped in French or in English. The Creole language became a spontaneous tool for verbalizing their way of life and their aspirations. From 1996 to 1999, Radyo Tambou became a vital crossroads for rap music in Guadeloupe. Even though the radio station was known for its nationalistic stance, it never considered the Guadeloupean Hip Hoppers to be American copycats. The owners considered these artists to be young Guadeloupeans articulating the reality of their country with its social, historical, and linguistic complexity. During an interview Missie GG, formerly known as Fuckly, the first Guadeloupean rapper to enjoy commercial success, admitted that hearing those radio shows from Martinique was a turning point in his personal career and in the way he was creating his art.

The first graffiti writers became visible on the walls in Guadeloupe around the end of the 1980s. Most of the images were painted by Guadeloupean youths based in France. When home for vacation, they continued what they were practicing in Paris. Other youths from rival bands would paint their names on walls in order to mark their territory.

According to my interviewee Exxos, breakdance arrived in Guadeloupe at the same time as the other elements of the culture. However, today what's

---

3. Translation: "to crush one's throat"; it's a time when rappers can express whatever they have on their minds, however they wish, without holding anything back.

noticeable is the fusion with local dance. Moves from traditional dances are incorporated into breakdance. A school of dance located in Goyave, a local town, invented a new dance style called Hip Hop ka. Another cultural association, Kamodjaka, well known for its defense of local heritage, integrates breakdancing into its presentations. Breakdance is not duplicated but is instead reinvented within the local culture that welcomes it. In that light, it becomes a vehicle for local cultural traditions.

In Martinique, breakdancing arrived during the 1980s but was reinforced during the mid-90s with the arrival of David Milôme, a young Martinican b-boy who was based in Paris. In 1995 he founded MD Company, an association of breakdancing, in order to organize their activities and to gather breakdancers in Martinique and throughout the Caribbean. In the same way that graffiti writing was promoted by young Martinicans from Paris who returned to the island and brought back the art and the techniques, breakdancing had a similar history on the island.

Hip Hop was sometimes seen as an alienating culture; thus, the older generation of Guadeloupeans and Martinicans have been leery of it. This was not always the case, though. Various Hip Hoppers on those islands have found a way to merge their traditional culture with the Hip Hop disciplines. For example, Exxos stated that he always wanted to do what he termed "Guadeloupean rap" in order to describe his reality because of the richness of Creole language and the pride he felt expressing himself in his native language. Doing so, Guadeloupean rappers realize that they have nothing to envy of American and French rappers. If Creole language is the backbone of Creole culture and identity, Hip Hop culture is engaged in a process of creolization. The language still plays its role by fulfilling the communication needs of these young people. Still according to Exxos, breakdance established itself in Guadeloupe at the same time as the other elements of Hip Hop culture; however, what is interesting is its fusion with the local dance called gwo-ka. Breakdance is not imitated but is reinvented within the expressions of the local culture that is receiving it. There are dancers and choreographers who are inventing gwo-ka's steps to rap music and breakers who are dancing to gwo-ka. This new hybrid dance is referred to as Hip Hop ka.

Within this framework, Hip Hop becomes a channel for local traditions. A cultural bridge is laid down between different generations through musical expression. This bridge brings together gwo-ka, dancehall, and Hip Hop artists. This artistic approach crystallized itself during a concert on August 1, 2003, in Pointe-à-Pitre. It was named dub-n-ka. This cultural, musical, and generational cross-fertilization is vital to the future of Hip Hop culture in Guadeloupe. According to LM Star Jee, an MC who participated in the concert, "Ka is the future of Guadeloupean Hip Hop; otherwise, we will always remain exotic copycats of the United States."[4] Similarly, François Ladrezeau, a major drummer and vocal leader of a popular gwo-ka act, Akiyo, declared, "Their music needs to feed itself from ours since it's also theirs."

This fusion of two worlds is well appreciated—even desired—by both parties, who are enriching themselves mutually. Rappers are going back to their cultural roots. As for gwo-ka drummers and singers, it's the recognition of their status as pioneers but also a projection into modernity. Hip Hop culture in Guadeloupe emancipated itself from its North American founders and began to penetrate Creole culture. As a result, while global cultural phenomena coming from capitalist countries via powerful culture distributors are understood within the dynamics of local cultures, the latter, while being transformed, also transform these foreign cultural products. In Guadeloupe, Hip Hop culture became authentic and Creole because it reflects the reality and the specificities of Guadeloupean society.

Emergence of Hip Hop Culture in Jamaica

I went to Jamaica in May 2007 in order to meet local Hip Hoppers. During my stay, I conducted a series of interviews in a recording studio in New Kingston. My contacts with the rappers who were coming to record facilitated other contacts with local composers and sound engineers. Gambling House Recordings was the name of the studio where many young reggae, dancehall, and rap artists come to lay their vocal tracks in New Kingston. It's also a record label, founded and run by three rap artists from the island: Alique Archer, also known as Julio Sluggs; Kimani, also known as Kjohn; and Sadike Johnston, also known as Hunka Gold.

When I asked them about the arrival of Hip Hop culture in Jamaica, I could feel the pride in their tone and in their answer. They were well aware of the role of Clive Campbell, also known as DJ Kool Herc, the young Jamaican who migrated to New York in 1967 and became the first Hip Hop DJ. I was told confidently that Hip Hop came from Jamaica and that without their musical heritage, Hip Hop culture would have never been. Even though I could understand their pride, being fellow countrymen of Kool DJ Herc, one must recognize that if Jamaica gave Hip Hop the "sound system culture," America gave Hip Hop its cultural and urban context, and the material and technical elements necessary for its emergence.

---

4. Denis, Jacques, "Sound-klash en Guadeloupe," July 9, 2004, http://www.rfimusique.com /musiquefr/articles/060/article_15060.asp.

Two factors are essential to the emergence of Hip Hop culture in Jamaica: cable TV and the frequent travels of local actors to North America as well as their thorough knowledge of the United States. Due to the proximity between Jamaica and the United States, both countries have a long history of cultural influence and exchange. Radio stations based in the United States broadcast in Jamaica. Since 1992 cable TV has perpetuated this tradition. The first Hip Hop television shows arrived in Jamaican households by the early 1990s (*Yo! MTV Raps* and *Rap City*). Through these shows, Jamaican young people familiarized themselves with Hip Hop culture, its codes, and its dynamics. The first households to have cable TV were those of the middle class. During the second half of the 1990s, cable TV became more popular and more accessible to modest-income households.

During the early 1990s the first rappers in Jamaica were influenced by the musical and the writing codes of North American East Coast Hip Hop. The beats are less melodious, the flows sharp—less dance music than West Coast Hip Hop—and the rhymes are much more poetic and thoughtful. According to one of my informants, during the 1980s, breakdancing had strong appeal, but nowadays the form seems to be fading away. In spite of my research and the interviews I have conducted, I was not able to get in touch with active breakdancers. Other informants have also stated that breakdancing had never emerged on the island or, if it did, it did not last because of the strong presence of local dancehall. Dancehall music is associated with the different types of dancehall dances, and because of its outstanding popularity, it infringed on the development of Hip Hop dance in Jamaica. At the same time, graffiti art never developed itself in Jamaica due to the difficult economic situation of the island and the high cost of the spray cans. Very few people would have been able to afford the materials needed to hone their skills. Another factor is that graffiti writing in Jamaica is closely related to politics. Very often, political activists tag the name of their party on walls in order to mark their territory.

The second main reason behind the emergence of Hip Hop culture in Jamaica is the length and the frequency of the contacts between the two countries through human exchanges. The majority of Hip Hoppers in Jamaica went to the United States for long or short periods of time. During their stay, they became more sensitive to and familiar with Hip Hop culture. As a result, they felt naturally attracted to it as a means of expression and social identification. Sadike and Kimani studied in Georgia and Florida between 1996 and 2001. Alique lived and studied in New York between 1995 and 1999. Frank Grizzy, a rapper, was born on the island but lived in New York between 1987 and 1995. He followed his father, a professional musician, to the United States when he decided to move. These travels and stays have helped nurture their attachment to Hip Hop. They allowed them to meet North American rappers and to bring Hip Hop cultural products back home (CDs, videos, clothes, magazines, etc.) Nowadays, there is still a large number of young Jamaicans from the well-off class who are turning to Hip Hop. They are more sensitive to it because they have more access to the culture. They can travel to the United States more often on vacation or to go shopping. Thus, for some of the upper class, Hip Hop is becoming a favorite means of expression. However, I'm not suggesting that all Hip Hoppers in Jamaica are from the well-off social class, since some are also from the middle and the lower social classes.

As everyone knows, rap is not traditional Jamaican music. Mento, ska, reggae, and dancehall are the leading musical trends of the island, the last two being the more influential and powerful nowadays. When rappers in Jamaica confess their attachment to the art form, they are accused of turning their backs on their country to the benefit of a foreign country. The United States is not always seen as a friendly nation, especially in terms of its cultural and geopolitical influence. While reggae and dancehall artists are using Jamaican Creole to pen their songs, rappers are using African American slang to write theirs. This is a bone of contention between them and a disapproving segment of the Jamaican people. Language is a vital element of culture; it keeps and carries the memory and the values of that culture. Their use of a foreign accent and vocabulary is perceived as a lack of personal affirmation and a betrayal of their cultural roots.

Nevertheless, I believe one can explain that behavior given that their references in terms of authenticity are the creators of the culture, American Hip Hoppers. That is why they want to be understood, rated, and approved by them. However, their lyrics do not reproduce the North American reality because they are living different experiences and, as such, they touch on different topics. Through the topics of their songs, their images, the words and expressions they choose to use, they are getting closer to the culture of their island. The fact that they are dealing with their day-to-day lives, their personal experience in spite of the language they use, is what makes their music original.

A great majority of Jamaicans do not see the purpose of Hip Hop culture in Jamaica and view it only as an invasive and alienating culture. According to Alique, even if they are criticized because of their North American accent, their talent makes the difference and will grant them the respect they deserve. Young Jamaicans appreciate their music and perceive themselves through it. Rappers gave me another explanation for the choice of language. Since dancehall artists are using only patois, it became synonymous with this musical genre. To sing in Creole is equivalent to making dancehall or being a dancehall artist. As a consequence, to distance themselves from dancehall music, they chose to use the North American English that goes better with rap. Their raps reflect their voices, coming out of Jamaica, but are destined for the ears of the whole world.

In general, the topics of their songs vary: gender relationships, political life dominated by two major parties for decades, the arrival of drugs and weapons on the island, night life, advice to young listeners, and so forth. All these topics distinguish their art form and allow them to label it "Jamaican rap." They are also writing, in the pure Hip Hop tradition, ego-trip songs in which they show their verbal dexterity. There are also active rappers (Beat, Cash) on the island who are using Creole, but they are less numerous, and I was not able to meet them while I was on the island to ask them about their motivations.

In the early 1990s, there were North American rappers with Jamaican roots (Smif-N-Wessun, known today as the Cocoa Brovaz, with the title "Sound Bwoy Bureill" in 1995; Originoo Gunn Clappaz, with the album *Da Storm* in 1996). This approach helped these Jamaican American rappers distinguish themselves in the United States and affirm their cultural origins. Jamaican Hip Hop culture was galvanized indirectly by Hip Hoppers with Jamaican roots living in the United States.

Nadirah X, the only Jamaican female rapper I have discovered, does not reside on the island, though she's known in the Hip Hop community. She grew up and pursued graphic design studies in Jamaica. She started rapping during the mid-1990s. Her parents were activists of the Nation of Islam and the reason she named herself Nadirah X after Malcolm X. She uses both North American English and, less often, Jamaican Creole.

When I asked my informants to share their aspirations for Hip Hop culture in Jamaica, their statements revealed several things. They want to export their art form and convey its difference. They also want to emancipate themselves from local prejudices and be recognized as full cultural actors. Next to the Rastafari movement, reggae, and dancehall music, Jamaican Hip Hoppers are trying to implant themselves in a cultural landscape that is under the strong influence of the first three. It is a challenge because Hip Hop culture is still perceived as a vehicle of North American imperialism.

Hip Hop Culture in Trinidad

In October 2005 I had the opportunity to conduct field research in Trinidad. Through several interviews with rappers (Be-Dangerous, Skeeto), local producers (Lamar Poland, also known as Beebo), and a breakdancer (Ahmed),

I was able to figure out the outlines of Hip Hop culture on the island. As early as 1983, a young Trinidadian named "Jus Jase" was already writing rhymes and rapping on the island. He is part of the first generation of Hip Hoppers in Trinidad. I was not able to interview him, but one of my informants identified him as a pioneer of the art form. Between 1988 and 1989 Jus Jase won many rap contests that allowed him to be the opening act for major American rappers performing in Trinidad at that time. By the end of 1991 he was hosting a radio show, *The Other Side of Midnight.* The arrival of cable TV during the 1990s brought Hip Hop culture into Trinidadian households. Through *Yo! MTV Raps,* many young Trinidadians became influenced by North American rap groups, Hip Hop clothing fashions, and language. Breakdancing emerged on the island during the 1980s thanks to a local TV show dedicated to local urban expressions.

Another group that was mentioned often during my interviews as legendary pioneers of Hip Hop in Trinidad was the Dreadthren. They are considered to be part of the very first generation of Hip Hoppers in Trinidad. They organized and sponsored many Hip Hop events. The latter were spaces where they could reinforce the spirit of brotherhood and the values of the original Zulu Nation, the first Hip Hop organization based in New York and created in November 1973. There are virtually no female Hip Hoppers in Trinidad. The culture is mainly male-dominated, and rappers are beginning to gain public exposure within the artistic sphere. Breakdance emerged during the 1980s with a b-boy called "scientist." He's known to be the first Trinidadian breakdancer. In 1989 the art form gained popularity owing to a TV show called *Party Time.* Young breakdancers would perform and compete on stage. According to Ahmed, most crews are of African descent and reside in the main urban center around Port of Spain (Outrageous, Fusion, Scientist Crew, Surge, etc.).

On the other hand, graffiti has never really emerged, for several reasons. It is considered an act of vandalism, and the latter is severely punished. Another reason is that potential graffiti writers could barely afford the spray cans. And last but not least, the urban constructions are smaller in size and scale than in a large urban metropolis of North America, where one can find large walls and varied types of spaces to paint.

Young Trinidadians who could afford to travel to the United States participated in the emergence of Hip Hop culture just like wealthier young Jamaicans did in Jamaican society. The first generation of Hip Hoppers appeared during the 1980s owing to migratory flows between the two territories. The second generation appeared during the 1990s owing to cable TV as well (Black Entertainment Television–BET, Music Television–MTV). Apart from graffiti writing, the expressions of Hip Hop culture—rap, breakdancing, and DJing—found open spaces in which to develop within less than thirty years. If they have definitely changed the cultural life of the island, these expressions have also been transformed by the local Trinidadian culture.

Globalization does not prevent a cultural movement from taking a local and unique shape. In order to grasp the relationship between music and local and popular culture, the arguments of the Australian scholar Andy Bennett (2000), exposed in his book *Popular Music and Youth Culture,* are insightful. He surveyed the different concepts that have been used over the years by specialists of culture, media, and sociologists to theorize youth culture and popular culture. In the process of cultural identification around the products of popular culture, manufactured and sold by the Euro-American creative industries, there is an interaction between local and global forces. In order to theorize this correlation, Bennett refers to a concept popularized by the English sociologist Roland Robertson. This concept, "glocal culture," refers to the fusion of these two drives. "Glocalization" implies that in spite of global economic and cultural mechanisms changing the world drastically, each cultural product is reinterpreted and used in a unique way within a nation and its people. Consequently, if Hip Hop culture within the Caribbean is a vehicle for the uniqueness of a nation, it can be considered a form of local culture.

In 2002 a group of Trinidadian breakers, The Eclectic Dance Crew, participated in the World Hip Hop Dance Championships in Miami, Florida. For the very first time, Trinidadian breakers were competing against international breakers. They finished in sixth place. Ahmed, one of my informants, confessed that they did not really know about breakdancing and that they were just trying to imitate North American breakers and their dance steps. They returned to that contest in 2004, in Los Angeles, and were ranked second after beating the North American breakers. The difference was that this time, they were able to outdo the North Americans when they danced without trying to imitate. This was a major symbolic victory. They were able to top the inventors of the art form when going from simple imitators to innovators. When Hip Hop culture is adopted and understood within its context, no matter what the origin of the participants, they can contribute with strong legitimacy and authenticity.

Jus Jase, one of the first Hip Hoppers in Trinidad, blends into his DJing performances the rhythms of soca, one of the leading local musical forms in Trinidad. He even goes so far as to rap on soca rhythms. His Trinidadian origins facilitated this fusion. Nowadays Jus Jase is the most popular DJ on the island. He is also a member of an international team of DJs. Without this original intercultural experience he would probably never have gained such popularity. His listeners, participants and nonparticipants in Hip Hop culture, were able to find their cultural roots in his performances.

In 1997 the leading rap group of Trinidad was founded, with five rappers and a DJ. Some are rapping in Standard American English, others strictly in local patois, and one is mixing both languages. The path of the group is unusual. One of the rappers, Nigel Telesford, also known as Be-Dangerous, is also a journalist. Being immersed in the media, he has a different outlook on Hip Hop culture. Telesford has been in touch with calypso and soca artists regularly; for this reason, he understood the importance of local music and Creole early on. Interviewing these artists and having to transcribe Creole in his papers nurtured his desire to use Creole in his raps. When he made up his mind to stop using the North American accent, he was mocked and ridiculed by the other members of the group. He realized that he was more at ease and had more confidence when using his native language and his natural accent. The reaction of the audience was more enthusiastic; the DJs would replay his verse on the group's songs. Trinidadian listeners were identifying more easily with the rapper using their vernacular language. Seeing Be-Dangerous's experience, another rapper from the group, Chromatics, developed this approach but decided to mix Creole and Standard English. The other rappers kept the North American accent in order to be more authentic in the eyes of North American rappers.

Thus, the Trinidadian rapping scene is increasingly gaining independence from North American standards. It is based on Trinidadians' language and reality. It is a state of mind that contrasts with popular opinion because, according to Be-Dangerous, many Trinidadians despise their cultural heritage. Through their musical influences, the importance they confer upon their sociocultural differences and their language priorities, Hip Hoppers in Trinidad are a mirror of the glocalization of Hip Hop culture in this territory. Even though it penetrated the country through global communication industries and its presence is a consequence of North American cultural imperialism, Hip Hop culture was recontextualized within the local specificities to fit local needs. However, Hip Hop is not taken into consideration by the Trinidadian government when it comes to official cultural policies. Nonetheless, companies that have understood its commercial appeal do not hesitate to use it to promote their products.

Hip Hop as a Cultural Bridge

The primary objective of this chapter was to show how urban cultural expressions could create bridges among young Caribbean citizens regardless of their ethnic heritage and the political status of their countries. Since I am a specialist in Anglophone societies in the Americas, I deliberately focused on these countries, but this in no way means that the Caribbean consists solely of those territories. Before going any further, I must repeat that Hip Hop culture emerged throughout numerous countries of the region in different ways and at various speeds but that its presence is quite visible nevertheless. It manifests itself in Spanish-speaking, French-speaking, English-speaking, Dutch-speaking, and Creole-speaking countries, from Cuba to Trinidad via Puerto Rico and the Bahamas. It means that these participants share similar codes of expression, sociocultural landmarks, and values that surpass their own ethnic and cultural heritages without negating them. In light of those observations, for more than a decade exchanges have been initiated to put in place artistic festivals, panels, and conferences to nurture more edifying relationships between participants. These events bring together Hip Hoppers from various countries of the region and various art forms of the culture. They expose their expressions to one another and discuss their practices, their challenges, and their local development. They also learn about their countries, their history, and their sociocultural specificities that, under normal circumstances, are very complicated for one individual once language barriers, ticket fares, and political status enter the equation.

In the Caribbean, there is a long tradition of culture and arts being used as links to bring people of the region together. This is not a new phenomenon. For the Hip Hop generation, the cultural bridge is different. This generation has begun communicating and exchanging their practices, their values, their traditions, and their heritage. In 2002 in Montreal, the Symposium on Hip Hop Culture was inaugurated at the University of Concordia. This initiative, begun in Canada, was relocated and held several times in the Caribbean. It is dedicated to the exploration of all aspects of Hip Hop culture. Renamed in 2009 the International Symposium, the last one was held in Havana, Cuba, from August 17 to 21, 2011. Rappers, groups, and breakdancers from Canada, the United States, France, Haiti, and Colombia took part in the Cuban International Symposium. The topic of the sessions was "Hip Hop for peace." It brought together in the Cuban capital seventy musicians, graffiti writers, DJs, breakers, and Hip Hoppers to participate on different panels. Hip Hop culture in Cuba is fifteen years old; it has gone from marginalization to institutionalization. For the fifth symposium, participants gathered to share their experiences and to talk about race, politics, gender violence, and the development of Hip Hop culture in Cuba.

From September 8 to 11, 2011, the very first International Symposium on Hip-Hop Culture in Haiti was held in Port-au-Prince. The theme of the conference was "Hip Hop for the other Haiti"—meaning the building of a more democratic, more stable, more dynamic Haiti, taking into account all its abilities, including what the Hip Hop generation has to offer the nation. In the actual context of Haiti, where more than half the population is under twenty-one, Hip Hop culture is gaining more and more popularity. During this symposium many professionals based in the Americas, the Caribbean, Europe, Africa, and the Middle East, from various fields, showed up (from Haiti, Canada, the United States, France, Argentina, Iraq, Brazil, Cuba, Chile, Algeria, Barbados, Saint-Vincent, and Mali). The topics discussed on the panels dealt with the relationship between Hip Hop culture and Haitian society: the emergence of Hip Hop in Haiti, the professionalization of Hip Hop culture, Hip Hop culture and social change, the role and representation of women in Hip Hop, the Creole rap movement, the place of Hip Hop and its participants within Haitian society and culture, the Hip Hop generation as a vehicle for social progress, the transgressive universality of Hip Hop, and so on.

Guadeloupe, Trinidad, Martinique, and Jamaica, like many other Caribbean territories, have high unemployment rates for people between 16 and 26 years old. There is a rampant delinquency that is becoming almost uncontrollable. Nowadays these countries have built urban areas that are densely populated and tend to be locations of social exclusion. This urban chaos was the cradle of Hip Hop culture, so I believe the movement, if supported and monitored, can be a vehicle for social change. It can help build bridges among young people in the Caribbean but also between the world of arts and creativity and the professional world.

More recently, a Hip Hop festival took place in Fort-de-France, Martinique, in January 2012. Its name, Caraïp'Hop, spoke volumes about the organizers' intentions: to use Hip Hop to bring Caribbean peoples closer. Hip Hoppers came to the French department from Saint-Vincent, Grenada, Guadeloupe, French Guyana, Germany, and France. They wanted this session to be Caribbean while still inviting pioneers from Europe. The association Version Hip Hop, founded in 1995 by David Milôme, a young Martinican breakdancer and choreographer born and raised in Paris, was the organizer. This fifth congress stayed in tune with the objectives of the very first one that was to build bridges between Hip Hoppers in the Caribbean. The guests are actually partners, students Milôme met during his different trips in the Caribbean. He had the opportunity to perform and teach breakdance in several other Caribbean countries (Dominica, Saint Vincent, Grenada, Saint Lucia, Guadeloupe, and Saint Kitts). In most of those countries Hip Hop culture is less structured. There is a real need for teaching and counseling, so he and his associates are welcomed. No matter the level of these Hip Hoppers, Milôme insisted during our interview (May 25, 2012) that the most important goal for his association was to share knowledge. As a follow-up, they are trying to bring these youth to Martinique in order for introduce them to other Hip Hoppers and to instill in them a desire to get organized in their own country with or without official cultural institutions.

When Caribbean Hip Hoppers travel to other Caribbean territories, it is a very concrete and vital way to foster their Caribbean consciousness. It also reduces the exclusiveness of postcolonial relationships between former colonies and former metropolises. Instead, youth learn to turn toward other Caribbean territories that do not necessarily have the same colonial heritage, language, and political status. There are special moments to discover the history and geography of one another's countries. These exchanges can lead to lifelong relationships. This experience helps them build their knowledge and their sense of belonging to the region in all its diversity. The association intends to make these exchanges durable instead of turning towards European countries that care less about Hip Hop culture within the region.

For example, I met Xän and Oshea, two graffiti writers from Martinique who traveled to Guadeloupe and were able to paint with Haitian graffiti writers. They also welcomed other Caribbean writers in Martinique and painted with them. Another popular Martinican MC named Mali who is also a young sports instructor was invited to French Guyana recently. He not only performed there but also mentored young Hip Hoppers in order to help them in their various projects. Once again, Hip Hop culture becomes a way to interact, to know one another, and to experience new human relationships in spite of historical, political, and ethnic differences.

In July 2012 another Hip Hop festival took place, with many delegations coming from other Caribbean countries, as well as South American, Central American, and North American countries. They met to perform, to discuss, to exchange art forms, and to get to know one another. This festival was organized by AGIC (Guadeloupean Agency of Cultural Engineering) and supported by official Guadeloupean cultural institutions such as la DRAC (Regional Committee of Cultural Affairs).

Conclusion

In the same way that it would be ridiculous to say that Caribbean kids will become more Japanese if they play with PSP video games, it is not reasonable to think that wherever Hip Hop culture emerges, it automatically Americanizes its participants. In this case, like the pioneer of cultural studies Richard

Hoggart (1957), I believe we underestimate the capacities of these young people to filter and reinterpret cultural products according to their context. We also overestimate the influence of North American cultural industries. According to Tricia Rose (1994), "In every region, Hip Hop articulates a sense of entitlement and takes pleasure in aggressive insubordination. Like Chicago and Mississippi blues, these emerging, regional, Hip Hop identities affirm the specificity and local character of cultural forms as well as the larger stylistic forces that define Hip Hop and Afro-diasporic cultures" (84).

During my various travels throughout the Caribbean, Hip Hoppers that I met expressed the desire to exchange with other Caribbean Hip Hoppers. These festivals and conferences are a unique way for well-off and modest-income Hip Hoppers to discover the history, the societies, and the people of the region; to nurture their sense of belonging and citizenship; and to build trailblazing perspectives in terms of education, professional life, culture, and societal issues. In the discovery of a variety of types of Caribbean nations, some postcolonial walls are breaking down and other paths of identity are invented. Using Hip Hop culture to foster new ways of approaching Caribbean citizenship will not solve the challenges ahead of us, but it can help. The groundbreaking universality of Hip Hop can magnify local culture if understood within the context of its emergence. Created by marginalized youth, it was a way to define oneself out of the mainstream society and values, to remain authentic in spite of poverty and lack of means. Hip Hop culture's expressions can also be a tool for cementing regional consciousness in the face of dissolving forces of capitalist development.

Bibliography

Alleyne, Mervin. 1988. *Africa: Roots of Jamaican Culture*. London: Pluto.

Barrow, Christine, and Rhonda Reddock. 2001. *Caribbean Sociology: Introductory Readings*. England: Markus Wiener.

Béhague, Gerard H., ed. 1994. *Music and Black Ethnicity: The Caribbean and South America*. Coral Gables, FL: University of Miami, North-South-Center Press.

Bernabe, Jean, Patrick Chamoiseau, and Raphaël Confiant. 1989. *Eloge de la Créolité*. Paris: Gallimard.

Best, Curwen 2004. *Culture at the Cutting Edge: Tracking Caribbean Music*. Kingston, Jamaica: University of the West Indies Press.

Bennett, Andy. 2000. *Popular Music and Youth Culture: Music, Identity and Place*. New York: Palgrave Macmillan.

Bennett, Hazel, and Phillip Sherlock. 1998. *The Story of the Jamaican People*. Kingston, Jamaica: Ian Randle.

Brathwaite, Kamau. 1971. *The Development of Creole Society in Jamaica: 1770–1820 Creolisation*. Kingston, Jamaica: Ian Randle.

Bynoe, Yvonne. 2004. *Stand and Deliver: Political Activism, Leadership and Hip-Hop Culture.* Brooklyn: Soft Skull.

Chang, Jeff. 2005. *Can't Stop, Won't Stop.* New York: Saint Martin's.

Dyson, Michael Eric. 2007. *Know What I Mean: Reflections on Hip Hop.* New York: Basic Civitas Books.

Dunn, Hopeton, ed. 1995. *Globalization, Communications and Caribbean Identity.* Kingston, Jamaica: Ian Randle.

Edmondson, Belinda. 1999. *Caribbean Romances: The Politics of Regional Representation.* Charlottesville: University of Virginia Press.

Hebdige, Dick. 1990. *Cut 'n' Mix: Culture, Identity, and Caribbean Music.* New York: Routledge, 1990.

Hoggart, Richard. 1957. *The Uses of Literacy: Aspects of Working-Class Life.* London: Chatto and Windus.

Kitwana, Bakari. 2002. *The Hip-Hop Generation: Young Blacks and the Crisis in African-American Culture.* New York: Basic Civitas Books.

Lirus, Julie. 1979. *Identité antillaise: Contribution à la connaissance psychologique et anthropologique des Guadeloupéens et des Martiniquais.* Paris: Editions caribéennes.

Nettleford, Rex. 2003. *Caribbean Cultural Identity: The Case of Jamaica: An Essay in Cultural Dynamics.* Kingston, Jamaica: Ian Randle; Princeton, NJ: Markus Wiener.

Perkins, Williams Eric, ed. 1996. *Droppin' Science: Critical Essays on Rap Music and Hip-Hop Culture.* Philadelphia: Temple University Press.

Perret, Delphine. 2001. *La Créolité: Espace de création.* Martinique: Ibis Rouge Editions.

Perry, Imani. 2004. *Prophets of the Hood: Politics and Poetics in Hip-Hop.* Durham, NC; London: Duke University Press.

Rose, Tricia. 1994. *Black Noise: Rap Music and Black Culture in Contemporary America.* Hanover, NH: University Press of New England.

Rubin, Vera. 1996. *Social and Cultural Pluralism in the Caribbean.* Annals of the New York Academy of Sciences 83.

Sheperd, Verene, and Glen Richard, eds. 2002. *Questioning Creole: Creolisation in Caribbean Discourses: In Honor of Kamau Brathwaite.* Kingston, Jamaica: Ian Randle.

Tafari, Seko. 1985. *From the Maroons to Marcus: A Historical Development.* Tunapuna, Trinidad: Research Associates School Times Publications.

Valdman, Albert, and Arnold Highfield. 1980. *Theoretical Orientations in Creole Studies.* New York: Academic Press.

chapter 18

AfroReggae and Grupo Cultural Afro Reggae

A Study of the Early Years

Sarah Soanirina Ohmer

The following study of AfroReggae and Grupo Cultural Afro Reggae (GCAR) calls attention to Brazilian presence and community organizing into the field of Hip Hop studies with a long memory framework: placing AfroReggae and GCAR in a long history of Africana resistance through music in Latin America.[1] The 1990s GCAR group arises when reggae and Hip Hop music had become new global forms of solidarity among urban marginalized youths worldwide, making use of old and new strategies of social healing (Fernandes 2011). A close look at lyrics from the Hip Hop fusion band and the associated nonprofit organization shape the concepts of *performance movement* and *re-membering in the flesh,* to support further studies on resilience through performance in the African diaspora. Like most Hip Hop and reggae music, the band and the organization choreograph what I call a *performance movement* of resistance against politics of genocide, and a movement that is both therapeutic and rooted in a tradition of resistance.[2]

---

1. There is a distinction in spelling between "AfroReggae" (the band; spelled with one word) and "Afro Reggae" (the association; spelled with two capitalized words).

2. Other studies on Afro Reggae, like Yúdice (2001), Neate and Platt (2010), and José Junior's *Da Favela para o mundo: A historia do grupo cultural Afro Reggae,* refrain from

From the late 1800s on, politicians, European Positivist architects, chroniclers, journalists, and Federal Police have had their eyes on favelizing—or keeping lower-class, Indigenous, and Black Brazilians outside of urban centers. Presented as a criminalized and/or a diseased space, the favelized space continually stands as a necessary evil in order to sustain the civilized yet tropical paradise myth of Rio de Janeiro, from hosting the World's Fair in the early 1900s, to hosting the World Cup in 2014.[3] In the 1990s, the focus of this brief study of the creation and first years of AfroReggae and GCAR, the impact of both entities shows an arguably limited attempt to deconstruct stigmas, through cultural projects that resist a government's policies to ensure that the favelized are never meant to survive (Costa Vargas 2008).

On Methodology: Favelized Spaces, Long Memory, and *Mocambo* Epistemology

In the 1990s' context of sociopolitical tension and physical survival, one of AfroReggae's songs, "Nenhum Motivo Explica a Guerra," establishes a global connection between urban marginalized neighborhoods in a state of exception.[4] The rapper's lyrics introduce the current conditions in United States, Brazilian, and British metropolises. The song, part of a transnational movement of Hip Hop, calls attention to war—urban wars in which youth battle one another, police, and/or military forces:

War, what is it good for?
Who is it good for?

---

outlining Afro Reggae's cultural contributions, or its therapeutic abilities. The following discussion adds to their body of work.

3. Although referencing different time periods, this study focuses on the early to mid-1990s—the conception and early years of AfroReggae and GCAR. The late 1990s through 2014 make up a second and third phase of the AfroReggae and GCAR, during which both witnessed a boom, then criticism, death threats, and radically different approaches. Associations with conservative presidential candidates and alleged associations with drug trafficking, and the overall direction of nonprofit organizations in Rio de Janeiro, make up the body of a forthcoming study on the reception of GCAR's activities in its later years.

4. The testimony *Nenhum Motivo Explica a Guerra*, by José Junior, one of the founding members of Afro Reggae, reveals the military state of the favela in the 1990s, with 48,000 men, armed, none of them belonging to the state's armed forces. This group of men makes up Rio de Janeiro's largest group of organized crime at the time, with three factions: O Commando Vermelho (CV); the best located group, Terceiro Commando (TCP); and the Amigos dos Amigos (ADA), the most violent group. Junior includes numerous examples of daily violence, where the state's law has been lifted, and citizens have become victims of any type of violence, never meant to survive, in conditions reminiscent of the Agambenian state of exception.

When is it good for?
You being good poor
Or me being good poor
It's never been good for
Us in the hoods
Or favelas

In the verse "us in the hoods or favelas," the British guest rapper highlights commonalities between United States and British "hoods" and Brazilian "favelas," slums, or marginalized or *favelized* communities. Instead of favela, I will use the term *favelized space*. A favela is a slum community, a populated and marginal urban space, very common in Brazilian urban areas, and comparable to other agglomerations worldwide. The term favelized space underlines the phenomenon whereby a group of people were purposefully pushed into the margins by the state. The favelized space is not just a symptom of global and local affective, sociopolitical, and economic marginalization, but also a site of subversive power, meaningful growth for solidarity, community organizing, and Black cultural renaissance. Where a war is waged that is not good for "us in the hoods, or favelas."

A hyperbole underlines the global spread of war waged on favelized spaces: "Every single inch of this earth is considered turf / to be fought to the death over." Marginalized urban youth, "the powerless," are the victims: "Who gets the left overs? / And who is left over? / The powerless while politicians brush their left shoulders / Now, wait a minute." In Rio de Janeiro, AfroReggae denounces the war's consequences on their marginalized communities, and ask youth to "wait a minute," or to vouch for alternative options and change their communities.

Historiographies of the evolution of favelas demonstrate that socio-affective marginality, living in a state of exception, and vouching to "wait a minute" and find another way to live, start long before the 1980s "war on drugs." Favelized spaces of Rio de Janeiro were originally *quilombos*, communities built by individuals of African descent who deservedly opted out of life in bondage, fought for their basic human right to life, and resisted the established socioeconomic system.[5] They called themselves *mocambos*.[6] Values

---

5. Campos (2005) traces connections between favelas and *quilombos*, communities of individuals of African descent in the seventeenth and eighteenth centuries in Brazil.

6. *Quilombo* originally means camp or fort in Bentu. In 1740 imperial legal terms, *quilombo* loses this meaning to refer to an illegal establishment consisting of any group of more than five black runaways, while they opted to call themselves *cerca* or *mocambo*. The first favela is recorded as a place where *mocambos* start a new life close to the city, where they pass easily

attached to their space labeled as *quilombo* were values such as group survival, communal living, and an alternative mode of organized living in contrast to the imperial order and life in bondage.

Later on, the values of solidarity, military resistance, independence from colonization, and interracial community (between Indigenous, Jews, Blacks) were added onto *quilombo*. The lyrics of "Nenhum motivo explica a guerra" promote similar values: group survival, communal living, solidarity, independence and an alternative mode of organized living in contrast to the neoliberal order and life in a space of exception. With performance at the center of their activism, AfroReggae and GCAR make up a performance movement that promotes the *mocambo* epistemology of resistance.[7]

Mocambo voices continue to be *favelized* in Brazil and around the world. Some members of GCAR travel to help other marginalized communities fashion their own tools for empowerment, while AfroReggae sometimes tours to perform their musical comment on the effects of neoliberalism. At home, in favelized spaces of Rio de Janeiro, Brazil, the band and GCAR both work to cultivate self-esteem in communities that have been historically marginalized and guilt-ridden.[8] From the labyrinthine favela often called *boca sem saída*,[9] voices of hope break through, and perform the Hip Hop philosophy of *doing*. *Doing* regardless of being *favelized*.

AfroReggae and GCAR breathe life into a long memory of community organizing throughout which musical communication played a role in fashioning an identity during and after the shock of forced migration from various parts of West Africa to the Americas. A metacommunication for survival, rebellion, and cultural rebirth, the foundational pre- and anti-discursive constituents of Black metacommunication in the Americas are the basis of Africana performance movements (Gilroy 1993, 75). Thus it is important to perceive AfroReggae as pre- and anti-discursive constituents of Black metacommunication that call attention to a long memory of Africana Latin American music (Aretz 1984), and at the same time to note how GCAR contributes to community activism in Rio de Janeiro that originates as *quilombos*,

---

as freed people, avoiding men who commonly chased *mocambos* in rural areas. There have been records of both rural and urban *quilombos*; the latter evolved, in several cases, into favelas.

7. In an interview, a member of GCAR also brought to my attention that there is a wide array of performance-based nonprofit organizations in Rio de Janeiro. I would point out, however, that GCAR was originally unique in its ability to propel its performers onto the global market and into global nonprofit organizations.

8. On the history of the stigmatization of the *morros*, or favelas, see Fischer (2008).

9. Translated literally, this means a mouth shut; but a flytrap, like the plant, could also serve as another translation.

outlying and outlawing spaces. AfroReggae and GCAR re-member traumas and addresses them with an empowering Black art form.

By the end of the nineteenth century, regardless of the abolition of slavery in 1888, Black Brazilians make up one fifth of the population in Rio and mostly live in spaces that the state labels a parallel state [Estado paralelo] (Campos 2005, 21). By the mid-twentieth century, urban spaces resemble modern European cities, while undeveloped favelized spaces look down on the upper class and administrators' obvious disdain for its wider population (Ventura 1994, 14). Meanwhile, Brazilian media portray individuals of African descent and other favelized inhabitants as guilty, diseased, lazy individuals (Campos 2005, 25–26). Groups working against marginalization and stigmatization historically mobilize with difficulty,[10] with community associations recorded as first established in the 1950s.[11]

Aside from distorted media representation, the once *mocambo* then favelized spaces remain devoid of a legal recognition, and activists often choose survival-based over ideology-based action (McCann 2006, 152; Zaluar 2003, 163). Neighborhood associations become increasingly authoritative and sometimes benefit from government collaboration (McCann 2006, 153; Perlman 2006, 161), although without the power to settle property lines, distribute state resources, appoint government employees, or drive out undesirable representatives (McCann 2006, 154). Organizations face difficulties in resolving major issues within the favela, like the problem of citizenship. AfroReggae's songs and GCAR's mission recognize this lack of legal representation and citizenship. Their social healing attempts to work on two levels, proposing an alternative citizenship of beat-citizenship (Yúdice 1994), and undoing affective marginality or stigmatization (Herlinghaus 2009). The music of the band AfroReggae reveals images of police violence, exposes and protests its cruelty, and overturns the marginalizing policies enacted in the favelas. One scene of the documentary *Favela Rising* portrays the band performing a song "Tó Bolado," about the massacre of twenty-three innocent residents. They perform at an elementary school. Their performance proposes something to get done while at the same time gives pleasure to those who participate in it or observe it (Schechter 2004, 69). GCAR and AfroReggae's work in the realm of the spectacle works at a level where stereotypes affect children, young adults,

---

10. See Fischer (2008), Perlman (2006), and McCann (2006).

11. The Associacião dos Moradores (1960s); the Federação das Asociações das Favelas do Estado da Guanabara held several associations; the FAFERJ, Federação das Asociações das Favelas do Estado do Rio de Janeiro (1975); later more "spontaneous" organizations—for example, Afro Reggae fits. See McCann (2006).

and their families.[12] The insertion of a group penetrates global civil society, wherein grassroots community movements facilitate what Yúdice (1994) calls "performative injunction," or what I call a performance movement—a form of mobilizing in the pursuit of social justice through performance (115).

AfroReggae illustrates a performance movement that resists forces that work against individuals of African descent, thus articulating a *mocambo* performance movement. I use the term "performance movement" rather than "performance" to denote a distinction from performance art, from staged performance and from street performance, for several reasons. Firstly, Afro-Reggae exists as an institution both on and off stage. Their message is political beyond being an art form that revolutionizes the aesthetic and institution of art; it is more than performance art.

Second, "movement" connotes both physical *and* ideological action, with respect to the organization's mission. And because it is more than activism or social change, the label performance activism does not fit either. AfroReggae encompasses a nonprofit organization, a band and other performance groups, and a for-profit organization. All entities work on different fronts, on sociopolitical as well as interpersonal and psychological levels. They pay specific attention to raising cultural, political, and historical consciousness, and cultivate self-esteem in the youth of slum communities. For all of these reasons, I propose to label them a "performance movement." Hip Hop is a movement that *does* rather than writes its manifesto as a cultural movement (Chang 2006, x). It is a *lived* culture, not carried over through written discourse. It is a discourse constantly in motion, it is an embodied discourse or a performance movement that re-members specific values into the flesh of young adults.

To this day, the main issues at hand for favelized-space dwellers are the lack of citizenship, basic needs and rights, and internal colonization. Daily issues are not limited to drug dealing and violence, but are also about changing an economy of affect that supports drug trafficking, an economy based on production and consumerism fetishism, and whose focal points remain far from the favela, and an economy of affect that blames one part of the population for urban mismanagement since the early 1900s, and currently for national, even global, problems (Herlinghaus 2009, 14). Work on self-esteem, creativity, education about African history and Black Brazilian history, cultivating historical consciousness, are values recognized in Hip Hop, that help translate ideas into clear agendas and action, and shape a performance movement.

---

12. On the "realm of the spectacle," see Yúdice (1994).

With roots anchored in *mocambo* traditions and values, over time favelized inhabitants have focused on meeting their basic needs in order to survive, rather than political representation. While many organizations had to choose between political representation and basic survival needs in Rio de Janeiro, AfroReggae and GCAR focus on identity transformation through embodied knowledge in the realm of the spectacle, and perform social healing by restoring beat-citizenship. Precisely because AfroReggae works both as an NGO and as a band, it enacts healing on several levels and makes room for ignored citizenships via the beat of youth's drum through batidania, or beat-citizenship: bodies that drum of citizenship of survival and empowerment.

Social Healing as Re-Membering in the Flesh

In the documentary *Favela Rising*, AfroReggae performs a song, "Tó Bolado," about their community's massacre, to an elementary school. Military police had allegedly responded to an influential gang's offensive, in which some gang members allegedly shot four policemen, by invading the favela and attacking several parts of the neighborhood, killing twenty-three innocent residents. In "Tó Bolado [I'm Fed Up]," Anderson Sá addresses this traumatic event, the consequence of living in a space of exception. This was the first song that he wrote, a first step to re-member trauma to his community and city's memory. Anderson's narrative is especially poignant since the event had barely acquired full visibility in the media when he wrote the lyrics. Citizens knew about the massacre, but only later did the hypothesis that it was an act of vengeance by the police come out in the media. The performance is a result of coping with this traumatic event, which directly affected the singer, who had lost his brother, and from some of the community's points of view, drug traffickers might not have been to blame.

The concept of re-membering in the flesh is used here to dialogue with voices of those who are marginalized and acting for visibility and true citizenship, working to become participants of a national community again, to be re-integrated into societies and nations, actively working to heal social and personal traumas.[13] The healing process requires a text that wraps bodies around memories, that includes *the pre- and anti-discursive constituents of Black metacommunication,* and that provides a possibility for bodies or queloids—deeply repressed wounds or forgotten inherited traumas—to heal.

---

13. The use of the word "flesh" echoes Black feminist and women of color discussions with/against the imposing logocentric system of written language.

The song's title, "Tô Bolado," (I'm fed up) alludes to the community's collective frustration. It is also the chorus of the song, and with a fast-paced rhythm and aggressive guitar riffs, it nudges the audience—in the *Favela Rising* documentary, the audience consists of elementary school students—to dance away the frustration. The first stanza states the date, time, and a short description of the event, setting up the song as a witnessing of a traumatic event.

The second stanza reveals more details: one verse is dedicated to the victims ("moradores assessinados") and another to the perpetrators ("o ódio e a violência de policiais vingadores"). Each verse is separated by the singer's breath. His breath breaks up the story into layers with first the cause of the trauma, the effects of violence, and the police force as a force of death—martial law in a space of exception or Agamben's (1995) "concentration camp." The third stanza has a similar construction, divided into effect and cause: "essa crueldade aconteceu porque [this cruelty happened because]," in contrast to "no dia anterior traficantes mataram quatro policiais [the day before drug traffickers had killed four policemen]." The relationship between effect and cause places the blame on the drug dealers' violence. Is Anderson Sá's frustration aimed at the drug traffickers? Are they to be blamed for this traumatic event? If so, then the song would only be replicating affective marginalization, placing guilt onto drug traffickers who live in Vigário Geral. Yet the last stanza debunks a rational cause–effect logic: life in the favela follows no rules.

Re-membering in the flesh denotes the ability to reintegrate traumatic memories into collective cultural memory and to repair identities through embodied narrative. A step away from the meaning of the common verb "remembering," usually associated with the idea that the mind stores memories, the act of "re-membering in the flesh" places emphasis on body movement and collective shifts from social dismemberment to "polyglossia of sociability" (Yúdice 2001, 56).[14]

In the early 1990s context of social dismemberment, a handful of young Rio de Janeiro inhabitants start a performance-based group for favela youths called Afro Reggae (1993) and create the association's trademark band, AfroReggae (1995). It all begins with a young José Junior trying to make ends meet by organizing funk parties. After an *arrastão,* or mass arrest, in October

---

14. New identities arise that are more readily and available for favela dwellers, and this is what Yúdice refers to as "polyglossia of sociability": new and multiple identities that disarticulate the national identity. Funk and rap paved the way to establish the polyglossia of sociability, he argues, to identify with identities other than the false unified national identity that marginalized and favelized them. In turn, this helps to work through the stigmatized identity and collective trauma.

1992, the culmination of a large fight between two factions at a funk party in Ipanema, the context for Rio mayoral elections seems fit to pass a law to ban funk parties. José Junior has to change his funk party organizing to a reggae parties, first a flop, but then a big hit (Neate and Platt 2010, 18–19). With friends, he decides to put together a free publication on reggae, music, and diaspora issues, *AfroReggae Notícias,* and to fund it with reggae party profits. Issue number zero comes out in January 1993. Shortly thereafter, the Vigário Geral massacre is the tragedy that sets forth more participation by the newsletter editors. They join Vigário Geral community meetings about how to cope with the aftermath of the massacre. Later in 1993, they establish the first Núcleo Comunitário de Cultura, precedent to the Grupo Cultural Afro Reggae (GCAR), aiming to give youth options other than joining factions in Vigário Geral.

In the context of the organization's foundation, Operação Rio ("Operation Rio") begins in 1994, taking away civil rights from favelized citizens. The social dismemberment persists. Military forces invade the favela streets, suspending favelized residents' civil rights as they point their artillery directly at the residents (Costa Vargas 2008, 63). This favelized space is in a postwar state at the time, comparable to how Agamben defines the concentration camp, in a state of exception where the law has been lifted (Agamben 1995, 29). Afro Reggae performs most of its activism, or re-membering the flesh, in a targeted part of the Vigário Geral district of Rio de Janeiro during the 1990s.[15]

Over the course of ten years, and until today, GCAR and AfroReggae act to re-member trauma in the flesh. AfroReggae's second album, "Nenhum Motivo Explica a Guerra," illustrates how the band, as an embodied performance movement, enacts a re-membering in the flesh or a healing process of remembrance and social inclusion, that re-members or reincorporates the diasporic foundational experience into contemporary music, and that helps

---

15. The group's performance and activism at this time can be seen as an attempt to redirect genocidal political projects that might affect community members' self-esteem, with Brazilian policies that function as genocidal politics that sustain the "fragmenting and domineering and globalized neoliberal heteropatriarchal capitalist White supremacist world" (Costa Vargas 2008), in contrast to a changing discourse that joins the White supremacist discourse today. Ten years later, the founding members have expanded into a large team, Afro Reggae has built four cultural centers that house events and workshops to connect youth to an Africanist style of performance, to provide a space and tools for agency in the context of a marginalized community, and to cultivate role models and upward mobility other than from professional sports or drug trafficking. Over the course of ten years, founding members of GCAR have learned to navigate the complexities of creating an organization in a marginalized space in Brazil, outlined in detail in José Junior's 2006 testimony *Nenhum Motivo Explica a Guerra.* Some have allegedly received death threats, and one cultural center has been closed in the Complexo do Alemão area.

individuals work through and witness personal and communal trauma. The album, analyzed in further detail at the end of this chapter, incorporates issues that have been widely discussed in the media, but from the standpoint of the band members and community members. The album mirrors the mission of the Afro Reggae organization. Both adapt foundational diaspora music to promote African diasporic values of self-esteem, cultural preservation, agency, and resistance as a part of Afro-Brazilian identities in the 1990s until today. In that way, Afro Reggae choreographs a performance movement to survive current challenges in Rio de Janeiro, and acts to re-member the community's voice in the flesh.

The dash in re-membering in the flesh recognizes palpable identities with bodily and/or psychological wounds, points to forgotten citizens that re-form part of a community *and* re-shape the heterogeneity of the African diaspora, and reflects the essence of Hip Hop as fracture. Hip Hop as fracture implies a broken bone, a wound and a point of tension that communities of African descent have carried throughout history (Rose 1994, 21). First there was the transnational colonial economy based on the slave trade and forced migration of individuals of African descent. Then the industrialization and modernization of the Western hemisphere continued to marginalize groups of African descent, while the abolition of slavery remained questionable in both the United States and Brazil. Postindustrialism witnessed oppression of Afro-Brazilians through urban segregation, drug trafficking, and violence. Each era witnessed a parallel African diasporic voice of resistance. In postindustrial New York, Los Angeles, and other parts of the Americas, Hip Hop artists speak up to denounce the continuing oppression of the postindustrial era. Hip Hop addresses the socially therapeutic role of performance as Rose presents Hip Hop at the fracture or tension between two cultures (Rose 1994, 21). The whole concept of re-membering in the flesh encompasses the tension, binding ties, and social healing through embodied expressivity.

In "Tó Bolado," Anderson Sá concludes that "o caminho certo é o caminho da sorte [the right way is the way of luck]," and the 'wrong' way, that is, the unlucky way, is the path to death ("o caminho errado pode te levar a morte"). This is the logic that makes the singer, and the favela community, fed up. It is impossible to determine what is lucky or unlucky at the site of the fracture or tension between neoliberalism and *mocambo* communities. The song ends with "my pride still resides in this community," replacing stigma, sadness, shame, with pride and a sense of belonging to a community. In 1993 choreographing to survive and to re-member pride in the flesh, the performance releases lingering frustrations after the massacre. The lyrics reflect the lack of logic that rules favelized spaces, and urge the young audience to re-member in the flesh a logic wherein the state of exception that governs their lives *can* be redirected, with pride.

Healing within the Realm of Spectacle: From Narco to Transformative Culture

A brief overview of the slum communities of Rio de Janeiro highlights a socio-affective context of marginality—marginalization through guilt—and a "state of exception"—a geopolitical space where the state's law no longer applies. AfroReggae and GCAR enact a resistance to both, in Vigário Geral, where a war is being waged to defend (the privileged) society against a contaminating entity (the marginalized of African descent). Rio, the divided city[16] with now two-thirds living in favelas (Ventura 1994, 13; Campos 2005, 92), is governed by genocidal policies (Costa Vargas 2008) and targeted abandonment by the state.[17] A decade before GCAR is founded, in the early 1980s, the media remains a counterproductive source of stigmatization as it earns a central role in the daily life of late twentieth-century Brazil.[18] In response, aside from working on material recuperation and survival, organizations in favelized spaces work on restoring empowering images within the realm of the spectacle, counter to the media coverage boom on drug trafficking in the favela (McCann 2006), in part due to a boom of drug trafficking in the 1980s, itself due to international policing changes, which turned Rio de Janeiro into an important export node for cocaine produced in Bolivia and Colombia. In a context of beach *arrastões* (mass arrests), onstage and street performances turn targets of moral stigmatization into vehicles of African diaspora culture and empowering tools for agency. They do so precisely in the realm of the spectacle, where the process of moral stigmatization occurs, where negative stereotypes have been reinforced, and police invasions have been legitimated (Yúdice 1994, 54).

---

16. Ventura (1994) outlines the history of Rio as a divided city, tracing the growing divide between "modern" Rio and "barbaric favela," throughout the twentieth century. Ventura refers to the Roman term "barbaric," which meant "foreign to the empire." Rather than stigmatizing the favela as backward, Ventura sets forth an image of the favela as *set apart from* the state, foreign to the empire.

17. *A favela fala,* a collection of testimonies from favela dwellers, describes ongoing abandonment by the state, and the struggles against such abandonment, with activists' stories and their efforts to improve local infrastructure, education, and public health.

18. Costa Vargas (2006) shows "the long history of negative racialized stereotypes associated with the favelas" and how the image of the favelized space has been "recycled by including the alleged effects of drugs on these supposedly already degraded, amoral, and violent communities" (63).

Anderson Sá, the lead singer of AfroReggae, addresses the same traumatic event in "Tó Bolado." When he founds the Grupo Cultural Afro Reggae, José Junior's actions and choices as co-creator and director of GCAR fit a paradigm that attempts to go beyond Westernized social circuits. Instead of prescribing immediate answers, the group looks for solutions based on social context.[19] GCAR members communicate with and recognize the culture of the factions early on, along with the amount of knowledge and training acquired in factions, to resist stigmatizing a part of favelized spaces' realities. For example, in *Da Favela para o mundo,* José Junior draws a line between the representation of the favela community in Brazilian films and AfroReggae. In response to critics of GCAR who would put AfroReggae and the film *Pixote* in the same category, Junior notes a difference in intentional meaning. The narrative in *Pixote* disallows favela dwellers, portrays dispossession and marginalization, and fits José Junior's metaphor of a net that traps a child in a character rather than giving him the tools to "transform into a fish." The mission of GCAR is to shape young adults into independent, skillful, educated, and empowered individuals, and to break the *Pixote* stereotypes. The analogy of transformation suggests a re-membering in the flesh: transformation comes from the child herself, agent in the act of re-membering empowerment and agency to her *favelized* self.

The words of GCAR's founder underline favela children's potential, without discrediting drug factions' influence on children's identity-formation. He respects some of the values, structure, doctrines, and rules implemented in the factions (Junior 2006, 119). Counter to the national media narrative that feeds affective marginality, and that labels drug trafficking as immoral, Junior states how ex-drug traffickers acquire valuable skills as reliable leaders in GCAR. At the same time, he rejects the concept of "anti-marketing." Group members consume and wear brand-name clothes in order to "combat the image of the poor favela dwellers with dirty noses and rotten teeth," questionably in line with consumerism and capitalism (140).

Within the favelized *camps,* GCAR organizes youth programs and workshops to teach policemen about theatre, graffiti, and music, and consequently, that children from the favela are not inherently part of the drug army. The

---

19. For example, for its first event, nonprofit organization Viva Rio organizes a house remodeling. A Casa de Paz (House of Peace), in which eight of twenty-three innocent residents were killed by the military police, becomes a space of cathartic commemoration. Military police had allegedly responded to an influential gang's offensive, in which gang members allegedly shot four policemen, and retaliated by invading the favela and attacking several parts of the community, including the house, taking away twenty-three innocent lives. GCAR and AfroReggae were inspired by the citizen action initiative Viva Rio. Working in the realm of the spectacle enabled performers and community members to cope with trauma.

funding comes first from the Ford Foundation, and over time has received sponsorship from Universal Music, Santander Bank, and Petrobras, becoming a business with an annual budget of 20 million Reals coordinated within the walls of a 5-million-Real headquarters office. The activities that take their community out of a state of exception, and out of socio-affective marginality, include music shows in marginalized areas, training in computer and employment skills for young adults, hosting and organizing academic conferences and workshops, and holding open discussion with and training for police. In an online interview, José Junior explains, "Why all that? Because we need to build something to impress and show off. We are competing against drug trafficking. Our objective is to attract and recruit young people earning, sometimes, fifty thousand Reals a week.'" Fostering projects that untangle the stigmatized identity of their community, AfroReggae musicians and GCAR talk back to stereotypes, and talk back to the favelization of their communities as spaces undeserving of protection, public services, or self-esteem. They work to heal affective marginality.

On AfroReggae's second album, *Nenhum Motivo Explica a Guerra*, the first track speaks to undoing the state of exception and stereotype of the favela—healing affective marginality within the realm of the spectacle. A fast-paced, live-sounding Hip Hop fusion track with spots from UK rappers Ty and Est'Elle presents the album's main argument: "War, What Is It Good For?"—a critique of the current global geopolitical order.

The critique begins with the first stanza of the first track, "Nenhum Motivo Explica a Guerra" ("War, What Is It Good For?"): "War, what is it good for? / Not for dough / Nor victory / nor vengeance, nor industrial progress . . . Nor territorial conquest" (v.1–4). "Conquista territorial" relates drug gangs fighting for territory with the global neoliberal world order, while the repetition of "nem (nor, not even)" emphasizes critique. The world order of war that marginalizes "us," individuals speaking from the "hoods/favelas," is ominous yet irrational.

Hip Hop demonstrates qualities of "flow, layering, and rupture" (Rose 1994, 22), which stand as both a reflection and a contestation of the roles that society offers to urban inner-city youth. Shifting power relations, establishing new configurations of knowledge and power, AfroReggae and GCAR use the two driving forces of Hip Hop defined by Rose to present the possibility of using performance and Hip Hop as a healing tool, specifically to heal affective marginality imposed through guilt (Herlinghaus 2009). There are two driving forces that fashion Hip Hop—social and political forces on one hand, and Black culture on the other (Rose 1994, 23). Afro Reggae and GCAR transform bodies that have served as "targets of moral stigmatization" into vehicles of African diaspora culture and empowering tools for agency.

There is both an ethical concern and an epistemological concern in the first track—finding the right solution and establishing new configurations of knowledge and power. "War, what is it good for," or the world order without a purpose in their community, relates to identity crisis—"No one needs to be something that they are not." This is the chorus of the song, and the only verse repeated in this song besides the chorus is "not race, nor faith." The song is about a preoccupation with the way war has affected identity, with some individuals accepting it as "national pride," "shame," or "population control." The rapper affirms an ethical stance against all of these discourses of socio-affective marginality.

With a world order based on "war," and individuals identifying with war for various reasons, lyrics urges the implicit audience—favela dwellers worldwide—to break free from both the stereotype—being a target of moral stigmatization—and the neoliberal world order that wages war and turns favelas into spaces of exception. The song concludes, directed at gang members: "Pull out your gun if you're looking for death / You're no better / you're as bad as the rest / Listen!" This call to the audience ("Listen!") is followed by a synthesis of the song's arguments; with a fast pace, the rapper lists all of the justifications to change and pauses to state his stance: "Nenhum motivo explica a Guerra! [No motive justifies war!]."

The song ends with the chorus fading with the Wailers' "We Don't Need No More Trouble." The two theses of the album are exposed. AfroReggae calls attention to their affective marginalization and to the need to change it in the public realm of imagined narratives, through performance and music. AfroReggae asks to end the affective and the physical warfare, to turn the image of narco-culture into transformative culture. Starting with and ending with a chorus of homage to Bob Marley and the Wailers' track, the first track, "Nenhum Motivo Explica a Guerra," is a cry for peace and an example of versioning in Hip Hop remixing. The reworking of a track redefines traditional notions of authorship and originality. The sampling of "we don't need" (in voice rather than technological sampling) recontextualizes, highlights, and privileges Bob Marley's message in a fresh context (Rose 1994, 90). AfroReggae's versioning breaks down the global order of an affective economy of guilt, where "a politics of foundationalist assumptions, together with a repertoire of images and symbols for rendering evident guilty territories and bodies, have succeeded in 'crowd[ing] out the possibility of reason, care, and collective responsibility'" (Herlinghaus 2009, 10). There is a possibility of reason, care, and collective responsibility. Though favelas have become increasingly stigmatized since the 1950s (and oddly a new destination for tourism in Rio), and the "repertoire of images and symbols" that renders favela residents guilty is part of a drug war associated with sacred symbols, while drug trafficking and drugs connote evil in global narratives (ibid., 9), AfroReggae crowds *in* collective responsibility, and asks for peace. AfroReggae musicians and activists chose to perform a narrative repair of community trauma and guilt in contrast to other works of art, to turn narco-culture into transformative culture (Lindemann 2001, 66).

GCAR effects a healing of affective marginality in its activism with their own repertoire of images and symbols. The image of Orilaxé attests to the importance of transformation: "a cabeça tem o poder da transformação [the head has the power to transform]" (Junior 2006, 197). GCAR named its yearly awards after this Orixá (a Candomblé deity) that, aside from supporting neighborhood activism efforts, promotes their African diasporic culture and underlines the importance of transformation. José Junior also associates GCAR with the "Shiva Effect," moving from chaos to destruction to change.

The performance movement's use of transformational symbols cultivates self-esteem. Transformation redirects the discourse of narco-culture into a discourse of nurturing Afro Brazilian cultures. José Junior explains in his testimony: "The fact is that GCAR is inserted into this reality [of narcoculture]. We developed two basic strategies to ensure that the 'AfroReggae culture' consume the narcoculture, supersedes it and rises from there, a positive path to action." This is a redirection of the affective marginality into social affirmation and agency. For Junior, the narco-culture is a network beyond the favela, with tentacles that allow it to touch upon different social instances. It does not necessarily imply violence or illegal acts, and can actually reject those very aspects of narco-culture. Novels, chronicles, short stories, and films such as *City of God* or *City of Men* and some Hip Hop artists can be a part of narco-culture. Vice versa, the larger profits from narco-culture go to individuals who barely interact with and live far from the favelas.[20] In that way, AfroReggae is a part of this culture, but at the same time, it reformulates narco-culture, recognizes the effects and reality of socio-affective marginalization, and proposes a nurturing form of culture: a Hip Hop–based performance movement that re-members in the flesh.

Rather than supplementing the neoliberal regime and feeding the tentacles that support narco-trafficking, AfroReggae embraces cultural values of

---

20. In mid-September 2005 several members of the upper-class Zona Sul *carioca* neighborhoods were arrested after 1.6 tons of cocaine were seized, along with 2 million Reals, later stolen from federal police headquarters, for which fifty-eight police were suspended. Later in December, a PSDB-party-related former mayoral candidate was arrested for trafficking 500 kilos of cocaine in Pará. The traffic in favelas was known to be much lower and local at the time: "It's the upper classes who send cocaine abroad, and what goes on in the favelas has nothing to do with it" (Police official Marina Maggessi, qtd. in Platt and Neate 2010, 89).

the African diaspora and performance, the same values upheld in the first *mocambo* favelas. José Junior and other organizers make use of drug traffic's organizational structure, having new members earn their way through the association by rewarding them with increasing responsibilities. Rather than earning a gun to move up from kite flying to watchman, they shift from *batucada* percussionist to *batucada* section leader, to workshop leader, and so on.[21] They shift from affective marginality to beat-citizenship.

From Affective Marginality to Beat-Citizenship

AfroReggae's lyrics denounce and overturn a state of ban into beat-citizenship or *batidania,* to use George Yúdice's term. Still with a theme of war, the third track of *Nenhum Motivo Explica a Guerra,* "Mais uma chance," conveys a strong political tone. The chords that open up the harmony are repeated throughout the song to build a harmonious, upbeat rhythm while a minor chord notes an unsettled feeling—the space of exception. The first verse presents a divide between the public discourse that describes his community, in contrast to his own life experience: "Porque nas segundas chegam notícias tão ruins / Quero expulsá-las da minha vida [Because in a matter of seconds we get such bad news / I want to get these news out of my life]" (v.1–2). He reveals how difficult it is to live in "bad news." One verse is repeated besides the chorus, "gerações sem chance (generations without an opportunity)." These two characteristics—having private life exposed in the public realm, and lived as bad news, and feeling like a generation without opportunities—establish the song's thesis. Living in a space of exception and affective marginality limits self-identity.

At the end of the song, the rhythm picks up for the bridge and rap "Damned heritage / Fighters, guerrilla fighters without a cause/ There are so many mothers who cry / When they lose their children / I pray to a God whom I don't know / But who surely knows who I am." A melodic verse follows: "I want to have a tomorrow," with this seemingly harmonious chord that ends on a sharp note—musical superimposition of hope in a space of exception. Backup singers wrap up with a harmony, with rapping reminding that "guerrilla fighters fight a war without a cause." The note of hope, yet lack of solution, resolves in the following track on community unity, or beat-citizenship.

---

21. See Platt and Neate (2010) for testimonies from GCAR members, and detailed descriptions of skills that they make use of in drug trafficking as well as in GCAR.

"Quero só você [I only want you]" shifts *Nenhum Motivo Explica a Guerra* from critique to desire—desire for beat-citizenship. This is the first song in which the direct object pronoun "us" is associated with themes of dream and hope. This song shifts the album's mood to one of a love song, first with the harmonizing backup voices at the beginning, then the chorus "quero só você [I only want you]" and the first lyrics "O que eu quero e o A do amor [What I want is the L of love]."

With this track, the sound clearly defines the band's heterogeneity. AfroReggae splices rock music with rap music, reminiscent of early U.S. American Hip Hop that sampled rock music (long before Run-DMC's use of samples from rock band Aerosmith's "Walk This Way" in 1986). "Beats selected by Hip Hop producers and DJs have always come from and continue to come from an extraordinary range of musics" (Rose 1994, 52). *Nenhum Motivo Explica a Guerra* also features sounds and influences from reggae music, dancehall, and drum'n'bass throughout the album, expressing a plurality of new forms of identities to relate to, in order to work through the stigmatized identity that had been imposed onto them, and in order to identify with something other than the falsely unified national identity that marginalized them. AfroReggae, by putting music at the center of its social activism movement, shifts the Western epistemology of social activism to fit their plural context.[22] Its fusion sound speaks for the "polyglossia of sociability" that is useful for their movement to work (Yúdice 1994, 56). In other words, GCAR's sociopolitical strategies, which included a hybrid music genre, spoke to the multiplicitous needs of urban youths, and met a need for heterogeneous strategies to provide social mobility to the youth.[23]

A desire for freedom, not charity, is a political message directed to the city's behavior towards the favela dwellers, and NGOs perform acts of charity that do not emancipate in "Quero só você." The chorus establishes that this

22. Context-based heteroglossic social activism also has a history in Brazil: funk and rap critiqued society, proposed antinational identities and local citizenship (Yúdice 1994). During interviews with Afro Reggae administrators and favela youth, DJ Marlboro's name came up on several occasions. He was a famous funk DJ over ten years ago whose name still resonates as a central figure to rejuvenate the favela's marginalized space, its state of constant war, and helps to transform it into a place where youth could find entertainment and come together to dance at funk parties. Other DJ names that were mentioned include Furação and DJ Romulo Costa.

23. Funk and rap critiqued society, important influences of AfroReggae, fashioning a new sense of antinational identity that claimed local citizenship, and providing a language that went against falsely unified national discourse, and spoke against the myth of *mestiçagem* (or race mixing), while providing favela youth with new forms of identity—pluralistic role models that fit their social context. Funk lyrics speak to the context of the favelas, youth came together to express themselves through social dance at funk dance parties. New identities were readily available and relatable to favelized youth (Yúdice 1994, 197).

song is about a way of life: "Quero liberdade / Não quero caridade / Que o vento nos carregue / Pra paz do nosso reggae (I want freedom/ I don't want charity / I want the wind to carry us / Towards our reggae's peace)." The association with the wind could be related to true freedom, being one with nature and unbound from a state of exception's boundaries. In the chorus, the possessive adjective "our" first comes up, which speaks to ownership, property, and is associated here with "reggae." Of what could "our" reggae—our beat-citizenship—consist?

The first stanza lists everything the poetic voice wants: love, good, a future with "you," well-being, no one else (other than "you"), understanding, peace helping "us." The first stanza sets up the utopia that the poetic voice strives for—a peaceful time, day and night, in which "you" would not abandon them. The lyrics in "Quero Só Você" set up the argument of the song to be about sanity, health, how beat-citizenship could flourish, or the product of beat-citizenship: "Quero o B do bem / . . . quero o bem estar (I want the G of good, I want well-being)." The bridge is made up of rap that breaks with the rhythm, and makes the song's main point. While backup singers accompany the harmony, they echo the beginning of the song and mark the poetic tone's changes. What was first setting up a romantic harmony now backs up a political stance: "I'm on a destination-less road / Where all the paths lead to one / Roaming between mind and hearts / I look back with dignity / Enough with the tears / Enough with the conflicts / I can't find what I'm looking for / But I insist, I won't desist." This new path is a path of desire, of dreams, and the lack of destination suggests the possibility of going on with hope regardless of the lack of opportunities and conflicts. "I insist, I won't desist" being the last verse of this stanza, the only one with a rhyme, underlines the persistence not to let lack of possibilities put one down. The anaphora of "Chega (Enough)" also puts the critique behind, alluding to the two previous songs. One looks back "with dignity," rather than the anger of reading the news in "Mais uma chance." After this bridge, the first stanza is repeated and earns new meaning.

The call and response between two singers in this song, with the harmonizing singer and the rapper as two different voices, transforms the "you" and the desire. "I want only you," the second time around, refers to the transformative ability to dream, the strength of a community able to dream. The chorus returns ("I want freedom / I don't want charity / I want the wind to carry us / Towards our reggae's peace") to introduce the rapper's voice. The rapper's voice reiterates a sense of dignity, "head high," and this time around, he is not lost or wandering but calling to seize the moment: "this is the time, the time is now. A call to follow faith and desire and strive for unity, "for me, for you and everyone," transforming the perception of the relationship from just a loving relationship between two people to solidarity within a community. "I want only you" now changes to mean you, a community full of faith, hope and pride, beat-citizens.

The two singers end with a call and response not stanza to stanza, but verse to verse, with the rapper saying verses first dedicated to the harmonizing voice. The song ends on a note of solidarity: voices intertwine, towards a hopeful future, resolving a questioning of identity prevalent in the previous songs as it defends historical agency, ownership, and the power to look back with dignity and look forward with hope.

Conclusion: Performance and "Collective Efficacy" as Social Healing

AfroReggae offers an Africana performance movement of empowerment in order to overcome affective marginalization and collective trauma. With components such as "our reggae," the polyglossia of Hip Hop sampling and beat citizenship, AfroReggae's Hip Hop imparts a discourse of hope, channeling an oppressive context and transforming it through performance, through embodied discourse. The performance movement echoes a history that to this day remains insufficiently heard, from geopolitical spaces that were once quilombos, spaces of political cultural resistances to the genocidal statist discourse, then and now. In a context of weakened or absent citizenship, under the threat of genocide, members of Afro Reggae and the community choose to re-member pride, hope, and agency to their identities. AfroReggae and GCAR create a performance movement that re-members in the flesh. With Hip Hop and performance movements that re-member trauma in the flesh, Afro-Reggae's performances and narratives promote a blend of Africana experience with a *mocambo* epistemology: survival, solidarity and cultural connection to Africana experience in order resist (neo)liberal and affective marginality and state political racism.

Bibliography

Agamben, Giorgio. 1995. *Homo Sacer: Sovereign Power and Bare Life.* Translated by Daniel Heller-Roazen. Stanford, CA: Stanford University Press.

Aretz, Isabel. "Music and Dance in Continental Latin America." In *Africa in Latin America: Essays on History, Culture, and Socialization,* edited by Manuel Moreno Fraginals. Translated by Leonor Blum. New York: Holmes & Meier, 1984.

Campos, Andrelino. 2005. *Do quilombo à favela: A produção do "espaço criminalizado" no Rio de Janeiro.* Rio de Janeiro: Bertrand Brasil.

Chang, Michael. 2006. *Total Chaos: The Art and Aesthetic of Hip Hop.* New York: Basic Civitas Books.

Costa Vargas, João H. 2006. "When a Favela Becomes a Gated Condominium." *Latin American Perspectives* 33(4): 49–81.

———. 2008. *Never Meant to Survive: Genocide and Utopias in Black Diaspora Communities.* Plymouth, UK: Rowman & Littlefield.

Fernandes, Sujatha. 2011. *Close to the Edge: In Search of a Global Hip Hop Generation.* London: Verso.

Fischer, Brodwyn. 2008. *A Poverty of Rights: Citizenship and Inequality in Twentieth-Century Rio de Janeiro.* Stanford, CA: Stanford University Press.

Gilroy, Paul. 1993. *The Black Atlantic: Modernity and Double Consciousness.* Cambridge: Harvard University Press.

Herlinghaus, Herman. 2009. *Violence Without Guilt: Ethical Narratives in the Global South.* New York: Palgrave Macmillan.

Junior, José. n.d. *Conexões urbanas.* http://www.multishow.com.br/conexoesurbanas (accessed June 1, 2007).

———. 2006. *Nenhum Motivo Explica a Guerra.* Rio de Janeiro: Ediouro.

Lindemann, Nelson. 2001. *Damaged Identities, Narrative Repair.* Ithaca, NY: Cornell University Press.

McCann, Bryan. 2006. "Review: The Political Evolution of Rio de Janeiro's Favelas: Recent Works." *Latin American Research Review* 41(3): 149–63.

Mochary, Matt, and Jeff Zimbalist, dirs. 2005. *Favela Rising.* Genius Entertainment. Film. http://www.favelarising.com/.

Perlman, Janice. 2006. "Metamorphosis of Marginality: Four Generations in the Favelas." *Annals of the American Academy of Political and Social Science* 606: 154–77.

Neate, Patrick, and Damien Platt. 2010. *Culture Is Our Weapon: Making Music and Changing Lives in Rio de Janeiro.* New York: Penguin.

Rose, Tricia. 1994. *Black Noise: Rap Music and Black Culture in Contemporary America.* Middletown, CT: Wesleyan University Press.

Schechter, Robert. 2002. *Performance Theory: An Introduction.* New York: Routledge.

———. 2004. "Liminality and Communitas." In *The Performance Studies Reader,* edited by Henry Bial. New York: Routledge. 358–74.

Ventura, Zuenir. 1994. *Cidade Partida.* São Paulo: Companhia das Letras.

Yúdice, George. 1994. "Funkification of Rio." In *Microphone Fiends: Youth Music & Youth Culture,* edited by Andrew Ross and Tricia Rose. New York: Routledge. 197–217.

———. 2001. "AfroReggae: Parlaying Culture into Social Justice." *Social Text* 19: 53–65.

Zaluar, Alba. 2003. *A favela fala.* Edited by Ducle Chaves Pandolfi and Mário Grynszpan. Rio de Janeiro: Editora Fundação Getúlio Vargas.

about the contributors

Editors

MELISSA CASTILLO-GARSOW is a Mexican American writer, journalist, and scholar, currently completing a PhD in American Studies and African American Studies at Yale University. For the past ten years she has documented and written on Latino/a culture(s) in a variety of forums, from CNN.com to *El Diario / La Prensa* to various peer-reviewed journals. She is co-author of the Hip Hop novel *Pure Bronx*, which was released in 2013, and is currently editing an anthology of Afro-Latino poetry for Arte Público Press. She is currently at her work on her dissertation, tentatively titled "The Atlantic Borderlands: Mexican American Container Cultures of New York City," a multidisciplinary work about Mexican cultural productions in New York. Her debut poetry book, *Coatlicue Eats the Apple*, was released in June 2016 by Pulse.

JASON NICHOLS has built his career around the studies of race, class, and gender through a Hip Hop lens. He earned a doctorate in 2012 with a dissertation titled "You Ain't Messin' Wit My Dougie: Black Masculinities in Post-Millennial Hip-Hop Song and Dance," and he is currently editor-in-chief of *Words Beats & Life: The Global Journal of Hip Hop Culture,* the first peer-reviewed journal devoted to Hip Hop studies, art, and culture. He is also an internationally known Hip Hop artist, who has collaborated and shared the stage with platinum rappers and producers.

Contributors

MARK NAISON is Professor of History and African American Studies at Fordham University. He is the author of five books and over 200 articles on African

American politics, labor history, popular culture, and education policy. Dr. Naison is the Principal Investigator of the Bronx African American History Project, one of the largest community-based oral history projects in the nation, and has completed work on a book of oral histories from the BAAHP, with Robert Gumbs. His articles about Bronx music and Bronx culture have been published in German, Spanish, Catalan, and Portuguese as well as English. He is also the co-author of the novel *Pure Bronx*, written with Melissa Castillo-Garsow, and published in 2013.

ROBERT TINAJERO earned a PhD in Rhetoric and Writing Studies from the University of Texas at El Paso and master's degrees in Creative Writing and Religious Studies. He is currently Director of Writing Studies at Paul Quinn College in Dallas, Texas. His research interests include composition studies, race critical theory, and Hip Hop culture, and he has published academic articles and two books of poetry. He is from El Paso, Texas.

PANCHO MCFARLAND is an associate professor of sociology and the author of numerous works including *Chicano Rap: Gender and Violence in the Postindustrial Barrio* (University of Texas Press, 2008) and *The Chican@ Hip Hop Nation: Politics of New Millennial Mestizaje* (Michigan State University Press, 2013). He is active in the food and environmental justice movements and is currently writing his first book about food justice, *Food Justice in the City: Essays on CommUnity, Autonomy and Struggle in Chicago,* and co-editing *Decolonial Food for Thought: Mexican-Origin Foods, Foodways and Social Movements* (University of Arkansas Press).

JARED BALL is a father and husband. After that he is a multimedia host, producer, journalist, and educator. Ball is also a founder of "mixtape radio" and "mixtape journalism," about which he wrote *I MiX What I Like: A MiXtape Manifesto* (AK Press, 2011), and is co-editor of *A Lie of Reinvention: Correcting Manning Marable's Malcolm X* (Black Classic Press, 2012). Ball is an associate professor of communication studies at Morgan State University and can be found online at IMIXWHATILIKE.ORG.

PETRA R. RIVERA-RIDEAU is Assistant Professor of American Studies at Wellesley College. She earned her BA in African American Studies at Harvard and her PhD in African Diaspora Studies at the University of California, Berkeley. Her research has been funded by agencies such as the Ford Foundation, the Social Science Research Council, and the Center for Puerto Rican Studies at Hunter College. Dr. Rivera-Rideau is the author of *Remixing Reggaetón: The Cultural Politics of Race in Puerto Rico* (Duke University Press, 2015), and co-editor with Jennifer A. Jones and Tianna S. Paschel of *Afro-Latinos in Movement: Critical Approaches to Blackness and Transnationalism in the Americas* (Palgrave Macmillan, 2016).

CHRISTOPHER DENNIS is Associate Professor of Spanish at the University of North Carolina Wilmington. His specific geographical regions of interest are Colombia and the Caribbean, and he has worked extensively on topics pertaining to Afro-Colombian communities of the Pacific and Atlantic littorals. In his book *Afro-Colombian Hip-Hop: Globalization, Transcultural Music, and Ethnic Identities*

(2011), Dennis explores how Afro-Colombian artists rework ethnic identity while using Hip Hop and digital media as tools for carrying their perspectives, histories, and expressive forms to national and international audiences. In addition to his research on music, Dennis has written and published on the gendered and racialized iconography used to represent the *palenquera* (female descendants of runaway slaves), Afro-Colombian narrative fiction, and the discursive representation of Black subjects in Colombian colonial literature.

HONEY CRAWFORD is a doctoral candidate in Performing and Media Arts at Cornell University. She previously earned her MFA in Critical Studies in Writing from California Institute of the Arts and her BFA in Acting from the Theatre School at DePaul University / the Goodman School of Drama. Her scholarly interests include feminist performance practices, public spectacle, protest, cultural theory, critical race theory, and postcolonialism. Her current research traces contemporary acts of public spectacle and street performance in Brazil's urban centers to legacies of resistance and identity making. She pulls from a repertoire that includes public protests, Carnaval, Candomblé, riots, samba, Hip Hop, and capoeira.

BOCAFLOJA is a poet, rap artist, scholar, cultural ambassador, and founder of the Quilomboarte collective. In addition to five professionally edited music albums and international tours throughout fifteen countries, Bocafloja in 2008 published his first book, *ImaRginación*. *Prognosis* is his second literary project. Race relations, decolonial narrative, and the African diaspora in Latin America studies are fundamental topics addressed in his body of work. He was born in Mexico City and lives in New York City.

LISSET ANAHÍ JIMÉNEZ ESTUDILLO is a social anthropologist at la Universidad Autónoma Metropolitana-Iztapalapa (UAM-I) and an investigator for the project "La Ciudad Transantional." This project has developed an investigation of youth who live on the border, focusing on youth practices such as graffiti and rap in Tijuana, Mexico. Other aspects of the project include the city, the border and migration, identity, youth practices and cultures, and masculinity.

DANIEL D. ZARAZUA draws upon a diverse background that includes more than fifteen years as an educator and twenty years as a writer, photographer, and DJ, an adventure that has taken him across six continents. His experience includes teaching at the Rock and Roll Hall of Fame's Summer Teacher Institute and working with the U.S. State Department as a "Hip Hop ambassador." He's currently working on a book exploring Black and Latino communities in Taiwan.

DIANA CAROLINA PELÁEZ RODRÍGUEZ is an instructor-scholar at the Centro de Educación para el Desarollo, Universidad Minuto de Dios, Bogotá, Colombia. She studied Language Philosophy and Sociocultural Studies at the Universidad de Los Andes in Bogota, where she researched female Hip Hop in Colombia. She then did a specialization on Cultural Policies and Cultural Management at Universidad Autónoma de México, Iztapalapa, where she created a project on memory and symbolic reparation of the armed conflict for communities in the outskirts of her city using Hip Hop arts as the means of expression. In 2012, she finished the Master's Program in Cultural Studies at Colegio de la Frontera Norte, in Tijuana, Mexico, where her thesis focused on female rappers of Mexican origin in Los Angeles.

JESSICA N. PABÓN is an Assistant Professor of Women's, Gender, and Sexuality Studies at SUNY New Paltz. She completed her PhD at NYU's Department of Performance Studies, where she specialized in Subcultural Aesthetic Practices of Resistance and Feminist & LGBTQ Performances of Community and Identity. She won a Dissertation Fellowship from the American Association of University Women in 2012 for her ethnographic work with female graffiti artists from over fifteen countries, which examines gender politics in graffiti subculture. From 2010 to 2012, she was the Director of U.S. Relations for Rede Nami (an urban art feminist collective in Brazil). She was also the curator and artist consultant for bOb gallery in NYC, showing artists including Shiro, ClawMoney, Anarkia Boladona, Queen Andrea, and Miss163, and an invited speaker at the 2012 TEDxWomen conference in Washington, DC. She has published in numerous journals and is now preparing her manuscript *Graffiti Grrlz: Performing Feminism in the Hip Hop Diaspora* for publication as a book.

SANDRA ABD'ALLAH-ALVAREZ RAMÍREZ has worked for almost ten years as the editor of the website *Cubaliteraria*, a portal for Cuban literature. She is dedicated to investigating themes relating to racial discrimination in Cuba, in particular, representations of race in the media, the production of art by Black women, and the impact of social media on activism for sexual and reproductive rights of people with non-heteronormative sexual orientations. As a cyberfeminist, she is a member of Proyecto Arcoirisis, a group of Afro-Cuban women who have documented the struggles against racism through art and culture in the book *Afrocubanas: historia, pensamiento y prácticas culturales.*

MARIA ANGELA RIVEROS PINTO is an Amayra anthropologist and lecturer at the Universidad Mayor de San Andrés (UMSA), Bolivia. Her areas of expertise include urban anthropology, youth identities, gender, and religiosity. She received her master's in "Investigación Social para el Desarrollo con mención en Identidades Culturales y Medio Ambiente" in 2009 from Universidad para la Investigación Estrategica en Bolivia (UPIEB).

STÉPHANIE MELYON-REINETTE is presently an independent researcher, writer, cultural activist, and performer. Her field encompasses issues such as diaspora (Haitian Caribbean), migrations and discriminations, integration strategies, Black art, gender studies, and sexuality. Her prominent work includes *Marronnage and Art: Revolt in Bodies and Voices* (Cambridge Scholars Publishing, 2012).

STEVE GADET is an assistant professor at the University of the West-Indies. He writes on culture, religion, crime, urban expressions, and social movements. With L'Harmattan (Paris), Gadet has published *The Fusion of the Rastafarian movement and Hip-Hop Culture* (2010), *The Multiple Faces of Hip-Hop Culture* (2010), *God and*

Race in the United-States: The Political Power of the Black Church (2015), and *Urban Cultures in the Caribbean* (editor, 2015). He's from Guadeloupe but resides in Martinique with his wife and his two daughters.

SARAH SOANIRINA OHMER is Assistant Professor of Spanish and the Coordinator of the Spanish Proficiency and Curriculum at the University of Indianapolis. She received a PhD from the University of Pittsburgh, and an MA in Spanish Literature and a BA in Spanish and English Linguistics from the University of Houston. A French native, Ohmer has directed one play and has translated/acted in several other plays for Et Voila Theatre in Houston. Her current book projects are focused on mirroring race and gender in non-English literature and remembering trauma in Afro-African contemporary literature.

Translators

JANELLE GONDAR is a PhD candidate in the Department of Spanish and Portuguese at Yale University who specializes in twentieth-century Latin American literature. She has a BA and an MA in Spanish from CUNY Hunter College in New York City, as well as an MA and an MPhil in Spanish from Yale University. Janelle is also an associate editor of the AATSP's graduate student journal, *Spanish and Portuguese Review*. Currently, she is working on her dissertation, "The Evolution and Revolution of the Haiku in Ibero-America," in which she analyzes how the Japanese haiku was introduced to and adapted by Ibero-American poets in both Spanish and Portuguese languages spanning across several major literary movements over the course of the twentieth century.

ADRIANA ONITA holds a MA in Spanish and Latin American Studies and an Honours BA in Romance Languages from the University of Alberta. Her research interests include female sexual agency in Chicana rap, visual culture, and SL pedagogy. Adriana is also a poet, art educator, and owner of a language teaching business.

JOCELYN LANGER is a graduate student in Translation Studies at the University of Massachusetts Amherst, with a focus on collaborative approaches to translation in social change movements.

MANUELA BORZONE is a translator and a doctoral candidate in Comparative Literature at the University of Massachusetts Amherst, where she also teaches a variety of undergraduate courses.

ALEXANDER PONOMAREFF is a doctoral candidate in Comparative Literature at the University of Massachusetts Amherst.

Index

Abd'Allah-Álvarez Ramírez, Sandra, vi, 14, 214–26, 300

abolition, 280, 285

Abya Yala, 43, 49–50, 52, 55

activism: African American, 173; and AfroReggae, 279, 281, 284, 289, 292; and blackness in Brazil, 117, 120; and civil rights, 184; and community, 36, 39, 279; and Hip Hop, vi, 14, 58, 148, 195–96, 200, 215, 200, 227, 275; and labor, 185; as performance, 117, 120, 148, 279, 281, 284, 289; and Supercrónica Obsesión, 215, 220; women, 195–96, 198, 200, 204n6, 300; and youth, 114. *See also* artivism; feminism

African American: African Americanization of Hip Hop, x, 143; African American Studies, xi, xiii, 297–98; and community, 29, 45; Hip Hop artists, 116, 120, 176, 253; influence of African American music, 68–69, 71, 84, 87–88, 116, 145, 173, 180; influence on Brazilian Hip Hop, 114–22; influence on Haitian artists, 253, 255–58; and Los Angeles, 186–87, 88; role in Hip Hop's development, 7, 24–26, 68–69, 71, 84, 90

African American vernacular English (AAVE), ix, x, 24, 137, 266

African, 55–56: Diaspora, ix, xiv, 45, 49–50, 55, 56, 59, 70–71, 78, 84–85, 88, 95, 101, 104, 130, 183, 185, 247, 276, 284–86, 288, 290, 298–99; Drumming, 137; African

heritage, 69, 81; African Heritage Knowledge (AHK), 54; African Slave Trade, 94, 285. *See also* Pan-Africanism

African National Congress, 46

Afroantillanos, 66

Afrocoloniales, 65–66

Afro-Cuban, 77, 220, 226. *See also* Obsesión Krudas; Supercrónica Obsesión; Abd'Allah-Álvarez Ramírez, Sandra

Afro-Diasporic: culture, ix, 274; identity, 183; roots, 137. *See also* African Diaspora

Afro-Latin American, v, 12, 61, 65, 77–78, 84. *See also* African Diaspora; Afro-Cuban; Afro-Mexico; Andrews, George Reid; Colombia; Gates, Henry Louis; Wade, Peter

Afro-Latino/a: AfroLatinidad, v, 61, 65; history in the U.S., 59, 68, 78; identity, 42, 64, 70, 74–76; invisibility in the U.S., 67–69, 78–79; identity for Los Rakas, 64, 66, 69–70, 73–76; in California, 12, 54, 64–65, 74–76, 79; experiences of discrimination, 12, 43, 49, 67; resistance, 50, 70. *See also* Afro-Cuban; Colombia: Afro-Colombians; Flores, Juan; Jiménez Román, Miriam; McFarland, Pancho; Ball, Jared; Rivera-Rideau, Petra R.

Afro-Mexico, 68n5; 78, 130–31. *See also* Aguirre Beltran, Gonzalo; Black Mexicans; Bocafloja; Gaspar Yanga; San Jarocho

303

GLOBAL LATIN/O AMERICAS

Frederick Luis Aldama and Lourdes Torres, Series Editors

This new series focuses on the Latino experience in its totality as set within a global dimension. The series will showcase the variety and vitality of the presence and significant influence of Latinos in the shaping of the culture, history, politics and policies, and language of the Americas—and beyond. We welcome scholarship regarding the arts, literature, philosophy, popular culture, history, politics, law, history, and language studies, among others. Books in the series will draw from scholars from around the world.

La Verdad: An International Dialogue on Hip Hop Latinidades
EDITED BY MELISSA CASTILLO-GARSOW AND JASON NICHOLS